Ex Libris

Dorothy M. Morris

BEYOND BELIEF

BY EMLYN WILLIAMS

Full Moon

A Murder Has Been Arranged

Night Must Fall

He Was Born Gay

The Corn Is Green

The Light of Heart

The Morning Star

A Month in the Country
(*Adaptation*)

The Druid's Rest

The Wind of Heaven

Spring, 1600

Trespass

Accolade

Someone Waiting

Beth

––––––––––

George: An Early Autobiography

Beyond Belief:
A Chronicle of Murder and Its Detection

BEYOND BELIEF

A CHRONICLE OF MURDER
AND ITS DETECTION

by Emlyn Williams

RANDOM HOUSE   *New York*

My thanks are due to Dorothy Bacon, Sally Cheadle, Leslie Clare, A. W. Cutler, Elsie Doran, Ann Downey, Caroline Flemyng, Robert Flemyng, Percy Hoskins, Jack House, James Johnson, Winifred Johnson, Nellie Jones, Sheila Kilbride, Ann Lansley, Elsie Masterson, Angus Morristoun, Gladys Newton, James Nicholson, Robert Perrin, Cyril Polson, Olive Purlow, Amos Reade, Joan Reade, John Roberts, David Scott, David Smith, Maureen Smith, Stephen Watts, John Weeks, Alan West, Cyril Wheeler, Brook Williams and Rosemary Wilton. I should also like to thank several people who wish to remain anonymous.

For permission to quote, thanks are due to the following: Criterion Music Corporation for "These Boots are Made for Walkin'." Words and music by Lee Hazlewood. Copyright © 1965–66, Criterion Music Corporation; all rights reserved; Sphere Music Company Ltd. for "Catch Us If You Can." Words and music by Dave Clarke and Lenny Davidson. © 1965, Sphere Music Co., Ltd., Regent, London, England. Sole selling agent (including world, excluding U.K. and Eire); Branston Music Company, New York.

To Detective Chief Superintendent Arthur
Benfield, head of Cheshire C.I.D., and to
Superintendent Robert Talbot, in charge of
the Stalybridge Division of the Cheshire
County Constabulary (1965–66).

AUTHOR'S FOREWORD

"BUT *how* can a self-respecting writer like you be spending over a year writing a book about such a ghastly case?" I have often been asked the question, mostly by women ("I wasn't able to read the details of it in the paper, never mind a book!"). And now that *Beyond Belief* is published, I have no doubt I shall hear the question oftener.

My answer is a simple one. For me, just as no physical aberration can ever be too extraordinary to interest the medical scientist, so no psychological phenomena can be forbidden to the serious and dispassionate writer, however "unsavory" the details. Who expects savor from a story of noisome evil? When a shocking scandal blows up, with all the attendant sensationalism, there is in some people an instinct to avert the head and shovel the whole thing under the carpet ("I don't want to know"). But some of us *do* want to know, and it is salutary to inquire: the proper study of mankind is man. And man cannot be ignored because he has become vile. Woman neither.

And when the phenomena have developed, over years, in two human beings appearing as ordinary as their surroundings . . . "I keep remindin' myself," Superintendent Talbot said to me, "that this isn't a tale—that it's been happenin', as you might say, *in our midst*. Even as a hardened copper, you just rub your eyes." The observer's interest has to be as absorbed as it is horrified, especially when the horror is matched by a unique record of detection.

In 1962 John Arlott said of William Bolitho's classic study of real-life crime, *Murder for Profit*, that "it has a dual accuracy, the accuracy of history and the accuracy of imaginative understanding." Ever since writing *Night Must Fall*, I have wondered if a murder case would one day present itself which would challenge me to embark on a book aiming at that "dual accuracy." *Beyond Belief* is composed, therefore, of three elements: fact, interpretation of fact, and surmise.

Marshaling the established facts of most "chronicles of murder," the writer is faced with gaps between those facts which it is doubtful will ever be filled, because the people able to fill them are either dead or unwilling to co-operate (in this case, the guilty man and the guilty woman). Hence the necessity for "surmise"; that is, between one set of established facts and the next, a reconstruction of behavior, conversation and thoughts *based entirely on the facts*, aiming at complete concordance with them, and in no way allowed to conflict with them. In such passages, moreover, indirect use is constantly made of authenticated details, statements, opinions and typical turns of phrase.

I have felt that in the cause of coherent narrative, this reconstruction should be incorporated into the text as smoothly as possible. At the same time, it is obviously essential that it should be clear each time "surmise" begins and leaves off. To make sure of this, I employ two familiar and unobtrusive devices: (a) for "surmised" narrative, the present tense, and (b) for "surmised" thoughts and even "surmised" dialogue, the omission of quotation marks. Several of these "surmises" are discussed briefly in the Appendix.

"I dream of moor, and misty hill
 Where evening gathers, dark and chill. . . .
 What have those lonely mountains worth revealing?"

E MILY B RONTË

CONTENTS

PART THREE

FLYIN' HIGH

PART FOUR

DOWN TO EARTH

PART ONE

MISSING FROM HOME

CHAPTER 1

THE LOVEBIRDS

"Catch us if you can . . ."
Pop song

SUBURBS make me feel at home. Working my way through a
maze of muted streets indistinguishable from thousands more all
over Britain, I ought to feel oppressed by the twentieth-century
disease which overnight, in the name of progress, turns grass to
bricks and mortar. But I like the bricks and mortar. The English
county of Lancashire being near Wales, the outer fringes of its
two great cities are peppered with cousins of mine, and as a child
I spent happy hours walking pavements and sitting in one or
another of the myriad little houses.

I feel comfortable among them. An empty mountain landscape, even under the sun, evokes wonder in me but not affection; by night, even bathed in moonlight it chills my heart. I
remember what my cousins told me, that up here live the
Bogeymen, shadowy giants with staring eyes who lurch silently
up and down the roadsides. The wind whimpers through the
stone walls, then from the dark beyond I hear ghostly rustlings
that press the fingernails into the palm. And I hurry down to the
horizon, to the reassuring glow of the suburbs.

"Greater Manchester," the map says. The city once named the
Cottonopolis of the North has settled into a formidable provincial

capital, which has meant the inevitable sprawl. Through a grey rainy afternoon in November 1963, we are heading southeast. Not that it looks any different from northwest or from any other city; it is the same endlessly straight arterial thoroughfare and it may be Stockport Road or Hyde Road or Old Ashton Road, hard to tell. It crawls with the same buses, trucks and cars, and the pavements jostle with the same shoppers, mostly middle-aged women, intent but unhurrying and—if you can only take a quick look—made of plastic: plastic hoods, raincoats, shopping bags, overshoes: the whole mundane pageant moving intent but unhurrying between the welter of signs fading up into the low ceiling of sky: CITY SANDWICH BAR NUT SCREW AND BOLT WARE-HOUSE CO-OP FOODS GENT'S HAIRDRESSER MUNICIPAL LAUNDER-ETTE FURNITURE MART ROSETTA MODES KAY'S MINI-MARKET YATES' WINE LODGE SELF-SERVICE MARK-DOWN JIM'S BED AND BREAK-FAST OO-LA-LA PARIS FASHIONS SHOE REPAIRS YOUR OWN GLAMOUR BINGO HALL.

Just when you are about to miss a feature you were waiting for, it looms up. As you get to traffic lights where a schoolteacher is shepherding a flock of children across the road, you wonder why you haven't spotted the familiar suburban place of worship —and here it comes, four-square, the Nonconformist church with the bad color and the sooty laurel and the jaded notice board: A SMILE FOR A NEIGHBOUR, TO A CHRISTIAN IS NO LABOUR. And just when you're thinking, Why isn't there a supermarket?—there it is: WHY SHOP IN TOWN. Even the two matrons waiting for the lights to change, weren't they hanging about two hours ago on the outskirts of Chester?

Behind them, the same Picturedrome as in Chester, looking like an outsize public lavatory, and the same film, *Dracula and the Werewolves,* there he goes riding the poster, his knife dripping gore into an open coffin. The two shoppers glance up and their bespectacled eyes meet his, dead on. "Ee, 'e don't 'alf look far-fetched, bless 'im," and they clatter over into the spicy warm supermarket bursting with good things that are truly household words. For at this moment, at the flick of a knob they are being celebrated, in jingle and animated picture, in living rooms throughout the land: Omo Washes Whiter . . . We Are the

Ovalteenies ("I'll 'ave that one, loov, I saw two beautiful kiddies eatin' it on the telly").

Behind the shops and the cinemas and the churches and the stray bay-windowed Victorian mansions converted into seedy offices lies the hinterland of the back streets. A wilderness webbed between the main roads, with at its heart—ironically—Manchester's ample and glittering playground of circus, ballroom, zoo and race track, Belle Vue. Long timid grey stretches of grime pierced regularly with square holes to make a window—one up, one down—and the front door opening straight onto the road: the whole row back to back with the row in the next street and with only the long narrow public "back entry" separating one lavatory from the one opposite. Line after line after line, some christened fancifully: Spring Street, followed by Summer Street January Street February Street Wheat Street Oats Street Rye Street; then a series unsuitably named after the spacious homes of a long-dead empress, Balmoral Street Osborne Street Sandringham Street Windsor Street. There is even Elysian Street. The only variation: some are dead ends, with perhaps a tall fence across and a drop to the railway, and others—quite a few— have a pub on the corner. Rows and rows of hand-me-down doll's houses.

But the people are mostly a cheerful race. Only twelve miles away is the Rochdale which first heard the laugh of Gracie Fields, and no dish in the world is more genially named than Lancashire hot pot. As in any underprivileged community, there are scabrous corners: a couple of dance halls where the police have the odd sticky Saturday night with the bad lads with the pep pills and the switchblades, but all fairly in hand. To a seaman straight from Port Said or Forty-second Street, it would be like coming home to Mother.

As you proceed through the maze, the thin winter light wanes, and low in the city sky the thicket of television aerials is dwindling into the dark. Schoolchildren wheel their bikes up back entries, the paperboy crushes the Manchester *Evening News* into the odd mailbox and saunters whistling on. Top bulbs click on in front rooms, and thin curtains close on tables laid for high tea.

The suburb of Gorton. Up Casson Street, corner of Bannock Street. In the first house on the left, framed in the lighted window, two children sit staring at something out of sight. A sudden shout, and two pistol shots ring out into the roadway.

The Lone Ranger is in full spate, and the paperboy lingers at another window for a quick look. The screen is filled with gun smoke, the little room echoes with violence, and the old pensioner sits finishing his tea as he pats the rapt grandchild perched beside him. You can follow the television dialogue from door to door. Bannock Street is in the daily thrall of make-believe.

Chatty Mrs. Matlock of Number 9A lands home from Bingo just as a young couple emerge from two doors off, he slim-legged with the fashionable pointed shoes, she dark with the fashionable bouffant hair—Evenin', Mrs. Matlock—and they are off arm in arm to Belle Vue. Ta ra for now, they call out, the warm casual Lancashire way of saying goodbye, "ta ra!" The paperboy hands Mrs. Matlock her *News*. Willie, anythink new 'bout t' missin' child? Oh yes, 'ere it is, SEARCH CONTINUES.

Mr. Weatherby, the new neighbor, approaches on his way to sample the beer around the corner in the Bessemer. Oh Mr. Weatherby, I got the names o' the tradespeople for you, the child's kidnapped I shouldn' be surprised.

The door of Number 7 opens and two young people come out and climb briskly into a little car. They are very like the other two, he slim-legged with the pointed shoes and she with the bouffant hair, only blond. Mrs. Matlock calls to them: I was joost sayin', I think that child's been kidnapped!

Says the young chap sitting next to the young lady as she settles behind the wheel, Shouldn' be surprised.

An' bein' 'id, continues Mrs. Matlock, by soom woman wi' no kiddie of 'er own which 'as sent 'er off 'er rocker. I mean, it's the poor mother you think of. Well, ta ra for now, 'ave a nice drive both, be good!

As the car slows down for the corner, the two neighbors just catch the driver's green-scarfed head as she turns to her companion and says something. Her laugh floats back, echoed by his deeper chuckle, and they slide off into the dark between more parlors ringing with horses' hooves and the cries of dying men.

Mrs. Matlock has the last word with Mr. Weatherby, who is itching to get to his pint: Aye, she lives with 'er gran, you see, so wi' bein' two women livin' alone she persuaded 'er young man to move in for safety. Oh, proper couple o' lovebirds, not like them rock-'n'-rollers, they keep themselves to themselves, do Ian an' Myra.

Ian Stewart Brady, born Sunday, January 2, 1938.

Myra Hindley, born Tuesday, July 23, 1942.

CHAPTER 2

THE PIED PIPER

"Oh whistle and I'll come to you my Lad."
Burns

FOR every British home with television or radio, the previous Friday evening, November 22, had been a shocking one. At seven-thirty stricken announcers gave the news that President Kennedy had been assassinated. And to the Kilbride family, of Ashton-under-Lyne, it was that bit more personal: not only were they Catholic, the father was Irish.

Ashton is another of the small towns so imbedded by now in Greater Manchester that it has to be looked upon as part of the outskirts. Smallshaw Lane, therefore, a couple of miles by bus from the central Market Square, can be said to lie in the suburb of a suburb.

The address is not as modest as it sounds, really more of an avenue with houses of a fair size—luckily, for Number 262 housed eight Kilbrides. Pat the father, Sheila the mother, in her thirties, plus four boys and two girls: John, then Pat ten, Terry nine, Sheila seven, Maria six, Chris four. Although Dad's job was on the roads as a flagman and he wasn't always working, they didn't do so badly: the house was Sheila's and she was an excellent housekeeper and mother. A buxom pretty woman with blue eyes and dark hair simply brushed out, she had a peasant dignity which among the tinted, back-combed coiffures in the super-market looked refreshingly old-fashioned.

John, the eldest, twelve, who attended St. Damian's Catholic School, was a cheery, friendly boy, big for his age and looking older in his long flannel trousers and rough teen-age jacket.

He had a square Irish face, short of nose and blue of eye, with a wide smile and an engaging gap between his two front teeth. Framed in the parlor, three enlarged snaps: one of John, aged eight, giggling awkwardly as train bearer to the May Queen; one of his mother as a very young girl and looking exactly like him, giggling awkwardly as a maid of honor. The third, John had prepared for her, as a surprise, in the summer four months before. At the garden party run by St. Christopher's down the road, where the family attended Mass every Sunday, her four sons had been specially photographed standing next to one another, John at one end and tapering down, through Pat and Terry to little Chris, and all trying not to laugh, especially John. It was a favorite present.

That Friday evening he had been sitting on their gate and talking to his mates, too dark to play tag, when he ran into the front room, looking—for him—concerned; "Mam, they said he's been killed, is it true?" They were all around the television watching the endless Dallas newsreels. Isn't it dreadful, thank God we don't 'ave that sort of thing 'ere. We'll make a novena for him on Sunday, that poor girl and her babies. Go in the kitchen, John, your supper's on the table.

But Mam, what about telly, *Bonanza?*

No lad, all programs suspended.

Oh but Mam, it won't bring him back to life there bein' no *Bonanza*, we 'aven't missed it yet of a Friday!

Never you mind, our John, p'r'aps next Friday they'll put two on to make up. You get your supper now. At nine John went up to bed, still missing *Bonanza*.

The next morning he was up early and off to breakfast with his gran in Rowley Street. He did this every morning because Mrs. Doran couldn't stoop and he put her stockings on for her. He also did jobs about the house and "kept the garden loovly for his gran." The morning soon passed for his mother, washing and shopping and dusting and cooking and the younger children all over the place, John home for midday dinner, fish and chips, and the kids squashed around the big table each in place.

After midday dinner he was to meet his mate John Ryan outside the Pav, his weekly treat, t' pictures, kids' matinee. He took up the Ashton *Reporter* and read out: " 'The Mongols' Jack Palance an' next week 'Hand of Death,' that'll be good!"

"Don't be morbid, our John, any news this week?"

He read out: " 'Man from Keswick Avenue Fell Thirteen Steps to His Death.' "

"Oh dear, I 'ope your gran doesn't see it, make 'er nervous, don't be late for your tea."

"No fear, Mam, can I have two boiled eggs instead of one? I'll be seein' ya," and he was off. 1 P.M. Chris, where are you, coom back inside our gate this minute, that poor Mrs. Kennedy.

Outside the Pav, John met John Ryan, they paid their bob and hurried in. John settled to the beginning of a good Saturday, for after the film, which finished at half past four, already dark, came the Market.

Ashton-under-Lyne is proud enough of its Market to feature it in cheerful colors across the cover of the *Official Handbook,* extending the length and breadth of the Market Square. Open Mondays, Fridays and Saturdays—especially Saturdays—it is typical rows of trim improvised canvas roofs, everything in the world for sale cheaper than anywhere else, from secondhand furniture to diamond-mesh stockings, and all offered by bawling, beaming, bawdy men exchanging impromptus with hawk-eyed housewives: "Coom on, missus, 'ere's a match, what d' you say you take that quid out o' your garter an' light your fag with it!" For a local child the market was a rowdy paradise, and this evening, in the incipient fog, the muzzy yellow lights looked especially exciting. Eddies of smoke got into the glare, it was like a daft dream.

His mam was never too keen on his coming here, but apart from the fun there was the chance of earning the odd sixpence by running an errand, and then he could blow threepence on an ice-cream cone at Roland Evans' stall. And his conscience was clear so long as he remembered what Father Kelly had said: If a strange bloke that's had a drink staggers up an' puts a mitt on your shoulder an' says you're a bonny lad, not even to look up, just run an' join your mates, promise? Anyway, they always expect you to get into trouble more in the summer somehow.

He and John Ryan did earn their sixpences, for running to the station and picking up a pushcart and bringing it back to the carpet stall. Then they mooched around, distracted by a scream of a row between two stall holders, then the fog seemed to be getting thicker and he told his mate he was off soon to catch the bus home for his two boiled eggs an' special Saturday cake. 5:45. The other John decided to wander around for a bit (See you Monday at skule, ta ra), and left John leaning against the big trash barrel.

Hungry. Ta ra to the lights and the bargaining and the fun and the danger, and down into the dark bit of Warrington Street on his way to the bus station. The dull, comfortable beckon of home.

The sound of gears changing. He turns his head. A car slows down, and stops.

John Kilbride, born May 15, 1951, died November 23, 1963, aged twelve years and six months.

6:30. Not like our John to be late when 'e's 'ungry. 7:30. Coom on, Chris, Maria, Sheila, bed, an' Pat, you pop 'round to your gran's in case an' I'll give 'im Ashton Market. 8:30. Not at 'is gran's? Oh dear, then Pat, run 'round quick to your Uncle Frank and Auntie Elsie. I'm not worried, but oh dear . . . 9:30. Elsie, I know I'm bein' silly but I joost can't keep still. 'Ow terrible if he fell in a ditch an' broke 'is ankle an' can't make anybody 'ear. Elsie, *what's 'appened to 'im?*

Panic. Dial 999, sleepless night on chairs listening for a step, first night he's ever spent away from home. If he was a girl three years older you'd think the worst but he's not, *where is he?*

Breakfast—no, couldn't touch a mouthful. Knock, uniformed police. Please coom in (What must the neighbors be thinkin'?) . . . What was he wearin', let me see, flannel trousers (Why don't they say what *is* he wearin'?), grey jacket I'd turned the hem, his dad's undershirt that I took in at the sides for 'im and black shoes I'd just 'ad mended at the Co-op . . . Aye, that photo on the wall I've got the negative soomwhere. (No good standin' at window, must get the Sunday dinner ready.) Answer the door dear an' stop asking where's our John . . . No, Mrs. Barlow, no news I can't oonderstand it, I just can't . . . Oh, turn the telly off, it's gettin' on my nerves. Frank, try John Ryan's house again. Sunday night, chairs again, no sleep. It's like your mind had screws on it and with every hour goes by, just to see how much you can bear, somebody's screwing it that bit tighter. Tighter. Tighter. Don't know what I'd do without you, Elsie, he only 'ad a shillin' on 'im. I can't understand it. Good mornin', Mrs. Tuohy . . . No, there's no news, must 'ave lost 'is memory, none of us can grasp it.

Monday evening, through the mailbox, Manchester *Evening News*, page 7: MASSIVE COMB-OUT FOR BOY. There he is in the photo, funny to see 'im lookin' straight out, smilin' an' yet tryin' not to, he might be in the room. Oh, John, John, don't tease me, coom back coom back coom back. No sleep no sleep no sleep. Okay, Elsie, if the doctor says so I'll try a couple, no sleep no sleep no sleep. Tuesday, the press. Yes, flannel trousers, his father's undershirt. Elsie, it sounds silly but I've offered anoother prayer an' I think there'll be a letter—the kids don't ask any more an' then you notice one of 'em's been cryin'—I mean, there's been these American kids kidnapped for the cash but this is a lad from *Ashton,* our John, it doesn't make sense. I'll brew some tea. Wednesday, the screw tighter. Thursday. Tighter.

On Friday the Ashton *Reporter,* which made it clear that nobody was talking of anything else: the front page was splashed with BOY VANISHES SIXTH DAY. Under it the familiar snap, enlarged and fuzzy, smiling away. His mother stared back at him. Was this the paper they'd taken every Friday for years, the same he'd read out of last Saturday, was it *only* last Saturday, sitting in yonder chair? She spread it on the kitchen table and five young Kilbrides crowded around her to look.

Photograph of "Police handlers with their tracker dogs." The missing boy had elbowed two items into corners: YOU WANT THE BEATLES! and WILL SINGER DENISE JONES BE TOP OF THE POPS?

"The police have been assisted not only by soldiers from the Royal Pay Corps at Ladysmith Barracks, cadets from the Police Training School at Preston but by police frogmen." Mam, they're *sure* to find 'im, frogmen can do anythink . . . Oh luke, Mam, what Dad said to the man! "My son is not in trouble he is always cheerful and known for his habit of walking down the street hands in pockets and singing or whistling." John had a nice soprano voice, and the tune he liked was one his mother had practiced with him, Comin' In on a Wing and a Prayer.

The picture of a stout-hearted little Irish pied piper, head of the Kilbride clan and whistling on his purposeful way, caught the imagination for miles around. But last Saturday night, after leaning against a trash barrel savoring the music and the fun, he had walked off piping . . . to where?

Tuesday the chief constable himself had held a conference: "Several new lines of inquiry are being followed up." He had then visited the Town Hall: "Oh look, our Mam, they've been to the mayor about our John!"

And over the page, the false hopes. A man had been seen threatening two boys with a knife, a lady at the bus stop had seen a boy leave the hot-drinks machine and bump into her daughter —nothing.

Finally Chief Inspector Stebbing: " 'I am appealing for volunteers for a search that will continue till dusk if necessary.' " It *was* necessary. On the bitter-cold Sunday, the Piper drew from their homes two thousand teen-agers, housewives, businessmen who brought their dogs, a cross section of Ashton . . . but where was the Piper? They scoured derelict houses, canals, reservoirs, parks, woods and every square foot of wasteland. Meanwhile a poster had been circulated of the same snap blown up to monster size: HAVE YOU SEEN THIS BOY? Where was he?

Another week. No news, Mrs. Barlow. No news, Mrs. Tuohy, "but after that they just didn't ask an' even looked away, which was better in a way." The Kilbrides never had much in the way of letters, just the odd Christmas card, but now they waited for the postman. Young Pat would station himself at the gate and call his man when he saw the uniform approaching. And every day he passed them by.

The *Reporter,* December 6. Another enormous headline; MASS HUNT FOR A BOY. All about last Sunday. Oh look, our Mam! The dazed Kilbrides pored over LORD LIEUTENANT OF LANCA-SHIRE ADDRESSING VAST CROWD THROUGH LOUDSPEAKER, BIGGEST SEARCH EVER MOUNTED FOR A MISSING PERSON, and in the corner "Ashton police announce that owing to pressure of work the Police Dance in the Mecca Ballroom is cancelled." Then, after the beatings and proddings up the highways and down the grubby byways—by now merry John's smile on the posters, straight on, was teasing beyond words—the official final state-ment was a stout gesture: "The boy is nowhere in the open, and the police will continue till he is found." The mayor had stated that "no news is good news" and had meant it. Through all this, in a decade of mounting alarm about violence threatening the citizen, and on the outskirts of a tough city, not one person voiced the worst fear. The boy had had an accident. The *Re-porter* even printed the remark of a neighbor: "It's as if the ground had opened, and swallowed him up."

In a desperate search for the accident, even the giant open trash barrel in the market, against which John had leaned, was suspected. The police thought that maybe high-spirited mates, in a game of I-dare-you, had tossed the chuckling lad into the flames, and were now quaking among secretive relatives; for days tons of charred rubbish were searched for human traces. None.

Another week. Somebody had told the postman that 262 was hoping for a letter, and he started giving a trying-to-comfort smile and shaking his head. After that they looked out for him from inside and just watched him pass.

The *Reporter,* December 13. Though the case still claimed the front page, ASHTON BOY STILL MISSING, it was clear that things were getting desperate. A description had been sent to the Catho-lic journal the *Universe* "in case he might have approached a priest." There had been inquiries all over southern England, an uncle in Dublin had been tried, ditches in Ashton Moss had been examined in case he had stumbled down and drowned: a truck driver was radioed for who had given a lift to a boy between Bristol and Bath. Nothing.

Even the supernatural reared its head in Ashton. Mrs. Anne Lansley, "psychic since she was a girl," kept mentioning a "concrete room." A storage tank? Sure enough, one was reported which had a dislodged lid. The crowds gathered. The high winds had done it.

The rest of Mrs. Lansley's vision was, months later, to be recalled by many with wonder, and by the family with a crossing of the breast. She saw the missing boy as "out in the open, some way down a slope, with the skyline completely barren, not a tree in sight, a road on the right, and near a stream."

Another week. A businessman offered a hundred pounds to anybody who would locate the lad: "If he is restored to his parents, it will be the best Christmas present I ever bought anyone." And neighbors had collected fifteen pounds "to give the family a better Christmas."

Without news to feed it, the biggest story starves. On Friday the twentieth, the *Reporter* front page blazed with THREE MILLION CIGS AND VAN DISAPPEARED, and the other mystery was squeezed between that and Landlady Asserts Workman Washed Socks in Bathroom.

December 27, something, but only because of a photographer's enterprise. The Kilbride living room with the family sadly arranged around the table, and in the foreground, its back to the camera, an empty chair. Underneath: "A place has been reserved for John, in case the prospect of Christmas at home brought him back." Underneath, news of an Ashton woman who had Found an Earwig in a Meat Pie.

And that was it. Shamefacedly, like a shabby bundle getting heavier every minute and which nobody will claim, the subject was dropped.

Then one evening late in the next year, 1964, a knock at the door. A large, square-faced man in dark suit and trilby, pugnacious-looking until he smiled. Detective Chief Inspector Joseph Mounsey had just joined Ashton police headquarters from Middleton nearby and knew the Kilbride dossier. It had absorbed him: he was a bulldog of a policeman, and the completely enigmatic character of the case caught his fancy. This missing person must be found.

He sat in the front room, and Mrs. Kilbride answered his questions simply, mildly, with a lack of bitterness remarkable in a woman subjected to such a calamity. She told him about John going to help his gran every morning: "The middle boy does that now." And then she said, "Things have to go on, don't they, we hardly ever mention John's name now." And just when he thought she was not going to go into whether he was alive, she said, "I don't know why, but I think he's been burnt."

"Burnt?" He remembered she was a Catholic.

She went on, "People should have a Christian burial, shouldn't they?"

Joe Mounsey did not consider himself a sentimental man, but as he walked away he realized he was moved. And back at the station he went into the whole thing again and even checked up on a couple of rumors. Then he made a habit of popping in to see the Kilbrides, in case he or they had anything to report. At the station, where the two impish eyes still beckoned from the poster to the defeated police force, his pertinacity became a joke, and the missing boy was never called anything but "Mounsey's Lad."

But there was nothing to report.

On April 14, 1964, the Manchester *Evening News* announced that Raymond Woodhouse, aged seventeen, was missing.

The police sent out search parties, and must have held their breath. The absentee was found sitting by his own fireside; he had gone off "for a ramble without tellin' nobody."

On June 12: Edward Bourkett, fourteen, missing. He was searched for, for six days. Then it was discovered that he had gone hitchhiking and was having a nice time with relatives in Plymouth. The police can sometimes relax.

CHAPTER 3

SO LONG AT THE FAIR

"They kept the noiseless tenour of their way."
Gray

THIRTEEN MONTHS after the disappearance of John Kilbride. Christmas 1964.

In the streets to which we are committed, Yuletide—as it is called on the frosted cards—can never be a spectacular affair. But the shopwindows are stuck with cotton wool and scattered with scraps of holly and mistletoe and little Santas. Stockings are tremulously hung at the foot of the brass bed, even though the empty grate couldn't produce a Father Christmas the size of our cat, and pinched carol singers huddle on doorsteps (There's a penny for you an' don't you lot coom back).

In Greater Manchester, the season's activities were in full swing. As itemized later in the Gorton *Reporter,* in Dukinfield the Old Chapel Sunday School put on its Annual Pantomime "Ding Dong Bell" and in Ashton the St. Christopher's Church Hall (the Kilbrides' church) held an Olde Tyme Dance, while for the industrious, Stalybridge Evening Centre offered a Course which included China Decoration, Woodwork, Beauty Course, Spanish Conversation, Ladies Keep Fit, and Scottish Dancing. And weddings: "The bride's mother wore a brown wool suit trimmed with squirrel and toning effects."

The pious side of the festival was also heeded: out of the treeless groves and the leafless lanes, on Christmas Eve young and old trudged intrepidly to the midnight service in St. Philip's Church, Gorton, which "drew a good congregation." On Christmas Day, at St. James' Secondary School the annual Nativity Play; and the All Saints Scouts' Band gaily toured the grubby parish, playing carols.

For the odd-minded, the Spiritualists' Church, Dukinfield, offered: Sunday at 8 Healing, Monday at 8 Whist.

Ancoats is a suburb five crow miles from Ashton, two from Gorton, and nearer the city's center than either. Mrs. Ann Downey, in her early thirties, was lucky enough to be housed high up in a new block of council flats, 25 Charnley Walk, Ancoats, with her four children and prospective husband, Alan West. Lesley, ten, the only daughter, with close dark curls over blue eyes, gave promise of turning into a delightful young girl. Her brothers spoiled her but she was markedly timid with strangers and close to her mother: last summer she had spent her first holiday away from home, at a Methodist camp in Rhyl, and the minister reported afterwards that every night before going to sleep she had said, "I miss my mam," and cried for a minute. But she was beginning to enjoy the unknown: a couple of weeks before, Alan had taken her and her little brothers to Henry's Store in Market Street and let her be photographed with Father Christmas, a nice snap, holding Thomas protectively by the hand and quite grown-up in her long winter trousers. But the best fun had been when her big brother Terry, fourteen, had squired her to her first dance, Church Hall—a skiffle group—and one lad had gorgeous long hair and Les thought he was like out of a storybook and Terry said would she like a lock o' the lad's hair and she said, Oh, I couldn't ask—well, Terry asked and got her a snippet and she kept it in a drawer.

For the Downey kids, this Christmas did not fail in the expected excitements. It was once more amazing how much fun could be got out of little—a foot-high tree, tinsel, watching the empty stocking till the eyes droop into sleep. There were the endless dawn surprises, the rubber ball, the space balloon, the Horror-Comic Coloring Book, the squeaking doll you could undress and put to bed. But Lesley's prize present was from her mother, a tiny electric sewing machine. And when the family went to the service at their Methodist church—the minister had said, would the children bring their best toys to be blessed—Lesley took her sewing machine.

Then telly, the Queen's Speech, Punch and Judy, special tea and she fell willingly into bed, more fun tomorrow.

Boxing Day—and why it is called that, nobody much knows—fell on a Saturday. Parties and excursions. Lesley's treat was to be a visit to the Christmas fair down t' road—so exciting that she couldn't concentrate on her midday meal and decided to save up for after the event: a big tea. The day brought the first snow of the year and Lesley didn't go out, played with her toys. The afternoon brought a surprise present, Terry put around her neck a string of white beads he had won at the fair. Then her mother promised her they would spend the evening with the new sewing machine so she could start making clothes for her doll.

The fair was excitingly near—down Iron Street into Hulme Hall Lane and there it was, overflowing the recreation ground. As the afternoon faded into the early snow-flecked dusk, in the sky you could see from the flats a deepening glow like the Fire of London: the giant Ferris wheel, and if you shushed everybody in the room—listen—the joyous shriek of the music. Nothing could have kept the kids away.

At four her friend Linda called from a few doors off, her mam helped her on with her blue coat over the new pink cardigan, gave her sixpence and they were off: Lesley, Linda, Linda's brother Roy, eight, her sister Ann, four, and Lesley's brothers Thomas, eight, and Brett, four ("They'll be all right wi' me, Mam, I'm oldest!") They all clattered down the stairs in excited convoy, skipped down Iron Street to the tune of Off to See the Wizard and Mrs. Downey relaxed. Nice to get shut o' kids for half an hour, nice cuppa, switch on telly, feet up, *Black Beauty* and then *Juke Box Jury*.

The convoy arrived at the magic place, all light and sound; the evening was cold without being raw, and the glitter of snow in the lights somehow made the darkness beyond less dark. It would be a marvelous half-hour and perhaps you could spin it out by saying the roller coaster had broken down just as you got on, and you had to wait or waste your money—and Mam, you wouldn't want that, would you?

Lesley waved to classmates from St. Mark's School, then a little girl holding a grown-up hand showed her a favorite present, then Lesley held out her white beads and took Ann and Linda on the Cyclone Roundabout, then the Whizzer and a look at the Waltzers, then the candy stall and suddenly it was after five and they'd spent their money and Lesley said, "That was super, now home." The group threaded through the crowd; then as they were getting into Iron Street and all turned for a last look, the merry-go-round started up again and the horses sailed up and down, slow and graceful. From a crashing Dodgem, a whoop of delight. "I'm goin' to 'ave a last look," Lesley said. "Linda, you see our Thomas an' our Brett to the door, ta ra, see you later!" She ran back into the crowd, and the others walked home.

She threaded her shy but confident way into the jostle; there were many people in it whom she knew well; for instance, young Bernard King waved to her as she stood hypnotized by the toy horses cavorting up and down and on, up and down and on, a gorgeous dream of rhythmic grace and light. Then they slowed down, down, down . . . Everythin' cooms to an end, it does an' all, got to git 'ome. Into the dark of Iron Street. Her mam had told her that the sensible thing when you were walking by yourself was to hum to keep yourself company, Good King Wenceslas.

The sound of a car drawing up. Lesley Ann Downey, born August 21, 1954, died December 26, 1964, aged ten years and four months.

This time the police gritted their teeth. God, we'll find this one or else.

Once the fair had closed down for the night, every square inch of equipment was stripped, with the distracted mother looking on. And on the Sunday evening, police photographers having worked overtime, men went from door to door showing the snap taken with Father Christmas. Monday, Manchester *Evening News,* across the front page: TRACKER DOGS JOIN GIANT SEARCH FOR GIRL. Police cadets and fire-brigade cadets were roped in, Philips Park Cemetery was searched, the Ashton Canal dragged and forced to disgorge the rubbish of years, every inch of wasteland scoured. On Wednesday the thirtieth, an event unheard-of in British television: little Linda appeared on a Granada children's program, with Lesley's mother watching at home, and appealed for information: "Last time I seed Les . . ." Then Lesley's face was flashed on, her friendly eyes in a thousand Manchester homes. But Les, loov, you're lookin' straight at me, *where are you?* Ah ha, eeny meeny miny where am I?

Holiday folk returning to shrouded houses were doubly chilled to find a note asking them to search premises for a missing child. And on Friday in the Gorton *Reporter,* the holiday activities noted above were pushed on one side by the one subject which blankly dominated the paper: HAVE YOU SEEN 10-YEAR-OLD LESLEY?

As policemen know, in every grim operation there is a loony episode. The *Reporter* reported that in Clayton Vale, a park a mile from the Downey home, cadets prodding in the snow mantling a rubbish heap had espied the shape, whiter than the snow, of a naked twisted leg. Part of a dismembered shopwindow dummy. Other bodies were unearthed in disgust. One item headed A GRIEVING MOTHER cannot have touched either Downeys or Kilbrides: "When Mrs. N. Hood visited her son's resting place, she found it piled with earth from another grave and was overcome with grief."

Another wife had forced her way into a house and found her husband in bed with another woman, whom she belabored with a chisel while he slept through the entire incident. The rest of the paper reflected the normal look of Gorton—alongside the front-page mystery: BOY THUMPED ON NOSE BY BUS DRIVER . . . FOR MEN ONLY, WHY NOT START 1965 WITH A NEW OVERCOAT? and the women's page asked: HAVE YOU MADE YOUR NEW YEAR RESOLUTIONS YET? From the cinema page it was possible to deduce that on the night Lesley Ann Downey was So Long at the

Fair, outside the Palace Stalybridge, on a route up to the moors, the films advertised for the next two Sundays were *Kill Her Gently* and *The Premature Burial*.

207 fairground visitors interviewed, 6000 others, 5000 handbills, 6000 posters. Everywhere the candid little face looked out from billboard, school noticeboard, bus front, station platform. A bobby can't stick 'is 'ead inside a bluddy café wi'out a kid that lukes like your own starin' you in the face.

On January 8, the very next week, the case was ousted from the front page by CIRCUS DOG SAVES CHILD and CONSTABLE GOT HIS MAN AT LAUNDERETTE. And lower down, readers learn that in Newton Heath a five-year-old girl had been accosted by a man, and kicked him so hard that he had staggered around the corner and never been seen again. The following week: WATER-IN-BEER RUMOR SCOTCHED; the one after, January 22, the paper not only had no mention, it carried a piece on Ten-Year-Old David Noone, missing for a day, who had been scared of his Eleven-Plus exam and gone to stay with a friend. The mother had said, "All night I was thinking of the other children who had disappeared without trace."

The next week, a flicker. "Missing for 24 hours, an eleven-year-old girl was found at Victoria Station, another Lesley Downey mystery had been feared." This struck numbly at the Downey family, for it implied that the subject was closed.

The rest, silence.

CHAPTER 4

THE LAD THAT LIKED TO MAKE NEW FRIENDS

"I'm off to the City Center
'Cos the pretty City Center
Lies in wait, all alight, for me tonight!"
                                    Pop song

NINE MONTHS and two weeks later, early in the evening of October 6, 1965, Edward Evans set out from his home in Ardwick. At the decisive moment of departure, he was five miles from the Kilbride house, two from Mrs. Downey's flat and two from Gorton. Apprentice machinist at the big electrical works of A.E.I., he lived with his parents and a younger brother and sister. He was seventeen.

This particularly dingy doll's house, 55 Addison Street (a regular poets' corner of Manchester, being next to Tennyson, Dryden and Shakespeare streets) was condemned and they were all to be moved out by the New Year. While waiting, this first-born had only lately tested his knuckles against the brick bonds of his home, and found to his amazement that it was not a bash at all, the walls were made of straw. So long as he went to chapel once on Sundays, now that he was a wage earner—only four pounds something a week, but still—he was free in the evenings. And in the evenings he was the typical youth of his time and class, the one who makes you wonder how that sedate couple could have produced a medieval page, a dark long-haired Blondel with frail good looks who seemed to need only an electric guitar and an agent to hit the jackpot.

6 P.M. In the little back bedroom he studies himself in the swivel mirror, under the fly-blown top bulb, and fancies himself, as youths will who are at the perplexed though enjoyable stage of not knowing which way to turn.

His was a simple frame of mind; he liked girls but was frightened of them, while men didn't scare him. As his workmate Jeff Grimsdale put it, Eddie was a lad that liked to make new friends. But this evening he was meeting Jeff, who'd got him interested in football, then off to floodlit Old Trafford, Manchester United versus Helsinki, he and Jeff to meet sevenish at Aunty's Bar. The name had to make you chortle but it wasn't what it sounded, just a straight men's bar with the occasional flotsam an' jetsam but mostly journalists, theater and TV, just Bohemian enough to make you feel you were downtown.

He got into his best faded tight jeans, suede jacket, couldn't find the socks his mam had laid out and impatiently pulled on old ones, then donned his best Italian suede shoes, took his comb, wet it, draped his hair in neat disarray over his narrowed eyes, and by the light of a no-good bulb he was set.

In the back kitchen, with his mam mending his spare undershorts, the quick tomato and cold ham. Then out into the ole backyard into that nasty lav he'd known all his life, but thank God in a couple of months we'll be out, in Withington with running water inside the house all the way. A graceful saunter back into the kitchen: "Ta ra, Mum, ta ra Dad, ta ra Alan, if you can't be good be careful, see you later." I.e, if they're not all in bed, I got me key an' I'll creep in. 6:30 P.M.

A wonderful evening, more like spring. He walks briskly, a third of a mile down mucky Dover Street and he is in Oxford Road, yet another highway out of Manchester. As he wheels to his right to the city's exciting heart, he glances up at the gigantic black Victorian fortress which is the University of Manchester. A poster advertising night classes in every subject under the sun:

ENROL NOW, WHY WAIT? Every reason, mate, pardon me—and the medieval page wrinkles his nose: Life, man, is for the livin', wouldn't be seen dead wastin' an evenin' studyin', let's go.

And the jeans, artfully tight at hips and crotch, made their provocative way under the glaring lamps, past the closed shops, past t' telly window with 'em all going at once, one girl smilin' at you fourteen times, past the chemist wi' Damaroids large as life, past CITY SANDWICH BAR CO-OP FOODS YATES' WINE LODGE SHOE REPAIRS BED AND BREAKFAST. After the mild day the pavement feels warm underfoot in the dark, the snatch of music from a coffee bar melting and seductive and you feel like it must be in New Orleans, all ripe an' ready, you an' the night an' the music. Ah well, football's better for you.

Aunty's, 73 Oxford Road. 7:05. No Jeff. Bitter please, George. Same again, George. No Jeff. Jeff had said if his mam wasn't any better he might have to stay in. Hell, look in t' paper. Palace Theatre down the road, *The Seekers*, goodo—no, they're next Monday, damn. Studio One, *Twenty-Four Hours to Kill*—nay, football's better for you. So long, George. Train from Oxford Road Station to Old Trafford, match started, standing room.

When you're by your flippin' self, after an hour the crowd gets on your flippin' nerves. The protective bass boom of a thousand fellowmen. Lonely in a crowd, isn't there a pop song 'bout that . . . Long before half time you're cheesed off, and you bugger off. Back downtown. Hell, you're only yoong once, let's case the Barrowford.

A bar in Sackville Street, attached to the Barrowford Hotel (respectable), but as often happens, attracting a subterranean clientele as separate as a tube station is separate from Buckingham Palace just over it. Enter Eddie, a twinkle in the apprentice eye, (I know the score fellers, here goes.) To cover insecurity, to get himself to the bar, he uses the Elvis Presley roll. Pint o' bitter, please, ta.

Two isolated customers trying to drink small whiskies like big businessmen, rather than like what they are: lonely individuals angling for the friendship of the flesh. And if the flesh is withheld with no offense meant, then just friendship will be accepted and the taxi fare pressed moistly into the tolerant young palm.

Eddie dismisses them as sinister and turns his back. Another beer, crisps. The businessmen, having stared long enough, seep separately away. (Ta ra, me lovelies, ugh.) You're saying good-bye, Ed, to two separate chances of life.

Let's go. Central Station buffet, you never know. Down Whitworth Street, the darkness still warm. Lower Mosley Street and a bound up the station steps. In chronological order, he is the third of three young people who walked briskly, as the moment of no recall approached, toward something they were looking forward to: a busy market, a Christmas fair, a pot-luck counter on a city evening, relaxed.

At the swing door, he barges into two men hurrying out for a train. Into the buffet. Empty. Hell. Sandwich and another beer.

Drink up, heigh ho, bus home up Oxford Road. Some night out.

Outside, out of cigarettes, thinks he sees a vending machine and is there before he realizes it's for milk. His sway up to it, after a dollop of beer, could slip a hint more positive than need be. A voice. The medieval page turns his head. Trains whistle.

Edward Evans, born January 3, 1948, died October 6, 1965, toward midnight, aged seventeen years and nine months.

But this time it went wrong.

CHAPTER 5

THE BREADMAN COMETH

"The army of unalterable law."
George Meredith

IT WENT WRONG, and at 6:07 the next morning, a beautiful autumn dawn on the farthest fringe of Greater Manchester, a telephone call was made from a roadside phone booth. A trembling hand, but 999 is easier than most.

A boy of seventeen stood hunched over the phone. Not Edward Evans. Could as well have been, another guitarless adolescent, but this one was fairer, taller, tougher, and outside the booth there shivered a frightened shadow of a girl with a hasty beehive hairdo. Stammering into the mouthpiece hardly above a whisper, he—as it was to be mildly put in court—"set the machinery of the law in motion" with the most banal five words in the language: "My name is David S-Smith, is that Hyde P'lice S-Station?" Young Police Constable Keith Edwards, still on night duty and in an early-morning doze: "What is it?"

"I'm speakin' from 'Attersley, there's been a m-murder."

Hattersley is one of those new things. It forms part of the long-overdue plans of the Manchester Corporation to bandage the running sores of a great city: by building on its outermost edges

what are called "overspill estates" for the housing of slum
dwellers.

Driving east from Gorton's decaying streets, you forge past
Audenshaw and finally reach Hyde, to which Hattersley is offi-
cially attached. There is nothing to tell you that you are not still
in the suburbs, but peer again and you will see that Hyde was
once a little country borough with amenities. The *Hyde Guide*,
1963: "Many stately homes are accessible, such as Chatsworth . . .
The countryside offers pleasant rambles . . . Outstanding events
have been visits from the Princess Helena Victoria in 1926 and
the Duke of Gloucester in 1930 . . . Noteworthy is the Town
Hall, which includes the Police Headquarters and the Magis-
trates' Court . . . Apart from the Pit Accident of 1889 and the
Flood of 1905, public disasters have been very few." The editor
of the next *Guide* will be forgiven for leaving this sentiment
intact.

A couple of miles east, the last straggles of suburbia give way
to gently rolling hillocks; on the eastern horizon, the soft line of
the moors. You can almost smell the healthy ozone. Region of
family picnics in summer, of athletic hikes, of God's fresh air, at
last.

And on these hillocks the Director of Housing had set out
Hattersley, and agreeably too. When the emigrant housewives
from Gorton and thereabouts hung up their fresh cretonne curtains, they must have felt they were in paradise. Little roads
wind up and around the hillocks, lined with houses which are
small but with large, plain windows and . . . *gardens!* The names
of the byways have a rustic ring: Hare Hill Road, Pudding Lane,
Sundial Walk, Sundial Close.

The wholesale emigration had been looked on askance by
nearby Mottram-in-Longdendale, a middle-class community as
settled as its name: doctors, lawyers, retired business folk. The
newcomers were certainly a mixed lot. To be sure, there are the
frugal decent families, usually church or chapel, the backbone of
the North, who have kept the delicate equilibrium, can use and
enjoy new amenities and are a credit to progress.

But there are the others. Mottram mutters that at the old New
Inn (on the edge of the estate) you used to be able to sip

your sherry in peace, and now it's long-haired Irish laborers and mums with drooling babies, and the NO OMNIBUSES sign's been taken down and gas meters broken into—what d'you expect, they've never had such things and there's even burglaries and I hear TV sets on the installment plan and washing machines arriving and leaving like clockwork. It's let the district down.

" 'Attersley," repeated the voice on the phone, "a—m-matter o' life an' death, 'Attersley Road West C-Call-box, an' 'urry!"

"Okay," said Police Constable Edwards, and hung up and blinked. Should he have said, "What d'you think you're playin' at, *Z Cars?*" Could be a joke, he thought as he dialed P.C. Antrobus, but a joke at 6:07 A.M.?

Could be a false alarm, Antrobus thought as he buttoned up his tunic, p'r'aps the bloke's found a drunk lying against their front door bleeding from a broken bottle. The car started like a bird, lovely morning sun just coming out, a pleasure to be alive, and four minutes later he was slowing up at the red phone booth.

For a moment he thought, Oh hell, it *was* a leg-pull, nothing stirring for miles except an early red bus with PICCADILLY written on it and containing a couple of workmen. But as his car came to a standstill, a slight figure darted forward from the shadows of Hare Hill Road, followed by a girl even slighter, the boy in spindly jeans under a short coat with a fur collar. They were cold and white to the lips, like children who have spent a homeless night after seeing a ghost.

Antrobus climbed out. "Mr. Smith?"

" 'Sright, this is M-Mrs. Smith."

Playing at mums and dads—well, let's see. "Mr. Smith, what's the trooble?"

"There's been a m-m-m . . ."

"Murder," said Mrs. Smith. There was a footstep and David Smith gave a gasp, turned even whiter and wheeled around in such a panic that he started to climb in the driver's door. "Okay, Dave," said the girl, "it's only two workmen," and he unstiffened.

"What's that you got," said the policeman, "hand over please." The boy did so: screwdriver and bread knife. "I brought them for p-protection." They climbed in, so relieved to be there that the polite silence was not embarrassing.

In Hyde Police Station, Inquiry Room, the two looked still so cold and hungry that Antrobus suggested tea all around. As they drank, David Smith, in fits and starts, in the flat voice which was never to vary, told his story. Little Mrs. Smith, clutching and reclutching her crumpled handkerchief, said nothing. But David Smith talked. And then stopped.

7:20. Police Constable Antrobus telephoned his superior, Detective Inspector Wills, at his home in Hyde, who after a flicker of hesitation telephoned *his* superior. 7:25. The flicker was because the super was all packed to leave with his wife for a badly needed holiday, three days with his sister in London and then ten at home working in his garden. "Sorry, boss, looks like a murder, and a sticky one."

Superintendent Talbot. He was still savoring the sound of it, he was newly promoted.

Mutterings are often enough heard against the British police ("Not all they're cracked up to be") for it to be fair to present Robert Alexander Talbot as representative of British law and order. A young fifty, tall and lean ("Played football till I was thirty-eight") steady blue eyes, he was a simple and serious family man. When he makes a joke you have to watch out, for he keeps a poker face that tells you nothing; correct to the point of dryness, wedded to the truth. But the manners impeccable, none of that bullying. It is likely that if he opened a door and found a cook holding a cleaver and glaring at him across six decapitated waitresses, Bob Talbot would clear his throat and fix her with thoughtful eyes: "Good morning, madam, I understand there has been an act of violence." A St. George of the North Country, astride the nag of common sense.

His career had been a local one of meritorious and uneventful progress. Started as constable, moving slowly from such country stations as New Ferry, Frodsham, Sale and Altrincham to Chester and Cheadle Hulme. Police Training School; after joining the C.I.D. (the Criminal Investigation Department; in other words, becoming a detective) was gradually promoted to detective constable, detective sergeant, sergeant, inspector, chief inspector in charge of North East Cheshire and finally, in July 1965, deputy superintendent.

By then it had become clear to him that the burden on the headquarters at Cheadle Hulme was getting much too heavy, and that to ease it there should be formed a new division centred in Stalybridge, a valley factory town beyond Hyde, the last grimy bastion before the country takes over for good. The chief constable of Cheshire agreed, and on September 1, 1965, just five weeks before, Talbot, after his years of plain-clothes detecting, found himself back in uniform as Superintendent Talbot, chief of the Stalybridge Division. His most important landmark so far. He was not yet to realize how important, or how mistaken he would be to imagine he had left detection behind. For the new division comprised not only Stalybridge, Hyde and Dukinfield, but Hattersley.

Bob Talbot looked at his wife, just waking up, then at the two suitcases, full but open and waiting for toothbrushes and all that. Some poor old body's surprised a burglar on the job and had to pay for it, damn . . .

7:26 A.M. "Sorry, Mum, got to get the uniform out, bang goes the holiday for today, back one o'clock wi' luck." The only meal he was to eat at home for six weeks was breakfast.

7:45, Hyde Police Station, already bustling. Wills had phoned Jock Carr, Talbot's detective sergeant, a chubby ginger-haired young Scot who was waiting to follow the super into the Inquiry Room. There Police Constable Antrobus was pouring out a fresh cup of tea for the Smiths, they were introduced to the super, he sat down and fixed them with impartial blue bobby eyes. They certainly looked poorly, what's it all about, lad? It's m-murder, sir, and he told his story again, his wife helping him out with the stammer.

Talbot looked up the right map and pocketed it. "Thank you, Mr. Smith, I ought to be gettin' along."

"I wouldn't go inside the 'ouse alone, sir, 'e's got g-guns." It was the familiar Lancashire voice he had heard all his life, and in the sunny light of a North Country morning a gangster crisis seemed improbable. "See you later."

But the word had to stick. Guns. Talbot lifted the phone, and like a housewife speaking to the grocer, ordered two dozen policemen and half a dozen plain-clothes men in half a dozen patrol cars at—where is it, Jock?—within twenty minutes—oh, and Policewoman Slater—and then for them all to disappear around the area, you get me? Then he pulled on his peaked cap and he and Carr were off. Just time to study the map before they left Mottram Road and turned up into the Avenue they wanted. No trees, just an ordinary new road on a hill; somehow from the word avenue you thought of trees. As they stopped, Talbot saw a couple of his cars arrive and steal unobtrusively past. He sat a moment to think.

8:19. With every minute the estate's daily life was quickening: a motorbike revved up, a housewife haloed in plastic curlers shook a rug out a window; outside the New Inn, bus queue for Manchester. A glorious morning, the sort when every child you see in the sun looks as if he'll grow up great and good. A bold billboard in a field: CITY OF MANCHESTER OVERSPILL DEVELOPMENT.

Whatever awaited him—and after stripping Smith's story, what was left was possibly a hysterical husband with a hangover and a boy friend dead in the wife's bed—it seemed safest to get at the place from the back. He and Carr got out and studied a row of four little terraced houses.

Perched above the Avenue, they looked squarely down and across at the highway—Mottram Road—the proud representatives of the other new homes clustered on the slopes around them. Number 16 was the last one of the four. The Smiths had assured the policemen that "he" left every morning at 8:20 sharp. And with luck "he" wouldn't have a gun on him.

Without luck he might. Talbot remembered the policeman at the Cheshire railway station when they had thought, Well, even if there *is* a gun, folk don't use them, not here—and the man was shot dead. He saw a door open, then another. Children with school satchels. Guns. More cars were disgorging policemen who dispersed as noiseless as morning shadows. And at each corner, just within view of the next, there seemed to be posted a young businessman who had forgotten what bus to catch, or indeed what his business was. Next to Carr's dark suit Talbot suddenly felt very conspicuous in his uniform.

8:25. And with every minute more was going on. Luckily folk on the estate seemed intent on minding their own business. Two more kids with satchels, "Got yer sandwiches?" Postman—perhaps somebody on the estate had won the pools. Then more kids. "Careful gettin' on that bus!" Kids, guns.

The paperboy dawdled—*Express, Mail, Mirror*—Rhodesia Crisis Tories Plan Jolt, what'll they be saying tomorrow morning? Talbot tried to think of something else.

8:30. A couple of mothers had a quick curious look at the two of them, one pointed them out to a neighbor. Talbot waved reassuringly, Carr yawned. They strolled a yard or two.

8:35. Must do something. Talbot decided to take a walk around the back; in Sundial Close he espied Craig's Pantry Van, the breadman climbing out in his long white coat. Talbot sauntered up. "I am," he said pleasantly if ambiguously, "in a delicate situation, would you mind lendin' me the coat?" The breadman looked at him; there'd been a car pinched perhaps. "Ee, I don't know, it's got me small change in it!" "Shan't keep you a minute," and Talbot hopped into the van, pulled the white coat over his uniform and climbed out again with a basket of fresh loaves over his arm.

A return stroll, Carr at a respectful distance. Then as he embarked on the footpath in front of the four houses (in the window of the first house, Number 10, a plaster cat and a plaster dog) he heard a snigger: out of the corner of his eye he saw two of his men watching him, hand to mouth. All right, lads, I don't want a bullet in me guts as I get to the gate, better safe than sorry. The smell of the bread reminded him of the breakfast he hadn't had, and of the comforts of country life.

He clicked open the front gate of Number 16. Nasturtiums. At the front door the mat was clean but worn, must have been brought from the old place. Still the humming tradesman, he walked along the left side of the house to the back door, which was overlooked by an amphitheater of houses, over twenty windows in all, and the sun was like a spotlight on him. He was glad of the white coat. But the tenants were busy emptying rubbish, hanging washing, beating a carpet. A radio played somewhere, must be *Housewives' Choice*. He knocked at the back door. 8:40.

The trash can was at his elbow, neatly closed. Outside the next house, a couple of feet away, a child's swing. He heard Carr's step along the side of the house; it stopped. He knocked again, no louder.

Suppose Smith's one o' these teen-age drug-fiend weirdies who's imagined the whole caboodle? Take it easy.

The door opened. The lady of the house. Blouse, tweed jacket and skirt, white high-heeled shoes, just off to the office.

Something stirred behind her, and a face peered inquisitively up. A dog. Mongrel collie, and neat, like her legs. "Puppet," she said, again the flat practical voice, "you hush now."

Talbot the policeman sized her up, swiftly. Local business girl, bettered herself. Thirty-five, strong chin, good complexion, woman's mouth. A smart secretary who, if she'd married the boss, would be in mink in the Midland Hotel, diamond earrings, the lot, getting the martinis past that square jaw and discussing her new committee, child welfare and all that.

As it was, she was a smart secretary whose coiffure and make-up almost made her a dance hostess living some distance from her job and up unnaturally early: a helmet of honey-platinum hair bulkily back-combed above a bold fringe, fashionably thick black eyebrows, handsome dark eyes fashionably rimmed by black lashes; pale cheeks, pale lipstick. Even the family man had to note that she was a bit on the bulgy side; if she'd been half an inch taller and a couple of pounds heavier she'd ha' been strapping. He was amazed later to hear her real age; less than three months ago she had reached her twenty-third birthday.

She looked from him to the loaves. "Would you be wantin' anythink?"

He was losing ground. "I'd like to speak to your husban', please."

The black brows contracted a millimeter, and she answered coldly (why not, it's a question you don't expect from a tradesman), "I 'aven't got a 'usban'."

A pause. What the hell, here goes but careful with it. He stepped past her into the kitchen and opened the white coat. "Sorry, madam, I am a police officer."

Her face had not changed a muscle. Neat roomy kitchen; on the gas stove, kettle and coffeepot, with next to them a tin of the salt his wife used. Beyond the tiny hall—four clothes hooks—the closed door of the sitting room. The dog passed them and scratched at it. She hesitated, passed him, opened it and went inside, the dog sliding past her. Talbot heard Jock Carr slip into the kitchen from the back, good old Jock. He put down the basket of loaves and followed her.

Inside, he almost collided with something. Eighteen inches off, a pair of eyes, unblinking, mad-bright. He realized they were staring at him from behind bars. A bird. A budgerigar. A budgie. (Just let me get at you, David Smith . . .)

The room was as neat as if Mary Poppins lived here. Rose-pink wall, red-flowered curtains, a rug in front of last night's dead fire, telly in the corner. Two boxes that looked like his son Dennis' tape recorder. Everything tidy except the bed. One of the two pillows retained the impression of a head. The housewife's. Who was not a wife. Sitting up alongside in his undershirt, the non-husband. But a bobby can't dress up as a breadman just to arrest a chap for writing a letter with a hollow in the other pillow. Potato crisps. A bowl of plastic chrysanthemums.

The occupant, green ballpoint pen in hand, raised his head to look inquiringly at the intruder. He was a lean, alert young man, with bright hollow-set eyes above high cheekbones: dark-brown hair sprang from an intelligent forehead. An up-and-coming bank clerk having a lie-in.

But something made Talbot persevere. "I understand that last night an act of violence was committed on these premises."

The young chap in bed went on looking at him, but the woman's look switched from Talbot to the bed and stayed there, steadfastly. The young chap did not speak. Why should he, wasn't he the righteous occupant, waiting for an explanation? Carr appeared in the doorway. Nobody said anything.

Talbot turned to the girl, might as well bluff. "I'd like to see upstairs, if you don't mind."

"Certainly." Cold, correct, like a receptionist. He followed her, leaving Carr standing before the fireplace, while the other finished his letter.

Up the tiny staircase. Nice pale walls, stair carpet gaily patterned with flowers. Landing. Bathroom door open, two doors closed. Just as he put his hand out to one of them, she stepped closer to him and whispered urgently, "No . . ."

He gave her a sharp look—hello . . . Past her, he opened the door, an inch.

The inch was far enough to see, in a bright morning bedroom, an old lady sitting up in bed in a frilly jacket, sipping from a cup. As she started to teeter an absent-minded head, he closed the door softly and turned to the girl. "It's me gran," she said, "it's her 'ouse an' she's not a bit well."

Two dogs, a budgie and a gran. The girl had now moved over to hold Gran's handle, leaving the third door unmasked. Mechanically—just as he was thinking, How can I get out without an action for illegal entry, she looks just the sort—he tried the door. It was locked.

Her expression still did not change, she was still the lady of the house who has been put upon, but he felt his confidence return. The landing was so small that he was closer to her than he wanted to be. The flat Lancashire monosyllables came out muffled.

"Could I have the key?"

"No, you can't, it's not coonvenient."

"Why can't I?"

"I keep me firearms in there for safety."

"I'm afraid I moost ask you for that key."

"It's at work. It's not coonvenient."

She was obstinate, but so was he. "I'm afraid I have to have that key."

She continued to look at him, without answering. He turned smartly and descended the steep flowered stairs. She followed him. Carr was still on the rug, and the man of the house was still writing. He looked up. She looked at him. Nobody spoke.

Then Talbot said, "I'll send one of my men down to where you work, to pick up the key." He waited.

The man spoke at last, carefully. A Scottish accent. "Ye best give him the key."

A pause. His hollow-eyed immobility was unsettling. She crossed toward the tape recorders, opened her handbag, handed Talbot a key ring and turned to the door. He followed her upstairs, thinking, Carr's down there with him . . . guns . . . God, I hope there isn't one under that pillow.

He unlocked the door. She opened it, like a landlady showing a room to a prospective lodger whose looks do not please her. He walked in.

Bare floorboards, and the furnishing so sparse that it might have been a storeroom: bare walls, narrow stripped bed, wardrobe, small table with lace runner, armchair with a dress on it, suitcases, on the floor a scrabble of polythene, cardboard boxes, large open carton with an old magazine crammed on top and printed across it FRESH FROM THE FARM, NEW-LAID EGGS and on the floor under the window—the same red cretonne as downstairs—a neat oblong parcel which looked ready for dispatch by rail, on it two or three paperbacks, looked as if they were left over from the packing. He looked at the wardrobe, then at her, and opened it sharply.

Clothes on hangers, shoes: man's and woman's. No go.

Then he looked again at the parcel under the window. It was covered in a dark-grey blanket. He tried to move it with his foot. Heavy, even for books. Under the blanket one small bulge, like an extra butt end sticking out of a well-packed swathe of firelogs. He bent down and felt it.

It was hard, like wood. Or rather, stiff. And yet when you squeezed, it was soft. He ran his fingers along. Under the rough cloth, it felt like marbles in a row.

Not marbles. Toes. A human foot.

Straightening up, he heard the sound of a child running for a bus in the sun. *Housewives' Choice* still on the radio somewhere. A woman in a back garden hanging up a shirt. Miles away on the horizon, the moors.

He turned to the lady of the house.

PART TWO

THE SEPARATE JOURNEYS TO THE APPOINTED PLACE

CHAPTER 6

WEE IAN

"Life is a maze in which we take
the wrong turning before we
can walk."

Cyril Connolly

THE WORLD ADVANCES, how it strides! Yearly, monthly,
weekly, yet another mystery of the universe is laid bare. Dare-
devils from Omsk or Oshkosh frisk like drunken balloons in outer
space, a billion miles from home. And any day now, while
frisking, they will exchange planetary trivia with their moist-eyed
families sitting around the new Fireside Intercom. "Guess what,
folks—I been signed by Universal Pictures!" . . . "Tovarich, this is
long distance!" The jokes will be described, a couple of days later
in *Time*, as cosmicalities. The week after, dogs will be baying
not *at* the moon, but on it.

We advance. But the one mystery we shall never solve is the
enigma of human identity.

What am I? What are You? I spell "You" with a capital because to you, you are as real as I am to me. What is your full
brother, brought up by the same parents in the same house and
educated at the same school? You meet him in the street and find
him so different from you, in instincts and in outlook, that you
might as well be greeting a pleasant stranger. Why?

Again, you may have another full brother, who from the day of his healthy birth has lived, and will live till the hour of his gentle death—hazily, monosyllabically—encircled by an invisible wall. He was touched, in your mother's womb, by a spell as weird as the curse cast by the wicked fairy. And as your mother sits holding the fingers of the sweet-faced grown man on the stool beside her, her eyes stray to the newspaper photos of the scientific geniuses who have made the latest miracle possible. But she can search their faces till doomsday, neither they nor their medical counterparts will ever be able to explain to her why this one son has to stay, all his life, an isolated child. It is not a case of finding the key to a locked door. There is no door.

A phenomenon as preordained as that one, riddle though it has to remain, is there for all to recognize, unvarying, stark. But there are stranger mysteries of identity. What of the spells which are woven after birth, the subtle processes working from day to day in the darkness of the young head, as it grows from childhood to adolescence and maturity?

There are the good spells, excitingly cast on future great ones and unheeded by the family. The boy of ten who, hearing the Sermon on the Mount for the first time, felt the first stirrings of his destiny as Albert Schweitzer. One of the two daughters of Mr. and Mrs. Nightingale, a Victorian miss who stunned them with the news that she was going to war as a nurse. The girl who seemed identical with every other peasant in Lorraine heard voices, rose and left for ever. Looking back on the faceless crowds, we watch the elect individuals stir out from the rest and step slowly forward into history.

But the spells working in the growing head are not always propitious. Ian Stewart Brady, born Sunday, January 2, 1938, forty minutes after midnight. "A Child That's Born on the Sabbath Day Is Fair and Wise and Good."

His delivery, in the Maternity Hospital, Rottenrow, Glasgow, was an easier business than his mother had thought possible. Having been assured it was a boy, she asked the inevitable second question, "Is he all right?" The reply was "Eight pounds and parrfect all over, only what a shame he didn't get here for the New Year!"

But for her, things were not so simple. She was down as Mrs. Maggie Stewart, Tearoom Waitress, Husb. Deceased," but the nurses knew she was Miss Stewart, such a pretty wee thing with her long fair hair like that film star Alice Faye or somebody, but no use pretending. These girls are either a tearful adolescent who didn't know what was going on, or a fly-by-night, or careless. Maggie Stewart, at twenty-eight, was hardly the first of those, there it was.

What a relief the baby was okay, but she had to wonder, guiltily, What if he'd ha' been stillborn? *He*'d never ha' kenned a thing, would he? For how was she to know the tearoom folk would take her back, and not a penny saved, and would her girl friend let her stay on with her at 8 Huntingdon Place, not that the postal address of St. Rollox was Buckingham Palace but moving's an expense.

Ah well, Maggie thought, wait an' see. She was, and would remain, easygoing and warm-hearted, a bit of a chatterbox. But one secret she was to keep. The identity of the father. All that is known is that he was a reporter on a Glasgow newspaper ("That's where Ian gets his readin' an' writin' "). The mother of his child has consistently maintained that he died three months before the birth. Did he? If not, is he still alive? Was there anything strange about him, or was Maggie Stewart's vanished lover a sunny and solid young man? There was certainly never anything out of the ordinary about her.

She had to leave Huntingdon Place, all right, and find a room quick-sharp in Caledonia Road, Gorbals. But she did get her job back. Only just, the baby meant she could only work part-time, and when she got the odd job waiting of an evening at a reception or a dance, there was the endless worry of arranging for various little girls up and down the street to watch over him; often at work she feared the worst until she got home and found he was still there and all of a piece. After three months she was worn out and had an ad put in a window: WORKING WIDOW WILLING HAVE CHILD ADOPTED. It was a long shot; families in the Gorbals are as teeming as in any other slum.

But a kind, vague little woman answered, over forty and slightly deaf, a Mrs. Sloan who said she'd take a chance, since the little lad was healthy. Maggie, not believing her luck, wiped away the tear and heaved the simultaneous sigh of relief, arranged her payments and said she was going to visit wee Ian every evening without fail and she would henceforth be Peggy, not Maggie, as Peggy was that bonnier a name. Ma Sloan called again, carried the sleeping baby down the alley to the battered pram and wheeled him to Camden Street.

The Gorbals is a poor and overcrowded district in the center of Glasgow, corresponding to parts of London's East End and of New York's West Side but carrying a specially notorious reputation. So notorious that when a man turns out to have been reared in the Gorbals, the reaction is, "What's his record?" The quarter certainly has bad slums and gang warfare, but there are also schools and hospitals and libraries; a child from a decent Gorbals home has as reasonable a chance as any other. And though Camden Street was a bad slum and Number 56 a sordid brownstone tenement, the Sloans' was a decent home.

They found him a good baby. As good as theirs had been, better if anything. Bouncing really, with his mother's hair, fair and curly, so he looked like Bubbles the Pears Soap baby, and bonny deep-set grey eyes.

As good as theirs? Not in the way of wedlock, of course, but the puir wee thing canna help that, can he?

No park nearer than Richmond Park, but the Sloan front window overlooked the little old Gorbals Burial Ground, depressing but nicely kept, and if there was a gleam of sun you could leave a baby. But a better bet, around the corner off Caledonia Road, was the Southern Necropolis, a big cemetery with wide paths where you could wheel a pram for a hundred yards. So on fine afternoons, her own children safe in Camden Street Primary, Mrs. Sloan would wheel the baby between the graves. Some people might think it a wee bit morbid but it's still fresh air an' a park really. While the gurgles were still straining to become speech, and the endearing smile, wind-induced, gradually became more wary as recognition dawned, words would drip down onto wee Ian in the shabby pram, as unimportantly as thin rain.

Gude afternune, Mrs. Mackintosh—Ian, wave your paw tae the lady . . . No, Mrs. Mac, it's no' our Jeannie, she's at school. This is an extra, as ye might say, nearly one of us by now, though the lady does try to get to us of a Sunday forenune, though she must be dyin' to get married, therrty she'll be any day. Hard to tell if he takes her in, sharrp though he is.

But unlike the rain, the words do not evaporate. The little ears catch the conspiratorial lowering of voices, and the words seep invisibly in. To be stored against the day of sorting out. Gude mornin', Inspector. Mr. Sloan's filled in the forrm wi' the ages o' the children . . . What's that? No, he's no' one of ours— Ian go find May's auld teddy bear—Stewart's the name. A long story, Inspector, let's step ootside a minute. Carry on, Ian.

The first two words he was to speak were "Auntie" to Ma Sloan and "Peggy" to her mysterious pretty friend who came odd Sundays and brought him a bow and arrow or something and once on a Saturday took him to the Circus. He was to go on calling her Peggy.

Minds are being broadened by the year, stretched so wide that you wait for a tearing sound. But in English-speaking countries the day when the Negro, walking in a white crowd, will be unconscious of its color and of his own, will come just as soon as the time when the bastard will grow up forgetful of his birth. In the instance of Ian Stewart, there were aggravating factors.

It was another case of well-meaning turning unconsciously into harm-doing ("We thought we was actin' for the best") and it is hard to censure. It had been infinitely good of the Sloans, with four children and depending on John Sloan's tenuous job with a firm of grain-and-rice merchants, to help out a young woman they did not know; and Peggy cannot be blamed either for her conscience or for her rumbling maternal instinct. But if only the foster mother had insisted on adoption, or the mother had made a clean break or even in the first place left her newborn baby on the workhouse doorstep, it would have been better.

Chance helped with the odds. If he had been a real baby brother, with a different permutation he might have found what he needed. The Sloans were all good people, and if the family had consisted of one daughter, she might have made the new-comer her own special brother; an only son might have done the same and become a protector and a pillar. Two daughters only even, or two sons, might have joined to champion the wee thing; they might have taken him by each hand and swung him down the stone stairs and into the adventure of the street, a secure child breathless with delight and trailing bare toes in the Gorbals grime. But there were two sons and two daughters, all older, and that is too complete an entity to reach outside itself, especially in a society where the fight for existence is unremitting. They were kind, as a family is to a pet: Tha's right, Ian, sit ye still an' play wi' yon bricks. D'ye mind the time he nearly fell i' the fire, he's really no' much trouble. Comin' tae the pictures, Jean?

There was never even the roughness which an overworked mother has to fall back on sometimes, the brisk smack-bottom and the lusty yell. Kindness all the time, even though it was, in the last analysis, the kindness of indifference. It needed one special arm around him, before he could even sit up; one face, loving and constant, heaving suddenly into view between pram top and slum sky: "I'm me and you're the one and only Ian, and when I'm not with you I'm always thinking about you." With that help, children stricken with physical deformity have scaled the barrier to adult happiness. Here was a perfectly equipped infant body, not a trace of asthma or even astigmatism. But through nobody's fault, where there should have been love there was only solicitude; they were sorry for him. The glass wall between him and the world was nebulously forming.

It would be foolish to maintain that this early situation is the key to "what caused it all." There are to be so many intertwining considerations that the case calls less for a blackboard than for a tapestry. But in that tapestry, the theme of the unwanted child is to trace itself indelibly. In and out it goes, out and in, the threads growing with every inch darker and firmer, until they run into other fearsome colors and the tale takes shape.

When the Second World War broke out on September 3, 1939, Ian Stewart was one year and eight months old; when it finished he was seven and a half. The war made less profound changes in the lives of the Glasgow poor than of the rich: the men were called up, and in the service they often got better money than they had in menial jobs. Clydeside was humming, crane and truck and screw and hammer, even Peggy had a job as a capstan operator. There was the rationing, but to families like Ma Sloan's there had always been curtailment, dictated by the household purse. And as for the blackout, the Gorbals side streets had always been twilit and unpredictable. There was talk of evacuating the children, but somehow it never came to anything. When Ian was three, Glasgow suffered its share of air raids, but Camden Street was never hit and the boy too young for the nightly strain to disturb his nerves or even his sleep, in the little back-room bunk behind a curtain.

The side streets were certainly unpredictable; having said that the child from a decent Gorbals home does have his chance, one must concede that temptation is only around the corner, and never more insistently than during the war. Smelly blind alleys, black as pitch, were suddenly stabbed across by a furtive beam from a flashlight or the quick open-shut of a bar door. Punchin' an' gougin'. A bairn of three was safe, but there were lads of thirteen running around ready and willing to prepare the scene for when the child of three would himself be thirteen. With Dad away at the war and Ma dealing with the problem of "just keeping going," the blackout became a joy forever. For the teen-ager, the thrill of the flashlight, the knife at the scout belt, the game of prizing open the windows of bombed or evacuated houses in search of the odd watch or even cashbox, the fire escapes, the footsteps of the exasperated police fading away in the dark—life was an endless adventure. And for many was to remain so.

The war settled down, and by the time wee Ian was five, his "Auntie" was walking him to the corner, tidy in May's battered old white sneakers, Camden Street Primary School, a godsend (get him oot o' the way 'stead o' toddlin' off into the street—with a war on, ye never know). One Sunday Auntie's friend Peggy brought him a kilt and a ruffled shirt, and trotting beside her in Richmond Park he was the regular Bonny Prince Charlie.

He was a quiet little boy, intelligent and obedient. He learned to read and write as soon as anybody—and independent! Had his tantrums: when he was crossed he would bang his head against a cushion and growl till he was red in the face. But hadn't the others done that in their time; isn't it supposed to be a healthy sign in a growing bairn?

On the morning of May 8, 1945, schools disbanded for the day, the war was over. Front page: royalty on a balcony, immense cheering crowds around Nelson's Column piercing the sky, very exciting.

In Camden Street Primary, the tired teacher looks along the rows of seven-year-old eyes, ye can spot the varieties in any classroom anywhere, and map out the course. The amiable little girl who has wife and mother written all over her, the red-haired biddy with the secret smile who is booked for the brothel before she's ever heard about babies, the lump of a lad with the eyes close together who'll go straight into one of the gangs, the boy always asking questions who'll forge ahead, the pretty little fellow who by the time he's in long trews will be sewing dresses for his sisters, they're all there.

Wee Ian? Well, Sloany's the type your eyes just skim over. Thoughtful, tidy, a sensitive face, serious though no reader. No' a merry lad and no' a mixer, maybe the makings of a parson. Illegitimate, poor kid. Merges into the crowd, really.

True, not a reader. Not yet. Except that he made the required Scottish contact with Walter Scott Condensed for the Young, where the lurid romance of castle and gorge and battle and dungeon caught his fancy. King Arthur and his knights did too, the all-powerful monarch with his Round Table of blindly devoted henchmen.

But in the first postwar and pretelevision years, over every city child it was the movies that held sway; on the lonely and imaginative one, their hold was especially strong. Saturday afternoons, sixpences were clutched in hot palms and pushed down the metal slope of a thousand pay windows, then the perch-up on the edge of the seat in the darkened shouting stamping arena. And each child found in the excitement what it suited him to find. One of them might be carried away by the horse riding across the great outdoors and the bravery and the chivalry, another not. All you can bet on is that if the child was really impressed by what he saw, however he saw it, he'd start noting down the fillums: PICTURES I HAVE ENJOYED. And if he's the sort that likes making lists, he can keep it up for years.

1947. Calder Cinema Govan Hill Jan 9 *Gunsmoke.* Feb 6 *Shadow of Terror.* New Savoy Feb 22 *The Killers.* Govan Hill Feb 27 *Appointment with Crime.* Mar 27 *Wanted by the Police.* One against the world, bang bang bang. Bang bang bang, one against the world.

Before the loneliest of boys settles for his own society, he is for a moment blown like a leaf into the social life; in this case, games in the street, harmless duels which several schoolmates remember, British Tommy v. Jerry. Nobody was willing to be a Jerry except the one boy who had had no relatives in the forces: Sloany. He even insisted on it, as if instinctively drawn to "the other side." The first symptom of what was to turn into a disease. Cranstons de Luxe May 9 *Odd Man Out.*

On a summer Saturday, when he was nine and had never been beyond the Gorbals, there was a Sloan birthday and out of the blue, Ma organized a family day trip to Loch Lomond, sandwiches and thermoses.

On the long journey through the same old streets, he sat staring out of the bus window in that sedate way of his, while the older four blethered about the fun to come. Then they got down and were suddenly faced with the towering majesty of the mountains mirrored in the great lake. It was spiffing to breathe the air in after the muck, and they all set off into the steep fields. They settled before a breath-taking view and picnicked, then the real Sloans had a family snooze in the sun.

It was when they sat up that they missed Ian. Five hundred yards up, against the afternoon sky, they spotted his silhouette, then the boys called, Ian Ian!, then tried yodeling, then scrambled up to him.

He looked at them as if he had never seen them before. "We're for hame," they said. "Go back," he said. "I'm fine up here by mesell, let me alane." They gave him ten minutes and went down again.

On their way home in the bus he was to talk, unusual for him; for he would be excited enough by those minutes to blurt out, to one of his foster sisters, his feelings about them.

He stood and stared at the vast empty hills as if they were staring back at him and holding his look. He had been a great deal by himself, on bomb sites or in the park, but the throb of life had always been on the corner. For the first time, he was alone at the center of a limitless territory. His own, it belonged to him. The revelation was the same breath-taking one that once swept the nascent Romantic poets with humility and love.

But this was no Wordsworth. He was never to forget the effect which "scenery" had on him that day, but there was little love and no humility. As the conviction overcame him that this empty domain was his property, his emotion was one of power. The lone Laird of all he surveyed. Flood that valley to make Ian's Lake, crowd that hillside with Ian's City, cap that crag with a Castle just like them postcards of Edinburgh.

On from there, the mind's eye bolstering up the names with the capital letters of the fairy stories. In the center of great Castle Square, atop a pedestal the height of Nelson's, the gilded statue of King Ian is unveiled, his good sword Excalibur high in the air above ten thousand cheering subjects . . .

"I reckon he enjoyed hisself," said poor Ma Sloan, whose failing ears were making her relationship with him even more tenuous, "ye nivver can tell wi' Ian." He never mentioned the outing again, but they noticed that whenever he came across a photograph of mountains, he would look at it for quite a time.

Later in 1947 the Sloans made a momentous move, out of the Gorbals and up in the world, to 21 Templeland Road, on an overspill estate three miles off in Pollok; the procedure which, seventeen years later, was to be repeated elsewhere. The house was a pleasant two-story semidetached house with indoor bathroom and front garden, in a nice clean sweeping road near golf courses and semi-open country; Pollok was a Tory stronghold. Ma and the girls felt a buoyant sense of release and self-respect.

For Ian, Camden Street Primary was replaced by Carnwadric

Primary in Capelrig Street, a pleasant two-mile ride by school bus. But the dual change meant nothing. It seemed, to the puzzled family, as if he felt himself to belong to a world so superior that the difference between slum and comfortable flat was negligible compared with what he was used to. And surely the lad should have felt the wrench of parting from Camden Street pals? He had no pals. And Auntie's friend Peggy had by now skipped enough Sundays for him not to miss *her*.

To be sure, there was the conventional sexless sentimental friendship "wi' one o' the wee lassies," characteristic of the little boy too timid for the rough-and-tumble camaraderie of the playground. For over two years, nine till twelve, he sat in the bus with his satchel jostling that of a shy little girl in a jumper named Evelyn Grant, who thought him as nice-looking as he was gentle. They became sort of sweethearts. He made a habit of sending her notes in class, such as "We'll meet behind the tree," then put crosses for kisses. They both liked pop music, Ian the more old-fashioned kind, Cole Porter and such, and also rabbits, which they kept in a hutch behind the Sloan home and which they fed together after school.

Then she would sit agog while he did his party trick. Unexpectedly, in her front room Ma had always kept an old upright piano, and Ian acquired the knack of picking out tunes on it. "Annie Laurie" would echo stringily across the road but more often than not it would be a rousing march, "Scots Wha Hae," or "Hielan' Laddie," thumpa thump *thump,* thumpa thump *thump thump: Daily Clarion* Edinburgh, King Ian's legions are now streaming into the Castle Square, banners flying, thumpa *thump.* It was hardly a talent in the making, but his was one of those excitable imaginations which react instantly to music so long as it is either martial or erotic. For Evelyn he would feel out on the keys any tune she hummed, and then give his wizard imitation of Billy Daniels singing "That Ole Black Magic."

Meantime in school, his teacher Miss Scott observed his delicate looks, his politeness (from the Gorbals too!) and especially his sense of order. His "jotter"—exercise book—was the neatest in the class ("For years after he left I used to hold it up as an example"). Little Lord Fauntleroy.

1948 Odeon Renfrew St Feb 23 *I Walk Alone*. Westway Mar 8 *The Outlaw*.

Go on, ye fule, kick him! Nae, no' in the face, ye fule, i' the balls—that's better, goodo wallop! Grand Cowcaddens June 21 *The Perfect Crime*.

Yes, we are beginning to look out—it is inevitable—for portents. When old schoolmates are quizzed about a Prime Minister or a mass murderer, details emerge which fit miraculously into the jigsaw. The P.M. was heard to say, "I'm bottom of the class now but one day I'll be at the top of the ladder," and the miscreant was caught pulling wings off insects, with a gleeful glare. Too good to be true. The future P.M. is just as likely to have been the fly baiter.

It has been constantly repeated that before Sloany was eleven he tied a boy to a post and set fire to him. The story was becoming authentic when John Cameron, a young mechanic from Allison Street, Glasgow, stated, "Well, I just remember we were playing cops an' robbers and it was my turn to be tied and there was a lot of smoke. I don't recall much about it."

But another boy, Angus Morristoun, tells a story told to him by Sloany, an account detailed enough to be credible. About a cat.

CHAPTER 7

SHADOWS BEFORE

"He bears the seed of ruin in himself."
Matthew Arnold, "Merope"

THE DAY this happened, he was ten and a half. And growing. Across the asphalt playground they used to shout "Lanky Sloany," but better than "Short Arse" or "Smelly" like they do after some poor kids.

The trough of the summer holidays, and an oppressive late afternoon. Pictures? Elephant Cinema Shawlands. Jeanette Mac-Donald and Nelson Eddy in *Sweethearts* (Ye can stuff that one up). Finished reading *Biggles Goes to War* and all the comics, a wee walk, Sandy Gowan an' Willie McEllan crossin' the road so they wouldna have to ask me to play cricket on the bomb site. I'd ha' said no anyway, all that butterfingers stuff an' orrderin' ye aboot like ye was muck. They both look like they got a dose, wha'ivver that means.

Ma Sloan asked him to do some shopping for her, and he was so bored he was glad. He made a list—tomatoes, peas, spuds—set out, did the shopping, then saw a bus and thought he'd kill time with a visit to a secret haunt. Rutherglen, four or five miles across town: next to the old bombed cemetery, a funny little old house, razed by a raid except for one little room which still had the four walls and the fireplace.

He climbs over the age-old rubble in the doorway, puts down the bulging shopping bag and flops onto the carpet of weeds under the canopy of blue sky.

A wad of stained wallpaper sags down into the nettles sprouting between the rotten floorboards, and the ruined hearth still shows the marks of the old dead family fires. In the afternoon light, the senseless destruction of the smashed home is so utter that it brings a tranquil satisfaction: chaos can go no further. A satisfaction which in the warmth of the sun on the weeds softens into voluptuousness. As grossly as he can, for the benefit of grownups who aren't there, he burps. Gowan an' McEllan—coupla sods.

The cat's eyes meet his. And fix them. The glare of an emaciated pariah, red of eye, mangy of tail and sharp of claw. But insolent. A look steady with contempt: What was the name again? you think you're special, do you? Well, I have news for you. You have no fun in you and that's why everybody dodges you; you're a bastard.

In one second, the mutual hate is as absolute as mutual love. This is the enemy. An aristocrat of a cat, come down in the world in a borrowed fur coat, but she knows a Gorbals nothing when she sees one. If it takes till morning, he'll stare those eyes out.

She? It? Somehow a she, an imperious queen of an English cat, doncher know, no ideah where the next mouthful's coming from, we lorst all our money in the war, you Scotch nit. He blinks. The eyes have outstared him. Won.

No, not won. The lazy boy with nothing to do notices something. The impoverished aristocrat is trembling. She despises him, but she is frightened. Trembling. He reaches out.

But she is too quick for him. Just as his hands, already large and bony and strong, are about to close on her, she is on the half-mantelpiece, triumphant next to a dandelion. Hissing, taunting. They look again into each other's eyes. The only two creatures in the world.

Carefully, without taking his eyes off her, he feels for Ma Sloan's shopping bag and carefully empties it, stacking the groceries among the nettles. Then as he creeps up, she leaps down to the floor. Then her mistake: instead of streaking for the doorway she flashes up the chimney, scrabbles wildly for a foothold and falls into his waiting hand.

Gently it encircles the poor starved body and draws it out. She claws at him, covering him with soot and drawing blood. A fatal move. He cuffs her sharply over the head, drops her neatly into the shopping bag and as he pulls the string tight across the mouth of it, he watches the bag rock and writhe over the floor, to the rhythm of short, terrified howls. The shapeless, heaving mass exudes fear, as sharp as a smell. He sits back in the last of the sun, utterly content.

Essential, somehow, to wait for the dark. He is quite happy waiting, watching the bundle in spasm. Hs listens, too, to the howls dwindling into a long moan, then into silence.

The sun gone at last. He emerged into the street of the living, a dutiful little boy with a laden shopping bag. The bag stiff and still, as if it knew its fate. By the time he reached his goal, the bombed cemetery, it was almost night. The dark had never frightened him, he felt akin to it. What's a gravestone but a slab with a load o' rubbishy auld print, the folk under it bundles of bones, and how can ye be scared o' ghosts when there's no' such a thing?

When he clambered over the broken wall he knew exactly where he was going, though when was it the idea came? Was it when she had clawed frantically upwards into the blackness of the chimney? Mind ye—as he was to remind schoolmates—the idea had been dormant for some time. Weeks back, just before Easter, Mr. Biddle, the auld twit who taught Scripture, had been gassin' aboot his nibs bein' buried in a garden but wasn't dead, only shammin', and after three days shoved the stone to one side an' was oot again as gude as new. It's just like Biddle the Piddle to expect kids to swallow a daft tale like that.

Enough moon for him to reach his corner, a cranny next to a smashed marble angel where kids had been excavating for mud pies. The hole was still there, a foot deep, oblong, neat.

He lay down the bag, which began to plunge again and cry out. Then—the details were to come out in the playground when he was challenged, how could he have managed this and that— he heaved up a jagged slab of gravestone and lowered it over the hole, leaving a couple of inches uncovered at one end. Then he held the bag over the aperture, upside down; then as the frantic animal crawled and slithered her way out and down into the hole, he slid the slab so that it covered the hole completely. He was an ingenious little boy. Silence, except for the distant city traffic.

Then she began to cry. A muffled howl of anguish, so faint that it could have been human. As clear as a message in words, one creature was begging from another. For mercy. In a world where up till now every voice addressed to him was already thinking of something it wanted to say to somebody else, he stood under the moon and drank in the first intensely personal sound he had ever heard. Master, Master, I am sorry I misbehaved, I lick your boots, my Master . . .

He is at peace. A peace with at its core a bubble of excitement which is placed somewhere at the very center of his perfect ten-year-old body. A bubble that bursts and re-forms so fast that it turns into a tickle. And that, he knows without knowing, is the beginning of the business the older gang are allus bashin' on about. It feels sort o' bad like they say, but nice too. I know, he says thoughtfully to himself, I know that I am doing wrong, but I am right to be doing wrong.

He walked purposefully back to his secret haunt, packed the groceries back into the bag and took the bus home. A glance through his comics, then the radio, *Just William, Take It From Here,* then bed, there to sleep as soundly as the boy across the road, who had spent the same time reading a library book about medicine and going to be a doctor. He only wakes once, surfacing out of dreamlessness to think pleasantly of his little friend—the enemy has mysteriously turned into just that—whom he has settled into the little home only he knows about. And he dives deep down again into sleep.

Crunching his breakfast oats, still at peace. But later in the morning he felt a nagging urge, and on the cricket bomb site he met Angus Morristoun, "I bet ye dinna ken how long a cat'll live after it's been buried?"

"And I bet ye dinna ken how long it takes a drowned elephant to come to the top—your turn, Sloany!"

"Shut your face an' listen. I'll be able to answer the question I just put, by tomorrow or the day after. Mind ye ask me." And he told the story. Kids tell tall tales—in Angus' time he had told a couple himself—and he didn't believe it. But that afternoon he and a friend happened to be near the cemetery and he thought to have a look at the corner Sloany'd told him about. And there it was, the stone slab.

They slid it aside. Out into the sunlight lurched the mute, drunken ghost of an alley cat, and limped back to the scavenging life of the streets.

Dogs are different, somehow. The Sloan girls acquired one, and Ian and he became good pals.

On February 1, 1950, aged twelve, he qualified (as a "top-quality pupil") for Shawlands Academy, a reputable non-fee-paying mixed school two miles off—another definite step forward. But to this dreamer, it was just another sea of faces. And getting dreamier every month. It was John Sloan's opinion, one of the few recorded, that bearin' in mind how queer the lad had been aboot that scenery, there was a risk he might turn into something tricky like an artist.

Marks, good. Quick at figures, tidy mind. Again his classroom schedules, tacked under the lid of his desk, were the trimmest in the room, crisscrossed with ruled lines. Neat.

Saw quite a bit of Evelyn Grant, who'd moved up into the academy with him and the others of their year. Took her to the pictures. Cranstons Mar 2 ROBERT MITCHUM TOUGH AND TERRIFIC in *The Big Steal*.

But that is just habit, with her sitting beside him he is still alone. He reads, but only what he is given to read, and then sees it his way. *Quo Vadis*, Christian nobodies being thrown to the lions before the roaring Roman VIP's, what a sight for sore eyes! *Robinson Crusoe*, alone and King of the Island.

There gradually evolved the oddest hobby, even odder then than it would be today. Just as other youths went in for cigarette cards of cricketers or pinups of Betty Grable, so this one started to collect Nazi souvenirs. Particularly knives. And it was not easy, people were sick of the war and the relics of victory—the Jerry cap, the bloodstained swastika blade, the rare photo of Eva

Braun—all had been thrown away or had to be unwillingly dredged from the bottom of trunks. A schoolmate, Frank Flanagan, had an elder brother stationed in Germany, and was pestered to no avail. People either thought Sloany soft in the head, or took offense. He didn't mind, he was used to being unpopular.

Cranstons Mar 9, doors open 12:30. Spellbinding and Fascinating *The Third Man*. He was twelve and a bit.

From the moment the curtains parted, and the great hands filled the screen and plucked at the zither with a weird throb never heard before, half nostalgia, half menace—dum da dee da *dum*, da *dum*—the boy felt the back of his neck tingle. This was for him.

All of it. The shadowed alleys and the rubble and the ruined tenements veering before him, to music: the Gorbals of a dream city. Mysterious shadows meeting in wet streets, commands barked out in a strange tongue which could be the Gaelic you hear on the radio: *"Warum antworten Sie nicht, WARUM!!!"* His mind refused the fact that it was the language of a people ignominiously defeated—no, it sounded proud and harsh and good. And then, to the gut-stirring throb of the zither, beat beat beat, the long slow walk through the cemetery, mourners around newly dug grave, priest sprinkling earth on coffin (*gekreuzigt gestorben und begraben*), the laconic exchanges in a sleazy bar: "Well, you could say murder was his racket . . . I was told that a third man helped to carry the body." The American hero and his girl he hardly saw, something was lacking—what was it?

The Third Man. The kitten between the feet, the lone face in the doorway—gone. Then the ghostly deserted fairground, dum da dee da *dum* da *dum*, then the lonely figure they thought was dead. Harry Lime. Slowly he sauntered, looking up at the giant wheel, black shirt and white tie, gross and yet elegant, cynical and all-powerful: Hallo old man, how are you? Then he talked easily (*Geht in Ordnung, geht in Ordnung*), then they went slowly up on the wheel and looked down at the people miles below, dots walking like flies. "I carry a gun . . . Would you feel

any pity, old man, if any of those dots stopped moving forever?
. . . In Italy they had terror, murder, and they produced Michel-
angelo; in Switzerland they had five hundred years of democracy
and what did that produce? The cuckoo clock, so long old man."
The twisted smile, the ruthless charm, the turn on the heel; the
zither music was beating around the boy's face like warm caressing hands. Harry Lime I love you Harry Lime I *am* Harry Lime
Harry Lime's a Scot. Wish they'd talk that German more, that la-
di-da stuff they're spouting gets in the way, leave that to flippin'
stuck-up London . . .

Wet streets, police on the prowl, mysterious man with toy balloons, dum da dee da *dum*, Harry with gun running from police,
and then—he turned a corner into Something Strasse, heaved a
manhole up, disappeared into the bowels of the city earth, and
the cinema reverberated with the boom of footsteps and of water
in subterranean caverns. The sewers! The sewers of Vienna! The
secret places, that the millions walking around have no knowledge of! Harry Lime, black shirt and white tie and cigar, strides
godlike past the plunging rats, a god at bay, one against all,
monarch of all he surveys. *Jawohl!*

Any facets of the film which did not suit him, he ignored.
Vienna? No, no, this was Berlin, and Harry Lime was not a
dapper Anglo-American but a ruthless Teutonic hero, the raised
eyebrow the symbol of amused power. And when he saw in a
magazine—"Twenty Years Ago Today"—the photograph of a
mustached and uniformed man on a balcony, holding out an
enraptured arm to a waving crowd of thousands, it was the Castle
Window in Ianburgh. The mustache didn't look so good but
what the hell, the uniform was smashing. The face merged into
the better one of Harry Lime, then into King Ian's; Sieg Heil it
said underneath. "'The English must be brought to their
knees,'" preached Hitler twenty years ago, "'just as the Jews
have been!'" Weel, what's wrong wi' that, snooty English bas-
tards all over the Central Hotel and a lot of 'em Jews too, half
the Gorbals owned by fat money-grubbin' Yids. Gude auld Hitler, he's not dead, ye ken, just bidin' his time in South Amer-
ica.

Embassy Mar 11 *Bad Men of Tombstone.*

Christmas 1950. Best present ever: Woddye think, our Stone of Destiny which the Sassenachs pinched a thousand years back an' had the cheek tu shove under their Coronation Chair in Westminister soddin' Abbey—guess what! Weel on soddin' Xmas Day some Scottish laddies pinched it right back an' they've got it right here in Glesga, gude werrk.

1951. Sloany shooting up, tall for thirteen. Regal Renfrew St Jan 26 *The Asphalt Jungle*. Elephant Shawlands Feb 6 *She Shall Have Murder*. One of the football team put a knee out and they gave lanky Sloany a try. An important match against an Edinburgh academy, and Sloany really meant to have a go. For a week he gave up the surreptitious cigarette.

And he did have a go. It wasn't easy to tell why he was no good. He ran fast and had a strong kick, but when a shoulder came hurtling his way he was seen to flinch, and he was so leery of the plunging leg that he actually swiveled to avoid it, a funny girlish movement of revulsion. He heard somebody laugh, then his face boiled with shame and from then on he took no trouble. As they walked off, the team joker called out, "Look at Sloany the lanky lassie!" He raced to the locker room, where the others found him with clenched hands beating the wall and pale to the lips.

Was the mold not yet set, still just soft enough to change? Suppose that match had turned out to be Sloany's golden day? Suppose, in the first five minutes, he had streaked past opponent after opponent, a winged Scottish Mercury with a magic ball, wham, *goal!* And on from there—miraculous passes, I am where I belong, Ian and his Merry Men, another goal, roar upon roar, girls in tam-o'-shanters waving tartan handkerchiefs, he is carried off shoulder-high for he's a jolly good fellow bound to get his cap, for Scotland and Shawlands is proud of ye, laddie!

Athletes go to pot like anybody else, but it would be hard to find one who went to what Ma Sloan was to call "the real bad." Would it have been in time? As it was, the episode probably precipitated things. Regal Apr 5 *The Elusive Pimpernel*. Elder Govan Apr 25 *Shake Hands With Murder*. May 17 *The Tougher They Come*. He was apparently having extra tuition from a master; it made him late home, sometimes not far off midnight, but it was a promising development and auld Ma left him his cocoa to warm up and went to bed with a tranquil mind.

Then, one night when she was doing the last washing up, a knock at the door. One of her neighbors sometimes borrowed milk or such, but wiping her hands she thought, But this is the *front* door. And as she opened it, she started at a sight which every wife and mother of her sort dreads all her life, and is relieved to have been spared. Against the background of respectable Templeland Road she was face to face with a policeman.

CHAPTER 8

QUEUE UP FOR EXHIBIT NUMBER ONE

"I'm in love wi' Somebody
An' that Somebody is Me . . ."
Pop song

WHEN A BOY is interested in neither books nor games, there is trouble. With the fine weather, he had got restless.

Among the lavatory smokers there had been chitchat about a milk bar where "the lads" gathered. Ian and his companion Dusty pricked up their ears. Sloany, are ye game? *Jawohl.* They dropped in.

It was worth it. Tough locals talked out of the corners of their mouths about "knockin' off jobs." Burglary. Raffles, Harry Lime in a mask, hands up, ye bunch o' piddlin' bank clerks, stand an' deliver if you don't want grapeshot in your guts. Hands *auf!*

Play it easy, Dusty, we'll keep ears open an' the auld trap shut. Then they talked to Hutch, a boy of fifteen who showed them something under the table: a lever thing for prizing open gas meters. A cinch.

To Dusty, a year older and seeing himself as seasoned, Sloany was transformed from a sullen recluse to a cool leader. His authority was unmistakable. He turned up one evening, Dusty remembers, carrying a mangled old exercise book, with among the usual silly drawings a neat list of addresses. Jottings. He had been on a reconnaissance the night before ("a recky" he called it, as if he'd been on this kick all his life) and these were houses whose owners were away for the Easter holiday. Two he'd crossed out; there was a dog. The other addresses had careful remarks and little plans: pantry window catch broken, small glass panels in front door, then "carry thin f.p. for blts plus p. bks false addr."

Dusty and Hutch were expected to ask what all this meant, and did. It meant that on the recky he had taken a thin sheet of foolscap paper to run up and down between door or window and frame, to check on inside bolts. He had also carried a parcel of books borrowed from school and addressed slightly wrongly in case he was questioned on a doorstep. Dusty and Hutch were impressed. They fixed on a couple of houses, Ian told auld Ma he had tuition till late Thursday evening, and met the other two. He was still armed with his parcel of books. It was dark and the street was deserted; it being Sloany's first job, he was stationed outside the gate to stroll up and down keeping guard while the others crept up the garden with flashlights at the ready.

That first job was like falling off a log: the gas meter had opened up sweet and quiet, twenty-four shillings, not bad, eight each. But when the two of them got back to the front gate, full o' beans, Sloany was nowhere to be seen. Then lo an' behold, he stepped out from some bushes across the road, said a bobby had come walking along, it was just too late to nip up the garden and warn ye without him noticing and I thought best to slip into the bushes. There was nothing they could say, except luck was with us with the meter not goin' off like a bloody pistol shot just as the cop passed the gate—no good pickin' an argument wi' Sloany when he's got his mitts up. He went off home wi' his eight bob, but it was plain to see he'd been rattled. He just didn't fancy the one thing all the boys go for, the danger. On mappin' it out he's dead on the ball, but when it comes to the night, you could tell he was sweatin' blood. That's why he got caught o' course, lost his nerve. A queer fish.

* * *

The bobby greeted Ma Sloan as a friend, he'd moved out from the Gorbals too. But he *was* a policeman.

Ian Stewart?

Oh officer, we've allus been respectable.

Dinna fash yersell, Mrs. Sloan, we got the other lad, a window smashed and a desk broke into and . . .

A step at the door. Ian. When he saw the policeman he stopped and gave the blank stare she was getting to know well, the deep, wary grey eyes, the hollow cheeks sucked in and the full lower lip thrust defiantly out. Then the stolid, stone-wall answers: No, nivver herrd o' Potterhill Road . . . No, Wiley's a liar, he should shut his auld gitter . . . No. No.

Okay laddie, let's see your jacket wi' the wee hole where the button was wrenched off. The bobby produced the missing button.

The juvenile court took a lenient view: on probation for two years. John Sloan delivered a lecture: Ye've disgraced us . . . are ye listenin' tae me? Elephant Aug 9 *Destination Murder*. Embassy Nov 19 *Pick-Up*.

January 1952, fourteen. Embassy Feb 18 *The Prowler*. Apr 21 *Gunman in The Streets*. May 20 *Flesh and Fury*. Elephant May 30 *Night Was Our Friend*. Embassy June 23 *Secret People*.

July, a knock. Again the silhouette of the law. Theft, caught red-handed, hauled up before the court in Govan, admonished, more probation, all for a measly twenty-five bob. Lad, are ye mad, people look at us in the street an' call us that Gorbals clan but haven't we lived there fifty law-abidin' years an' what o' the decent lads in your class like that Andrew Bates gettin' that scholarship? John Sloan thought of a good thrashing, but Ian was a big lad and those unblinking eyes gave him pause. And it wasn't as if the lad was under a gang, just a couple o' strangers he'd gone to with a plan, is he mad?

Fourteen and a half, and a big lad. A lad who was arriving at the crossroads where the signs point to different directions. Puberty.

In most boys at this time, and girls too, the restlessness and the mutinies are, without their realizing it, the preparation for the first bodily explosion. When that has happened, the air is cleared and the emotional chart of a lifetime proceeds peaceably to plot itself. To the relief of parents, things sort themselves out.

But this was already a special case. There is one school incident, recounted now for reasons which will become clear. It is recalled, without inhibition, by a former schoolfellow.

At the academy—as in any boys' school—there was for the nonathletes and the secret smokers, especially on a warm summer day, the lunch-hour vacuum when the devil found work for idle hands. The furtive conclave in the lavatories.

It usually started with one of those grubby photographs which between 1910 and now have been handed up the low road and down the high and in this case finally got to Scotland. Every schoolboy knows the sort of thing. A faded study, say, of a young woman perched on a swing, in what looks like light rain and with nothing on but a sun bonnet, against a backdrop of Windsor Castle. One hand on the rope, she looks soulfully up at a man standing sideways to the camera, naked except for his socks and with hands on hips. His absent eyes are lowered on to her other little finger, which is curved daintily in midair as if the rest of the hand were encircling a teacup instead of her visitor's protuberant person.

"Aye, I remember Sloany weel that time. Mind ye, them sessions was few an' far between an' though ye couldna call them innocent, they wasn't sinister eether. Two ringleaders I mind there was, everybody foolin' around for laffs, like: 'D'ye mind So-an'-so when he went for his National Service, doon to his knees?' That same day there was a boy called Wullie, big hefty guy but shy. 'Come on, Wullie,' says one, 'bet you got a nice bit o' goods!' Weel, Wullie goes red as a beet an' backs away an' that was allus the worst thing, ye was for it. In twenty seconds flat his arms was behind him and his trews 'round his knees—well, ye nivver got such a shock, the bit o' goods was all bit an' no goods, if ye follow me. 'Ladyfinger!' somebody shouted an' Ladyfinger he was for the rest of his school time and to this day for all I ken, poor Wullie.

"Then another laddie draws the attention o' the court by 'is obvious state of excitement. Weel, he was embarrassed an' yet half proud to be in the public eye. 'What's the matter,' he says, 'I'm built the same as all o' you silly buggers'—aw, what the hell, I may as well tell, it was me. Weel, I wasna averrse to developments so long as I could pretend to struggle an' have me cards as it were put on the table for me, and for a minute the fun was fast an' furious an' no harm done i' the long run—dinna mention me name, the wife might no' like it.

"Then a ringleader calls out, 'Look who's in the corner all on his Sloansome!' an' it was Sloany, drawin' on his cig like he was a provost in a pigsty. Come on, they call, see if ye can beat poor old Ladyfinger. Come on, Big Lassie, show the gang!

"Weel, they was just aboot to pin him doon when Sloany says, in one o' them quiet voices on the fillums that stop everything i' the saloons, 'Okay,' he says, 'okay.' Now, in this game nobody ever said okay, ye pretended to struggle like a steer, this wasna right. Then he plants the cig between his teeth so as to leave both hands free an' then he goes into the imitation he was allus doin', o' that big chap in *The Third Man,* an' he says, 'What can I show ye, gentlemen?' 'Yer cock, mate,' somebody says an' we roared. 'Okay,' says Sloany. An' then, as slow as the slow motion on the flicks, he runs his zip doon an' then, as if he was unpackin' somethin' o' value out of a crate—cig still in his mouth, mind you, smoke up into his eyes—he takes it oot without a word. And for a growin' lad it was bonny. An' no' even awake, which didna seem right.

"Well, we had to give him credit: 'Sloany's in the finals, hot favorite, goodo!' 'Thanks,' says Sloany, an' takes a drag at his cig. An' then, if you please, he slowly bends his knees for more easy fumblin' an' brings out the entire box o' tricks as it were, the brazenest action I ever seen by any boy or mon in me life. No' a syllable frae the gang, we was a row o' mesmerized rabbits i' front of a conjurer. A bunch o' kids oot of our depth. 'Finished wi' me, gentlemen?' he says, an' packs the property away again—ye expected him to fish oot a key an' lock it up an' flick the combination. Then the bell goes and nobody brought the subject up thereafter. But ye couldna forget it. He was respected for provin' his manhood errly, but there was somethin' in the way he done it that stuck in the gullet. I do remember thinkin', though, Well, no problem for Sloany when he grows up, not like poor auld Ladyfinger—dinna give my name will ye—it was weird . . ."

But he wasn't weird to the Sloans. After two sharp knocks at their door, they were only relieved there hadn't been a third bobby to say there was a lass around the corner in Lyoncross Road cryin' her eyes out an' her dad fit to tie (Man to man, Mr. Sloan, but this time your laddie's broke into more than a hoose . . .) No, in that line of country Ian wasn't involved with a soul, the boy-and-girl thing with Evelyn was so healthy, what a blessing.

The blessing had a simple explanation. Ian was involved with himself.

From factual evidence which will materialize later, as well as from the incident above, a picture emerges. Every boy at his age has at recurring moments an interest in his own body, but this was not interest. It was love.

Systematic as always, he wedges his one chair against his bedroom door, lifts the shabby swivel mirror from the chest of drawers and sets it on the floor. Then he takes off all his clothes except his undershirt, lays them neatly on the bed, sits on the floor in front of the mirror, pulls the shirt up under his arms, then swivels the mirror to such an angle that from his eye line his middle is in the foreground while somewhere up in the background a face returns his own Peeping Tom grin. Strong white teeth. Then, methodically assuming poses, some facing the mirror and some with his lower back to it, he watches himself make love to himself.

Nothing wrong, you'll never find the police at your door for it. But for your own gude, laddie, grow out of it.

Apart from his lapses, though, nothing could be less odd than the daily life he led, from his waking to his fall into dreamless sleep. Porridge with auld Ma, the others already at work, bus to school, lessons, lone sandwiches, lessons, home, high tea with meat pie and canned salad, homework, the Harry Lime theme thumped out on the piano ("Don't, Ian pet, puts me doon i' the dumps"), more homework, the Sloans doing the pools, *Lives of Harry Lime* on the radio, bed. Saturday, the fillums. Kelvin Jul 9 *Murder Inc.* Elephant Jul 14, *Five Fingers.*

Fourteen is an average age for the assessment not only of the sexual future, but of the mental and moral outlook. His spiritual future simply does not come into it. Though the Sloans were a conventionally God-fearing family and there seems to have been, from outside, no whisper into his ear on the subject of atheism— from the moment he could think, he had displayed an active hostility toward religion and its laws. His rejection of it was as spontaneous as a child's physical throwing up of wrong foods.

But he was ambitious, and so conscious of himself that there must have been a moment when he examined his prospects. And he was astute enough to gauge them. His intelligence at school was by now reported as "just about average." He certainly didn't try hard. He had a reason.

His self-assessment, in his moment of honesty, must have faced the fact that while brighter than they said, he was not bright enough to get out of the rut without help from other assets: wealth, influence, dedication, charm. With his passion for lists, he separates the pros from the cons. Pro: good appearance, perfect health, application. Against: money nil, influence nil, dedication nil—not interested enough in any one thing—and as for charm, he suffered not so much from a lack as from a ferocious determination to obliterate it. It hurt him to smile. And all this meant that as far as worldly success was concerned, whether in business or the arts or even socially, he was not equipped. If he wasn't careful, before he ever got started he'd be marked a failure.

Ambition without prospect of fulfillment. Millions of normal boys with just that, make their attempt, come a cropper, shake a sad head and settle for the weekly stipend and retirement with pension at the expected age.

But when ambition is interlocked with a desperate inner uncertainty which has cut itself off from the nourishing affection of fellow beings, and in panic feeds endlessly off itself, the idea of failure is intolerable.

So cover up, cover up. In class, do it by ignoring the fact that the teachers are there to help a pupil make the best of himself—

do it by refusing, out of pride, to work to the utmost, because that would lay limitations shamingly bare. Give the impression that if you tried, you could wipe the floor with pupils *and* masters, but are posing as a mediocrity to save embarrassment all around.

Out of class, cover up with ridicule: Shakespeare an' all that's a load o' bombast, the Bible one big tranquilizer for the feeble-minded, if people don't like me because I don't turrn on the big smile, why the hell shude I, when I don't like them? Cover up. And when later you hear of school contemporaries who went meekly into banks and offices and are now soaring into affluence, turn a deaf ear, it isna happening.

The moral aspect? Here is the reverse of a normal phenomenon. Often at this sort of adolescent stocktaking a physically unattractive boy will look at his naked body in a mirror, be discouraged by it and never look again, setting out to comfort himself with the riches of his mind. Sloany is more than happy with his body, but having given one cool glance at his undressed soul, he has found there such enormity that in his nakedness he hastens out of pride to pull on protective garments. And those he will wear to the end, so skin-tight that long before that end they will have become his skin. Cover up, cover up.

Elder Cinema Govan Nov 5 *Killer With a Label.*

December 15, 1952. Dear Sirs, Being fifteen on the 2nd of next month I am leaving Shawlands Academy and herby make inquiries concerning the job advt. in the Manchester *Evening News,* Yrs respectfully etc Ian Stewart.

There were several such letters—to offices, to shops, to factories —but the applicant had no concrete qualifications, and the sprawling childish hand cannot have helped. And though hardly anybody knew of "Ian's troubles," you never could tell whether discreet inquiries might have been made at the academy or the police station, and that would be that.

But he did land a job. In a big shipyard with a smashin' sound to it: "I starrt Monday, Harland an' Wolff, openings there." This particular opening, however, was the smallest, for King Ian went among his subjects disguised as an apprentice plater. Tea boy most of the time, fetching and carrying (Ye've spilt it again, ye blitherin' idiot!). Left after nine months "owing to insufficient wages." "Dear Sirs, Being nearly sixteen . . ." Errand boy to Messrs. Wallace, Paisley Road. Butchers.

1954. With his first Friday-night pay check he bought Evelyn a rabbit's foot as a lucky charm and took her to the pictures. Embassy Jan 25 *A Blueprint for Murder*. Mar 2 *Life After Dark* ADULTS ONLY.

Butchers. The first sight and smell of blood . . . The reports are less than sensational: "I mind little aboot him. Fred, was he the gangly 'un moonin' aboot wi' a fag allus in mouth?"

"Ay, shorrt o' speech an' shorrter o' temper."

"Nae, he'd 'a been allowed naethin' to do wi' the slaughterin', that calls for trained skill, ye ken."

But every day a butcher's mooning assistant does get more and more used to the mechanics of carnage. Used to the innocent eyes one moment liquid with life, the next—at the hefty flash of the axe—glazed with sudden eternal disbelief, the blood spouting red and smelling warm, the thud of the carcass; used to the swift expert dismemberment, the rhythmic crunch of bone and parting of tissue to the accompaniment of a jaunty whistle, the Harry Lime theme was as likely as not to shrill across the smoking bodies. Not that this particular assistant needed to harden his heart. Aren't they animals, in a coupla nights won't they be stuffed as portions down a bunch o' greedy-guts in the Malmaison Restaurant, so what? Regent Apr 5 *They Gave Him a Gun*.

The butchery even bored him. After six months of it he needed something to look forward to beside the fillums, in the long winter evenings. Back to the cafés he knew, back to the smash of the windows and the sharp instrument and the gas shillings. What the hell, I am Harry Lime an' I got the meat i' the mornin' an' the meters at night, goodo! Embassy Oct 6 *Lone Gun*.

For Evelyn, perfume and brooches and bangles (Ian is so sweet and generous when you think he earns so little). She did notice he was reading nothing but "crime books." Then came the evening she skipped a date and he was "really nasty." Then she went to a dance with a new boy friend, and when she came out there was Ian with a knife and she was so scared she took refuge in somebody's house and that was the end of the romance of wee Ian and wee Evelyn. The Little Lord Fauntleroy side of him had gone, forever. Evelyn: "Perhaps it was lucky for me that we split up when we did."

November 1954, seventeen any minute. John Sloan noticed he was flashing pound notes, and sure enough, this time the policeman took him away. Sheriff summary court: several cases of housebreaking and theft. The welfare officer was as sick of Sloany as the Sloans were, his real mother must take him over.

The Sloans had completely lost sight of Peggy Stewart since her letter four years before, to say that for two years she had been "courtin'." Ma had to raise an eyebrow, for Peggy was then in her forty-first year and a late entry for the respectability stakes. The courtier was an Irish laborer, ex-Army, and he had a new job down south. She had left her hometown for good and on May 16, 1950, became Mrs. Pat Brady. It is doubtful whether Ma Sloan even mentioned it to Ian. If she did, he can't have been that interested, as he had still never been told anything about Peggy except that she was Peggy.

After hesitation the welfare officer wrote a letter. Routine, and far-reaching: "Dear Mrs. Brady, We are willing to put your son on probation for the third time, but on condition that he moves from Glasgow to cohabit with you and your husband." Peggy Brady had no alternative but to heave a sigh, agree, and hope for the best. Ian, in Pollok, was told that he was going to live with Peggy (You remember Peggy?).

There wasn't much packing to do: a suit, a pair of overalls, crumpled newspaper cuttings about Hitler, and a ragged paperback of *The Third Man*. One of the gang was struck by his jaunty parting shot: "I've been deporrted, fellers, but ye haven't heard the last o' me. I'll be in an' out o' the sewers down south." The Sloan farewells were perfunctory, auld Ma—was sad and puzzled. And in mid-December 1954, three weeks before his seventeenth birthday, Ian Stewart entrained from Central Station, Glasgow, and the same evening arrived at his destination as Ian Brady.

Victoria Station, Manchester.

CHAPTER 9

IDLE HANDS

"Naebody cares for me,
I care for naebody."
Burns

HE HAD WELCOMED the change of name. *After a nationwide poll,* Picture Show *announces that Britain's new heartthrob will henceforth be known as . . .* IAN BRADY!

To a new arrival, Manchester looks much like any other British city. Smoke, clangor, a chaos of besmirched public buildings usually scowled at by a sooty Queen Victoria; cars, trams, buses, pedestrians hurrying with no look to the right and left. Ian Brady, an adolescent already hardening into a criminal, was still naïve enough not to realize that a day's outing to Loch Lomond is no preparation for a two-hundred-mile migration to the heart of England.

His stepfather's postcard had said the Oxford Road bus. When he asked the woman conductor how far tu Whitwerrth Parrk, she looked at him as if he had said it in Turkish: "Coom again, loov!" He repeated it, she looked at the girls opposite and they laughed.

From his later references, their giggle was to echo for a long time. It was then that the Scot, his pallor flaming angrily into a blush, knew how hard it could be to change from a Stewart.

Around him, the flat vowels reverberated. Uncouth. Lancashire.
As the bus lumbered on past the endless stream of faces, into the
suburbs which were to be, from now on, his fateful habitat, he
resolved once and for all to stay what he was, in accent and in
mind. A foreigner.

After the amenities of Pollok, 132A Denmark Street, Moss Side,
was a jolt. Worse than Camden Street. Its inside: identical with
the interiors of all the doll's houses for miles around. As these
interiors differ only in degrees of cleanliness, some being spot-
lessly run by a brave woman who deserved a better deal, others
exuding the hopeless smell of disease or drink—Peggy did her
level best, not easy—one description will serve the several addresses we are to know.

The front door—brown peeling paint and rusty knocker—
opens straight from the street onto the tiny, narrow, dark lobby
with a rickety hat stand. You pass the door of the tiny parlor—
the word "tiny" has to recur—with a fireplace as big as your fist;
up the tiny staircase, narrow and dark, the tiny front bedroom,
tinier back bedroom, each provided with one tiny window with a
panel which should slide but mostly doesn't. Tiny scullery
kitchen, with battered range and one cold-water tap dripping
into the worn sink. Tiny backyard, with coal shed knocked together, tin bath hung behind the door, and the one water closet
which not long ago was an earth privy.

The first evening was easier than any of the three had expected. Pat was a solid, forthright workingman in undershirt and
trousers who loved his wife and wanted to like her son and be
liked by him. After he had gone up to bed, Peggy told the boy
she was his mother. ("He didn't say anythin', just luked. He
seemed to have worked it out for himself.")

Pat was a porter at Smithfield, a vast market in the heart of
Manchester, and he managed to get his stepson a job there, at
Howarth's Fruiterers, as "loadman and stall hand": an errand
boy again. The inevitable lecture ("If Oi catch you at your
Gorbals capers, mate, I'll wallop ye") was received without com-
ment, the face impassive.

As far as Pat could tell, the lad settled down to his job, with a sullen acceptance. Punctual at home, he tolerated the Bradys with an indefinable condescension. Spent long evenings in his bedroom. More like a lodger, really. A loner.

"What was he like at that time? Well . . . seventeen in Denmark Road—wasn't he, Peg—an' looked much as he did later, big-boned, slim and nearly as tall. Not far off six foot, though never looked his height as he allus 'ad a stoop, as if to look a scholar or summat. Good brown hair; just to be different he never would put a brush to it or even a comb, combed it with his fingers so it was inclined to spring up and back. Big hands. 'Keep them hams off the table,' I used to say.

"Always pale, though not as pale as later, and eyes sunk in his head and yet they were prominent somehow, big eyes they was, grey an' with extra long lashes that he got from Peggy, so she tells me, though it's no use pretendin' his ears didn't stick out, is it, Mither? Smudges under his eyes as if he hadn't slept, and a thin back of the neck as if he was delicate, but he was as strong as a horse.

"Mouth? You got me there. No, not thin, always juttin' out the lower lip and pursin' it up, as if he was sizin' up everythin' 'round him all the time, so the mouth looked smaller than it need. You hardly ever saw it stretched and up at the corners in a hearty laugh, that'd be a red-letter day . . . Oh, he'd laugh at the rummest things, wouldn't he, Mither? I'd come home with a tale o' some comic at work having said a funny thing about a foreman, and Mither and me would be in stitches with Ian lookin' us over as if we was common as dirt. Then Peggy would tell some sad tale, about an old lady down the road who'd been run over by a bike an' her hip dislocated, and there the lad would sit with a grin from ear to ear. 'What she want to do a thing like that for,' he'd say, 'silly old bitch!' Shows you how little he did laugh, 'cause when he did you'd be struck what good strong teeth he 'ad.

"Dress? Well . . . To work, 'e wore overalls o' course, but even then particular. None of this beatnik stuff, though it was well in the wind then, always neat an' tidy, even his ordinary suit he wore a waistcoat with, looked old-fashioned even to me. In the summer, open white shirt and a scarf, though he was never sporty even to the length of a long walk. Oh, he could look quite the gent, shoes always polished an' ballpoint in his breast pocket next to 'is 'andkerchief, which he would take out an' press onto his mouth for no reason and then put back in pocket still folded. Didn't fancy the lav i' the backyard not one bit, very la-di-da— oh, a rum card. No, not rum if you didn't know 'im, only if you did, see? Would wave the Scotch flag right, left and center, not easy for the Irish likes o' me . . ."

The Scot, for him, was taking a sentimental turn. Living in Glasgow, he had never felt warmly surrounded by his own folk, and had even retreated from them into willful isolation. But because they *were* his own, he had never had an excuse to turn that isolation into antagonism.

At exactly the right moment, the move to Manchester had furnished that excuse. Scotland, softened by the haze of distance, became Home, and he the proud exile in a sleazy clime. "Jock" Brady to his workmates, and proud of it. It was the first stage in the steady journey of a permanently adolescent mind into a fantasy of its own.

Wycliffe Cinema Apr 20 *Three Steps to the Gallows*. Regent May 18 *Naked Alibi*. No friends. And no hobbies: Snooker's for auld men, jivin' clubs for kids, chess for eggheads, they'll suggest pigeons next.

Girls? The odd saunter into hot-stuff dance halls, but ye can't get far with a bird on a glass o' pop and a bag o' crisps. One casual encounter with a number named Reeny. As another boy friend of hers put it; "Jock had the occasional in-an'-out at t' end o' the old cool-dee-sac when the moon was low."

Reeny took a shine to the tall, mysterious stranger and for a coupla Sats they were a twosome; then he got casual, so she acted very come-hitherish to another chap to see if North-o'-the-Border would register.

He did. Told her to come outside, pinned her arms black an'

blue, then hissed like on the pictures, only Scotch; if you so much as luke in 'is effin' direction again I'll effin' well murrder ye . . . What did I do? I said, Just 'cause I don't come up to yer shoulder in me 'igh 'eels is no reason to treat me like you picked me up in the bargain basement in Adsega's, an' no sooner he let go me arms I ups on the tip o' me toes an' smacked 'im in the chops an' stalked off.

As far as could be gathered from this stout-hearted little bantam, he was a satisfactory lover—as satisfactory as the conditions allowed: No trimmin's, if you follow me, none o' the fondlin' an' fiddlin' an' whisperin' a girl enjoys, whatever folk say . . . No, not rough. Just sort of absent-minded, like he got his mind on summat else, but he did stand me a port an' lemon at the Royal George an' told the plot o' soom daft picture full o' sewers but after I slapped 'is face I never seen 'im again.

In the same year, 1955, the Bradys moved a mile and a half, to Grammar Street (now Cannel Street), to exactly the same house they had left. Not long after, another mile and a half, to 36 Cuttell Street, three quarters of a mile from 7 Bannock Street, Gorton, the home of a thirteen-year-old schoolgirl named Myra Hindley.

The lad stuck it out at Smithfield. Natty as ever, strolling down the street, he would bow politely, not quite superciliously, to Mrs. Singleton of Number 19, who thought you'd never think he was a market porter. Carried on as if he owned the street. Like he was too good to be true. He was.

Olympia Sep 13 *Killer At Large*. Corona Gorton Oct 31 *Companions in Crime*. Met Dec 19 *The Tougher They Come*.

Though the Bradys were to stay two years in Cuttell Street, Ian was not to see much of it. He got restless. Where had he got the money for a record player? A blow had to fall. On January 10, 1956, a week after his eighteenth birthday, he was hauled before the Manchester Crown Court Quarter Assizes for "petty larceny as a servant"; he had been caught trying to smuggle out of Smithfield a bag containing forty-four pounds of lead seals filched from boxes, lead being "a disposable commodity." And so run-of-the-seedy-mill did he seem that the welfare officer has no recollection of him.

Pat's anger, at a lad with his name who wasn't even his kin making a mickey of him where he worked, was acute. If they hadn't shipped the boy off to Borstal he'd ha' turned him out. "What d'ye expect," retorted Jock, "from a mon borrn in Rottenrow?"

Waiting for Borstal, the culprit spent two months in Strangeways Prison, Manchester, less than a mile from Smithfield, where his stepfather found the disgrace hard to bear. Reg Vachel, a resident prisoner: "Jock Brady kept himself to himself, and the conversation was restricted to crime. He said he might write me if he wanted me to do a crime with him, but never discussed violence."

Borstal is a tiny Kent village in which experiments were made, at the beginning of the century, to reform juvenile delinquents rather than punish them; after the Borstal Act of 1908, the "Borstal System" created all over Britain institutions providing a special form of detention devised to develop "inmates"—not prisoners—"mentally, physically and morally, with the idea of their becoming good citizens." The system has its successes and its failures but has flourished, and by the sixties there are in Great Britain twenty-seven Borstals.

The Borstal at Hatfield, Yorkshire, is a camp of wooden huts built on flat marshlands. "The type sent here is the boy of better than average intelligence with a relatively light criminal record. Emphasis is placed on activities which make for self-confidence; teams engage in cricket, soccer, rugby and athletics." It would be fair to say that every chance is given; it is up to the "inmate."

Of this particular old boy there is no record, except that he deliberately spurned his advantages and went the other way. And on his own, which explains the lack of information. Moody, wouldn't attend church, sat outside; prone to drinking a sort of "red biddy"—which he called his "hooch"—made by him out of lemon, sugar and surgical spirit, and hidden in a trench alongside the cricket-field. Turn your back on clean livin', into the

ditch wi' the hooch. When under the influence, he would play
the piano and pick quarrels. An inmate of the same mess, having
stated that once on a workin' party Jock crucified a frog, confessed that it was "gossip"; but Jock, again when the surgical
spirit had entered into him, was heard to boast of homosexual
adventures, and "gettin' paid for it."

Jock, *Goons* comin' up! And for *The Goons* he dropped everything: an offbeat radio program, impressionistic quick-fire comedy with crazy sound effects and nightmare voices from a dream
world often hilariously comic but more than grotesque, which
appealed irresistibly to Jock's fairly special sense of fun. His
imitation of "Neddie"—created by Harry Secombe, a shrill,
epicene voice with a maniac laugh—was as wizard as his Billy
Daniels act had been.

After a year he was moved to nearby Hull, and after another
year returned ingloriously home on November 14, 1957. This
two-year period was the only time in his "free" life which he
spent out of Glasgow or Manchester.

The Bradys were temporarily at 97 Grey Mare Lane (mortgage
trouble), around the corner from Cuttell Street, same doll's
house, shabbier. No question of the market, not mentioned. His
Borstal report was fair: "Application, Good at Figures."

He studied the Manchester *Evening News* and smartly answered three ads for a bookkeeper. Pat told him to mind he
enclosed the report. What, mention Borstal, d'ye take me for a
dunderhead? Hell of a tussle. Ian mentioned Borstal. However
much employers try to be fair about "corrective schools," there
has to be prejudice. No go. No go. No go. He blamed Pat.

Christmas 1957. Not his favorite season, come all ye faithful—
Christ. Lodger in disgrace, too broke to pay Peggy any rent,
never mind presents.

1958, twentieth birthday. For a couple of weeks he was a "steel
erector," one of those made-up names to bolster the ego of a
laborer. For another week or two, worked for the Gas Board.
Then not, became "redundant."

March. Out of work, sound in body and mind and reasonably intelligent, twenty and adrift.

His only recurring date was the Labour Exchange: the weekly dole, two pounds ten shillings, enough to contribute to his food and the odd shoes and socks and fillums and cigs and the odd drink and the odd shilling on a nag. He had started to bet.

Nothing to get up for, so he lay in. Then, alone in the stale, empty little house, he made his own breakfast porridge. His stepfather and even his mother had long ago gone off to work, he to the market, she to her factory where she had a job as a precision worker—not exactly a boost to young morale. Slop around, stare at the *Mirror* from end to end, ads, the lot. Bar the comic strip an' the sex pics, what a load o' tripe. Forenoon over.

Bet placed around the corner, then fish an' chips in Stockport Road. He was never one for food; if it had been the Midland Hotel he'd 'a been damn choosy, but short o' that, anything goes. Then a fillum, then home, high tea and the Manchester *Evening News*. Racing results first, then SITUATIONS VAC., then the front page in case of an air disaster or the atom bomb gone off at last an' serve the nits right.

Through cig smoke he looks emptily at the big black names of the famous and successful: MACMILLAN ANSWERS CRITICS–MIKE TODD–EISENHOWER–DR. FUCHS AT SOUTH POLE–TOMMY STEELE TRIUMPHS. And according to his custom he stares hard until another name appears, bigger and blacker: IAN BRADY ANSWERS CRITICS–IAN BRADY TRIUMPHS. Then the racing page. His nag nowhere again.

Then, in the close-quarter shuttle rhythm of the story, yet another move. A little over a mile, to 18 Westmoreland Street (not Westmorland), Longsight, a backwater off Stockport Road. On the day of the move, a quarter of a mile away off the same road, in an identical backwater named Aked Street, it is likely that a boy of ten was playing tag outside Number 39, David Smith.

In Westmoreland Street, Ian was to be domiciled, with the Bradys, for the best part of seven years.

The street is particularly narrow and short. As you lean

against the rickety lamppost outside Number 18, you can hear and watch the endless traffic of Stockport Road. The house differs from past homes only in being up a couple of steep steps, over a pygmy's half-cellar for coal and rubbish. The other end of the street is blind except for shortcut alleys to endlessly straight South Street and Earl Street. The usual back entry runs between the Brady backyard and the backyards of Upper Plymouth Grove: an alley crammed with overflowing ashcans and stray refuse. This was the view from the Bradys' upper back window, Ian's bedroom.

The sight of this thoroughfare, meaner than mean, in the half dark of a winter drizzle with old soggy newspapers and eggshells soaking into the puddles, is only equaled by viewing it on a hot summer afternoon. That is when a merciless dagger of sunlight shafts between the grey cowering chimneys and strikes the ashcans and winkles out the sour smells of cabbages and drains. Standing just here, you would say that in this place any young spirit, without resources, must needs wither and die. To survive, that spirit has to flee to some heaven of its own: the concert hall, the gym, the prayer meeting, the youth club, the public library, the picture gallery—in Manchester they are all there.

And if the young spirit spurns this?

A grey afternoon, one more dawdle, just won seven bob on Great Scott and off to blow it on one large whusky, what the hell, then we'll sample a fillum. Stockport Road. Cars, whizz whizz. Traffic wardens shepherding kids across (The bleeders look like dolls wound up and oot for the day). Take your fill o' the sights, Jock, this is you for the rest of your free life.

NUT SCREW AND BOLT WAREHOUSE GENT'S HAIRDRESSER SECOND-HAND FURNITURE MART OO-LA-LA PARIS FASHIONS CITIZENS' ADVICE BUREAU YATES' WINE LODGE FREE TRADE HALL MOZART CHAMBER MUSIC *chamber aw piss off ha ha* CO-OP FOODS SHOE REPAIRS ROSETTA MODES CHRIST CAN ANSWER YOUR DEEPEST NEED *sez you* OLD PEOPLE CROSSING *step on the gas kids for a load of auld rubbish* SELF-SERVICE MARK-DOWN SHOE FAYRE JIM'S BED AND BREAKFAST. On the corner, a worn-out church that's been turned into Piccadilly Motors, *nice bit o' conversion ha ha, queue up for the font and have your bairns christened wi' crude oil.* Then the fillum, Shaftesbury Longsight Mar 3 *The Depraved.*

It is simple.

It is a level at which a starved young spirit cannot stay. If it refuses to rise from there, then there is only descent.

But not yet. On one of the lowest of the drifting days, the welfare officer called. Boddington's Breweries, a major business in Central Manchester, wanted a laborer in the wash house. Could a Scot sink lower, except to become a lavatory attendant? Ah weel, Roll oot the Barrel. They weren't that particular about references and he reported for work on April 28, 1958.

"Bottle washer, eh?" said Dad. "Wear an apron, do ye? Any lead seals on the bottles?"

"There's one thing" was the answer, he sure had a tongue in his head, "it's dead handy, next door to Strangeways."

He stuck to the job. One lapse, minor, June the ninth. Was it a night when the dreariness by day and the nothingness by night was just too much? Drunk and disorderly, fined one pound.

Shaftesbury June 12 *Violent Playground.* Kings Jul 17 *Orders to kill.* Jul 30 *Blood Is My Heritage.*

"To I. Brady, Laborer in wash house. We regret to inform you that as from 3 Oct. we shall be dispensing with yr services owing to redundancy, p.p. Boddington's Breweries."

Well, he'd lasted five months, and as Pat remarked over high tea, better to be redundant than in the dock.

As the drift started again (Light ale please, got a match, mate?) what's gone wrong wi' me? When does the action start? Kings Oct 9 *The Last of the Fast Guns.* Queens Nov 2 *Ride a Violent Mile.* Dec 12 *How To Rob a Bank.*

Xmas, flippin' Xmas, 'ark the 'orrid angels sing. And on January 2, 1959, he attained his majority.

No bonfires on the estate. But from the Bradys—no ill feeling —the cash for a new suit. And he needed one.

Then, as if the thought of now being a grown man had sobered him, he announced he was going to borrow the right books from Longsight Library and brush up his bookkeeping and accountancy, ye never know. And he did. Queens Jan 14 *Intent to Kill.*

February 2, 1959, Manchester *Evening News,* SITUATIONS VAC.: "Male clerk required for office, 20–25, should be neat writer and accurate with figures and able to keep stock records on own initiative."

He applied. King's Feb 3 *The Cop Haters. Edge of Fury.*

Answered by return. Interview on Monday. Yrs faithfully, T. Craig.

CHAPTER 10

HE TO THE APPOINTED PLACE

"Books are not absolute dead things, but do
contain a potency of life in them."

Milton

HE bought an exercise pad and spent the weekend studying.
"Millwards Ltd Levenshulme Rd Gorton, Chemicals Soaps
Produce Oils etc, Est. 1810." Greater Manchester being by now
his own revolving parish, it was no surprise that it was a couple
of miles from Westmoreland Street.

Under his raincoat he wore his suit, sponged and cleaned by
his mother. It was wet underfoot, so to save the look of his shoes
(They allus look ferrst at your feet) he took a bus. It was to be
his route for many a day: the walk between the rubbishy houses
at the end, through to Hyde Road, the 57 bus east, then off at
Knutsford Road. He told a workmate later that he asked a postman where "Leevenshullum Road" was. The man looked puzzled, then "Ah," he said, "you mean Levvens-hume, you can allus
tell furriners by the way they can't say Levvens-hume!" It didn't
rile him. On the contrary. Walking down Knutsford Road and
past a bleak little park, he felt an alien glow.

The letter had been on good paper and he had imagined

Millwards would be in one of those smart new blocks, elevator, fluorescent lighting, smart secretaries, the lot. He got a shock. Over a railway bridge, the houses on the left ended in an untidy little parking lot and a group of shanties with blackened, broken windows and dozens of rusty, discarded oil drums. Next to this the backyards and back entry of a street exactly like his own. He asked a passing boy, who pointed to a small sign, MILLWARDS LTD, PRIVATE. A narrow passage led to the shabby door of what looked like another shed; on a bleak winter morning it was wholly depressing. He opened a door: a handful of people at desks, mostly older, surrounded at first sight by hopeless disorder, which at second sight proved to be a diffuse tidiness based on long usage. They all looked as if they had been sitting there since 1810. They were helpful and told him where to go.

Even in 1959 Tom Craig, a warm, simple man, had been at Millwards for so many hard-working and uneventful years that he could claim much credit for the friendly integrity of the old-fashioned little business. Its setting may have been ramshackle but its character was rock-solid, nine till five Mon. to Fri. and alt. Sat. mornings. Most of the fourteen or fifteen employees, men and women, had been with the firm many years and the atmosphere was a family one; Craig was "Tom" to all who worked for him. Most of the staff was from surrounding suburbs, and from solidly respectable backgrounds.

Weekly football pools, the occasional office picnic, more like a family treat, and on Christmas Eve there was the early break-up and "a bit of a do," drinks and eats around the corner at Haxby's Pub, and in the old days "before the old man went" there were even circus parties to nearby Belle Vue. On working middays, some of the staff went out to cafés or sat around while Mrs. Egerton, the cleaner, brewed tea and cooked bits of lunch while they played checkers, chess and cards for harmless stakes. The women would gossip: Tennis on Sunday was super except Reg got high at lunch . . . Rehearsals for *Charley's Aunt* are gettin' me down . . . Bingo, that's all me mam talks about and if I'm not in by twelve me dad's on the doorstep with a strap.

Sometimes it would get personal, but not very: Why's old Clitheroe ratty today? . . . Millie looks washed out wi' them slimmin' pills . . . If I was ten years older I'd fancy Tom . . . Oh, Irene hasn't spoken to Sandra for a week, I woonder what's up. Of real scandal there had never been any, though there were still whispers about nice, popular Dessie who left two years ago on sick leave, though every soul knew it was an illegal but thank goodness not a Millwards chap. Nothing else, bar the one-too-many at the club and the black eye. A nice place to work.

The applicant was shown in. Craig took to him at once: serious, a lad who took pride in himself. The lad was deferential without being nervous, even smiled and chatted; the Bradys would have been amazed. It was typical of him that unlike most young men in his position, with new people whom he was anxious to impress he was at his best, because he did not know them well enough to despise them.

He showed Tom his exercise pad and was challenged on the spot to work out a problem in ready reckoning. Tom was a football fan, and the Glaswegian was able to explain that the rivalry between Rangers and Celtic was based on religion, Protestant v. Catholic. And it was a firm mark for him that he was a Scot: Cabinet ministers, empire builders. Jock got the job (Go in and see foreman Bert Mathews, start Monday the sixteenth).

Queens Feb 14 *The Fiend Who Walked the West*. Ian Brady, stock clerk. Kings Feb 18 *Man on the Prowl*.

Somehow the "Jock" got dropped, though he stayed as Scottish as ever. He was determined, if only to show those two in Number 18, to hold down his job. And he did—with only a handful of days on sick leave—from February 16, 1959, to October 6, 1965. Once he even talked to Tom of quitting unless he got a raise, got it and stayed. Stayed for six years and two hundred and thirty-two days. His employer had undoubtedly to do with it; the combination of dignity and lack of boss's "side" was respected by a difficult boy. There were often to be words; if he thought he'd been slighted he'd go off into violently crude tempers which with many superiors would have meant the boot. It is clear that Tom Craig was the only man Ian Brady ever liked. If the one had been born the son of the other, and had lived a family childhood in his benevolent shadow . . .

But even now, can't there be hope? Nine pounds a week

mounting to eleven, living at home, a white-collar job in congenial surroundings, self-respect—the start of a success story? Two years of this, plus night school, leading to a Chartered Accountant's Certificate at the Manchester College of Commerce, then straight into a firm like Whinney Murray and Co. . . .

Could he have taken off? At just such a moment in life, many a young man in his position—uncertain which way he wants to go, disgruntled, getting "into bad company" even—meets his future wife. And years later, when he has become a successful citizen, he realizes that it was her advent, at this time, that gave him the providential nudge in the right direction. If she hadn't turned up . . .

During this year, Ian Brady's twenty-third, could something like that have happened to him?

No.

It is not even a question of its having been too late. From the day of his birth, the spell had been woven. And nothing could have changed him. Nothing.

Anyway, he didn't have much use for feminine society. With the girls in Millwards he passed the time o' day but couldn't tell one from t' other, and those he could tell were courting.

Shaftesbury May 8 *Two-Headed Spy*. Gaiety Peter St May 23 Two Tough Violent Films!!! ALAN LADD *The Man in the Net!!!* Shock-by-Shock Story!!! *Riot in Juvenile Prison!!!*

One evening, date at the Dolphin, pub in Clowes Street, with two mates from Hull Borstal, Vic Linters of Huddersfield and Greg Patch of Leicester, all three wearing the invisible old-school tie. He had written to them in the jaunty highfalutin' style he would adopt even in conversation: "I venture to put you in the picture by suggesting it would be to our advantage to grasp the opportunity of a quick trip this way, I'll sign off now, Jock."

One idea he sketched out was to lie in wait for a woman about to deposit money in a night safe, and snatch it from her; another, to pinch a revolver from a gunsmith's display cabinet. But Vic and Greg were going straight: Sorry, mate. Jock was glum over his beer; in his mind, as like as not, he had made lists. He gave them a baleful parting look which washed his hands of *them*.

In Millwards he was tolerated, humored even. But, the old story, he made no friends. At the moment when he should have come out of his shell, he was retreating farther into it. When he did talk, it would be about how much better things were orrdered in Glesga. (Old Ian was okay if you didn't rub him the wrong way—you try winning from him at pontoon, watch out!) And he not only didn't save, he gambled. Not just cards, the nags, bettin' shop around t' corner, Tommy Gibbons'. Typical of the sense of humor of a man who had none: his code name was Gorgonzola, later shortened to Gorgon. He was a cool bettor too, dashing for a clerk, and one week when it was five quid down the drain, was he mad. (Now, you don't often see a gambler that's a bookworm, but he's that too, studyin' German in the lunch hour, I ask you.)

Shaftesbury Jul 22 *Grip of the Strangler*. Kings Sep 3 *The Child and the Killer*. But the fillums were not enough.

Needs a lass, does young Brady. The awkward type, bit of an iceberg, but with a chap who's got himself a dog there's not much to worry about.

But there was. Only one eighth of the iceberg was showing. He hadn't only acquired a dog (christened, predictably, Bruce—after the great Scot Robert), he was also painstakingly collecting, in his back bedroom, a small library.

On a rainy Saturday morning, the bookworm alights from his 97 bus in Stockport Road; brown-papered under his arm, he hugs his latest acquisition from Manchester's leading booksellers. And quite a dip into the week's wages, for his library is not cheap.

Then up the bit of Westmoreland Street, in the unfashionably long and tight black overcoat he has acquired, in order to look different. He does, enough to make the two girls down the road snigger; they have nicknamed him "the Undertaker." He gives them a look of cold disapproval before mounting the steps of Number 18 as if he were in Pall Mall ascending into his club. The dark little passage, up through the familiar smells of the dark little stairs and into the back bedroom. Away from it all.

Small libraries have been the making of great men. A clear-eyed youth who is above his blighted surroundings, he draws the rag of curtain over his cell window to shut out the hideous city day, clicks on the standard fly-blown bulb in the middle of the cracked ceiling, sits back against the one scraggy pillow, takes up a new book he can ill afford, and loses himself in it. How promising he looks!

The collection started off on one subject, then gradually a second one took over. First subject first.

Childhood memories . . . The grown man of normal development reverts to them with nostalgic affection. But it *is* a reverting, he has left them behind. Ian Brady was not a grown man of normal development. His was not a whole mind. Cut neatly in half, right down the middle. The division between the adult and the permanent child.

The adult half, as if by native cunning, formed a façade which masked the other with complete success. His lithe co-ordination of eye and limb and tongue was matched by everyday behavior which was markedly conventional, almost debonair. At any gathering he passed invisible muster: Now, to *me* the solution to Manchester's traffic problem is, bla bla bla.

But behind this, there was Harry Lime and King Ian and the martial music and his sword Excalibur all swirling around trying to fuse into a solid power that would stifle forever something he hated: the dire knowledge of his own inability to come to terms with the real world in which his body happened to be placed. At all costs, he had to forestall humiliation at the hands of that world. And the only way was to get in first. First stage, aggression.

Verbal detraction. I, Ian Brady, belong, my friend, to a werrld superior to yours, thereforre I am superior to yu. It had started with "Glesga is tops," by now that was tame. He needed a weapon that would bewilder and anger. Glasgow was ousted by Berlin. Nazism.

It is difficult, but not impossible, to grasp his erratic logic. The observer's first reaction is: But Brady, if you want to be contrary, why not at least be up-to-date and join Russia? Why boost a setup which exploded in its own face when you were seven? Where's the sense?

There *was* no sense, and that was what suited him. Join Russia? He did not want to join anything. On his own, at the top. He might one day agree to *being* joined. But joining—no thanks a million.

And Berlin did the trick. For the proud ego, faced with sickening failure and determined to shy away from the sight, the only medicine—the one efficacious flattery—is the reiterated assurance that one is born out of one's time. A fascinating misfit: thirty years too late, in the wrong country.

The Scourge of the Swastika, The Eichmann Trial, Six Million Dead, Pogrom, Mein Kampf. Except for the last, all these works are so against the Nazi phenomenon that the choice of homework must seem baffling. But we are seeing the student as ourselves. Poring over his tomes in his secret room, he might have been a Christian in ancient Rome deciphering pagan diatribes. Remembering his sewers, if Manchester had offered Nazi catacombs, Ian von Brady would have been the first to report.

"The defeat of Hitlerism was a signal to every British subject to thank God . . ." (Bluddy superior Blimpish balls) and so each paragraph, through his distorting lens, jigsawed hither and thither till it acquired a meaning directly opposite. The monstrous Nazi power became the sternly righteous expression of the only civilized creed: *Herrenvolk* on top, the rest under, and if necessary, weeded out. The photographs too he transformed: above the bemedaled chests of the great, the smug conceited faces grinned at him splendiferously. And the same faces under trial, haggard and haunted, spelled for him noble resignation.

When the subject ever came up, if sober he would confine himself to disapproving silence. But with drinks under his belt he would open fire: What aboot auld Göring at the last minute, diddlin' the lot of 'em, kaput, *aus*. Can ye imagine that auld Blimp Montgomery havin' the guts, he'd most like lose the poison down the toilet, blah blah blah . . . Ignorant vulgar jabs, hit or miss, designed to infuriate.

One photograph he particularly extolled, and he was once

nearly beaten up for it. It shows a man looking like a displaced person, a shapeless uniform hanging on him, standing next to a young woman, with fair hair pulled back and then down to her shoulders. She could be a strapping schoolgirl of twelve— wellington boots to bare knees, shirt under a black sweater tucked into a short plaidlike skirt—until you see that the sweater hugs a bold pair of breasts.

She and the man stand with hands listlessly down, as they look into the camera with the stolidity of peasants who have been asked to straighten up from their potato picking and pose. *They*'re no' beggin' for mercy, see? The accent gets more histrionic: Now, tharr's a bonny lassie for ye, in a tartan too, take a look at them knockers!

Under the photograph: "Immediately after the camp was released: Josef Kramer, the commandant of Belsen, with the notorious woman guard Irma Grese."

Queens Oct 16 *Passport to Shame.* Kings Oct 26 *The Terror Strikes.* Dec 7 *The Young and the Guilty.*

1960. The little library was enlarging its scope.

Politics and sex. They seem incongruous items: polling booth and double bed, election and erection—it is only when a Member of Parliament forgets himself and is found out that the two find themselves in sudden juxtaposition.

For the bookworm, however, they began to intertwine. A passage from one volume ("As we go to press in 1960, members of neo-Nazi groups are chalking swastikas on walls") is followed by a victim's account of his sufferings at the hands of the Gestapo: "I heard the lash whistle, the breath was instantly dashed from my body but the excruciating pain of the second lash stifled it. When it was over, they told me with coarse oaths to cover myself decently." You might think this goes further into details than seems necessary in a study of Hitler's Germany. The book is entitled *The Kiss of the Whip.*

As it is typical of a kind of publication which, in the sixties, features in certain British bookshops, and even in their windows cheek by jowl with straightforward pornography, it is worth looking at. The author is Mr. Edwin J. Henri, the publisher the Walton Press; it is in hard covers and costs twenty-five shillings complete with Index and Bibliography.

On the inside of the jacket, a long blurb which gives a good idea of the complete two-facedness of the text: it is like watching one of those fascinating music-hall mimes dressed and made up on one side as a professor and on the other as a pimp, the act finishing with the two apparently waltzing together. It is the professor we are shown first. "Throughout mankind's history of crime and punishment, torture has played a prominent part . . . The old Mosaic injunction of 'an eye for an eye' has held sway not only in primitive tribes . . ." One would hardly guess from this that the front of the jacket is a color drawing of a naked woman with abundant, outflowing hair and breasts, the latter highlighted, arms held aloft and chained together, and ample buttocks encircled by a red whip.

In the second paragraph of the blurb the professor slips a little, and we glimpse the pimp. "A cavalcade of notorious methods of self-abasement and corporal punishment, particularly with the whip . . . Flogging is still lawful in the Royal Navy; this is the kind of interesting information the present work provides . . . The public schools of England come under the relentless scrutiny of Edwin Henri, being notorious for their birchings, which survive from an era that has fortunately disappeared." The word "fortunately" does not look as if it belongs just here.

"The perils of sexual aberration are clearly pointed out, and homosexuality, incest and masochism are openly paraded." The professor has slipped again. "Lesser known aberrations such as necrophilia, vampirism and scopophilia are clearly defined . . . Flagellation in brothels comes in for its fair share of the lurid limelight and makes diverting reading"—slipped again—"with descriptions of the armouries of instruments used by prostitutes to satisfy the peculiar cravings of customers with perverted tastes."

But the professor takes sternly over once more, with a paragraph the first part of which must have caught the Brady eye, though it was too soon for the second to engage his interest: "The proposal for new Borstals is discussed, then well-known views on a burning topic—whether to retain Capital Punishment or abolish it." The blurb ends on an exalted note tinged with nostalgia. "This book is a panorama of Man's upward advance from cruelty to the loftier heights of humane treatment . . . The kiss of the whip no longer lacerates human flesh as it once did."

Chapter headings: Pleasure, Pain and Propitiation; Flogging in the Army; Flogging in the Navy; The Whipping of Male and Female Servants; Educational Flogging in Fact and Fiction. And while the historical character of "the present work" is upheld by a series of immensely crude and innocuous woodcuts, in the very first sentence of the text the author makes himself clear: "The idea of pleasure being associated with severe floggings strikes one, at first thought, as wholly incomprehensible. But after due study, one perceives that *pleasure* may be of different kinds."

But the professor is quickly back with "Among the Indian tribes of Guiana . . ." and quotations from *Julius Caesar*. Then follows a bland piece of name-dropping, not a name one would expect to find in *The Kiss of the Whip:* "Even Christ used the scourge on the money-changers in the Temple."

The opposite page describes a "whipping club" formed in ages past by "a group of society women, and named the Merry Order of St. Bridget," though the author does conscientiously warn us that he has this information from "a publication which must be suspect."

Third-rate double-talk makes the dullest reading, and the normal reader surely finds it impossible to believe that such a book could hold the attention of a young man, never mind arouse slumbering propensities. But there is no getting away from it, this particular reader, much more likely to have put the money on a horse, spent thirty shillings on *Pleasures of the Torture Chamber,* thirty on *Corporal Punishment Through the Ages,* and thirty-five on *The History of Torture and Cruelty.* (Brady, in court: "Ye'll find much werrse collections in lorrds' manorrs all over the country.")

There was an element of posturing: Ian, what you got your nose into? . . . Good God, torture, are ye kinky or summat? He enjoyed the ribbing, it was attention, set him apart. And the scholastic pretensions of the books, far from making him smile—the absurd never did that to him—gave him a good feeling: Am I kinky? Weel, mebbe aye an' mebbe nae, but I don't sit on parrk benches gettin' a thrill out of a derrty buke published in Paris, I know literature when I see it, the subject intrigues me.

It did intrigue him, but the "literature" simply could not have made serious impact. The author who would do that was to come.

Kings Feb 29 *A Bucket of Blood.* Cinephone Mar 22 *Dolls of Vice.* Kings Apr 22 *Desperate Man.*

Warm evenings, too warm for the fillums. Hobbies . . . Tennis? Swimming? Chess?

The young insecure arm themselves with what they believe to be symbols of individuality. He gave up smoking to save up for a motorbike. But that was his only concession to fashion; turning his back on long hair, beard and sandals, Ian Brady conveniently based his symbols on his flair for machinery and gadgets. The installment plan was his boon and his curse: after the record player, a smart little transistor radio. Then a tape recorder.

Plaza Sep 14 *The Creature Walks Among Us.* New Oxford Sep 30 *Psycho!!!* Theatre Royal Oct 9 *Three Came to Kill.* Shaftesbury Oct 27 *A Lust to Kill.*

1961. January 2, Ian Brady twenty-three. "To Mr A. Marsh, Deroy Sound Co., Hest Bank, near Lancaster. Dear Sirs, Having seen your advt. I should like a copy of the American record 'Hitler's Inferno,' thank you Meine Herren, Ian Brady." "Meine Herren, I enclose 3 tape-recordings of German music broadcasts which I would like turned into an L.P. at yr convenience." The writing was so immature that Mr. Marsh judged his correspondent to be a "schoolboy picking up the language."

Walls are thin in Greater Manchester, and the evening din of the marching songs and the strident German voice, mounting to hysterical climax after climax, got properly on the nerves of the Spilsburys next door: Didden we get enough o' that before the war, the lad's bluddy mad . . .

To someone who spends hours alone, a tape recorder is an

engrossing toy. And especially to someone who is interested in himself.

Speak into the machine, go on . . . How weird weird weird to say softly: Sieg Heil, I am Ian Brady. This is my hand. I am sitting in Westmoreland Street on the ferrst of November . . . Then, seconds later, to hear the voice tell you from the empty air, intimate, caressing: *I am Ian Brady. This is my hand* . . . And a week later you can still turn it on: *Sieg Heil, I am Ian Brady. This is my hand* . . .

And the moments when you are *utterly* bored . . . What's wrong wi'— Wait a minute, let's get some sexy music on the record player, Bolero, right . . . Drum, drum, drum, drum . . . *This is Ian whisperin' Brady, and this is my hand, which I am holdin' in the other hand, it feels gude an' warm* . . . Drum, drum, drum, drum . . . *An' this is Ian Brady's hand unbuttonin' his waistcoat* . . . Drum drum . . . *This is Ian Brady's hand unbuttonin'* . . .

Playback. Mmmm . . .

Passes the time. Kings Jan 9 *Half-Human.* Jan 14 *Never Take Sweets from a Stranger.*

On January 16, Ian Brady walked to his desk as usual. In his awkward, noncommittal way he bowed to the female faces, which by now he knew so well. Shirley Gain having left to get married, there was a new girl standing next to the others. "Funny," she said, in the level local voice he automatically felt was beneath him, them long vowels and pronouncing "us" as "uzz" and so forth, "but I was at the school across the road from 'ere, Ryder Brow School, funny . . ."

Tom Craig walked up. "Graham, Tony, Ian—this is our new typist, Myra . . . sorry, love, I didn't catch your surname . . ."

CHAPTER 11

LITTLE MYRA

"By my sooth! She'll wait a wee . . ."
Burns

MYRA HINDLEY was four and a half years younger than Ian
Brady. Born Thursday, July 23, 1942. "Thursday's Child has Far
to Go." The spell passed over this baby, born in the Greater
Manchester which during the first twenty-three years of her life—
her free years—she was never to leave.

She came of Lancashire working folk—Hindley is even the
name of a town in the region—a class respected for its practical
humor and adjustment to hardship. If you went canvassing from
door to door you would meet them in their hundreds: poor,
respectable or trying to look respectable, nobody clever, nobody
original, nobody sinister; a multitude of warily conventional
human beings with a vocabulary just capable of communicating
the small talk of the day.

Not one word richer than that, a diet of common sense.
Monotonous but keeps you going, the fish and chips of the mind.
A few rogue polysyllables from newspaper, radio and television
stick out like sharp pebbles on a highway, but soon file down.
No, uzz lot don't 'ave mooch to do wi' church goin', y' know what
it is wi' what I call the pace o' modern life an' so forth. My point
is, everybody 'as their own psychological idea o' God sort o'

thing. Oh, I like to see the yoong girls gettin' rid o' their com-
plexes wi' the Twist, joost the job so long as it don't go too far, a
woman's place is in the 'ome, it is that . . . Aye, proper Manchester weather—and on and on.

The Hindleys lived at 20 Eaton Street, Gorton, a mile and a
quarter east of the Brady home in Westmoreland Street and one
mile north of Millwards. They had lived in Gorton all their
lives; as a boy Bob Hindley had attended the school attached to
the Catholic Church of St. Francis, around the corner along the
thoroughfare misnamed Gorton Lane. The Hindley surroundings, the usual nest of tiny dwellings, were rendered particularly
dreary by the presence, along the lane as far as you could see, of a
black domain called the Gorton Foundry: a thudding, reverber-
ant wilderness of brick and iron.

Eaton Street was shorter even than Westmoreland Street, and
also a cul-de-sac. Number 20, the last house at the blind end,
suffered a distinction: not only did the back bedroom overlook the
backyards and w.c.'s of adjoining Beasley Street, but the front
bedroom also overlooked the backyard of a house in Casson
Street. On top of this, in the callously casual street-planning
years ago, this backyard had somehow spilled over onto the
Eaton Street roadway, so that its w.c. (and it had not always
boasted "w.") is four yards from the Hindley front door. An
invasion of privies.

At adjacent corners of Gorton Lane, like casualty stations in a
permanent battle—which indeed they were—there stood no
fewer than three pubs, the Bessemer, the Steelworker's Tavern
and a third which displayed on its front lintel, unexpectedly, an
elegant little bust of Shakespeare: the pub is named after him.
Perched above the miles upon miles of commerce-ridden squalor
—no leaf, no flower, no sprig of wild thyme blowing—he looks
down at the listless passer-by with a gaze of deep compassion.

Myra, a first child, had been conceived in mid-war, when Bob
Hindley was on leave from his parachute regiment. But she
showed no aftereffects of strain, being a placid child and no
trouble. At the end of the war, by which time she was three and
had hardly ever seen her father, he returned home, got a non-
descript job on building sites, and on August 21, 1946, Nellie

Hindley gave birth to her second and last child, Maureen.

It is typical of this kind of city working family that the generations stay in close touch geographically. Nellie's half brother, Jim Burns, married, lived in Dukinfield, four miles away; her full brother, Bert Maybury, in Clayton, hardly one mile; her sister, Annie Cook, in Railway View, Gorton, nearer than that; and her mother, Mrs. Ellen Louisa Maybury, one minute away, around the corner at 24 Beasley Street, back to back with her street.

Bob Hindley, after a bad accident at work, for which he was compensated, became an invalid and something of a shadow, occasionally seen limping across to the Tavern for the half pint. Nellie was not a Catholic (her brother Bert had also married a Catholic, Auntie Kath) and the girls were christened in the Protestant faith.

Not that their mother was a dominant figure. As ordinary as her family and relatives and neighbors, she differed in being a frail young woman with delicate good looks and a timid dignity too tenuous for her surroundings. Between her and her husband the tie was not strong, but she tried to do her duty by him and it would be many years before she decided on separation. She tried with her daughters too, tentatively, but had not the strength to inculcate any definite moral code. As she was to say later in the face of catastrophe, with a bewildered pride which was poignant: "I did the best I could for all o' them." She became the overworked mother used by everybody as a matter of course.

After Maureen's birth the family acquired a way of life which was later to be misunderstood, the impression being that while Maureen was cherished, Myra was packed off to her grandmother —the classic example of the rejected child storing up fatal resentments. One story is that with the arrival of a second child "the house wasn't big enough," but in a community where families somehow housed four or five children, the arrangement that two little girls should share the back bedroom would hardly be thought overcrowding. What happened was that Mrs. Maybury, a lonely widow still in her fifties, adored her three-year-old granddaughter and begged for her. Nellie had to get back to her job as a machinist, the care of two babies was a taxing prospect, Gran was so near that it wouldn't really be a move at all, and it happened. The following year Gran herself moved, but only next door, to Number 22, then later to Number 7, by which time the street had been rechristened Bannock Street.

As it happened, Myra spent as much time in Eaton Street as with her gran, skipping easily from one to the other and seeing as much of her mother and little sister as if she slept in the same house, which she often did anyway.

If a house is impregnated with family character and tradition, it is valuable for a child to grow in it; but in Gorton this could not apply. Myra was never conscious of any difference between Gran's place and her mam's, even a couple of photos in the two parlors were the same. It was an easygoing way of life, but definitely not conducive to instability. Health excellent, slept well, ate well, a square determined little girl. And there was no question of jealousy of her young sister, she was even protective toward her: Dad and Mam called Maureen "Mo," and at the age of five Myra called her "Baby-Mo," then "Mo-Baby," then "Mo-Bee," and Mo-Bee was to remain her name for Maureen.

But the two homes did mean disorientation: a lack of the parental hand, flexible but firm, pointing out to the questing mind the difference between right and wrong. Gran, a pretty and gentle creature and no matriarch, had nothing to do except run her house for herself and her little darling, and while Nellie would have seen to it that her daughter learned to sew and cook like any other girl, little Myra sat back, waited on by a doting old woman whom she took for granted and later despised. She became that rarity in her world, a spoiled child. And for a self-centered girl already showing signs of a strong will, it was a bad beginning.

But not to worry, yet; she used to join all the other kids on the couple of neighboring vacant lots and bomb sites they called crofts, and romp and shout and tear her pinafore and play tag and field at rounders and come home all dirty so Gran had to wash her face while she'd stamp wi' temper, a real tomboy, but kids will be kids.

At five, school: Peacock Street County Primary, a three-minute walk from the child's double domicile, along Gorton Lane. The usual asphalt playground. Then, at eleven, to her mother's gratification she was bright enough to get into a secondary school. With luck, it might have been situated in some fascinating new clime, opening the world out to a teen-ager: no, one mile away.

Mixed, boys and girls, always a good thing. To walk down Levenshulme Road over the railway bridge and suddenly come upon playing fields which here seem vast is a pleasant surprise; behind the goal posts stroll animated groups of young people, the girls in white socks and dark coats. Ryder Brow could take a girl with the humblest background and prepare her to become qualified teacher, nurse, private secretary, cultivated wife, to be recorded in the Gorton *Reporter* as "Local Girl Makes Good." A good, solid Lancashire school. Without losing the flat Manchester voice—as hard to discard as any Middle West speciality—Myra acquired a couple of long words "for conversational use" as well as, intermittently, the sort of careful speech which sounds like walking on eggs.

From this childhood, too, one half expects the anecdote, the flash across the landscape of the future. Nothing. She was in the A stream (We're told that means our Myra's bright). Good at Maths and Eng. When the class was asked to produce an essay on "A Dangerous Adventure," Myra penned one which Maureen avers was good enough to be "bound and put in the school library." Calf or leather? Apparently she chose "A Shipwreck." The subconscious? It seems hardly enough. The girl next to her, now a wife and mother, possibly wrote about Jack the Ripper.

She walked the mile from home, and back. Two places, her family remember, she made a habit of glancing at, every journey. First, on her right by Glencastle Road, the little Church of the Sacred Heart, Gorton, three statues high over the door, Christ dying on the cross with a disciple on one side and his mother on the other (Ooh, it does look sad, what a terrible way to go). She would think about the nails and give a little shudder, then cheer herself up with tiny Sunny Brow Park on her left, a hollow which on fine mornings lived up to its name, with its miniature lake and dwarf waterfall a foot high and the swings and kiddies rolling down the sloping lawns (I'll make it *my* park). She specially liked the waterfall and took to saying to herself each time: Mornin', thou Sacred Heart; mornin', thou waterfall.

Otherwise she was a stolid, gawky girl of twelve, thirteen, fourteen, looking neither to the left nor right. Less interesting, really, than the one being helped along by friends, the wicked pretty girl who'd been passed a miniature bottle of gin and drunk it under the desk and was to be kept in for a week.

Myra was a good fielder at rounders, and later played netball: long legs, excellent at defense, strong swimmer. Gran had a framed snap of her at the pool among a bunch of girls, Myra leaning forward and grinning gauchely into the camera. Even threw the discus and the javelin. A boy, she might have turned into a passable athlete. If Lanky Sloany in Glasgow had had exactly her qualifications . . .

IQ of 109, slightly above average, and only failed the Eleven-Plus because of "unsatisfactory attendance." Gran again.

Summer 1957: she would be fifteen at the end of term. In the A stream or not, she was just not outstanding or keen enough to be one of those working-class pupils whose teachers try and persuade the parents to let them stay on with a view to the university. It went without saying that she would leave now, and like the other girls, get a job "to help things at home."

But before the term finished, there was an incident which was as significant a pointer to the future as the one or two in Glasgow. This one, however, was of a diametrically opposite character.

In spite of her dash and self-sufficiency—having more than her share of what even local men call in their women "Lancashire toughness," her mind already on leaving school (It'll be super to be grown-oop), she was completely unsophisticated. She knew there was to be a new world, in the next year or two, filled with "boys," and who's clicked with who, But it was still the future. Her body was changing; she knew about that, but nothing about the emotional upsets. No strong sentiment had ever brushed her, neither grief nor love nor hate; even in a community with no time for sensitive upheaval, she stood out as prosaic as a healthy calf.

And she was so ungrown-up as to befriend a little neighbor in Taylor Street, a boy of thirteen—two years her junior—and a childish thirteen at that. Michael Higgins was the sort of shy, delicate lad who would appeal strongly to the latent maternal instinct in a forceful older girl with no young brothers who has not yet come to the time of channeling emotions she is not yet aware of.

Although not at Ryder Brow with her—a Catholic, he was a pupil at St. Francis' in Gorton Lane, her father's old school—he became her constant companion. She shared her candy with him, took him for walks as if he were a puppy and defended him against bigger boys. His initials were the same as hers, M.H., the two were a team.

Friday, June 14, was a day of steaming city heat, and after school Michael raced around to Gran's: Myra, what about a swim? Walter an' Ed 'Ogan an' me's off to the Station Road rezz. The rezz was a disused reservoir a mile and a half away, behind the vast posh part called the Melland Playing Field: a strip of forgotten water amid a desert of rubbish heaps, disowned bricks and abandoned barbed wire, with behind it the inevitable backyards. But the cool water beckoned and it was a favorite forbidden playground. Myra the swimmer was tempted, but it was so hot that she felt too lazy to do the walk, so (Ta ra for now!) the boys raced off. At seven, a knock—Sally Cheadle from Taylor Street, Mrs. 'Iggins is that worried, Michael's not 'ome yet from the rezz. Myra set out with her, running most of the way.

In the late afternoon light, a crowd of thirty stood silent beside the water, including police with grappling irons and a frogman. Sally followed Myra as she ran into their midst; it seemed incredible the sun could still be shining. They looked down and Myra saw the first dead face she had ever seen. It was the color of the slime that still glistened all over it. Myra clasped her hands and whispered, "Michael come back come back come back," over and over again. He was gone, forever. She went into violent hysterics. "If I'd 'a gone, 'e wouldn't 'a got the cramp, I should 'a gone . . ." It was the sort of holiday tragedy which can strike any waterside group at any moment, leaving an impression for months. But this was a permanent shock.

For days she walked in a trance and did not sleep. The lifeless grey face haunted her darkness; she heard that ghastly gurgling for air air air, then held her breath to feel what he had felt until she was dizzy and her heart pounding. Her only activity was to go from door to door collecting for a wreath for the coffin. Gran thought it a beautiful action, but her mother felt vaguely that it should have been performed by a schoolmate less prostrate than Myra. When housewives opened their doors to be confronted with her pale and stony face, they were taken aback. "She wasn't like a little girl needin' sympathy, she made you feel sort o' guilty, like as if it was your fault 'e'd gone drownded and you better fork out for them flowers or she'd go an' tell on you." It sounds as if it ended up a good-sized wreath.

The funeral service at St. Francis', conducted by Father Theodore, left on her an indelible impression: the candles, the chanting, the warm smell of incense which somehow seemed a melancholy emanation from the dead boy himself. At the funeral in Gorton Cemetery, she stood alone in her black. To the other mourners, seeing her stare down at the soil raining onto the little coffin with her own initials engraved on it, it seemed that to herself she was in a mourning deeper than that of the Higgins family. Her parents accepted her reaction as natural; Poor lass, give 'er time an' she'll shake it off.

But she didn't. The self-indulgence deepened into morbidity. She wore the black till it had to be taken from her; when she left her school she could hardly be bothered to say goodbye to her schoolmates, then sat in the front room in Bannock Street "lollin' about." It was a relief to the family when she started her first job, junior clerk at Lawrence, Scott and Electromotors in Louisa Street, one mile away, and half a mile from Westmoreland Street. She was able to walk home to midday dinner.

The neighbor who had diagnosed her little caller as resentful was a shrewd woman. As the months went past, the girl's attitude hardened into a facet of permanent character: an important one. Where a girl of normal sensibilities would have thought—and gone on thinking—as much of the dead boy's tragic cutting off and of his parent's loss as of her own grief (Poor Mrs. Higgins, we know it was an accident an' nobody to blame, but Mam, my heart goes out to her), this girl's heart stayed exactly where it was: broken perhaps but immovable, right in the center of Myra Hindley.

Somebody was to blame. If she had ever thought about God—she had never been pressed to, and hadn't bothered—she would have blamed Him. As it was, she censured everybody she knew—how *dare* they stroll about when this terrible thing had happened to her? Her friend, the only one she has ever loved or ever will love—*why?* She behaved like a mother whose child has died and who can never bear another, a child snatched from under her eyes by wicked forces with a grudge against *her*. It was a conviction all the more dangerous for never coming into the open, there to be massaged away by sympathetic argument, or exploded by ridicule. It lay dormant, like a foetus.

And like a foetus, it grew.

CHAPTER 12

SHE TO THE APPOINTED PLACE

"What shall be the maiden's fate?
Who shall be the maiden's mate?"
Scott

TO THE CASUAL EYE, she came back to normal. At Lawrence, Scott she did quite well, running errands and brewing tea and typing the odd letter, though she was still a sloppy attender and was scolded for it. Not popular, not unpopular. Played netball for the office team if she didn't scratch at the last minute, and even dabbled once a week in judo. In the midday break loved listening to pop records, and it was then she learned to jive and was noticed: the strong adolescent body stirred, the somnolent eyes flashed, and to the blaring, barbaric rhythms she swiveled hips in the half-conscious simulation of an abandon she would have denied.

But comfort came from an unexpected source. From Gran. Not directly. Mrs. Maybury, as a girl, had been trained for a "vet's assistant" and loved animals. And Myra suddenly became aware of a personality in Number 7 which she had always taken for granted. Gran's dog, Duke. With an excess quite disconcerting, she flung her arms around him and wouldn't let him alone; he became her life. She couldn't understand why he couldn't sit at her feet in the office, loving eyes looking moistly up.

Evening lessons, eighteenpence a time, at Stan's Dancing School off Knutsford Road near old Ryder Brow. Christmas 1957, fifteen and a half, powder and lipstick, dance hall, first time: the local Alhambra. She went with a sort of boy friend, a perspiring youth she told her friend Pat Jessop about: Gigglin' an' 'oldin' 'ands an' that. Pat, I don't see anythin' in it, honest—I mean it's daft. I only go for the music an' he's a good dancer, I will say that.

The usual girls' escapades. It was easy to kid her gran that she was spending the night at her mam's or vice versa, and once, for a dare, she and Pat took a bus to Ashton-under-Lyne—nearly five miles away!—went to a dance and spent the night at the house of a girl friend. The mother found out, there was hell to pay and each "got a clout," even mild Nellie Hindley being roused to wrath by what was obviously not to be countenanced. But Myra spent her summer holiday with Pat and her family in boisterous old Blackpool, forty miles off: the first of her three brief recorded escapes from her suburban enclosure. She enjoyed it, swimming once more in a rowdy populated ocean which could not evoke the memory that darkened the back of her mind. And the roller coaster was a terrifying thrill.

In the office tea breaks she lent a wary ear to the giggle talk: Myra, don't you go 'and in 'and to a bomb site with 'im, 'e'll 'ave the knickers off you 'fore you can say French letter . . . Never you mind what it is, Myra 'Indley, it's summat that's been posted from Paris. Myra, try my eye black—just the job—an' wi' the right bra you'll be a hit, you got good ankles too but you 'ave got long feet. Myra, 'ave you clicked with a boy yet? . . . Oh, you will.

But she didn't. The two at work who were supposed to be smashing looked like shopwindow dummies, one of them never stopped gassing and the other half daft (Eeh, that's raht, ba goom)—no, not for Myra. Leafing the magazines, she mooned for hours over the illustrations of troubling young men as they loomed powerfully over their girls, hair short, mouths sensual but firm, eyes smoldering. " 'I want you,' he breathed, she could smell the tweed as he steered into the Promenade des Anglais, 'but I can't trust myself alone with you. Let's get back to books, do you know Sartre?' " From the mags she derived highfalutin' phrases which she mixed in with her own idiom: No, I intend to wait till I reach twenty. Then it is my eedy-feex to marry a steady boy and have two kiddies, a boy and a girl.

In the meantime she was going to be good, "keeping oneself for marriage." One unexpected side effect: when one evening Maureen entered Gran's kitchen and found her elder sister standing naked in the family tin bath brought in from the backyard, Myra squirmed and turned her back and said, "Don't coom in, our Mo, you can see I 'aven't got a stitch on." "It's only your sister," said Mo, sensible Lancashire, "don't be daft." This modesty was to crop up later.

Her vision of herself as wife and mother was a vague one, but it meant she enjoyed baby-sitting. She was a gift to Joan Phillips and her husband, with three little boys; patient and reliable, on an early summer evening she would be seen standing little Dennis up in the backyard, then sitting on her knees in a corner and coaxing him to totter into her outstretched arms.

Then Duke was run over and killed. Gran was greatly upset, dried her eyes and got another dog, Lassie. But Myra was desolate (You'd think her family'd been wiped out in a plane crash). Again she took it personally. What had who got against her?

Restless again, kept saying she wasn't doing well enough for herself. A girl had returned from a Butlin's Holiday Camp at Pwllheli, thrilled with the time she'd had as a Redcoat—a sort of sexy waitress; then there was a neighbor's daughter working outside Philadelphia (Ooh, where Katharine Hepburn and Bing Crosby and Grace Kelly hang out), a nurse earning oodles of dollars and her own car. Myra said she might apply to be a children's nanny and emigrate.

Drifting.

Then, toward the end of 1958, sixteen and a half, she called at the "Monastery" attached to St. Francis' and asked Father Theodore for instruction in the faith. This sounds more dramatic than it was: her Catholic Auntie Kath, the one she liked, had been concerned about her restlessness and suggested that religion might help. Myra scented again the poignant incense; besides, she had leafed through an old tale of Gran's called *The Rosary* and fancied the role of tragic withdrawer from life. ('Ave you 'eard, Myra 'Indley Bannock Street's takin' the veil or summat, an' 'er so yoong too. Never been the same since 'er tragedy, fancy a *nun*, never another dance nor one luke at the lads, ooh . . .)

She promised Auntie Kath she'd drop into the Sacred Heart by her old school to see how she felt. And she did, she told them after, one Saturday, good mornin', thou Sacred Heart. The agonizing Christ had to remind her of Michael Higgins, and she herself became the mourning mother. Loovly porch, Catholic Needlework Guild, Marriage Advisory Council, Pilgrimage to Lourdes. Funny in Gorton somehow, and so quiet made you feel all 'ushed up an' 'oly. She opened a book; "Commemoration of the Dead: Remember also O Lord thy servant who is gone hence and sleeps the sleep . . ." Michael. Ooh it is sad.

She did take instruction, enjoying her special name, Veronica, and in November, Auntie Kath and Uncle Bert were happy to present her with a prayer book ("souvenir of your first Holy Communion"). But the "Monastery," in November, must have depressed her: dingy hall with paint chipping off the dusty Virgin, little brown cells with kitchen-chair table and stool for confession. Of the mystic drama and glorious organ music she had seen envelop Ingrid Bergman and Deborah Kerr, not a trace. She lost interest, and Father Theodore (who remembers nothing of her instruction) recalls running into her in Gorton Lane and asking why she hadn't been to Mass lately: "She just hung her head and mumbled something."

And mid-'59 saw her back at Stan's gyrating and stamping to Bill Haley and his Comets, or under the drier at Maison Laurette in Taylor Street: I fancy a fringe, Mrs. 'Owells, an' what's more I'm sick o' bein' dark. I don't think it's me image, could I 'ave a root tonin'? If I won the pools I'd buy a car, I may still emigrate, I'm fed oop.

She once startled the neighborhood by emerging from the Maison, not yet seventeen, with a pink rinse (Myra is funny, seems only the oother day she was goin' to 'ave it all shaved off).

Kids playing tag on the corner, where she had played donkeys
years back. They yack after her, "Ooh, 'er 'air's caught fire!"
(Cheeky lot, that one's little Pauline Reade off of Wiles Street,
an' Jimmy Tate off of Casson Street, an' who's that lout of a lad
with a cig?) "What-ho, Myra, I've got a job for you in B-Belle
Vue, in a cage at sixpence a b-bluddy time!" (Ooh, it's that
other kid off of Wiles Street, that David Smith that's illegitimate,
a real Teddy boy, only eleven an' *smokin'*, an' there's our Mo!
I'll tell our Mam about her, this minute.)

It would appear that our Myra was becoming a prude frown-
ing on vulgarity in any form. Except hair.

1959, July 23. Seventeen. She went through the motions of
being engaged (Me fioncy's savin' oop for the weddin'); she even
sported a "diamond" ring: Ronnie Sinclair from Dalkeith Street,
practically a continuation of Bannock Street. Dances. Shiny
hands held over coffee and pop. Ronnie was a fresh-faced youth
who wasn't interested in saving, but did like a smoke and a
drink. Not for me, said Myra, and as for that smoochin' oop them
dark alleys, ach. The romance that never got started ended coolly
on the corner of Bannock Street: I sincerely 'ope your mam
doesn't smell the beer on your breath, ta ra for now. Ronnie was
very cut up.

She had been at Lawrence, Scott for a year and a half, now
became redundant and got a job, again as junior typist, at
Clydesdale's Furniture Supply in Ashton Old Road. Half a
mile.

1960. The junior typist moved again. To Bratby and Hinchliffe, Bottling, etc. Engineers, Gorton Lane. Up the road.

July 23. Eighteen. Gordon Eyers: "I was a lad of eighteen
meself, ran into her a couple o' times at the old Alhambra, tried
it on i' the car but no go, it was like pressin' yourself against a
shopwindow . . . 'Er looks? Well, I never recall mooch about a
bird excep' tits, not that I was ever allowed that near but looked
okay. Tallish, square, broad bum but broad shoulders to match
but not mannish, black eyes, chin wi' no nonsense. A well-built

bird, no doubt o' that, long legs but what's t' use o' legs when t' flippin' knees are glued together?

"Looked older'n eighteen 'specially when she talked all cut-glass . . . Oh, you know, sounded like you hear on t' pictures— I'm a girl who dreams of a boy with a brain in 'is 'ead, there's more to love than just the physical—you know the sort o' balls, an' 'er wi' that 'air all them colors gave you the idea she might be same inside, just 'ad no idea what she wanted.

"Last time in the car I pass a remark about 'er 'ands, an' she waves 'er fingers about: 'Yes, they're good 'ands,' she says, an' then I says, 'Different than mine which are very bad 'ands an' you never know where they'll land next,' an' suited the action to the word. Well, I got a stingin' wallop across the kisser an' she was out o' the car, bang, an' off on them 'igh 'eels an' that's the last I 'eard of 'er."

Drifting. It got bad enough for her to be sacked for absenteeism. No job, and nineteen next birthday.

December 15; Manchester *Evening News*; SITUATIONS VAC.: "Typist required, excellent prospects for chosen applicant."

Don't apply, Myra Hindley.

Could *she* have taken off?

If she had met a man at Bratby and Hinchliffe who was interested enough to pursue her and finally beg her to marry him? A junior partner in the firm, say, grammar-school type, doing well, "bettering himself," and likely to do still better. A good man even, though good men are not always interesting. One can safely wager that Myra Hindley would have found goodness, in any form, as dull as ditchwater.

But the prospects might have tempted her. A convenient marriage. (I don't mind if I do).

Give her the benefit of the doubt. It might have worked.

She was, at that moment, in a state of abeyance. As unconscious as an empty goblet ready to be filled to the brim, whether the potion is to be harmless wine, or arsenic. If—it might have been possible, *just* possible—if she had grown to take pride in her position as the wife of a successful man and had become determined to share in that success, she would have exercised every ounce of will power to bring her character into line with his. She might not have been the most popular wife in their set, other women might have found her disconcerting, but her children would have helped. If it had been possible to acquire a sense of humor by buying a set of Humorphone Records, she would have done it. And she'd have had a fifty-fifty chance, or even the odds in her favor. She might have pulled it off.

"Dear Miss Hindley, Thank you for your application, I should be pleased to see you here on Thursday the 21st, if you would kindly bring your references, Yrs faithfully, T. Craig."

She did not have to ask where Levenshulme Road was; she walked the route she had always walked, to school. Her hair wasn't too much between colors and she looked striking without being a sketch, just enough make-up and sensible in coat and skirt and bit of fur (No brooch, it kills the ensemble).

Crossing the bridge, she looked over at the playing fields, at her former self multiplied by fifty, running and strolling. (What has happened to me since? . . . Not half enough. You can't play netball all your life. Am I frigid . . . Where *is* Millwards?)

Mr. Craig? Yes, it is cold but you expect it this time o' year . . . You mean you want to dictate to me *now*? Okay. Dear Sirs, As we are chemical merchants we stock numerous acids such as Formic, Acetic . . . She got the job.

1961, Monday morning, January 16. Cold. Briskly she walked the mile. Like being back at school, quite exciting really. Mornin', thou Sacred Heart; mornin', thou waterfall; mornin', thou Ryder Brow, bring me luck. If you walk right to the bottom of Levenshulme Road, you're almost at the reservoir. Funny I should think o' that now. Bring me luck, my darlin' darlin' M.H. . . .

What a way in, but they make you welcome I must say. "No, I'll keep me coat for the moment, thanks. I was at the school across the road from 'ere, funny . . ."

Tom Craig walked up. "Graham, Tony, Ian—this is our new typist, Myra . . . sorry, love, I didn't catch your surname . . ."

PART THREE

FLYIN' HIGH

"A quiet couple, flyin' high . . ."

Phoenix Braithwaite,
(Chapter 25)

CHAPTER 13

DEAR DIARY

"He who believes in nothing
still needs a girl to believe in
him."

Rosenstock-Huessy

"HINDLEY," she answered, careful to aspirate the *h* as she always did unless with her family, or in a temper, or both, "Myra Hindley." 'E's a sulky one, the others seem okay.

She followed Mr. Craig, he pointed out her desk, a couple of girls showed her the cubbyholes to use and the typing paper and the tea things for her turn to make the tea, crummy view but not too bad.

Yes, Gran, it was okay . . . No, I just said hello to one or two. No, Gran, *nobody*'s asked me to the pictures . . . oh Gran, this meat *is* tough.

My godfathers, the first two weeks 'ave flown . . . No, Gran, I 'ave *not* clicked. A couple o' the lads got a bit fresh, I just said no thanks, I don't go on dates. There's one potty on Christian Science or summat and the other football, Manchester United till you could scream, but they're okay. There's all sorts, one Welsh an' one Scotch, daftest way o' speakin', only the Scottie just doesn't—talk about dour! I don't take any notice of any of 'em really; they're okay.

Kings Jan 25 *Young Sinners*. Feb 6 *Murder by Contract*. Shaftesbury Feb 8 *The Great St. Louis Bank Robbery*.

When did she first take notice of him? He was so uncommunicative that it may have been weeks. Not shy, just self-sufficient. Was it one chill March day when she looked up from her typing and saw him across the lobby, one knee high against his desk, doodling, and then turning to look out of the window, proud, challenging? Lively grey eyes, face coming to a bit of a point at the chin, so wi' the ears sticking out a *bit* he looked like them Pipes o' Pan lads wi' the goat's feet—fauns are they, satyrs?

She waits for him to move. He does not move. Absorbed, as if nothing around him exists, neither the delivery notes nor the pinups nor the streaked window nor the old oil drums. He is away. Where?

Or was it the day she first saw him angry? The afternoon he stormed in to Vernon, his face glittering with rage and unrecognizable: "I herrd ye call me a silly bastard, who the fuckin' 'ell d' ye think ye are?"

The shocked gasp of the girl next to her, then Tom at the door, pink and stern: "Now now, Ian, I don't stand for that sort o' talk around here, you get back—"

"Not before he bluddy well apologizes—"

"Aw, coom on, Ian, I was only . . ." Mutterings and arm-takings, it was over.

But he had made him apologize. And as she walked home through her sad little park, the fiery, contemptuous face stayed with her. Fancy old Stick-in-the-Mud. Of course that language was disgraceful, like a road mender, and he deserved to get the sack for it. But coming from those haughty lips and with that outlandish way of speaking, it was somehow not so much vulgar as forthright. Perhaps there had been a tragic love affair up in the Highlands, with a sort of an Annie Laurie, funny lad.

Whenever it was she noticed him, the moment she really stared was the morning by the parking lot just before nine o'clock when she saw something roar over the bridge and past her old school and he stopped dead in front of her, astride his new motorbike. Two hundred c.c. Tiger, on the never-never—in other words, on the installment plan. A creature from another world, crash helmet, goggles, belted leather coat, top boots, the lot. And yet underneath all the gear, once he got to his desk there he was, business suit, waistcoat, spotless shirt and tie, double vent back of the coat, chic.

Having noticed, she went on noticing. Not that there was much to observe and then ponder on her way home. Nobody knew even where he lived, somewhere Longsight way and she couldn't ask Tom. Brothers, sisters? Girl friend? Tony told her Ian's dog Bruce had died of a tumor and Ian was proper upset—well, if he loved his dog he must be nice. He went to the pictures a lot, but apparently alone.

Queens Feb 20 *Violent Moment.* Kings Apr 10 *Gunman's Walk.* Then the red-letter week of May 15: Kings Return of *The Third Man!!!* Dum da dee da *dum* da *dum* . . .

As the summer advanced, he seemed to retire further away from her. With doors open she could hear him dictating, in his deep measured voice: "July the ferrst, 1961, Dear Serrs, We are in receipt of your suggestion for a renewal of the perfumery contract from the therrd of August next . . ."

She liked the way his hair grew, like a mane. Once she heard him blow his nose, just like anybody else. And he used a nail file. When bored, flicked fingers. When tired or thinking of something, rubbed bridge of nose between finger and thumb. He was miles away—no, miles *up,* had to lose height to focus on an interruption.

July the ferrst, she mouthed as she crossed her summery little park, good afternoon, thou waterfall, kiddies swinging, July the ferrst. Fancy studyin' a German grammar in your dinnertime. Would a *certain couple* ever sit joost 'ere, Myra and Ian, Ian holding Myra's fingers in that large sinewy hand with the clean nails? Back to high tea with Gran and the new Woman's Mag. In the illustrations she substituted his face. Sometimes dreamy, sometimes white with rage. Myra love, your 'ot pot's gettin' cold.

Any other teen-ager with a crush on a bloke would have confided endlessly in a girl friend, such as in Olive Purlow, who worked next to her. But this early, Myra's confidante was herself. In one of the office shorthand notebooks, on her nineteenth birthday she started a day-to-day journal.

Writing on her knee in a lull, in her small, back-sloping hand, with short-sighted eyes bent low, she looked sophisticated enough. Older than her age, hair now a settled blond, generous make-up, smartly shod foot plus elegant ankle crossed over the other knee. But the notebook, lying about four years later, could have been penned by a schoolgirl of twelve stammeringly in love with a choirboy. If proof were needed that before Ian Brady, Myra Hindley was sexually inexperienced . . . Professional writers apart, only virgins and generals keep diaries.

Never can a calamitous obsession have found its initial voice in so banal a document.

It starts, as if she cannot bear silence any longer, abruptly: *JULY 23rd '61. Wonder if Ian is courting. Still feel the same. 25th, Haven't spoken to him yet.* This was after exactly six months of watching and waiting and gleaning an occasional grain of information to press to her skimpy pillow: he'd been with somebody to the dog races at Belle Vue, liked spaghetti and macaroni cheese out of cans, boiled ham, cucumber. Couldn't abide a black pudding, after a haggis it's obscene; was comically terrified of any winged insect, such as a cockroach or particularly a daddy-longlegs; didn't dance.

The twenty-sixth she must have spent with a beating heart, for she was preparing to make the first move. Was the plan as girlish as the diary? Graze her finger and ask him to bind it up? Borrow a German grammar from Cambert Lane Library and ask him what *Liebe* meant? Whatever it was: *27th, Spoken to him. He smiles as though embarrassed.*

"Embarrassed" can mean what you want it to mean: the shyness of a man's man faced by a female who attracts him, or the polite stare of the stranger on his guard. This last interpretation she side-stepped. No, wee waterfall, he *smiled!*

Then she adds: *I am going to change, you'll notice that in the way I write.* Was this a vow to get onto paper thoughts that would one day impress him into looking at her as if for the first time, and lean over her like the boys in the Woman's Mag? If it was, no go, she continues in exactly the same style: *28th, Irene Eccles has clicked with a lad she met in April.*

Then somebody must have dropped a dark hint to explain Ian's indifference to the female staff: *30th, Ian isn't interested in girls.* But overnight, she cheered up. AUGUST *1st, Ian's taking sly looks at me at work.*

Sly? He could not fail to guess, from the blushes and the clumsy coquetries, that she was attracted to him, and he had to be laconically flattered. For months she had been to him a blond shadow among shadows, though a good solid one, could be a Les. Then that first day when she had said hello, stammering and giggling, he had seen that this was a young girl on the edge of desire. (Weel, weel. Bide a wee.)

2nd, Not sure if he likes me. They say he gambles on horses. 3rd, Ian likes Boddington's Beer. 8th, Gone off Ian a bit. 10th, Tommy is scared of Ian. Then a statement as simple as it is pathetic: *11th, Been to Friendship Pub, but not with Ian.*

But the pendulum swings back: *13th, Wonder what Misery will be like tomorrow?* And back: *14th, I love Ian all over again. He has a cold and I would love to mother him. 19th, Visited Belle View* [sic]. *Tony Prendergast and Eddie were there.* Carnival night in the Elizabethan Ballroom, where she must have danced, around the Dancing Fountain, to the music of Johnny Drake and his Crewmates. Tunes new and old, gorgeous: I'm Breakin' in a Brand-new Broken Heart—The Very Thought of You—You're Drivin' Me Crazy—You'll Never Know—oh but The Very Thought of You's the best . . . why doesn't *he* ask me to Belle Vue? We Present Lancashire's Foremost Ballroom Dance Team HINDLEY and BRADY . . .

24th, I am in a bad mood because he hasn't spoken to me today. Four days later, a little girl's prayer: *29th, I hope he loves me and will marry me some day.*

30th, Ian and Bert have had a row. Tommy sided with Bert and said Ian loses his temper too soon. SEPTEMBER 2nd, Sivori's Milk Bar in Clowes St. Less than a quarter of a mile from Westmoreland Street, but she still did not know he lived there. *4th, 5th, 6th, Ian's moodiness. Don't know anything about Ian's parents, background etc. 9th, Ian mentioned Hadfield to George,*

I think it's near Glossop. It is; obviously Ian had spoken of Hatfield, Yorkshire, omitting the Borstal part. *Ian wearing a black shirt today.* A month's gap.

OCTOBER 8th, Ian never talks about his family. But she did find out his address: *9th, Eddie lives in the next street to Ian. 13th, Ian hasn't spoken to me for several days. 18th, Ian still ignores me. Fed up. I still love him. 19th, Ian lives with his Mam and Dad and hardly ever goes out.* One evening, had she stood opposite Number 18? Two days later, another simple statement which, from another girl, would disarm: *21st, Somebody phoned Ian at work and Ian arranged to go to them for drinks . . .*

Then a toss of the head, and fitful attempts at extrication: *23rd, I fancy Eddie. I could fall for Ed. 25th, Ian and Tommy had a row. Ian nearly hit Tommy.* Then the heart seems to harden: *25th, Ian swearing. He is uncouth. I thought he was going to hit Nellie.* Nellie was Mrs. Egerton, the cleaner. Ian was fond of her and every Christmas gave her a bottle of port, so it is probable that his turning on her was for the diarist's benefit. *28th, Royal Oak Pub in Wythenshawe.* Another suburb. *NOVEMBER 1st, Months now since Ian and I spoke.*

Another attempt. *2nd, Met Bob, pub crawl, went to Ashton-under-Lyne, Dukinfield, Denton. Quite a good night. 3rd, Ian swearing at work, using crude words. 4th, Rodney had drinks at Plough.* Rodney surely wanted to tell about himself, but no, *Rodney said "All Ian is interested in is making money."*

Regal Oxford Rd Nov 4, All Thrill-Horror-Shock Show *Jack the Ripper!!!* He Prowled the Dark Streets Mauling . . . Ravaging . . . MURDERING!!!

5th, Have finished with Eddie. He is courting another girl. Next day she lost her temper, and must have regretted it bitterly. *6th, Ian still not speaking. I called him a big-headed pig.* Crude, but genteel enough to save her face. For three weeks, no entry.

Manchester *Evening News*, November 22, DUKE OF MANCHESTER'S SON WEDS TYPIST. Ah well. Like winnin' the pools, I suppose. *28th, I've given up with Ian. He goes out of his way to annoy me, he insults me and deliberately walks in front of me. I have seen the other side of him* [when had she seen a first side?] *and that convinces me he is no good.* The next entries lurch

between the cry of the soul and the social snippet: *DECEMBER:
2nd, I hate Ian, he has killed all the love I had for him, visited
Empress Club Stockport with Joan and Irene.*

15th, I'm in love with Ian all over again.

Then suddenly, during the next week, he made a gesture. On
the twenty-second, the diary records triumphantly, *Out with Ian!*

How has it happened? Did she—as he once more turned aside
at her approach—did she burst into tears? And then did he at
last take pity?

No. He was no fool, and it must have been much more deliberate than that, starting from the first day she said hello, when he
thinks, Bide a wee . . . Realizing at that moment that she has a
crush, the next moment he guesses further: that her feeling for
him, while composed of the usual romantic yearnings, is laced
with something more special. Fascinated by his elusiveness, she
senses without knowing it that the mystery is more than reserve.
She scents the dark.

And the dark, while frightening her, draws her. He knows that
if he took her dancing to Belle Vue and in the waltz pressed his
lips gently to hers, she would be dreamily happy; also that if in a
corridor at Millwards he were to stage a fit of rage, grip her arms
hard and glare into her eyes as only he could, she would be
terrified. But he knows too that she would be physically roused.
And the thought of it rouses him. *Ian's taking sly looks at me.*

From that moment on, for five months, he has "played her
up," done everything he could to humiliate her—torture, subtle
systematic torture. And now, out of curiosity, he moves to the
next stage. *Out with Ian!* Probably a cup of coffee, but a heavy
date was made.

Sunday, New Year's Eve. To a Scot whose birthday was as near
as dammit, Red-Letter Night. At six o'clock, high-tea time, the
knock at the door (of her parents' house, in Eaton Street) which
she had thought of every day for twenty-three weeks. Ian, this is
me mam, me dad, me sister. Maureen an awkward sexy fifteen.

He did it in style. *Ian had bought a bottle of German wine
and whisky,* and whisky was a top luxury. She did know, from his
own address, that she could relax about frayed linoleum and
stains and stale air an' that. Anyway, the visitor had turned into

Bonny Prince Charming. After the weeks and months of love and hate and hope and despair, it must have been the miraculous evening of her young life. No mention of popping around the corner and saying "This is Ian" to loving Gran. After tea, a tiny sip of the wine, ooh it is sharp. Prosit, he says, all staccato, and Prosit she echoes as they clink, loovly private joke. Then off on the bus into the humming, glamorous hub of Manchester.

"King of Kings," no ta very mooch. Gaumont—that's better. QUEUE UP HERE FOR CHEAPER SEATS, but Ian bought two of the best, front of Royal Circle 7/6. First the lushy indoor twilight was inundated with golden stereophonic music that turned her heart over, The Very Thought of You, she looked at him and he looked at her. Then the ads, sexy people in color eating chocs and drinking soft drinks, then the twilight was alive with Glorious Technicolor, then the big film, triumphantly recorded in the diary: *EL CID!* Romance. Like Walter Scott. Castles in Spain. Invincible Heston, sexy sulky Loren. Music sex blood. Blood sex music music music.

Out again, glamour everywhere, raucous crowds waiting for midnight. But if they only knew—they're celebrating much more than the New Year. I want my 'ead on his shoulder as we walk along but he *might* jerk it away and I couldn't bear that. I'd kill meself, I *would*. Charlton Heston's smashin' but Ian's more than smashin', he's *interestin'*. I love the slow way he walks, almost a slouch, as if he had all day and the place belonged to him.

Standin' room on the bus, loovly, it means you can snuggle up without seemin' to, and his face slightly above like in the movies which is dead right. Irene Eccles said he was sallow; well, she ought to get specs, it looks to me more like Italian tan. Good old Gorton Lane, off the bus at the Shakespeare, lit up for New Year. Back to Eaton Street.

Just before twelve o'clock Ian's whisky was opened, her first taste of spirits. By 1962 Bob Hindley was, for him, glowing, and overworked Nellie flushed and pretty. Maureen of course was out, not wi' that David Smith we 'ope. As for Prince Charming, he was getting Bonnier. Out of the Woman's Mag. The diary, a couple of days later: *Dad and Ian spoke as if they'd known each other for years. Ian is so gentle he makes me want to cry.*

Midnight. Scraping of chairs over the threadbare rug, toasts, holding hands, Auld Lang Syne. No no, he says, holdin' hands, it's no' *"Lest* auld acquaintance," it's *"Shude,"* then he sings it in a daft way half-Scotch and half-German I love it. The bottle has to be finished, he has the most because he's got such a strong head. Gude night, folks, I'll whistle a taxi and see your wee gerrl home, ha ha! Laughter and unaccustomed embraces all around, though if you watch him he manages not to touch *any*body proper, so it's not only me.

The Hindleys wave them down the street from the front door, ta ra ta ra ta ra, well she's not done too bad for 'erself 'as our Myra, only 'ope Mo'll 'ave the same sense.

He walks her around to Bannock Street, ooh the cold air does make you giddy. A lurching trio of revelers wave and snigger. Common lot.

He takes her arm (Now we're engaged. This is Mr. Brady, my fioncy). At Number 7 she looks quickly up at Gran's window, no light, dead asleep, even on New Year nowt wakes *her.*

She fumbles with her key. Soundless giggles, they tiptoe into the little front room and she clicks on the light. She never dared hope he'd see her home, but earlier she did tell Gran to stoke up the fire and Gran has. With the bits of holly and the two streamers Gran brings out every Christmas, the room looks cheerful, the dead spit of the one they've just left. Ian, luke over the dresser, d'you ever see such funny ole-fashion faces, Gran's mam an' dad staring you out wherever you are in the room an' sayin' I wonder what our Nellie's lass is up to, couple o' nosy old parkers.

Not nosy. Just impassive. As impassive as the gods who arrange the direst mischief, and then watch it happen.

The room is the twin of Eaton Street, except in one respect. Gran's front room lacks the standard hard sofa. Instead, a sofa bed.

For a healthy girl the first full sexual encounter is a tricky emotional event; in a calm sea it is the first big wave, one which can threaten to capsize. For a highly sexed **young woman of** nineteen who has willfully adopted the pose of prudery, it can be a rough passage. If she is a girl who has—side by side with the prudery—allowed herself to sink into an advanced state of obsessive love, there is immediate danger.

A few days ago, he was so far out of her reach that she had not even considered the feel of the flesh of his fingers in a handshake. Suddenly, he is here, in her home. Alone with her.

And he? He has ventured agreeably into the little room, fomented by drink and the need for stealth, flattered by the idea of an easy encounter. While she is pale and tense and dry-mouthed, and her heart is beating, his eyes are as guarded as ever. Large hands steady as he lays down his overcoat, his breathing normal. *Alles in Ordnung.*

He sits opposite, and looks at her—yes, severely. Almost like those angry times in the office.

But she knows, somehow, what his next move must be. And she leans forward to whisper—so low that she has to say it again—that it will be "the first time." Her voice and her face carry a humble entreaty. The age-old plea for gentleness.

It is doubtful whether, on his few forays with girls, he has ever deflowered one, or that this time it has crossed his mind that he has a novice on his hands. It is a discovery which has caused many an ardent pursuer to lose his ardor, even to stumble off into the night.

But there are other kinds of pursuers. Not so timid.

In the last century a husband would find himself, on his wedding night, faced more often than not with just this situation. If he was a good man, he would coax his frightened bride, step by step, with love and understanding, along the road that led, ultimately, to mutual ecstasy. But if the bridegroom was the exception . . .

He looks down at his wife. A new look, very different from the face he used to put on when saluting her with the chaste kiss of betrothal. The hood has fallen, and the heart begins to beat. The lips moisten. The breath comes quicker. This is it.

She is like a soft and frightened bird, please, please be gentle. Then . . .

The bird is ensnared, in the all-powerful trap of male arms and legs; the well-mannered suitor has turned into the savage invader. Hanging wings of hair, and the pulsing neck utterly at his mercy, *please* . . . And like the invader with his sword, the bridegroom drives brutally home.

The lacerating agony is followed by a scream. Struggle, frantic beat of broken wings, scream, struggle, blood. Then the moans of frenzied pain. Then silence. The man hears his own spasmodic breathing, feels the stern throb of the conqueror's heart.

Then, in that Victorian bedroom, there would come the sounds of sobs: weeping which meant, too often, the foundering of a marriage for a wife who was to remain, through years of patient childbearing, quite frigid and as apprehensive of the sexual act as she would be of a minor surgical operation.

But suppose she had been the rare, rare exception? The woman in a thousand? In ten thousand? Suppose the terrified bride, in the midst of her agony, had suddenly realized—without knowing yet *what* she was realizing—that the brutality of the naked beast above her was mysteriously arousing, in her, a new and exciting servitude? That bride too, after the scream and the pain, would lie still.

Silence. Is she dead? Wake up the dead. Gently, carefully, the conqueror moves. Moves. Moves. Relax, my bride, relax. The hoarse babble of desire, mmmmm . . . Moves. Moves. Moves.

The dead bird stirs. And awakens. Moves. Moves. Moves.

The moans again. But different. Frenzy again. But a different frenzy. Mounting, mounting, mounting, and with it the moans, until the moment when the moans rise to a cry. But this time it is the cry of love—the consummation of a marriage which will be, of necessity, a strange one. The deed is done.

And the hearts of the dazed doers slow down to the pace of ordinary life.

Gorton life. The house must be put in order.

Does Fate sometimes, long before an event in store, arrange an ironic rehearsal?

Ooh, put the cigarette butt on the fire . . . Crumbs, look at the divan, kitchen mop pail ooh she's callin' down. All right, Gran, it's only me, I dropped soomthink on me toe. Maureen's here, she coom back for a tick an' we're brewin' up some tea . . .

Overcoat back on, the new cigarette lit. Then he runs his fingers through his hair and the face is in place, the careful watching look. Her face is in order too, and her voice; they speak low, and intimately, but in the flat currency of every day: Lucky it's not rainin' . . . Whatever's the time, two-therrty . . . Sure you won't have another cup? . . . Well, see you at the office, be good, ta ra.

And from the later testimony of those who spent time with them or, at a time of tension, overheard them talking, it is fairly certain that when alone together, at moments of the highest stress and even of the deepest horror, their language and demeanor was never to depart from the norm.

But on this first night, at the front door, although her face and voice are back in order, her eyes cannot help but speak. As she coaxes his tie straight, they meet his: Happy birthday tomorrow, my love my darling my love. And he knows that from now on, forever and ever, she is his. Not only a New Year. A new life.

CHAPTER 14

IAN BRADY,
PHOTOPHILIAC

"A big smile now, for the dickeybird!"
Anon.

*JANUARY 1st 1962, I have been at Millwards for 12 months
and only just gone out with him. I hope Ian and I love each
other all our lives and get married and are happy ever after.*

She could not have imagined anything different. It would have
been absurd.

New Year's Day, the office. Olive, when later Myra confided
fitfully in her, was to recall that she herself that morning noticed
nothing new, "he didn't speak to Myra any more than he ever
had, just passed the time of day." *'As though embarrassed'*? . . .

Dear Sir Dear Sir Dear Sir I'm taking down flippin' shorthand
notes from Bert wi' no idea what I'm doin'. I keep 'earin' bits o'
tunes, he's behavin' as if last night 'adn't 'appened. Oh, but I do
appreciate it, me darlin' Highland laddie, you don't want to
make things awkward for me at work, it's thoughtful really.

I can hear you dictating now but, love, I know you are
thinkin' of last night just as I am, it's telepathy that's what it is.
And your voice is thrillin' me. Dear Sir, Regarding Delivery Last
Thurs of Twenty Drums of Glycerine, the Very Thought of You

and I Forget to Do my Office Work. My darling, your voice
sounds deep an' posh an' tight-lipped, as they say, an' so business-
like, last night it wasn't tight-lipped, oh no, croonin' in my ear
like a wee baby only deep How Deep Is the Ocean . . .

At lunch time, flanked by card players, he was at his German.
One day she would suggest a honeymoon on the Rhine. Silly, but
she couldn't remember exactly what they'd arranged about
tonight.

Five o'clock. She couldn't find him at first, he was collecting a
betting win, then in the parking lot she saw him getting astride
his motorbike, Spaceman Brady off to his planet. She couldn't
believe it, ran up to him; Ian . . .

Oh hello, I'm off to meet a pal at five-therrty, we're goin' to the
dog races. Cheerio!

She must have looked ill, to make Olive run up and ask what
was the matter. "Oh nothink, let's go to the pictures," then on
the corner of Sunny Brow Park she burst into tears and said she
was too tired to come out and hurried home.

The next week it was all to pour out, in spurts and spasms.

"Olive, now I can tell you. Next day was the same only worse,
and I just had to face the truth, that he isn't interested. I joost
went about like a doll that you wind oop, and in the afternoon,
when Irene switched on Music While You Work, they played
The Very Thought of You and the tears were rollin' down an' I
was dead scared Tom Craig'd catch on . . .

"Then at five I didn't give so much as a glance at the parking
lot, two can play at that game I thought, Mr. Hoity Mac Toity.
Well, back 'ome I was pretendin' to read me Mag when rat-tat
front door. I thought, My God, don't say it's a telegram to say
somebody's gone drowned! I opened the door. An' there he was,
across his motorbike, helmet on, goggles on top. Smilin' . . .
Olive, you never seed him smile nor anybody at Millwards has,
ooh it's like anythin' rare, it's *loovly!*

" 'How about a spin,' he says. 'Oh, it's bitter,' I says, I thought
best to act hard to get. And then he says, "Oh come on, that's just
like a gerrl,' and I ran upstairs an' got into me slacks an' me
thick coat an' settled be'ind him and we was off. A wonderful

rider but mad mad mad, up into some hills somewhere. My godfathers, the corners we cut!

"Then on the way back he bought some German wine in an off-license joint in Grey Street, and we went in a milk bar and he drank it out of a cup with hot water, it's called Hot-White, sounds a pain in the neck but it looked super, oh a true Bohemian. Then he says, 'Myra baby,' he says, 'I'd like you with your hair even fairer'—when he's 'ad a couple he goes all Yankee, fancy German wine in cups!"

Next day at the office, again for him the night before had not happened. As you were. This time she was certain he was being tactful and wanted to skip the inevitable office jokes, and enjoyed avoiding him. At first. The enjoyment soon wore off.

On the sixth she took up her pen, the first time since New Year's Day, when she had written *I hope Ian and I love each other all our lives.* It reads as if she had decided that a pub crawl might help, even if it was with her mother. *Went with Mam to the Shakespeare, Haunch of Venison* [Dale Street] *and the Royal George* [Lever Street]. There, as abruptly as it had started, the diary ended.

No rat-tat, no knight-errant in shining leather. Nothing. That was when she broke down and told Olive everything: "If I don't, I'll go mad." Not quite everything. But enough.

Then, on an evening of defiant despair—not even misery, with this girl it was despair—his rat-tat. Mam had come around after work to bleach her hair for her, they were in the middle and she was then meeting Pat Jepson to go dancing at Belle Vue. Drop everything. Three days later, back in the dumps.

"Olive, we broke it off . . . Last Sunday, a loovly ride over to Glossop, like spring, an' we stopped at a wine place an' he sent me in for a *Flasche* of the German wine—what? . . . Oh ya, I'm allus the one to go in an' pick up the stuff such as drink an' cigs, p'r'aps 'e thinks 'e better stay on the bike in case it's pinched.

"Well, we got to a gorgeous bit o' country, I knew he was in a tricky mood 'cause up comes a hiker in shorts an' settles to eat 'is sandwiches, oh two hundred yards off. But if there's one thing Ian can't stand out in the country, it's seein' even one person, he says it spoils the scenery, p'r'aps it's 'is 'Ighland blood. Well, he says a terrible swearword, and ups an' walks right over. Then the person gets up like 'e's been shot an' races right out o' sight, an' when Ian comes back I says, 'What did you tell 'im?' I says. 'Just that right under 'is bum there's an unexploded mine'—you 'ad to laff.

"Then he give me the bottle. 'Swig it,' he says. 'No thanks very flippin' much,' I says, 'what an idea, like gypsies or summat!' Then he takes three or four tremenjous gulps an' 'ands me back the bottle. 'Go on,' he says 'swig it'—ooh, I was mad. 'You got a nerve,' I says, 'what d'ye think I am, a doormat wi' no mind of its own?' Well, 'e gets up, opens 'is eyes wide an' fixes me with a sort of a stare, then walks off wi' yours truly still talkin'. An' out o' the corner o' me eye I could see 'im astride of the bike an' finishin' the bottle. Then 'e smashes it straight onto the rocks, ye could 'ear the crash for miles, one sarcastic yodel an' roars off. I 'ad to walk to Glossop for the bus an' that was last Sunday. Olive, 'ave you got a Kleenex?"

The next evening. "Olive, I *am* glad I caught you in. Sorry, love, but I can't manage tonight, you see he's waitin' on the bike . . . I *know*, but it was just a lover's tiff, I bought a bottle o' the German wine an' left it in his drawer, ta ra for now!"

Into the night, shave the corners, the feel of the slippery leather. I forgot me gloves, so my wee darrlin' laddie, I'll have to slide my 'ands under your warm slippery leather armpits and me legs around *you*, oh what am I sayin'? Thank God it's only to meself—whoops, nearly ran over both moother an' child, serve 'em right, keep to the pavement.

Double and indivisible, the four-legged juggernaut plunges dangerously into the night. United we stand, together we fall, Ian and Myra, Myra and Ian, Brady and Hindley, Hady and Brindley. Here they come, King Ian and his Consort—scatter, ye pedestrians. Get a move on, ye hoi polloi. Off.

From despair to bliss and back, daren't make plans, will he speak or won't he? Gran, was that a knock? "But Olive, he told me he was stoppin' 'ome last night, are you *sure* it was 'im, who was he with, a *girl?"* To and fro, to and fro.

New Oxford Cinema Jan 27 *Judgment at Nuremberg.* "Olive it was a smashin' fillum, shameless Allied propaganda o' course, ooh my 'ead! . . . Aye, I know I didn't fancy it at first as a wine but it's got such a good bookay . . . I know, I *know,* me dad said the same, that it's not patriotic to drink German wine. I said to 'im, 'Rubbish, just 'cos ye was a flippin' parachutist,' I said, 'if the Germans 'ad won the war we'd *all* be drinkin' it!' Ooh, me dad was mad—well, it's true!"

It's true . . .

A little learning is indeed dangerous: halfway between the educated and the uneducated, there are the talkers, half-baked pickers-up of unconsidered truisms, just sharp enough to acquire surface knowledge and a run-of-the-mill vocabulary. These layers-down of the law are heard in pub and club, in plane and train: Why not utilize the trade unions, I visualize it this way, take the threat of the atom bomb, take sales tax, take the Holy Ghost. Brady the silent onlooker was too astute to go in for all that in company. But in private, with the chosen listener, his line of talk was embellished with the threadbare turns of speech acquired thirdhand from Madison Avenue via films and television: I reckon it's a case of self-survival, it doesn't implement anything for me sexwise.

"Olive, when he's sniffin' the bookay o' the wine, it sort o' loosens his tongue an' he's *terrific,* utterly diff'rent than in the office and he'd make a smashin' after-dinner speaker, not like that ignorant bunch across the corridor, Ian 'as a *turn* o' phrase . . . Oh, words like ideology, sterilization, orgasm an' that. An' with 'is eyes flashin' an' smilin' he's a smasher.

"Oh yes, gets moody but what clever chap doesn't? An' when that scowl comes I think, Ooh, run for shelter, an' then the sun's out again—sterilization? Well, sounds a shock at first but does make sense. Wi' the population explodin', you see, the world'd be better off if some folk was liquidated by coppin' the old needle . . . Well, such as them Jewish profiteers and niggers in South Africa, I mean, there wouldn't be all the racial headaches.

Aye, I know it sounds a bit off, but if you 'eard *him* you'd see it through his brain . . . Sex? Mind your own business, Olive Purlow, an' I'll tell you no lies!"

If she had whispered that the sex part was super, that they both liked it better every time, would she have been telling the truth? Would she have been nearer the facts if she had confessed that after the pain and joy of that first time, she had taken to it more and more, got proper hooked, but that he was finding it more and more humdrum, because it lacked something?

Kings Mar 27 *Curse of the Werewolf*. Apollo Apr 17 *Candidate for Murder*. Bert Mathews retired and Tom promoted Ian into his job, which meant he was now in charge of orders and was expected to exercise his own judgment as to renewal of yearly contracts and replenishment of stocks. Important.

"Olive, you'd *insist* on marriage? Ian says the blessin' o' God on man an' wife an' all that jazz is balls—what? That's not shockin', it's plain speakin', the only religion is 'edonism, enjoy yourself, there's no God. Ooh, reminds me, Ian made such a sick joke about something Christ said to the thieves! . . . Olive, don't ye know what a sick joke is? Well, it's a crack against religion or people wi' diseases an' that, I couldn't latch on at ferrst—what? Why, *do* I say ferrst, I wasn't aware of it . . . No, I'm not tryin' to talk posh, Pat Jepson said the same daft thing, it's just that when ye're with a perrson all the time ye start talkin' like them I suppose."

All the time? No. And the intervals, which would come upon her without warning and last for days with no guarantee of an end, must have been agonizing. It was during these waits that she was unable to keep at bay the one fact, dreaded by the hallucinated lover, which on the first sleepless night rises in shadow at the foot of the lonely bed: the fact that while the loved man was becoming as necessary to her as breathing, he was not only able to live without her, he was a stranger.

Then panic sets in, and on the ceiling's blackness plans of campaign eddy and disappear. "Dear Editress, How can a girl make sure of her man? Should she give 'im the idea there's another chap?" He'd see through it, and even if 'e didn't 'e'd just hunch his shoulders, get that faraway look in his eyes, good luck and he'd be away. They sometimes reply, "Be more demonstrative"—crumbs, aren't I that enough already, might be better if I 'eld back. Show 'im I got a mind o' me own? No thanks, not after that German-wine bit. Suppose I 'eard 'e was sleepin' with—after all, if he did wi' me—no, all *that* with another woman, I'd kill meself, I would I would, I'll emigrate. Oh, if only I could wake up one morning and find I had some spell which meant he could never get away. Oh, I am talkin' daft, Ian Ian Ian . . .

Kings May 14 *The Outsider.* Essoldo Gorton June 19 *Night of the Demon.* Kings Jul 12 *Homicidal.*

Mid-'62, and her twentieth birthday. Fine weather, the last summer of her innocence. Good weekend times, off on the bike into the country. He bought a little box camera.

Snap snap snap. Myra peeping roguishly from behind bushes, in what she called her doodle skirt, a dirndl he had made her buy (Ye look a proper Teuton). Ian squatting on a boulder with the mountains behind him, in his top boots and black shirt and helmet, grinning like a merry troll who owns as far as the camera's eye can reach; another mischievous one of Myra curled up on a rug fast asleep in the sun with her mouth open, perhaps sleeping off the Liebfraumilch or the Amoroso. A couple of high-spirited holiday makers, mad about the open air.

Marriage may have been out, but as the months went by, it would seem that though God had joined them not, they were daring man to put them asunder.

Move One. "Tom, this is Ian, can I come in? Sorry the typin's been lousy, the new gerrl seems bothered by my accent, d'ye mind if I try Myra? Thanks." He tried Myra, she wasn't at all bothered, and they worked side by side for over three years.

Move Two. "Listen, Gran, to this in the *Reporter,* two 'ouses burgled this week, one in Taylor Street on the corner an' wi' the nights drawin' in . . . Aye, makes *me* nervous too, two women alone in a house—I tell you what! If you ask Ian very nicely, he *might* agree to stop with us two or three nights a week, just to ease your mind. Okay?"

Two or three nights a week. Four or five. Six or seven. Seven.

Kings Sep 17 *Walk on the Wild Side*. Oct 8 Return of *Jack the Ripper!!!*

"Oh, Mam, don't ask me about Gran, she's crackin' up. She says that with Ian stayin' with us for protection the cookin's too much for her—well, Ian and I feel we should get somebody to cook for us. Yes, Mam, but you know I've never done it an' never liked cookery at Ryder Brow, I can do the odd egg for Ian but I couldn't for the three of us—what Ian and I agreed was for you to cook meals for us an' bring them over an' I pay you three pounds a week, right? Yes, I know you're workin' but *we*'re workin' as well, three quid is three quid. Well, that's settled . . ."

Through some quirk, the only geographical corner of him into which she was never to venture was 18 Westmoreland Street. He was determined she should not see him in the setting of that house: No, Myra, ye've lived twenty years without clappin' eyes on my lot, ye can bide a wee bit longer, I like to keep my environments separate.

Ian, ple-e-ase . . .

But he was adamant: the faraway look. When she walked him there, he would make her wait for him around the corner in Dallas Street. His mother once said, "Ian, have you got a girl?" He said, "Weel, sort of," and she said, "Oh, I am glad." But she wasn't allowed to meet her.

Essoldo Oct 29 *Deadly Duo*. Nov 5 *Wings of Death*. Nov 14 *Guns in the Afternoon*.

December 31, Happy New 1963, *"Shude* auld acquaintance . . ."
Prosit. Remember?

Ian, I heard a girl say, "Oh, look at Number 7, it's the only house without an aerial!" . . . Yes, love, I know there's a lot o' rubbish on TV but you do get good things . . . Look, there's *All Our Yesterdays* next Friday, documentary, all about Germany an' that.

It was worth it, and on Friday, Myra wore her black turtleneck sweater and new leather jacket and looked real striking. For Ian it was a real gimmicky night; while Hitler postured and screamed in the little front room, Ian was registering postures with camera and screams with tape recorder. And every vulgar gibe from the wartime commentators only served to consolidate the strange affiliation: "This Austrian paperhanger . . . Look at these prisoners of war, hangdog Huns, wait till our Aussies get at them!" He got an excellent close-up of handsome Hess, in uniform, to be duly pasted into the family album. The telly might have been a wartime radio set under the bed.

And until the days got longer the goggle box did pass the time, though there was a lot of crap. *That Was the Week That Was* was worth waiting up for, some fair sick jokes and they send up the government something chronic and that suited the Brady sense of humor. When the news came on, with the stirring music and the picture of the globe revolving to the music, you felt there was action even though all you got was a quick shot of Harold Macmillan. *We bring you the red-hot news—Ian Brady, first man on the moon* . . . Passes the time, does the telly.

There was also the Goons record, which he played to her over and over again, giving his wizard Neddie impersonation ending in the mad cackle; Filthy swine, ha ha HA! She got so gone on it, she started calling him Neddie, and it became her love name for him. His name for her came from a typical sardonic juggle with the names of a great pianist and of the notorious Nazi: Myra Hess. Hess for short, sometimes Hessie. If the pitiful old prisoner of Spandau knew, would he be interested?

"Olive, I'm that vexed with our Maureen, just seventeen an' goin' with a kid o' fifteen, only he looks older—David Smith . . . If I'm wanted, say I'm in the toilet, I'm just poppin' over to Tommy Gibbons to lay a bet for Ian . . . What d'ye mean how it's goin', i' the mornin' he calls for me at me gran's an' we walk to work . . . Oh no, all that's over, what d'ye mean 'secretive'?"

But secretive she was. Something was happening which she did not understand, and yet it had to happen. If she was to keep this thing going, it seemed the kick to be on. Play it cool.

Ooh Ian, you got grease on your book off the fish an' chips, 'ere's me 'anky. What are ye writin', 'omework?

Four neat columns, ruled with one of the two dozen ballpoint pens in the special drawer. Paper werrk. . . .

Neddie, what's P-R-J mean? Payroll job, I'm no wiser an' what's g-n-s? Guns—ooh, sounds like cops an' robbers—

She gets no further. Across the miserable kitchen table he has her arm, his nails dug in viciously, while across the empty bottle the eyes are blazing: None o' yer fuckin' smart-aleck chat, this is ferr reel. A long pause. Over to you, Neddie.

Nivver mind if it *is* the therrd bottle, open it. I'm silent 'cause I'm deliberatin' how to tell ye the truth aboot myself—what? No I'm no' married, d'ye remember askin' if I had a gerrl at Had- field, it was *Hatfield* I'd spoke of—Borstal, two years . . . 'Cause I'm a rebel against society, are ye shocked? . . . No, bank rob- beries. Big stuff, an' if my stooge hadn't squealed I'd be i' the south o' France, too long a story, the trouble wi' this country is the money's in the wrong hands, all these mergers an' monopo- lies, pass the bottle.

New food for sleepless thought. O' course this bank business is a shock, never anything like that in our family but *'e did tell me.* 'E just came to Myra like a naughty little lad, I wanted to take 'im in me arms an' I could feel me heart beatin' in the naughty way, *'e did tell me.* Ooh, if he'd told me he was married, oh God, mind you it needs guts to rob a bank, makes ye feel like a gangster's moll.

"Oh, Mr. Clitheroe . . . It's Myra, you're dictating, I won't keep you a sec. Irene told me ye used to be an international marksman or soomthink—are ye to do wi' the Cheadle Rifle Club? . . . The president, oh my! It sounds a funny thing for a gerrl to want, but I used to love fun fairs an' I'm mad to have a go meself. Next Sunday, super."

Mr. Clitheroe drove her out to the open-air range at Crowden somewhere up on the moors. He arranged for her to buy a .22 rifle from Stensby's, gun merchants in Withy Grove, but why did she want one, she wasn't a good shot and anyway was dead scared of the noise. Before every try she would shut her eyes tight and kept asking, "Will it kick?" Yet behind Mr. Clitheroe's back she bought a .45 pistol from one member, in a handsome holster, and a .30 Smith and Wesson from another, and even asked about German Lugers. Very queer.

In April, Neddie, driving into Belle Vue on the bike with Hess on the pillion, crashed into some railings, injured a woman, had to report at the police station and was off work for a couple of days with a bad ankle. "4/16/63. Well Myra, *Ich habe meinen Fuss verbrochen* . . . However let us capitalize on the situation, I shall grasp the opportunity to view the investment establishment situated on Stockport Road next Friday. I shall contact you before then to go over details . . . Well Myra just wanted to put you in the picture, Ian." Not even "Yours, Ian."

"Myra knew my views at this time, though I gave her no details." But she realized surely that "investment establishment" meant a bank. Did it get her hot and bothered, or did her woman's instinct guess the truth which must not be acknowledged?

Which was that with all his boasting and planning ("I'm only interested in makin' money"), after the miserable pre-Borstal shillings he was never to make a penny out of crime, and no gun would ever be even pointed. No swagman he.

Robbery, on any self-respecting scale, is an immensely professional business, involving as much training and nerve as mountain climbing. And Brady's sinuous nature had a core of Scottish realism which knew something the rest of him would not face: the knowledge that he was neither clever enough, nor courageous enough. So unable was he to face it that in court the only unproved admissions he was to make had to do with "jobs"; the crimes he had had no intention of committing were the ones he claimed.

And inside him the knowledge festered. For he was as ambitious as ever. To make his mark in the world. Determined. And again drifting.

Strolling along Gorton Lane, and stopping at a shabby little paper shop which, three years later, in 1966, will still be there.

Ian, I'll just pop in for the Woman's Mag—ooh *look* what's in the window! Yankee mags, an' in stuffy old Gorton too! . . . What? . . . Oh Neddie, I *couldn't* read it aloud, I'd blush . . . For a dare? . . . Okay . . . "Sexual Misfits—Heritage of Shame—My

Perverted Lover Made Me Pose for Dirty Movies–I Abandoned My Clothes and My Morals." *Now*, Mr. Bighead, are you satisfied? Woman's Mag, please.

April the twenty-first, clocks pushed ahead an hour for summer time. With every evening that grew a few feet longer, the air lost its bite and dawdled warmer and warmer over grass and peat.

And the guns were supplemented with a healthier hobby. Ian, who had been put off the bike by his smash, suggested a car.

On installment. Ooh Ian, what a lovely catalogue, where's the two-seaters? . . . But why not? . . . What d'ye mean, a *Traveller*— but love, where the 'ell are *we* gonna travel to? . . . You mean those two back seats joost fold over flat? . . . Which doors—oh, you mean at the back, but what for? . . . Luggage? But that's what I mean, where are *we* off to? . . . Slide a *mattress* in? Ooh Neddie, you are wild . . .

And she had a couple of driving lessons from Harold Rainger in Preston Street, who found her an excellent pupil. There was never any question of Ian learning, it was as if he felt that riding a motorbike was the man's job and driving a car the woman's.

Ooh Neddie, the forecast said it'll be the 'ottest weekend in May for donkey's years . . . Aye, wouldn' it be looverly but we 'aven't *got* a car, I 'aven't even taken my test! . . . Drive without a license, ooh Neddie, dare we, you mean '*ire* one? . . . A Traveller, oh yes, an' I can try it out for when we get our own. I'll call in at Glazier's, the hire place, on my way to work.

She settles into the driver's seat, he settles beside her: I'll stop ye at a good picnic spot. That's the way it is, and will remain. Turn there, second on right, first left, draw up to the side.

They reach the highest moor point which is next to a main road: in front of the parked car, the breathlessly generous sweep of mountain and sky and valley is shadowed by cloud and crossed with great majestic shafts of sun. Above them, against the sky, a black silhouette of rocks, like bared teeth, which could be the rim of a fortress. The occasional car. But with the glorious sunset the passing hoi polloi packs up. Then the moon rises over the battlements.

Turn the transistor on an' open the bottle. Pom pom *pom,* pom pom *pom,* drums an' percussion, that's great, livens up the countryside no end, feels like scenery on the Cinerama, dramatic like. Mmmmmm . . .

All tidy again, lipstick and comb, while he runs fingers through hair and straightens the tie.

No thanks, Neddie, not another glass for the driver, lemme light your fag 'fore we start for home. Ooh, that was lovely . . . How right you are, I *don't* mean just the wine, cheeky monkey, we're off. I'm gonna ask you a question, 'ere goes. Do you like *it* better up there i' th' back o' the car than home in bed—there, I've said it . . . I *thought* as much—well, I like it too . . . Why? . . . 'Cause we're on our ownsome with our music i' the middle of our lovely moors an' you can't say we didn't keep strict time when the occasion arose—ooh, what am I sayin', it's takin' me mind off of my steerin', wanna land us t' police station—wha' did ye call it Neddie, the cop shop? 'Ere coom the bright lights, ah weel . . .

Down from the great fresh air, the little car picks its careful way down into the stagnant summer city. And on their frowsty pillow they sink into the invisibility of the slums.

Then mechanics-minded Neddie bought a magazine called *Popular Photography* and extravagantly changed the little box camera for a Ross Ensign. And one Saturday he arrived back at Bannock Street with some sort of "electric bulbs and stooff."

You come over after tea, Mo-Bee, Ian's goin' to take some snaps. The camera's got funny little things that click out into three long legs called a tripod. It's got another thing on it that he can set for the timin', then he joomps to the front an' sits between us, then the flash goes pop an' the camera takes the snap all by itself, super! . . . No, *don't* bring that David Smith, Mam's givin' my hair a nice bleach, I want it to look nice for the snaps.

It had been a good idea, to emigrate. An idea she had long ago forgotten.

Bide a wee, Hessie, I thought I herrd the ole gerrl, where's me pants . . . No, nivver mind the match, I have 'em, where's the door . . . Okay, I been right up to her door—sleepin' like a top. Turn the light on, *bitte,* I wanna take me pants off again, that sounds funny, ha ha. Open 'nother bottle an' kindly remove the bra . . . That's better.

Now . . . Just for kicks, baby, a wee experiment, pass me my case . . . There . . . But can't ye see, they're briefs, what the ad said: Black-Lace Tantalizers to Keep Your Man from Strayin' . . . I ken weel there's nothing in the middle, use the ole crranium an *put it on.*

I don't care if we do wake her up, are ye goin' to obey me or d'ye want something whistlin' around your back? . . . Aye, I *thought* ye'd notice it, weel—no, that's no wee serrpent, it's a four-letter werrd, w-h-i-p. An' now stop snivelin' an' stan' up straight! . . . Okay, ye asked for correction an' here it comes.

That's better, now stand wi' feet apart . . . That's the ticket, now the tripod, clickety click, then the flashlight an' we're all squared off . . . Wha'm I gonna do? I'm gonna take a snap of you, baby, to send hame to the auld folks . . . Come on, it's for a giggle . . . *Come on* . . . No, take your hands awa' from the main perrpose o' the exercise, put 'em out over the sofa, *d'ye hear?* . . . Now light a fag an' then a shy look at how excited the Snapshot Man is to be snappin' ye, see? Big smile for the dickeybird, ha ha—click! 'Nother glass o' vino, an' now, ladies an' gents, we stage a li'l number entitled Two's Company.

The camera obtrudes more and more into our lives. One afternoon in a sun-soaked beach hotel—it has happened—a honeymoon couple, asleep after the fun, wake drowsily to more fun. What's my foot on, the Polaroid, *not* the moment for a snap . . . Oh, but it is, sit there, I want this for my wallet. The joke dissolves into laughter and love-making, and the snap, if it has been taken, is torn into pieces and thrown into the wastepaper basket.

Imagine, too—suppose the husband were not just the party standing behind the camera taking the snap, but had a machine which allowed him to be in the picture as well? Suppose he were the libertine who has—as it were—to get his kettle to the boil, leap to his feet, rush naked to the back of the camera, adjust the timing device and hop back to business. Partner, how long—if you'll excuse the expression—how long can one keep this up? Then a collapse into ridicule.

But these two were not like that. He was inventive all right, but it was not for a giggle; there were thirty poses. And not even in extravagant mood in a holiday setting. Photographed in the front room of a slum house long lived in by both, at this moment condemned to be pulled down, and with Gran's parents watching from the faded wallpaper just out of camera.

Copies of the pictures are in the possession (or were, he was thinking of destroying them) of a colorful character with one foot in the Manchester underworld, call him Bill. When he showed them to me, he insisted that he had not acquired them in the pornographic market ("Who'd want to pay for thirty dirty pics of the same couple?") but from an acquaintance of a friend of Ian Brady's.

Thirty. Twelve of female model alone (striking match to light cigarette in mouth, etc.), five of male alone and thirteen of both, mostly navel-to-thigh close-ups of the normal sexual act. Three of the last, full-length studies, are grotesque to the point of comicality, both partners being naked except for—over the head—a kind of homemade white cloth bag, with slits for eyes and mouth, which gives them the appearance of a couple of absent-minded Ku Klux Klansmen off to a rally who have forgotten to finish dressing up. In the pornography market, photographs are common in which the models disguise their identity in this way, but copies of these particular ones have not materialized. Even in this field Ian Brady, photophiliac, was to make not a single dishonest penny.

In quality the pictures are no better but no worse than most obscene photographs, surprising when one thinks that the lighting facilities in the little condemned house fell far short of requirements which the Victorian builders had not envisaged. How to distinguish the pictures from "professional" pornography? Not by the physique of either partner, both being adequate to the demands of the operation; and the girl's figure, without the ludicrous black-lace knickers and away from the situation, could be attractive. It is the poses in which the features are seen that give away the amateur status: while moneymaking models tend to an air of sullen resignation, these two are keen on their work. The pleasure written across their faces is as willfully immature as the hilarity of spoiled brats sitting among valuable china which they have broken piece by piece.

In two of the single-female poses, the model is completely nude. In the one she lies on the floor, face down and head away from camera, feet together in foreground; in the other the same position except that she is kneeling. On the buttocks, in both poses, several very faint horizontal lines. In the corner, the dangling end of a knotted whip. In another corner, on the floor, a page that has drifted from a daily picture paper; with the help of a magnifying glass obligingly furnished by "Bill," I was able to make out the pictures on the page clearly enough for me later to look up the date of the paper and then roughly place the date of the thirty photographs, mid-May 1963. The soles of the feet—when it is remembered what a barefoot walk across the average floor will do—unusually clean.

The single-male poses are markedly narcissistic. One shows the model standing full length with back to camera, strong legs apart, arms flexed: give him jockey shorts and he is out of *Health and Strength*. In another he is lying on his stomach, body facing away from camera, vest tucked up under his armpits, bottom in foreground, urchin face grinning over shoulder into camera; while a third shows him half lying, facing camera, same impudent snicker in the middle background, while in the immediate foreground he is gleefully grasping himself. "In that 'un 'e looks to me," said Bill thoughtfully, "like a kid that's got 'old of 'is first lollipop."

And Gran slept through it all.

CHAPTER 15

FOR KING IAN AND COUNTRY

> "People who feel themselves to be exiles in
> this world are mightily inclined to believe
> themselves citizens of another."
>
> *Santayana*

DEAR SIRS, In reference to yours of the fifth inst., oh crumbs . . .
Every time Tom Craig looks at me I see them panties, it was the
wine, I don't recall the half of it. Ooh, he is naughty, you'd never
think to 'ear his voice to me now, Dear-Sirs-we-suggest-that-a-
consignment-of-shaving-cream . . .

He'll ha' developed 'em by Wednesday, fancy fixin' up the
scullery as a darkroom—oh, 'e is sly. But you can't deny it's
clever. He wants a good smack-bottom Dear Sirs I've a good mind
to turn to 'im an' say, "You will destroy the negatives *tonight,*
what d'you think I am, a tart?" Ooh, but I dread that stare that
says watch-out-you're-tempting-your-luck, though it's better than
the faraway look 'cause when he's mad at me I go all goosey . . .
Ooh, if one o' them pictures was thrown on a screen 'ere now, the
faces! But anything's better'n vegetatin' like all o' them are, Dear
Sirs.

. . .

Olive, what d'you think? David Smith, the one Maureen goes with, was up before the juvenile court for larceny, if you please. I said to Maureen she'll get the Hindleys a bad name she will an' all.

Weel, ma wee Hessie-get-your-gun, how's lessons? . . . Gude, we'll be needin' ye. Noo, let's stroll up this side street, this is a recky. *Reconnaissance*, stoopid. That's the back door o' the Midland Bank; now of a Saturday forenune when the staff's comin' out, I'm tying a shoelace while you ask 'em the way to the Catholic church and I nip inside. I got it all figured, should be good for a coupla hundred quid, so keep them lessons up.

In the small hours of August 8, 1963, the Royal Mail train from Glasgow to London was stopped, in the heart of the English countryside, by armed robbers who successfully stole over two and a quarter million pounds. Later that day, over the startling front page of the Manchester *Evening News,* the mastermind is on the silent side.

And remains so. September, October. The faraway look is back. Nobody notices but her, and even she does not see how much farther away it is getting. From day to day, the glass wall between him and the world is closing in, until it forms a sealed bowl in which he can turn slowly and look around him. And while the glass daily thickens, every day his vision through it grows clearer. In the city murk, he picks out the rough grain of his desk, the ladder in a woman's stocking across Hyde Road, the hairs Lassie left on the brown cushion. And if you stare through glass long enough at folk looking kinda worried and jabbering stuff you can't hear, like watching a film with the sound off, in the end they turn into a bunch of dolls pulling faces for your benefit. It's a show.

Get this straight, it's not that ye *can't* hear, it's that ye're too strong-willed to listen. Ye switch off. If anybody asks ye something, ye automatically switch on, click, and understand the question better than they do. *And* answer it, clear, to the point. And by eleven o'clock, when the wee wine hangover's oot o' the way, the work's better than ever it was, not one boob this week, one hundred percent. Top o' the form.

A feeling of waiting. The camera? Put away for the present. The titillation of the thirty poses has worn off. Dirty pictures is for the birds. September.

Rainy Saturday morning, a squelch down into town to the bookshop. The fourth along the top shelf, *Erotica Erotica*. Thanks, would ye wrap it up—what? This one? I dinna fancy paperbacks, d'ye recommend it? . . . A translation—well, I'd sooner ha' had it i' the original but nivver mind, wrap it up wit' the other.

Sunday, still raining, *Erotica Erotica*. Same old corn, thirty bob—Christ! He'd have done better with a lady novelist from Longsight Public Library, with her panting breaths, aching groins, taut nipples and all for free.

Monday morning, still raining. A paperback slips easily into the pocket. After the big orders have been dealt with, Allen an' Hanbury's and Boots an' all that—it'll be a slack afternoon. An' we'll improve the shinin' what-not with a gude buke, though the title doesn't do much for me.

Justine, or *The Misfortunes of Virtue,* by the Marquis de Sade.

The events which threw their shadows before are not far off. The Lancashire landscape is to darken.

A seafarer who knows he is leaving for a hideous ocean, waves a fond goodbye to his shore. We are soon to cross the frontier into a fearful country, and it would be well to reassure ourselves with a last look at what we leave behind. The territory of human kindness.

Even in our age of fear and frustration, there live—in village, town, garden city, suburb, in health and sickness, in prosperity and adversity—ordinary men and women who love each other in a union simple, ardent and fruitful. Their children grow up just as unremarkable, and in their turn fall in love and go through the civilized motions. In all that, there are dull patches, sometimes very dull, but as we advance into our deep waters we shall be glad now and again to remind ourselves of the mainland.

Of the Galways, for instance. Two years married, with a baby, he is a cheery young man working in the Foundry and taking an engineering course, she has a singing voice and plays soubrettes in the Openshaw Opera Society; you can sometimes hear her from next-door's backyard singing snatches of Puccini as she does her washing. Next door being 7 Bannock Street. We shall not meet the Galways, but it is good to remember that the three of them are the other side of the wall, you can even hear them poke the fire. Look well upon that picture. Now on this.

Impossible though it is to fathom the spring that feeds the normal nature, never mind Ian Brady's, we can at least scan the dark waters swirling nearer the surface. We have to identify with him. If we do not, at one move he will turn into a body as foreign as a tiger waving a slow tail and baring hungry teeth at the headlights of a car in Gorton Lane. An unforgettable moment, but if the moment became an hour, one blood-freezing snarl would be very like another. The tiger is a young stock clerk employed at Millwards Ltd. *We have to identify with him.*

By first taking a look at the subject of the secret agent.

In fact and in fiction, the spy story has always been irresistible, from Spy Number One—the serpent in Eden—and the Trojan Horse through to *The Moonstone,* Dreyfus, *The Scarlet Pimpernel,* Roger Casement, Mata Hari, *Ashenden, The Riddle of the Sands* and finally to the phenomenon of the mid-twentieth century, as it succumbed to a cult mounting, in the sixties, to a rash of spies, or perhaps a hush. A noun which was once as malodorous as "conchie" (deplorable slang for "conscientious objector") has been dry-cleaned, "espionage" conveys glamour and the secret agent is a sexy adventurer, with nerves of steel and a cruel mouth, more devastating than the sheik or the Legionnaire ever was.

Any frustrated young man of the sixties, normal and good-hearted but looking for daydreams, turns to the spy. Next war, parachuted into enemy territory. The constant challenge—often in crucial peril—of passing unnoticed in an everyday world in the presence not only of strangers, but of near acquaintances. Tough, but if you last—lives saved, weeks lopped off the war . . . a decoration?

A good dream. But pin it down.

The grim demands. In the enemy darkness, under the bridge, you hear the sentry's step die away, you light the fuse, and by the time he turns to come back, you are fifty yards off in the bushes, the timing perfect. The doomed bridge stands against the moon, and the feeling of power rises in you like a forbidden drug. Except it's *not* forbidden, you're doing a great job . . .

Then onto the bridge steps a civilian holding by the hand— God, no—a child of ten, you hear the piping voice. Run for it, you fools! *Wallop.* The bridge spews roaring pieces of itself all over the sky, and Operation Ironside is ticked off. An hour later, in the house where you live disguised as a government agent, alone and toasting your success in an enemy liqueur, the vision rises before you. Father and child. Poor devils. But *they are not on your conscience.* Here's to 'em both, *c'est la guerre.*

The spy cult has worked on Ian Brady too. The difference is that he does not need a world emergency to fulfill *his* dream. Inside that glass bowl, the swirl is acquiring a shape; after years of battening on a feed of resentments, with every day that floats past he is slowly swelling a fad into a fantasy all his own. And that fantasy is now turning into the real thing. The shape is growing steadier, steadier. The shape of war.

Not even a war that has just been declared. There has never been any peacetime. And the enemy is the world in which he circulates. He is in their midst. Greater Manchester.

Knowing that his history has so far provided him with no motive, we cannot understand why he feels as he does. We can only attempt to imagine *how* he feels, by placing ourselves in his situation, armed with our own rational motive for revenge. Suppose . . .

Suppose yourself in a world ravaged by a war grimmer than any yet known. From the age of sixteen, you have been exiled in the enemy territory. Alone. To the populace around you, you are

an indistinguishable fellow citizen, speaking their language better than they do. And that becomes invaluable as you grow more
and more dedicated to your gospel of hate. *Why* the hate? Because every time you walk down a main street—let us call it
Marketstrasse, in the city of München in the province of Langkasche—you can never look at any of the strange faces in the
crowd without thinking of what they have done to you.

For when you were five—and this is where we have to create
motive—your mother, father and every living relative were de-
ported with thousands of others, brought to München, housed
in a gigantic camp outside the city, herded into slaughter houses
and exterminated. And you have secret information that every
adult person you pass in Marketstrasse has at some time or other
worked in that camp, voluntarily.

The taxi driver whistling at the curb was in the Electrocution
Wing, the beaming mother holding a little girl was a guard in
the cellars where your mother died in agony. And the wee child,
if she lives, will grow up like her mother—would it not have
been better if she had never been born? . . . And that clergyman
—no, the more they look too good to be true, the worse their
record—the young, the healthy, the do-gooders, all guilty. Each a
reminder, every waking minute, of your destiny.

From week to week the war is moving toward an impasse so
bitter that something has to happen. You don't know what.
Headquarters are aware that you're here and rarin' to do your
bit, it's up to them to get instructions to you. Patience. The
patience of the spy.

Mind you, ready for when the showdown does come, you have
another attribute. Some very brave soldiers are useless because
they are squeamish. You're not.

All right, callous. One dark evening you are sauntering down
Marketstrasse, a secret agent off duty, when you come face to face
with a man stepping out of a car—the human being you hate
most, the ex-Commandant who sentenced your family to death.
It's a posh car. As he strolls down a dark alley to a night spot,
three men leap out, overpower him and make for his wallet; he
struggles, thud of a blackjack, he falls, they run. As you approach, his head teeters up and just as he focuses on you, you too

focus, on the picture of your family queuing up for death as if for bread. And you raise one foot.

He slumps forward, you walk on. Is he dead? The papers will tell you tomorrow. What matters is that you have done your war work for the night. And you feel stimulated. *Sexually* stimulated? God no, not by that ugly mug—but now you come to think, you wouldn't say no to a woman, this minute, right here, standing up. Headquarters will be gratified.

Yes, possible. Because the "you" in the case is an average hater with a low percentage of abnormality.

We have to go further. Much further. Multiply that believable instinct for revenge a thousand times, and watch it hardening daily into a permanent state of mind. Granite.

Justine, or *The Misfortunes of Virtue.*

CHAPTER 16

UNHOLY WRIT

"This books can do. . . . They give
New views to life, and teach us how to live."
Crabbe

THE FRENCH ARISTOCRAT whose adherents, decade after decade, could never dare to speak his name, has in this century—in particular after World War II—undergone a unique promotion. His name has acquired a freakish celebrity by discarding its capital S, acquiring an -ism, and filtrating not only into literature but into daily chatter. But most people's picture of him is vague, and even those who know the violent facts tend to fall into one of two prejudiced categories: the defenders, insisting that he is a great writer, and the detractors, dismissing him as a mad bore too grotesque to corrupt a fly. He was neither.

Donatien-Alphonse-François de Sade (1740–1814) was born in Paris, in the Hôtel de Condé, where his mother was *dame d'honneur*. His father was *grand seigneur* and diplomat, his uncle an abbé. All very lofty, but this was France under Louis the Fifteenth; the escutcheon, for example, lost a little of its luster when the abbé's cloth was unable to save him from prison for taking part, with a number of prostitutes, in a *"partie de débauche."*

An only child, the Marquis seems to have been cold-shouldered by his mother, and biographers suggest that this might be the Freudian origin of his implacable contempt for women. He was, moreover, spoiled to death by his grandmother, who inculcated in him a pride which was to sprout into violent arrogance and life-long atheism. Matters cannot have been helped, either, by the fact that between the ages of six and ten he was entrusted to his uncle the abbé.

Sade was educated at the (Jesuit) Collège Louis-le-Grand; then from fifteen, starting as a *sous-lieutenant,* he served through the Seven Years' War, ending up as captain of a cavalry regiment, a young man of strong character and vivid intellect, and, in spite of his birth, a fierce libertarian. At twenty-three he married a gentlewoman who bore him three children. This again sounds an irreproachable dossier.

During the first year of his marriage, however, his zest for liberty rapidly overreached itself. He was imprisoned for indulging in "extreme debauchery" with young girls in the *petites maisons* which he maintained in Paris and Versailles.

The idea that sex can be tinged with cruelty has never been new—the permanence of many a marriage is based on love play in which one partner consciously simulates brutality while the other simulates the fear of it—but the Marquis overstepped the mark by kilometers. Two typical incidents, early on. First, the sealing-wax affair. One day in the street he picked up Rose Keller, personable and penurious, and she arrived gratefully at one of the *petites maisons.* He locked the door, ordered her to strip, flogged her with a knotted whip, carefully flayed off pieces of her skin and poured heated wax into the open wounds. Sentence, six months.

Next, the Marseilles scandal: a sexual merry-go-round involving three adolescent girls, a strapping broad-minded valet, a whip weighted with nails, and—for good measure—a box of poisoned lozenges. Even that complaisant century found it all a little fierce for its taste. Sade was sentenced to death, fled abroad, stayed away for a tactful interval, and returned.

It seems unfair that sexual indulgence, bought at such a price, should give so little pleasure to any of the parties. The terrified victims can be excused for not joining in the fun; never can there have been *filles de joie* less deserving of the name. But even the Marquis and his fellow revelers seem to have entered into any free-for-all in a glowering rage which precluded any sort of orchestral climax. *Faute de mieux,* the last resort was masturbation. A good time was had by none.

In between his adventures, the Marquis found time to cause a society scandal by seducing his wife's young sister, a nun. From then on, prison alternated with lunatic asylum, with deplorable regularity, for the rest of his life, the sentences growing heavier: five years in Vincennes, five in the Bastille. In one of the madhouses, Charenton, one doctor stated, "This man's affliction is not that he is insane, he is not; it is that he is intoxicated with Vice." And Sade's letters display an indignant self-justification which he was never to lose. "I have all my life had leanings towards Vice; and any fellow-creature who gives proof of a gift for Vice, I look upon as a Great Man."

As month followed month, he applied himself to feeding the taste of his age for pornography. He wrote. *Justine,* and the lesser-known *The 120 Days of Sodom,* set in (of all places) Switzerland. In a castle, each day there is staged a new and detailed variation in mass debauchery, "resulting in the deaths of thirty-odd persons." Odd's the word.

The 120 Days remained unfinished; after thirty orgies our author gave up. It is not surprising that even such a dedicated organizer as this one ran out of sodomitic inspiration: Nature, niggardly for once, has endowed the human body, the male one especially, with orifices which can be comfortably counted on the fingers of one hand. The project seems oversanguine from the acrobatic point of view alone; faced with a challenge of this order, the most ingenious of porno-choreographers must find his invention first flagging, and very soon expiring.

But as Ian Brady, one murky afternoon in the autumn of 1963, prepares to steal an hour of office time for a quiet bit of a read, it is with the other Sade product that we are concerned, held behind Spicer and Pegler's *Book-keeping.* In paperback, five shillings, stocked by reputable booksellers everywhere.

It is best to look at the book first through the eyes of the normal intelligent reader. To begin with, *Justine,* like most of the Sade canon, is a dirty book without dirty words. If anything, the language is pretty lofty, one of the reasons why the work is defended as literature. The flights are as high in translation as in the original, often sounding like bad Walter Scott: "She sought a place where she could be alone with her thoughts, and free the clogging feeling in her breast" . . . "She procured some writing materials and wrote a short note cloaked in an air of mystery."

But the grandiloquence cannot keep up for long; you never know the minute when the high-flown will take a sickening swoop. The bathos is recurrent. Justine, leafing through a newssheet, "is surprised to learn that a gentleman who once tried to murder his own daughter, has just been appointed Head Surgeon to the Empress of Russia at an enormous salary" . . . "The colour in Justine's face turned blue and her senses slowly slipped from under her . . ."

The effect is often enhanced by the constant bumpiness of the translation. " 'Have pity,' she aspirated, 'have pity' " . . . " 'He is in love with you,' Madame Dubois said, 'he thinks you're awfully nice . . .' " A girl friend of Justine's has displeased the wicked hermits: " 'Omphale, the society is fed up on you' " . . . " 'I will die a thousand times rather than submit to such tripe' " . . . " 'That coffin was just made for you,' he snarled, 'you look swell in there!' "

And if any schoolboy, in search of four-letter words, locks himself in the lav with *Justine,* he will only find a couple he hadn't bargained for. " 'The justice of God?' countered Madame Dubois, *'bosh!'* " " 'Paradise, sweet lady, may console some, but it's the bunk!' "

Sade makes continuous savage digs at Justine's virtue, but they are not funny and not meant to be; no author has ever sat down, in prison or out of it, with less of a gleam in the eye, and the horrors become more and more wearisome. Never can a girl have been so put upon. The hair-raising adventures of Pearl White, the silent-serial heroine, were nothing to the Perils of Justine.

Between the covers of one short book she is bled, branded, bitten, scourged, flogged, lacerated, pinched, opened vein by vein, dashed savagely against a wall by the head, dragged by the hair four times around a prison, flung bodily into dungeons, coffins and even horse carriages, struck violently "by the battering-ram of an open hand till she is black and blue," and (the last straw) "saluted" with twenty stripes from a bull's pizzle, whatever that may be. Twenty-four hours a day are spent between pillar and post; in this odyssey of insult, you would think that by Chapter Four not a square centimeter of unmarked flesh would be left on her. But no. Her tormentor suddenly compliments her on her appearance, clearly one of his off-days. " 'That lovely skin is far from being as callous as Suzanne's, one could set fire to that girl's rumps and she would not feel it!' "

When she reaches wooded hills and espies a belfry, " 'It must be,' hummed Justine, 'the retreat of some holy hermits.' " No such luck. The "church" is bedizened with every appurtenance of Gothic shockery: black hangings, skeletons, switches, daggers, pistols. " 'Religion? You will find here only cruelty and debauchery, *submit!*' " As is her wont, submit she does, and at the supper table her place is under it, "like a dog." On top of it all, not one of her utterances is anything but forgettable. " 'He is a ferocious beast!' retorted Justine" . . . " 'Oh good heavens!' cried Justine, 'you make me shudder!' "

She is also given to addressing the Deity, undeterred by His consistently deaf ear. " 'Almighty God, is it thy decree that the shivering innocent shall become the prey of the guilty?' " No, whether *Justine* is turned, in the unpredictable future, into a spectacular film or into a musical (*The Quaking Girl?*) it will never be a rewarding role.

"But surely," you may say, "it sounds more a silly book than a sinister one?" Silly only in spots. It's a long haul with very monotonous scenery. "But scenery is at least harmless?"

To most people, yes. But along this road, for him who stops to pick, there are clumps of deadly nightshade.

The discarded cigarette bounces across parched grass and starts the chance spark which starts the smolder which starts the forest fire. The same with the opening of a stray book: it seemed preordained that the adolescent Keats, after reading Chapman's *Homer,* should feel "like some watcher of the skies, When a new

planet swims into his ken." And now another young man hears
an author "speak out loud and bold." Across two centuries the
elegant monster, on horseback between the sunlit colonnades of
Versailles, waves recognition to the sullen stock clerk playing
truant on a gloomy afternoon, in a Manchester which mostly
wouldn't know the Marquee de Sade from the marquee of the
Belle Vue circus.

The idiocies in the text will pass right over the head of this
particular reader, because he and his author have in common
two negative traits: a want of literary taste, and a lack of humor.
More important, they share a propensity. A very positive one.
The reader settles down.

He looks first at the cover: a drawing of an indeterminate
woman with purple hair and a terrified bright-green face. Unim-
pressed, he opens at the Dedication, which doesn't make him sit
up either: "To my Lady Friend . . . who will value the sweetness
of Virtue's tears." He cannot know yet that the Marquis never
writes of goodness except with his tongue—and for once it is a
simple matter to specify its whereabouts—in his cheek.

The very first sentence of the (paperback) Foreword is an example of the indoctrination of an immature mind: "This is one
of the great forbidden books of all time." Then: "Its underground popularity . . . Stimulating, mind-prodding . . . A curious
and powerful book . . . Its publication at this time is an important cultural event . . ."

The Marquis is then given a personal build-up of exactly the
kind to seize this imagination. "Even in boyhood, evil seemed to
surround him . . . Of startling beauty . . . Acquired a flamboyant
reputation as a beater of women . . ."

Once the absurdities pass by, whole sentences leap up with the
impassioned conviction of the printed page ("O' courrse it's true,
it's oot of a book, this mon is *somebody!*") A look at two sentences from *Justine* and two from Holy Writ will help us hear
what Ian Brady heard: the ringing voice of authority. "God is
love"—"All virtue is born from a false principle" . . . "The
Kingdom of God is within you"—"Scorn the laws—scorn God!"

Then the note of sacrilegious antihumanity grows more insist-
ent. "Nature is sufficient in itself, and needs no creator. *There is*

no God!" . . . "For outcasts like ourselves, there are only two
courses, crime or death" . . . "If you have remorse for anything
you do, do it again and again and you will see how easily you
forget about your conscience . . ." Then the voice sounds lower,
insidious: "If crime is seasoned by enjoyment, crime can become
a pleasure."

Pleasure. The chord is struck; he hears it reverberate softly
through the office, and almost lifts his head to hear it die away.
Glasgow, the cat in the cemetery. "The consciousness of doing
wrong is what excites us. The greater the atrocity, the greater
the passion." His heart misses a beat, the color mounts to his
cheeks. "In sensual pleasure, the most intense sensation is produced by pain." He passes the tray of letters to Tony Prendergast
without looking up.

And at last, the voice at its most personal, whispering by now,
close to his ear. Irene Eccles is humming again and Mary Web-
ster is cracking her finger joints, but to all that, more than ever,
he is blind and deaf, hypnotized by the one quiet voice. And
turning a page, he reaches one sustained passage which hits him
like the tolling of a bell, every sentence a resonant stroke.

"The crime of destroying one's fellow-man is non-existent."
The heart of the matter. At last. "Do we not see how Nature
herself destroys, in the most wanton way by earthquakes, vol-
canoes, gigantic accidents—all to redress the balance between
creation and destruction? In the eyes of Nature, all living matter
is equal—all fashioned out of her immense crucible, and then
maybe destroyed, only to be re-created in a different shape . . . *So
when a human being destroys another human being, it is impossible for him to offend Nature."* How do, Constable; nice day,
Inspector . . .

"Indeed, such destruction does good, what does it matter to
Nature whether a certain mass of flesh which is today a living
two-legged animal should, by the action of another two-legged
animal, be destroyed? She knows well that in time to come, she
will reproduce it as—say—a thousand insects. Why should Nature find the life of the two-legged animal more valuable than
the earth-worm?"

The point is rammed home, over and over again. "It is man's

vanity that says murder is a crime—since such ideas come to us from Nature itself, how can they be unnatural?" ... "If all the decomposed parts of any one body only await their rotting away in order to reappear under fresh forms, how can men have the impudence to find any harm in murder?" Hear that, Judge? *"The crime of destroying one's fellow-man is non-existent."*

Particularly striking is the repeated suggestion that children should be done away with, at will. "A country which, for its own whim, can in one day sacrifice twenty or thirty thousand subjects —and to think that a father cannot be master of the life of his own children—what an absurdity! ... There are more people than are wanted anyway—what difference does it make if there are fewer? Did not Romulus permit infanticide? The Persians? The Greeks? Among the Chinese, weak children are constantly put to death. Why let such creatures live?"

His pale cheeks have reddened, his eyes are bright, he crosses his legs the other way in telltale fashion; from now on, the master is preaching to the converted. Passages which a skeptical reader would skip with impatience are, for him, charged with the erotic: " 'Now take your things off!' She threw herself at his knees. 'Have pity! Do not force me—please, *please*—when you have finished your crime, will you find happiness in my tears and my disgust?' "

Even the bathos exerts the baleful effect. "They were almost through with their dinner. Justine saw by their manner, and the delirium into which they were working themselves, that Rosalie was to be sacrificed that evening ... They stretched her flat upon a table, lit wax candles and desecrated upon her the most solemn of mysteries ... He tied her arms, and with quick birdlike movements started pricking them. Never for a moment did he take his burning eyes from the blood that dripped from her."

And as a shadow crossed between him and the grimy window —his typist taking the day's work over to Tom Craig—can his eyes have been racing along the words "Notwithstanding her knowledge of the Count's cruelty, she could not resist her passion for him ... He outlined to her his horrible scheme, she begged him to wait. 'Wait?' he replied, 'you forget I am already growing old—I am twenty-nine!' "

Or this: "At last she completely fell in with his ideas . . . 'It is a complicated network,' he explained to her, 'but with help, the machine works perfectly. I want an intelligent, spruce female who has herself passed through the path of pain . . . in short, an efficient young woman without pity, who'd know her job.'"

Myra Hindley, do now what you nearly did.

Emigrate.

CHAPTER 17

DESIRES AND DREAMS AND POWERS

"Come live with me and be my love
And we will some new pleasures prove . . ."
Donne

"Wherever he has gone, I have gone."
Myra Hindley

THE FIRST AUTUMN DAYLIGHT, creeping through paper-thin Gorton curtains. She has brewed up his cup o' tea, and brings it to the bed. He is still asleep.

Schlafen Sie wohl, mein Liebling, never seen him proper asleep. Or anybody bar Maureen. An' Mo sleeping wasn't the same lass as had been jumping and giggling, but looked all posh and inside herself. But Neddie looks the same as when he's awake —miles away—I wish I could follow him, I think sometimes if he saw me in a crowd he wouldn't remember me. Anyway, I do know he'd never look at another girl. Open your peepers, love— tea.

Taking the cup, still half in dreams he hears, faint and far away, the drums. Harry Lime's, the Devil's, King Ian's as his army approaches—take your choice. Getting nearer. And nothing can silence them.

It's a long wait for the word of command, from HQ to him who waits at the heart of the enemy capital disguised as a stock clerk. Messages, of course, constant and urgent: HATE HATE HATE. And any minute now, the signal. After the hanging about, what a relief. What will the contact be? How will the signal come?

Through the sewers, of course, that flow deep under Market-strasse. Carried perhaps between the teeth of a rat swimming against time. And what will the order be? Weel, call it a Payroll Job, "investment establishment," though mind ye, in a war you gotta be ready for anything.

A step in the street, a worker off to the foundry. Then a whistle, the paperboy. Cheeky little boogar, 'ell grow up as dead rotten as the rest of 'em. A scratch at the door and a whine. Come in Lassie, ye're okay, ye're no' one o' the voters in this borough. Hessie makes up her mouth. Neddie sips his tea. Miles away. Yet the two are indivisible.

They wake side by side, side by side they walk to the office, side by side they work. He the Dictator, of letters to purveyors of soaps and acids and oils, she the bowed First Lieutenant writing the orders. At midday they sit side by side over fish and chips, home by five-thirty to high tea brought over by her mam, then side by side in pictures or in the red-letter hired car up to the secret place. They take their annual holiday, of two separate weeks, together.

Every hour of every day seven days a week, and the weeks are passing. No married couple of their age, in the history of the world, have spent so much time together for so long. If they were handcuffed to each other, they could not be more inseparable. Gran thinks it's nice to see a lovin' pair but Myra's mam thinks it's funny: Don't know why, 'ave you noticed he never kisses her? Why don't they get 'itched up?

Indivisible. Yet he, every day, is more on his own.

And every day more of a tormentor.

No ta, Mr. Bighead, not another drop. I do 'appen to be your shawffer, 'as *that* slipped the royal memory, *and* in traffic . . .

What's up wi' me? I'm 'oppin' mad, that's what I am, *I* saw you
when we was waitin' for the green light, lookin' at that tart's legs,
an' I saw you wink back at her, yes you *did*, you'd be photographing her in bluddy black knickers before you could say
Kodak, an' you in the buff behind the camera. I know *you* . . .

I don't care if I did jump the light—what d'ye mean stop the
car, take that cigarette off of my arm, you fuckin' sadist. Well,
now we *'ave* stopped, what d'ye wanna tell me? . . . Don't say
shut up to me an' never you mind my language, who the hell
learned me the words anyway—what d'ye wanna tell me? . . .

What? Ye *would* like to do your nut with her, I *knew* it, I'm
gonna chuck meself under that bus. Leggo—you've broke my
heart an' turn that bluddy sexy music *off* . . . 'Ow'd I like to see
you *what?* Watch *you* with *'er?* I'm gettin' out, never been so
insulted in all me—what d'ye mean it's one or the other? You
mean, if I said I wouldn't watch for all the tea in China, you'd
walk into that pub *now* an' pick 'er up and go back with 'er? Ian,
I'd kill you both, don' touch me mmmmmm . . . You shouldn't
ha' kissed me like that, you know what it does to me . . .

Neddie, ye mean you couldn' do it to 'er *unless* I was watching? Well, Massa Brady, 'ow kinky can ye get? Ooh, they're playin'
In the Mood an' you've lit a cigar, you devil, you know what
that does to me. Stop actin' about now, back into traffic before I
lose me 'ead. Is it to the left? 'Ere put your 'and out, love . . .
Page thirteen o' what? The Woman's Mag, it's at 'ome—oh no,
it's there in the glove part, show me . . . What do I see? Well, an
ad, that's all, a knittin' ad . . . I don't get you—ooh, 'ark at that
music . . . What? Well, like I said, an ad for a sweater . . . The
photo? Why, it's of a schoolboy an' 'e's wearin' the sweater—ooh,
I do fancy you with a cigar, an' lookin' out o' the window, like
you owned the town . . . What? Well, 'e's smilin' at the camera,
like he's sayin' "Won't you buy my nice sweater, mm?"

Neddie, what *is* this? . . . Yes, he *is* a nice lad, but we don't
want marriage or kids, you know that, an' stop blowin' smoke in
me face . . . *What?* Ian Brady, you are the limit—why o' *course*
I'd turn me face away, what a thing to say in a traffic block. If
that couple i' the next car 'ad 'eard they'd ha' froze right up,

fancy gettin' an idea like that out o' the Woman's Mag. 'Ave the lights changed? . . . 'Ome, James, an' don't spare the blushes, you are the giddy limit.

October 6, Summer Time Ends and fab programs coming up on TV. *'Itchcock Hour* and *Espionage* and *The Avengers,* which is gettin' real kinky: Cathy Gale in that leather an' high boots lukin' as if she'd like to give ye twenty strokes o' the best.

And as the heather thins out, so do the hikers. November Saturday, nobody, only the stray car traveling to or from Langkasche or Yorkasche. With the clouds tumid with rain and the wind like the crack of whips, the sun sets early, by five it is dark on the moors. By six the blustering blackness is impenetrable, except when the clouds tear savagely apart and our winter moon, on its way to full, sheds enough light for us to pick our way from the parked car, to the edge of an immense wilderness. There we gaze our fill at our private lake, which by day the enemy has the impertinence to call a public reservoir, and where our moon is reflected. And the moors as deserted and mysterious as the moon.

The whole lot is private property: the moors, the moon, and the cold, *alles ist wunderbar.* And at the center of the cold, warm and protective as a womb, the dark little car throbs with music and smells of leather and spilt wine and sex. Aye, it's a good healthy face in the sweater ad—that's right, laddie, give Harry Lime's dickeybird a nice big schoolboy smile *click.*

The brain is ticking, steady as a bomb. Ticking to the tempo of the distant drumbeats. Drum, drum, drum-drum. Nearer. Waiting for the signal. No' tae worry.

Ooh, Olive I'm *ashamed,* I knew it was a mistake gettin' our Maureen a job 'ere. She's no' been bad makin' tea ecksettra, but *who* d'ye think just forced his way in bold as brass? That David Smith, still only fifteen an' burstin' out of 'is jeans. "I want Maureen," he says, and Tom Craig says as cool as a cucumber, "You can 'ave 'er at five," an' Smith says, "Where's that Fred Huddam that's been tryin' to date 'er, 'cause I'm goin' to beat 'im up!" . . . No, thank God Ian didn't 'ear of it . . . Oh no, me mam's no good with er—ooh, I was so embarrassed I could **blush** all over.

Achtung. There are indications that the signal is within sight. Messenger Rat, little eyes glittering like gimlets in the sewer dark, little feet splashing and teeth firm into the magic message —Messenger Rat approaches the enemy capital. *The crime of destroying one's fellow-man is non-existent.* Paddle paddle. On November 7, Myra passed her driving test.

Studio One Oxford Rd Nov 18 James Bond!!! *From Russia with Love!!!* HE DEVELOPED THE TECHNIQUE OF LOVE TO AN ART AND THE ART OF MURDER TO A SCIENCE!!! Also showing: *So Evil So Young!!!*

Ooh Neddie, *next* Saturday? Loovly, I'll pop into Glazier's, and order one for the full twenty-four hours . . . Yes, I *will* make sure there's a heater, cheeky, *an'* the same stretchin' room for when we get cramp—a couple o' bottles o' vino an' we'll be in business.

Just another outing it'll be. Yet somehow not. Something's trying to come through. Sure of it.

Friday afternoon. 'Bye Tony, 'bye Irene, 'bye Olive, have a loovly weekend. Ta ra, see you Monday, be gude.

Ooh Ian, I hope it's fine tomorrow, I'm pickin' it up at ten, he let me try the gears, what's the time? . . . Gran, stop fussin', we'll leave the washin' up till after *Bonanza,* I'll turn the telly on to get the time . . . What's this though, moost be an old fillum or soomthink . . .

It was very jerky, quick shots of city streets with crowds seething and waving and streams of cars, then the announcer broke in, something about a hospital. The President of the United States had died in Dallas, sounded as if he'd been bumped off by gangsters. Och aye, what a spanner in the wheel o' democracy but no reason to cut off all the bleedin' programs, the werrld hasna come to an end, let's have a game o' pontoon.

But switching on the news much later, they learned that a young man named Oswald had stepped from black obscurity into the permanent glare of world fame by taking careful aim out of an upper window. The most spectacular coup ever achieved by any Secret Agent.

Profession? "Order filler in a book depository." Parents? Father died before he was born. Wife? One year younger than Myra. And here in Manchester, right next to Westmoreland Street, we have Dallas Street. Weel weel weel.

Penny for your thoughts, Neddie. . . . Okay, don't get steamed up, it's joost that for the last hour you haven't uttered— Pencil? Here's one I'll sharpen for you.

Saturday November 23, 1963.

Front page Manchester *Daily Mail,* in letters that looked a foot high: KENNEDY ASSASSINATED. "A young man is being questioned"—yes, but Ian, *wait* for the afternoon papers, it'll be all Oswald Oswald. Terrible thing o' course, but what a super shot he must be! Quite a nice day, I'll be back by ten-thirty wi' the car, anythink you want? . . . Pro Plus, what's that? . . . Pills, why, aren't you well? . . . You mean the pep-up sort you said you—You're not by any chance plannin' a bank job today? . . . No, silly, I was only jokin'. Gran, have the sandwiches ready an' don't dally. I'll be back, ta ra.

On the table, the ruled lines are crowded. Jottings. Just like any other Saturday, pulse normal, large white hands steady, brain neat as apple pie. Remember the code an' keep saying I'm-not-me, I'm-a-humble-stock clerk, eyes open, trap shut and all will be well.

Just one thing, while we are in conference, secret, top level. The First Lieutenant at the wheel, taking orders from the Commanding Officer in the shadows . . . *will that work?*

It had better.

Glass o' wine? Bit errly i' the day, but this is *the* day an' nobody knows it but me. There's daft auld Gran hummin' tae hersell an' cuttin' sandwiches for the picnic, recheck list.

Funny how on a special day your hearing's twice as sharp. Radio next door. Car coming. Stops, bang goes the car door. First Lieutenant back.

What d'ye mean, Hess, what's wrong with a drop in the morning—we's on our holidays, aren't we? All on aboot the assassination are they—ah weel, it isna every week things happen—what? I'm just lookin' at the fire, that's all, the coal they serrve your gran is goin' frae bad to werrse, look at all that slack! . . . No, Hess baby, not a skerrt for you today, I feel it in ma bones it's the day for tight trousers. We're off.

Ooh, what's the matter with him today? It's not just the wine, nor that Pro Plus eether—didn't the chemist say it's not much more of a stimulant than black coffee? He's sort of excited, as if he's hell-bent for you-know-what i' the back o' the car. I must say I won't say no neither, seems ages. 'Ark at 'im—self-survival, question of the colossus-astride-the-metropolis—it's his swallowed-a-dictionary day. But I do like him in a good mood, an' I *do* like the way he says forenune instead o' 'mornin', an' moo-errs for the moors. Moo-errs, it's nice.

No, Hess baby, this is a *mystery* tour . . . Weel, is there a *law* agin smilin'? I just feel a bit mad . . . Am I gonna take ye to a *what?* A register office, God no, I'm no' as mad as all that. Into town ferrst, spot o' shoppin'. It amuses me to scan the crowds of a Saturday, the silly respectable expressions on the mugs, cabbages an' cretins. Look at those three starin' at the newspaper—"Terrible aboot the President, isn't it, ooh terrible"—the silly twits, give 'em somethin' worth cryin' aboot. Ah, now parrk just here by the ironmonger's, here's a quid, nip in an' buy me a spade.

A *spade*, Hess, you heard, we're goin' up to dig some o' that gorrgeous peat an' bring it hame an' dry it for fires, better than that mucky coal. You didn't know your Neddie was a nature boy, did ye? Nature is sufficient in itself and needs no creator, *there is no God!* Just a quotation, I got millions.

Lemme see . . . aye, it's the spade the gardener ordered, shove it i' the back wi' the sack an' the rug on top, we're off.

Weather for today, Sat.: cold. Moon will be at half, visibility good, some clouds.

The peace up here, ah . . . Prosit. Jus' enough wind to keep trespassers off, let's turn the heat on an' the musica an' climb into the back. There we are, snug as a coupla bugs, 'nother bottle, drum drum *drum* . . . Ye ken the trouble? Too many people i' the world, luke at Manchester doon there—now, now, Hess, take your wee hand awa' 'cause Neddie gotta conserve the auld energies for the P-E-A-T—peat. You herrd me, Hess, *drop it!*

That's better, I scared you, didden I? You currl up your tight li'l ass in your tight long trews an' I'm off wi' me spade, gotta do a spot o' diggin' to keep the auld home fires burnin', I'll be seein' ya.

What *is* the matter with 'im? P'r'aps 'e'll feel more like siesta when he's done 'is stint, he's queer for *peat* . . . He *as* traipsed a long way, looks a proper farmer diggin' there wi' the scenery be'ind . . . Funny, every time a car passes, 'e straightens up so they can't see the spade, an' then puts 'is hand over 'is eyes like he was lookin' at the view—I know, it's 'cause it's not legal to take peat 'ome, you have to giggle. I'll 'ave another drop, won't be drivin' for ages . . .

Ooh Neddie, I dozed off, it's dark! Where's your sack, is that all ye got—an' ye're all mucky wi' clay an' stuff an' all over our new spade . . . What? You want to see *what?*

The big city? Neddie, ye mean *now*—don't tell me we're goin' dancin' at last? . . . *Shoppin'?* But you got three smashin' shirts already that I laundered yesterday . . . Well, the best, on our way 'ome, would be where I got me diamond-mesh nylons that time, Ashton Market, you are funny . . . What? Neddie, ye'd like to come back up, 'ere? For a *session,* what a way to put it. Okay, shall us be off 'fore it gets dark?

Down from the heights they go, wheeling slowly down into busy roads. The Saturday-night cars endlessly restlessly dipping and veering and winking, but the little chariot where sit Adam and Eve, upright and owning the earth, is sacred. Palace Stalybridge, *South Pacific.* Stop on the corner, Hess, get out an' buy two things of ice cream an' don' ask why. Got 'em?

Market Square, Ashton. Bursting with stalls, streaked with foggy light; balloons, shouts, gaiety, brisk commerce, snatches of songs, men women children, enemy-humanity nudging enemy-humanity.

Now proceed slowly by the poster where it says: "THE MAN WHO MURDERED J.F.K. YESTERDAY." Look, Hess, the office of the Ashton *Reporter* where it says: "All The Local News Every Friday" . . . Now draw up here in the shadow, an' we'll jus' sit sippin' our ice cream as if we bought it over at that stall. An' now we take a look at the crowd. *Candid Camera* stuff, who shall we introduce to the waiting millions? Eeny meeny miny, eeny meeny miny, eeny meeny miny . . .

Hess, these are the orrders. An' ye may discard the smile, this is serious. See the kid standin' at the toy stall, i' the cap? Dinna look now, but I want you to—hell, his father come up that second an' took him by the arm. Have another spoonful of the jolly old harmless . . .

Ah . . . See the other lad over there? No, the little 'un leanin' against the trash barrel. Aye, in the flannel trousers, dead right, Hess, ferrst time—the pale ole tight ole trews! He's askin' the man the time, that means he'll be leavin' for his bus. Aye, there he goes, gimme your ice cream, now drive slowly around an' there where it says Warrington Street. I thought so, d'ye see the bus station, way down in the lighted part, now stop slowly, how the hell does this window werrk . . .

Hiya, laddie, the missus 'n me wonderred wi' the fog if we could give ye a lift home? . . . Splendid, ye'll be there in no time, nip in between us, d'ye fancy a mouthful of ice cream?

As easy as if you'd leaned out of the car and plucked a tame bird off a hedge.

As they pass the line at the bus stop, idle looks slide over the car. They see a young father, leaning between those looks and his smiling young twelve-year-old son, help the boy to ice cream while the efficient young mother drives them home. If Dad hadn't been leaning, the one or two possibly on their way to Smallshaw Lane might have glimpsed a resemblance between the lad and the one who lives at Number 262.

That's right, sonny, sit ye back—what's your name? . . . *John,* what d'ye know, same here, only mine's the Sco'ish verrsion—Ian. . . . To the right, ye say?

Sharply she remembers something. This incalculable man, who all day has been flashing uneasily between randy elation and

temper, is now as gentle as he was with her dad on that New
Year's Eve two long years ago. Except this time *he* is the dad. A
father's gentleness which would have put a terrified lost child at
its ease, never mind a broad-smiled, sociable boy who has been
given a lift home by a kind couple. She winks back a winey tear.
To the right again? A quiet darkish street. Then *he* remembers
something.

Gosh, Myra, I promised your mother we'd pick her up in Stalybridge on the dot o' six! It's five to now—sorry, laddie, but if we
miss her by two minutes she'll panic. We'll give you an' her a
quick cuppa, an' then whisk ye back hame before seven. Myra
dear, ye turn right, again here, dear, at the lights.

The lights are red. The car stops, she turns and looks. Across
the boy, who is finishing his ice and talking: Quite good picture
it was, but the one next week sounds smashin', *Hand o' Death*.

The man turns his head, she meets his look and her mouth
goes dry. His eyes are caught in a thin bar of livid street light.
They are arctic-cold, glittering with the icy fire of two diamonds.

She jerks her head forward again, her attention forced onto the
crossing traffic. The decision of a lifetime, and she has thirty
seconds to make it. She need only snap open her door, step out,
bang it shut and walk smartly up that dark alley and she will be
forever the wholesome North Country lass, so reliable with her
shorthand, who'll marry any day now. She needn't even turn the
engine off—he'll just stare after her, get out and walk away. Then
the bewildered child will clamber out and hurry home with a
garbled story of the missus walkin' out on this chap an' he
couldn't drive for toffee—ooh, 'e was mad. Her hand is on the
door.

But I'd never see him again, never never. I'd die. Ian, I can't
do without it and I can't do without you, I love you I love you.

The lights change to green and the car swings slowly away
from the home of John Kilbride.

Mister, is that a transistor? ... Oh yes, mum, I like a bit o' pop
music, ta ... Oh yes, I like the telly, *Bonanza*'s best but last night
in our street all the kids got mad, it was switched off on account
o' Kennedy but our Mam said they'll do it again next week, so

we may see two together, smashin'! My mate said the feller must ha' bin a super shot with a movin' target—what time is it now, please?

Drum, drum, drum HQ? Message received, code word stock clerk, hostage captured and proceeding east, *alles in Ordnung*.

Here we are, John—Palace Stalybridge, *South Pacific*. This is where we allus pick up Myra's mam when she's been to the pictures. Ten past, damn, she must ha' given us up. Never mind—John, ever been around here before? I tell ye what, laddie, for a treat we'll take ye hame the top road, takes no longer an' the view is tops. Myra, to the right here . . . No, laddie, we're still on your way hame, it's just that the road curves all the way around, verra deceptive.

The little family car—young Dad, young Mam, and young John—swings out of the town street and gently into the upper darkness. It climbs past slumbering farms which for centuries have housed families of simple hard-working people. At the wheel, mechanically changing gears, a trained and platinum-rinsed robot. The shawffer.

But it is a double image. While the robot is in faultless control of a car, behind the blank eyes and the strong chin there cowers a terrified woman. (I'm sittin' on a roller coaster like that one in Blackpool with Pat Jepson, only this one ends with you being hurled into the air a mile above Manchester wi' no parachute. God, make him change his mind, God God . . .)

The grunt and snarl of machinery, we're off. Over the roller-coaster hump, eyes shut, stomach in mouth, off. And at the same time, at the touch of the hands and feet of the robot, the Ford Anglia climbs obediently to the moon and to the moors. Miles away and down, the twinkling lights of the unsuspecting enemy.

He stiffens. What's that clanking—God, engine trouble? Relax, it's in the back. The spade.

Here we are, Johnnie laddie, now we'll tarry just here for the view, the moon's just out, see? Thirsty? Try this, we'll all have a swig . . . What? No, your mam won't be worried yet about a big boy like you, tastes a bit sharp but after a minute ye feel great, have another swig. That's the ticket, quite warm are ye?

Warm as a bird. A bird tame and trusting, until the voice of the tamer sharpens and the hand that strokes the feathers begins to tighten.

"Moon at half: clouds." So the light is mercifully averted, and the lone, motionless car melts into the blackness of the hills. And if after a moment the clouds move on, the moon's face will tell nothing. Too old for shock, or even sorrow. If it were not, tonight the puzzled world might stare skyward, and point in awe.

In the still-warm twilight of the car, she is alone. Hands clasped on the wheel in cataleptic trance, her eyes staring ahead. Zombie.

God, please God, do something. Stop it. Stop time. Turn it back. Stop time. Stop it stop it stop it.

Then her fear. The fear of the dark which is never to leave her, and which her sister is to be puzzled by over and over again.

Outside, blackness. And the full silence. No, not quite full. From the upper air, a sound. Calling, in a low long moan, to her. My-y-ra Hi-i-n-n . . . No, not the wind. The Bogeymen. Twenty feet tall, leaning over, red eyes. Bending. Nearer. My-y-ra . . .

How long since she watched the flashlight zigzagging away from her, flicking on and off like a firefly? Minutes? Half an hour?

The flashlight again, zigzagging nearer. The Bogeymen don't like lights, they glide back a step. The flashlight off, on, off, on. Nearer. He passes her. They might never have met. She hears the back doors open, then a clank. He has come back for the spade.

The doors close again, he passes her, zigzag, flick flick, gone again. The moon out again and far below, the gleam of the lake. The reservoir. A drowned boy spouting water. Michael Higgins. The moon gone again, silence and blackness. Alone, as they say, wi' the old thoughts. But she hasn't any, except to feel that *they're* there, outside, nearer, bending over the car. Check the fuel—where's the little light?—aye, we're okay, we'll get home, life goes on.

On the horizon, a shaft of moving light. The stray car, she is glad of its tranquil approach . . . Hello, thou light, sorry to see thee swallowed in the night. Blackness.

Then the firefly again. How long has it *been?* He gets back next to her and slumps like a man who's been working against time, such as fixing a tire in traffic. And it was work that had to be done, like the orange having been a pretty sight but you can't leave peel all over the place: NO LITTER PLEASE.

As she fumbles for a cigarette she thinks, heck, I saw meself jump wi' no parachute and I'm sittin' here alive, shock I suppose —but I haven't even twisted a muscle, how has it happened?

She lights the cigarette, places it between his lips, then he switches on the transistor and she lights her own. In the sudden flare they look at each other to the music like a mysterious pair in the movies, Bogart and Bacall. He feels for the bottle, takes a deep swig, hands it to her. She gulps. They are warmed together by the familiar acid glow. Life will never be the same again. Start the engine, lights on, into gear, out of the eternal blackness, awa'.

Down into the valleys. At the traffic stops, up with the music, all the colors of the rainbow, and the little car bursts with the distorted rhythms that by secret radio are telling the news to HQ, *alles in Ordnung*: mandolin, glockenspiel and drum, an' hark at the flügelhorn, Blowin' in the Wind, drum drum drum, Elvis Bossa Nova Baby, and then a relay from HQ, Shirley Bassey singing "Goldfinger" from King Ian's balcony to the cheering thousands, each his subject, superrb, all celebrating the coup which cannot be dimly guessed at, this end, look at those lighted windows, the morons and the cabbages bumbling into bed. Streets, houses, bridges, while the beat thuds triumphantly through them, drum drum drum. Churches, shops, lamps, railways, cars, people, the enemy. The Most Daring Coup of the Century.

They get to a pedestrian crossing and see a couple arm in arm nearly half across, the car just shaves them. The man yells, "Hy, who d'you think you are?" They almost look at each other. The car sails on, drum-drum, drum-drum. Traffic lights. A policeman strolls by, then stops to try a shop door. Simultaneously, they do look at each other. He smiles. She smiles back. Home in time for *The Avengers*.

But the blackness they have left up there is not eternal. Behind the slim television mast of Holme Moss, the morning light breathes everyday life into the eastern sky, and the everyday air blows fresh over the peat. The birds sing, and the animals begin their inoffensive day. The horse on the skyline raises his gentle head and sniffs the wind; the humble sheep bends and nuzzles the familiar earth for morsels of nourishment. And the first cars, very few because it is Sunday, appear from both horizons, cross in the virgin autumn light and go peaceably about their business. Soon, sweet and far away in the churches of moorland villages, bells will ring in praise of God.

Another day has begun, nothing has happened. The secret is so secret that there is no secret. Out of sight, out of mind. In the same Sunday light which filters into the million houses sleeping below, a young woman lies awake by the side of her unconscious lover. A girl really, twenty-two next July. A new day.

She wonders again, How did it happen so easily? The roller coaster was hell. Yet at the end, just as they jumped, he'd grabbed her hand tight and they'd just slid off and floated. Floated. Floated, to the ground.

But she does know that life will never be the same again. The frontier has been crossed. And there is no return ticket.

Soberly she tells herself that she should feel shame and remorse, any girl would. But she just doesn't. Only feels sort of bruised, like after a shake-up, it's like the naughty pictures, only more so, it's just one o' those things. And it's over. That's all. Ye're in a sort of trance about it. Oh, if it wasn't Neddie I'd feel terrible o' course, an' go straight to the police. But then if it wasn't Neddie it wouldn't 'a happened. Some people are special, I'll make a cuppa tea.

Before she does so, she looks down, as she has done before, at the sleeping face of a stranger. For two years she has shirked the fact that he was not hers, and that unless a miracle happened, he never would be. The miracle has happened. He is hers, forever.

CHAPTER 18

FROM GRAVE TO GAY

"Come ye here to drink good wine
Upon the weddin' day?"
The Oxford Book of Ballads

SUNDAY BREAKFAST is earlier than usual. Hurry oop, Gran, the
car got to be back at Glazier's by ten. Gran, 'ave you seen the
peat in the scullery, Ian's goin' to dry it out and use it on the
fire.

Out in the prosaic morning light, to the tinkle of distant
church bells, they examine the car to make sure it goes back as
good as it came. It wouldna do for folk to think there'd been fun
an' games up in them thar hills, dear me no!

And for good and all, the sly joke sets the convention between
them: there will never be any discussion of the secret. No need.
They behave about it, and always will, as some proper couples
might the day after marriage: something had come to pass on the
wedding night, something sudden and violent which other people had experienced but which neither of them could ever have
imagined happening to them. It has happened. And although it
has united them for all time, it is hardly a subject for daytime
conversation, except obliquely via the occasional risqué joke and
the naughty wink.

Ian, I'll be back on the bus—ta ra, be good. (Ooh, I do love
drivin' along me own streets! It's a funny thing to think, but I

am thinkin' it, so there—I've never seen him look so well. Usually on rotten Sunday he's proper dopey—oh, there's Ronnie Sinclair, been out to get *News o' the World*.) Hello, Ron. (To think I might be married to 'im now.)

Funny 'ow you get used to something bein' over an' done with. Like Fate or something. You just take your life up again. An' anyway, with 'im takin' it all so calm, *I* can't go faintin' all over the place, I mean what good did broodin' ever do, what'll be on the telly tonight besides Kennedy?

And home on the bus, Ashton Old Road. In front, two schoolboys on their way to church, bouncing and larking.

If Ian Brady's library had included the Gospel of Sri Ramakrishna, would he have now recognized the parable of the baby tigress?

Once upon a time, a flock of sheep found a newborn tigress and adopted her. She grew up with the lambs; when the lambs bleated she bleated, and when the lambs ate grass she ate grass. One day a Tiger attacked the flock and seized the baby tigress, who started to bleat. The Tiger dragged her to the river and held her over the water: "Look at thy reflection, thou art a tiger like me, taste this meat." The baby tigress whimpered, the Tiger forced a dripping dead lamb into her mouth, the baby tigress gagged, bleated, gagged, bleated, swallowed. Gradually she came to know the smell of blood and to relish the taste of meat. And then the Tiger said to her, "Thou art no different from me. Behold the forest over there. Follow . . ."

Monday morning, walking to Millwards—like on your way to work with a hangover, really—at the newsdealer's in Hyde Road their eyes travel together sideways to the scrawled poster, with their minds mutely speaking the name John Kilbride. And together they halt: WORLD MOURNS J.F.K. They stare again. J.K. Quite a coincidence.

Kennedy, Kennedy. But at lunch time, the Manchester *Evening News*. Good God—and a quickening of hearts. Page 7, a spread across five columns. Peck peck go the typewriters. Irene Eccles humming As Long As He Needs Me. DOGS JOIN IN MASSIVE COMB-OUT FOR BOY. And in the middle of it there he is, laughing up past them and trying not to, good likeness. Myra, Ian, 'ave you read about that boy, oh you've 'ad your 'air done, isn't it a terrible thing . . . I know, it's like an accident really.

And yet it isn't like after the naughty pics, when you imagined the faces in Millwards if they were told what a certain couple had been up to. *This* just hasn't happened. A dream. A *bad* dream? Oh yes, of course. And yet . . . oh dear, difficult to put it. *Special.*

The next morning before work, Myra went over to Glazier's and ordered a car for the following evening, the twenty-seventh. By six she had it parked outside Number 7. Wine, sandwiches, transistor. Evenin' Mrs. Matlock . . . Kidnapped? Aye, shouldn' be surprised . . . It's the poor mother you think of, ta ra and off. Checkup night.

And as they leave the streets and the farms and climb, they are conscious of a mutual and tranquil glow, impossible to mention, which makes them more truly one than they have ever been. The secret place is theirs absolutely.

Paper cups of wine, then without saying anything he opens his door. And alone the Master walks into his background of mountain and mist. This is the only bad time, lock the doors and turn on the headlights.

He returns, flicks Monday's *Evening News* over to the back, climbs in again, then without looking at her, turns up a thumb and pours fresh wine for them both. Prosit.

Transistor on an' Move to Rear . . . you ken well what I mean, ye're goin' to terrn into a back-seat driver. Siesta. But not to sleep. And to music. Ugly. The occasional car swishes by. But fab. This is for real. The *News* torn to a frazzle.

Friday, November 29, Ashton *Reporter*: BOY VANISHES, SIXTH DAY, ALL-OUT HUNT, "impossible to solve the mystery of a schoolboy who seems to have vanished into thin air." Lord Lieutenant's Speech Through Loudspeaker, Sunday, Biggest Search

Ever Mounted. Saturday night, *Avengers, Espionage.*

And Sunday, as he sits by the fire, his face has the relaxed look of a politician who has read a favorable account of a crucial speech. HQ send congratulations, operation impeccably carried through. They are not looking at each other, but the room is pleasantly crackling. An excitement not confined to the head. To be sitting with your stock clerk's feet up, your eyes shut and imagining hundreds of strangers who if they ever acknowledged your existence would consider themselves your superiors—bank managers, M.P.'s, parsons and, above all, oh above all, police-men—all about to waste a futile and uncomfortable Sabbath because of you . . .

Essoldo Gorton Dec 10 *The Mongols.* Hey, isn't that the fillum John went to see on the Saturday afternoon, must get a load o' that.

She begins to notice that he tolerates company more than he did. He favors sitting in the background of a group, in a pub, a club or even in Millwards at lunch time, observing the banter and the stupid arguments with the wisdom of the mystery man. The stillness of the strong. When he does put in a word, he is likely to steer the talk into dangerous waters—kidnappings, hikers, sex maniacs—then she finds it ticklingly difficult to meet his eyes. Next thing is, somebody's bound to propound an opin-ion on the Kilbride case, and lo and behold, he answers with a reasoned theory, near enough to the secret to make her hold her breath.

Then there's the evening you're strolling together to the pic-tures and straight into Ken and Marge from the office, and just can't avoid walking with them for a coupla blocks. And smack into that huge poster of Johnnie, HAVE YOU SEEN THIS BOY, same half grin, like he's got your number, makes you feel quite peculiar. As if he was a relation somehow, like a little brother, only you mustn't say so.

But it is in the cinema that the complicity is at its speechless strongest, for there it is enhanced by the dark and the reverberat-ing music. In close-up, the actor-murderer stares petrified at his bloodstained hands: "God, what have I done! I didn't mean to, I didn't . . ." She steals a look at the face next to her. On his other side, a bespectacled woman sits holding a forgotten ice cream as she looks horrified at the screen: over the tips of his long strong fingers he is studying the actor with the modestly amused look of the professional cricketer who finds himself guest of honor at a school match.

But the excitement has to die down. The poster gets more and more frayed, then comes the windy day when it disappears. Ashton *Reporter,* Dec 27: ELDERLY WIDOW BURNT TO DEATH. The paper is about to be crushed up as usual when the eye is caught by the photograph of the Kilbride family sitting at Christmas with John's empty chair, they do look sad, no there's nothink else at all.

Neddie, look, I'm wearin' your Christmas present. Aren't they a marv'lous fit, just right, up to just above the knee an' shiny black leather just like the Avengers! . . . Gran, don't be soft, they're just the thing for winter 'ikes, you shurrup.

And still more excitement for her, to make Christmas even more bearable. For unto her too a child was born, in the shape of a beloved new puppy, one of a litter delivered by Gran's Lassie. Just as after the Higgins drowning she had fallen in love with the dog Duke, so now she loved again to excess: a little mongrel half collie and half sheepdog. She took him to her breast and crooned over him in mixed-up baby talk, so that his name became a mixture of Puppy and Poppet: Puppet. The excess was to last. Can psychiatry connect it with a delayed and deep-seated shock sustained on the night of the secret?

Ian bought him a tartan collar.

With the New Year, 1964, his twenty-sixth birthday. Then in February, at last—the car, rented but for a time their very own, green Austin Traveller, again nice and roomy. Saturday outings, snaps against the snow. Ian was getting so keen on scenery that he invested in an expensive pair of binoculars. Then big news.

Housing. The Gorton slums were falling apart. The wallpapers, pasted one on top of the other over hopeless years, were leaving the damp, crumbly walls and curling like putrid leaves above the diseased floorboards. Bannock Street, doomed, was ready to be pulled down and Gran had been allocated a house in Hattersley. Ian read out from the paper: "Overspill estate, completed by September, within eight or nine miles of the moors" —good show, Myra.

Drifting. First week in May, gorgeous with the coming of the nice weather: the green Austin's three months was up and Myra invested in a smart little white mini-van and pickup. "Pickup," what was that again? "Ready to Go Anywhere and Do Any Job you have in Mind, Roomy Enough for Transport of Livestock," ha ha.

And then, within the mind's eye a summer of outings and then the move, the blow fell. The bash Myra had felt, in her bones, would sooner or later come clonking down. Her sister was pregnant.

That David Smith. Mam was tearful; *Joost* like our Maureen, no harm in her, but not that bright, and too easygoin'. Never got to Ryder Brow School and look at her now.

Myra's reaction was in blunt idiom: "Can't she shift it?" No, she couldn't, the little so-an'-so had just mooned about an' done nowt. Baby due in October. Neddie, she'll 'ave to leave Millwards *now*, she's showin'! Worse, Maureen—eighteen—wanted to become the wife of a good-for-nothing of sixteen.

Well, said the mother with a troubled shake of the head, we'd best do the best we can. Myra, don't be too 'ard on 'er. Ian, you tell our Myra she mustn't be narrow-minded.

And Ian, without ever having exchanged a word with the male culprit, did. "Aw, come on, Myra, I don't approve o' marriage but leave 'em to it." And Myra honored him, obeyed him, and left 'em to it.

David Smith had lived every day of his sixteen years within a radius of four Manchester square miles. Born on January 9, 1948, exactly ten years after Brady, he was the illegitimate child of a girl named Joyce Hull and of Jack Smith, a Manchester laborer who had been married and divorced. The parents lived together at 1 Lamb Street till David was two and then separated, upon which the boy was legally adopted by his father's parents, John and

Annie Smith, 39 Aked Street. He never saw his mother again.

From the age of five he attended the Infant School down the road in Ross Place; at nine he was removed from his grandparents by his father, now a long-distance truck driver, who took him to live with him in lodgings at 13 Wiles Street (landlady a spinster, Miss Jones) around the corner from Bannock Street and the Hindley house in Eaton Street. It was a savage adjustment; the child had become devoted to his grandmother and at fourteen he was to cry bitterly over her death. From nine till fifteen he attended the same school as Maureen, St. James' Secondary Modern.

Father and child stayed together. It would at this moment be a heaven-sent splash of sentiment to picture the Smiths *père et fils* as a devoted couple, with Dad arriving home from grueling all-night drives to cook his little lad's breakfast, and then taking him through his homework with a view to a more refined sphere: a proletarian Sorrell and Son. No, Smith was a rough diamond, and Son—if anything—rougher.

Just as well, because for a boy of nine, with a father constantly on the move and relying on the chance help of a landlady, the prospects were daunting. Compared with him, Ian and Myra had led sheltered childhoods; he was to grow up entirely deprived of any form of feminine attention, never mind affection. When at home, his father treated him like a baby, sending him to bed at nine o'clock, going out to the pubs, coming back elated and then waking the boy for a chat which frequently ended in fisticuffs. A delicate boy might not have survived, but this one, smoking at ten and drinking at eleven, hit back so successfully that at thirteen he knocked his dad out. At fifteen, the strongest head in Gorton: eight pints without turning a hair.

Agile of brain and wit, he was nevertheless bored by school; if he had not been, his future might have been different. He grew to adolescence in the streets of Gorton, a corner boy leaning with crossed feet against derelict walls, in the company of older toughs who could defend themselves with their fists and were not above the last resource: a length of bicycle chain. By nature easygoing, a shrugger of shoulders, when goaded he was a bruiser, and one thing was guaranteed to goad him: "Anybody that calls me a silly bastard gets a clout in the puss, see?"

City juvenile court, aged eleven years and nine months, charged with wounding with intent; at ditto, aged fourteen years and nine months, charged with assault causing bodily harm; at ditto, aged fifteen years and five months, charged with housebreaking and larceny, put on probation for two years. At fifteen, left school, then apprentice electrician at A. E. Sudlow's, losing his job after seven months because of "bad timekeeping"; apprentice glazier at Messrs. Armstrong, Salford; then after twelve months, ditto. It is on record that one night he threatened to "slash 'is ole man's wrists with a broken teapot," which sounds a basis for a play on parricide neatly fusing black comedy with the teacup sort. Perhaps Dave's old man had called him a bastard too.

August 15, at All Saints Register Office, quiet wedding. Did Ian realize that here was where, fourteen years before, his mother had married? It had been arranged for a Saturday so that the workers—Nellie Hindley, Myra and Ian—could attend. But none of them did. Nellie just didn't like any of it, and as for Myra, "Ian and I don't approve o' marriage."

The Smiths apparently did: Jack, the father; John Richard Smith, cousin; Mr. and Mrs. Albert Smith, cousins—so it's nuts to the 'Indley lot. The atmosphere cannot have been warmed by the fact that two months earlier the bridegroom had again been before the crown court, breach of probation. The couple were going to keep house at 13 Wiles Street; Miss Jones had left some time ago, and Nellie Hindley could imagine the state the place must be in with 'im and that father.

Back to Number 13, drinks, visitors faded away, and in the evening . . . what? Anticlimax. Pub crawl, Three Arrows as per usual. Tell you what, Mo, I'd like to meet this Scotch bleeder face to face, sounds quite a character . . . Likes the old wine does he? Well, let's make the big gesture, spend a bit o' that wedding present on 'alf a dozen bottles an' pop over to Bannock Street. What d'ye say, Mo?

Ten o'clock, the exhilarated bridegroom knocked at Gran's door. Myra opened. Oh hello, Mo, if you want our Gran, she's gone to bed. *Six* bottles? Oh well, I suppose you better come in. Ian, this is David Smith.

Under the steady gaze of Myra's ancestors, face to face at last.

Half an hour later the four were sitting around, the ice breaking chip by chip with every mouthful of the wine. For the first time Myra took a good look at her brother-in-law. Slim but husky for sixteen, not as tall as Ian but five-nine and more, brown eyes, dark hair with fair streaks, nice straight nose, big sulky mouth till he smiles, then it lights up. And when he giggles, sounds like a kid.

He and her Neddie made a remarkable contrast. The older one reserved, conservatively garbed, pale and spare, a curiously potent young tutor. Dave, on the other hand, wore a leather jacket and hair flopping over the back of his neck and into his eyes and constantly being tossed back. It was the first big year of the Beatles from nearby Liverpool, and Dave looked as if with guitar and microphone he could make the wedding go with a swing: a brash, shiny-faced adolescent animal, father and baby in one, one cheerful foot in the meadow of sex and the other in the bog of petty crime.

After an hour the ice had melted. The front room was drab, but it was a sunny evening and they were all young. And all that wine. Myra was appeased to hear that Dave was devoted to his dog, Peggy (Same name as Ian's mam, what d'ye know). Maureen sat podgily serene and happily fingering her ring: I'm older than you now, our Myra. Dave's inevitable jokes about shotgun weddings and the frustration of the randy bridegroom. He and Ian, of course, did most of the drinking. Dave the life and soul, clowning and leaping, excited to be married, excited to be alive.

He's 'oppin' about like our Puppet, any minute you expect him to wag his tail. What's goin' on wi' Neddie?

Ian is smoking a cigar, and he only does that when he wants to impress. And when he sits like that with his chin resting on extended thumb and index finger, and his other hand spread strongly on his knee, he's thinking. He is the older young man, the superior, giving the whippersnapper the once-over.

And the whippersnapper is keeping his end up: Me believe in G-God, never worried me eether way. I mean, if 'E's that keen to interest me in a p-proposition He damn well oughta communicate wi' me direct, I'm not goin' to be the one to write first, enclosin' a stamp, no ta, got me pride, my idea is that worry makes you old. I mean, m-money's gorgeous, I love it, but never worries me 'cause summat'll turn up, such as another drop o' wine in me empty g-glass. Oh ta, Ian, cheerio an' pleased to meet ya.

Then they got on to telly and space and war and then Ian started about Hitler, Dave all ears while the two girls fiddled with their hair as if to say, Leave the brainy talk to the men.

But Neddie wasn't being brainy all the time. He would suddenly unbend and evoke Dave's childish chuckle. Once when Myra said, "Oh Christ," Ian raised a finger and said, "Myra, watch that language." And when she retorted, "Watch that *what,* I like that from you!," he said, "Dave, I have a strong Gaelic temper which I endeavorr to control, so I keep a swear box. An' every time the auld tongue runs awa' wi' me I contribute to it. Actually I spend half my time emptyin' it." Dave roared.

Then, a few minutes later, Ian knocked his drink off the side of his chair. He looked from the broken glass to Dave, fished in his pocket, brought out a silver coin, looked at it and then in his dry deadpan way he said, "Two bob for an outburrst," spoke the old four-letter word slowly four times and put the coin away separately. It was dead funny.

Then back to the brainy talk. Home Rule for Scotland. Dave, like millions of boys in his position, had never been addressed in conversation by an intelligent human being. And he was impressed. He could hardly be expected to spot that the brain was not a first-rate one, and warped. The long words issuing in the measured Scottish voice to the rhythm of the pedantically waved right hand (the sign of a bad speaker), it took him in. Words like "administration," "approximate," "eugenics," I mean he talks like on the telly! Hook, line and sinker.

On the doorstep, a flushed Ian had an idea. A startling one, for Myra had never heard him extend an invitation. Tomorrow, Sunday, if fine, as a wedding present from him, they will all four drive for the day to the Lake District in the white mini-van, Myra'll pop over at noon and confirm.

The *Lake* District? Only sixty miles off, to the north, but for this claustrophobic group it was a project. Dave enthusiastic: It'll be fab!

Myra, your brother-i'-law's okay, raw but it's materrial. Gude night.

Good night, Neddie love—an' Puppet, you get to the bottom o' the bed. Not that there's much love these nights—is there, Puppet?—but no use bein' greedy.

Not that she's worried. In the dark she can feel the warmth of him, the light, downy hair of his leg just like James Bond, not too much—'night 'night, Hairy—and he is hers, As Long As He Needs Me . . . Her man and her child. But this David Smith business . . .

Going to sleep she thinks, It's been ages since Neddie mentioned Germany, an' tonight he was doing a spiel about it, soft-sell sort of. When did she last hear him do that to somebody? Funny. Only heard him do it to one person. Herself.

CHAPTER 19

FRESH FIELDS, AND A WEE PAL

"Anybody can be good in the country."
Wilde

WAKE OOP, Maureen Smith, this is your 'usband. You are a size, love, too bad but it's a gorgeous day for our 'oneymoon to the Lakes . . . Careful, girl, gettin' out o' bed or you'll wake the baby.

Myra, around the corner in Bannock Street, making Ian's tea, does a little wondering. Suppose, on that doorstep last night, he had said, "Dave, can you drive? . . . You can? Well, you and me's goin' on a spree and the girls'll stay at home." And suppose she had seen on his face the look that meant she dare not utter?

She would have been furiously jealous, o' course she would.

But the answer is that it couldn't happen. She doesn't know much about homosexuality; and in this context the secret, lying in its shadowy lair at the back of her mind, is much too special for her to feel it stir in the dark and move forward. Those books of Ian's have reams about it, but she could never be bothered; Neddie says there's bars in town, but she does know enough to realize that Dave isn't *one of those*. That big floppy mouth, sexy bastard—oops, I said bastard, sorry our Maureen. And Ian isn't a homo either, he's just . . . "Vicious" is the word she can't find, doesn't want to. And even she feels that "naughty" is an understatement. "Kinky" really. Suppose . . . Yes, there is another alternative.

Suppose Maureen had been bad wi' that morning-sickness bit and not able to go and *then* Ian had suggested the trip? Just him and her and . . . a passenger? A lift, laddie, to the Lake District . . .

No. She somehow knows—*no*. But she had to *think* of it. David Smith, been around the corner for years and suddenly . . . he's there. Funny. Kettle's boiling.

After midday dinner, off. Maureen sat in front next to Myra. In the back, with the partition closed between them and the girls, and the canvas bit at the very back rolled up for the view, Dave lay sprawled with Ian and half a dozen bottles of wine. Ian wore dark glasses, and around his neck a cord with binoculars, terrific. It was just what David wanted, the canny Scot fascinated him.

The wine flowed, half-doz. red, and so did Ian's conversation. He was dryly amusing about Borstal, frank about "clashes wi' the police" and implied that as a man o' the werrld, it amused him to go straight until he had decided what he wanted to launch into. He disliked work, he said, but found it useful until he had perfected plans to make money, crime is easier moneywise. Religion's the bunk, we all ken that, but to make your marrk you have to have something in its place—your own perrsonal philosophy, which takes working out, with the aid of bukes . . . Prosit.

Gliding in the sun through Preston and Lancaster in a winey haze, and with the laconic Scots voice holding forth, Dave felt woozily flattered. It was like discovering a big brother who treated you as a bright pupil, and nice to feel you're each other's brother-in-law like. God, don't mention that word "law," the way they run this country! I saw a phrase in a buke the other day, it said laws were made by Jim Idiots to be broken by geniuses—and isn't that something? Drink up, kid.

In an idle moment Dave noticed, neatly bored in the partition, two holes the size of pennies. Ian, what's them for?

In answer Ian put his binoculars to the holes; they fitted perfectly. Then he explained that he liked to "obserrve the man in the street without bein' obserrved," either by squatting where he was and looking through to the front, or by sitting in front on the half-turn and reconnoitering the prospect at the back. Some hobby.

But Ian makes you think. An intellectual, yet one of uzz. An' come to think of it, I *'ave* 'ad a raw deal, we all 'ave, and 'e's right too about a philosophy, woonder what 'is is.

Lake Windermere, lunch in a Bowness café. Change of pace, a monosyllabic Lancashire meal outside Lancashire. But German wine. Dave could tell Ian liked scenery, the way he gave the mountains the once-over, he came all over dreamy.

Ride in a boat ("Wordsworth's cottage, no thanks, too mooch like school"), and on the evening ride home, a snooze in the back. More *Wein*. At Preston, Ian felt the need for a snifter of the hard stuff (Hello, thinks the shawffer, we're off) and Dave was given a quid, to pop into a pub for half a bottle of whisky. The messenger. Which does not escape the shawffer.

A couple of gulps of the Johnnie Walker, the drink for a mon. With the summer darkness the philosopher became taciturn. More gulps. Then a strange thing happened. They were in hurrying holiday traffic when they stopped at lights, next to a posh sports car driven by a dandy—cap, bushy mustache and cut-glass girl friend. The two glanced idly at the mini-van, dandy said something and girl friend laughed.

It could well be a remark about stopping at a hotel and getting into the hay, but Ian was determined that they had laughed at him, for sitting in the back being driven by a woman. Dave heard him mutter, "Fuck them," the lights changed and they went on. The racer accelerated and overtook them. Quick as lightning Ian, white to the lips, leaned forward and called to Myra, "Pass 'em."

She stiffened, they were already traveling at quite a speed, thank you, and pressed down. As they passed the others Ian drained the whisky, flipped open his window and with all his strength hurled the bottle. If Myra had not, the second before, put a spurt on and got a foot ahead—which meant that the bottle streaked across the other car's hood and into a hedge—the other driver would have been hit full in the face and anything might have happened. As it was, the man didn't even notice he had been overtaken, and for all you could tell, Myra hadn't seen anything either. Then Dave said, "Ian, ninepence-ha'penny for swear box," and it all passed off with a laugh.

But Dave had taken it in. And it did not make the new brother any less interesting. Later Maureen was to notice that Ian never again swore in front of her husband, not until the last night the two were to spend together. It seemed as if he was seeking to "project an image sort-o'-thing." Dignified, top brass, Brother Superior.

Back into the smudged evening rabbit warren of dear old Gorton, and after the hot day Greater Manchester smelled a bit phewy. Lake Windermere might never have been. Back into the Bannock Street front room (Gran abed, whoopee!) and while Ian opened more wine Dave loped around t' corner for fish 'n' chips. Second messenger. Then supper and drinks: "There was more drinks," Dave said later, "than supper." Yak yak, good old Ian, swallowed a dictionary. Two A.M. Only a coupla corners to negotiate an' we're home, our Mo. The expectant father tottered carefully on the arm of his pregnant bride instead of the other way around.

As they moved away Dave muttered to Maureen, "Mo, what's this Ian's name, MacDoonigle?"

Standing at the door, Myra called out, "Mo-Bee, what did he say?" And when Dave called out what he had said, Myra died laughing and said, "No, his name's Ian *Brady,* you filthy swine you," and ran back in to tell Ian he was Ian MacDoonigle. He's tops, is Ian. Born in January too, we're both Capricorns.

And from then on, there they were. The Four Musketeers, Wiles Street to Bannock ditto, Bannock to Wiles, shuttle service nightly or damn well near it. Many the time that Mrs. Reade, two doors from the Smiths, would see the white mini-van parked outside Number 13 waiting for Dave and Mo-Bee to come home from the pictures, Ian and Myra inside munching their fish and chips. (With so much bad blood about, nice to see families being friendly.)

Suddenly the move was upon them. Myra was thrilled to bits, felt they were setting up house and—goodo—it meant getting away from David Smith. And what's more, Maureen was getting to look a proper sight.

But the Saturday when the house was finished, the Smiths did drive out with them. A beautiful day, and as the dwellings they had lived with, all their young lives, thinned out and they saw the skyline, the two realized this was indeed a new lease on life. Hattersley.

Four little houses in a terrace raised above the road. Ian worked out from the plan that theirs was the far-end one, their front gate approached by a dear little white-railed path running in front of the other three. Inside their gate, their own ten-foot path leading, between the two halves of the front garden, to the front door, with over it a *porch roof!*

Wardle Brook Avenue, doesn't it sound posh? Between the avenue and the main Mottram Road, where the cars and buses coursed by, to and from Manchester, Stalybridge and the east, there was a delightful patch of green which had just been planted with a couple of dozen baby ash trees (Ooh Ian, Puppet will loov that). They walked all over. The other houses behind and around made a big toy village, and the seven thirteen-story apartment houses, rearing heads on the various hillsides, got you feeling you were outside Manhattan not Manchester (Ooh listen, Mo-Bee, to the tinkle, it's the Tonibell ice-cream man).

And Number 16, after Gorton, was a little dream dwelling: a sitting room the length of the house, with a big window at either end, a roomy kitchen with gas cooker and every sort of convenience, and upstairs—the luxury never dreamt of—a bathroom with wash basin, built-in bath, and *toilet!* And look, Neddie, a red doorstep, and on the roof a live *bird,* just like Walt Disney, and even a *back* garden! They were so elated they had a bottle of wine, there and then, to christen the house.

And Myra arranged, for the following Saturday, to go shopping with Mary and Winnie Hill, two Gorton neighbors who were moving to Wardle Brook Walk, just behind Number 16. She needed a tea set and two fireside chairs, one for her and one for Ian. Which sounds as if they were setting up as Darby and Joan. For the shopping spree the Hill girls suggested, as the best bet, the market at Ashton-under-Lyne.

And Saturday afternoon found her, in her red autumn coat and green head scarf, moving from stall to stall, scrutinizing prices. A couple of the schoolkids scampering about possibly offered to deliver for her on a wheelbarrow. She got her tea set, and a chair for Ian and a chair for her. Ashton seemed lucky to them.

The week of September 4, Ian had arranged with Tom Craig that he and Myra should have, for the move, half of their annual fortnight's holiday. With Dave's help—he had one of his jobless spells—they worked hard and enthusiastically. The builders had distempered the sitting-room walls cream: Ian gloss-painted them rose-pink, then decided to vary the result by papering the wall around the fireplace with a pattern of imitation brick, and the opposite wall with imitation streaked wood, a completely professional job.

The house had two drawbacks, and the first was to be a constant irritation to Neddie. Whatever the inadequacies of the slum houses, they had offered visual privacy: you stepped off the street and shut your front door behind you, and even the backyard had its high brick walls. But the new home was very different. In the front garden, apart from the low white railing flanking the gates of all four houses, there was no attempt at seclusion: the "wall" between his front garden and Number 14 was a few inches high, and during those days of preparation it riled him to see the delivery boy at the other end house, Number 10, and then with an impertinent whistle step over each "wall" and through each garden, including his.

At the back, it was even more noticeable. Preparing the back garden or even standing at his back door, he was overlooked by a

barrage of windows, more than a score: the backs of Wardle
Brook Walk. But what really disconcerted him was that while
each of the four back gardens was surrounded on three sides by
railings, the railings afforded no outlet. And yet a paved path
ran along the backs of the four houses, which meant that anybody from the other houses was entitled to walk coolly past Ian's
back door and around his gable end to the front.

It made it doubly important to have a next-door neighbor you
could tolerate. From the office he rang up to ask the names of the
future tenants of Number 14. A Mr. and Mrs. Braithwaite.
Sound okay, gude Yorkshire name. Anyways, they can't be Yids,
but if they was royalty I wouldna want 'em on me flippin' back
doorstep.

The second drawback was one they made light of, not realizing
that one night it was to prove fatal. The avenue sloped enough
down—from Mr. and Mrs. Fryer's house, Number 10, which was
near the sidewalk, to theirs, Number 16, the end one—for the
latter to be atop a ten-foot brick wall with a railing. It was such a
nuisance to leave the car each time near Number 10 that they
formed the habit of parking under their own house, scrambling
up the shelved corner of grass and baby shrubs ("oop the slope")
and vaulting the railing to their front gate and vice versa. Passers-
by thought what a bright young pair they made.

By the eighteenth, the Saturday of the following week, they
were in. Gran and Maureen and Puppet and Lassie all sat looking on while Myra arranged pictures and books, and told Dave
where to shunt the furniture while he cracked the jokes. Ian dug
the garden. The spade had naturally traveled with all the Bannock Street bits. By dark they were able to sit down to the house-
warming wine. Even Gran had a sip. Oh Myra, this is the 'ouse
I've dreamt of all me life . . . Now, aboot the front garden. Ian
arranged that the right side of the path would be his and Myra's,
and the left side Gran's, to be tended every Monday by Myra's
Uncle Jim with strict instructions not to meddle with the other
side.

Ian was wearing his black shirt and white tie, sign of high

spirits. Then they heard something. Next door. Knocking. Pictures going up. The Yorkshire Braithwaites were building up to the move-in. Weel, if it's gonna be that damn easy for them to take a look at us, we can take a look at *them*. German-wine-happy Ian swayed to his feet and through the kitchen and scullery and out into the mellow September evening. He was in luck, Mr. Braithwaite was emerging, eight feet off, to deposit corrugated paper in his trash can. In the evening sun, the two neighbors stood face to face. Brady and Braithwaite.

Braithwaite was a little taller than Brady, who was not short; not much older, and handsome in a gentle, dreamy way. A dazzling smile and an elegant figure, aristocratic really when compared with some of the Gorton rubbish moving in right and left.

One drawback. Mr. Phoenix Braithwaite from Jamaica was as black as Ian's shirt.

Ah weel, said Ian philosophically into his whisky—he had to have the hard stuff after that—just as well we're the end house, or we'd be findin' Isaac Solomons on our other side. Jamaica Inn's enough to go on with. Prosit. And "Jamaica Inn" stayed the name for Number 14.

Five Braithwaites: Phoenix, the father, who worked in an engineering firm; Tessa, the young mother; Donna, four; Carol, two; Barry, one. Beyond the cold nod of "Good morning" and "Good evening," Ian and Myra were never to talk to any of them. While the two were at work, though, Gran would stand at the back door chatting with Tessa, then bring out Lassie—and even Puppet—for the children to play with. Gran's attitude was characteristic of the neighbors, who thought Ian and Myra "stand-offish." The Braithwaites kept a tactful distance, and seemed not to notice when Mr. Brady spent two noisy weekends knocking up extra railings around his garden (or rather Gran's) front and back.

What a smashing little home! Comforts undreamed of in Gorton, sitting room bright with cretonne curtains, motif sort of red tulips, blue door, rugs on shiny composition floor, Gran's armchair, dog basket, hassock, little dining table for two under the front window, Joey the budgie's handsome new cage on its stand, under the back window a long "coffee table" for drinks with a bowl of plastic chrysanthemums, telly in the corner, and between telly and fireplace something novel: a "hatch," a sort of window, painted a cheerful red, opening onto the kitchen, which had all the fittings.

And what Myra called "the accessories" were pleasing. A flowered wastepaper basket, on the telly a shaded lamp; on the low mantelpiece an ornamental clock and twin ornaments of a mare and its foal; on the wall a print looking like Stratford-upon-Avon.

Gran loved the little staircase with its flowered carpet: Never seed anything so cheery. She had the best bedroom, at the back because it faced the sun; after all, it *was* her house. Myra's was the side room facing east, but it is indicative that Gran's two lodgers were never to refer to it as anything but "the first bedroom."

Although it contained a Spartan single bed, there was never any pretence at furnishing it: plain table and armchair, couple of packing cases, two boxes containing the all-but-forgotten guns, large wardrobe for Myra's clothes and—sh—Ian's. "Myra's bedroom" was never really to be slept in, for the living room had against the main wall an attractive piece of furniture more important than it looked, a couch which at night opened into a double bed, cushions becoming pillows. This, for the benefit of callers, was "for putting Ian up." Folk at Millwards could think what they liked; he was still domiciled with the Bradys in Westmoreland Street, "where Myra called for him on the way to work." A fiddle-faddle of prudery and instinctive secrecy.

After the excitement of settling in, the settling down. It happened quickly. Their daily life resumed a rhythm practically unchanged: the only differences, a little more help from Myra with the cooking—no Mam popping in—the longer drive to the office (six miles as opposed to one mile) and the fresh air in the evening. And of course the absence of the Smiths. If there was nothing on the telly, they just sat around till Gran started her noddin' and went up to bed. Then they sort of still sat around.

Ian still bet every day, sometimes quite a flutter, five or six quid at a time, but kept an even keel. He seemed to have read all his special books.

As she gets a bit of supper for him, through the hatch she glimpses him in his chair, looking abstractedly out at the sky darkening around the heights called Harrop Edge; the long fingers are touching at the tips and he's flickering them together, the quick nervous movement she kens so well. Then he rubs his eyes with his fists.

He's bored.

And in one of her looking-at-the-ceiling moods when it's too dark to see the ceiling, she realizes that she is bored too.

Three weeks after the move. Myra, what a shame, dear, about your brother-in-law, that Smith lad. Manchester Crown Court, October 9, two assaults, fined three pounds and on probation. October 26, Ancoats Hospital, Maureen's baby born. ('E might 'a waited with 'is assaults.) Angela Dawn Smith. One evening Ian and Myra popped in on the way from work—a courtesy call, as she couldn't take to babies and never would. Mo the mother remarked how her big sister had changed since her baby-sitting days an' her talk of going to the States as a nanny: Myra, not likin' kiddies isn't natural.

Oh, said Myra, I don't mind 'em when they get older; for instance, Ian and me are pally wi' Pat 'Odges.

A little girl next door but one, the other side of Jamaica Inn. Number 12. Daughter of Mrs. Elsie Masterson, now wed for the third time and expecting.

Elsie was an irrepressible city dweller whose translation to the genteel outskirts of Hyde and Mottram had in no way subdued her interest in the life around her. Dark, wiry, in her forties ("Don't you give my exact year, this is in confidence"), in between looking after Jim eighteen, Edwina thirteen, Pat eleven (Patty to her mam), Elsie nine, Ruby five and Peter three, kept her pulse on daily events. Asked later by reporters if she remembered the boy who delivered the newspapers, she answered, "I watched 'im personally to see if it was 'im that was takin' Mr.

Braithwaite's milk." "About Myra's Gran's first name," she wrote to me, "there, you see, I am treading on delicate ground. I did ask the old lady and she said Ellen. Now some people do not sound H where it should be, and the question is whether her name is Helen or not, I dare not ask again."

She was a cheery and cheering soul, but the last neighbor to become the only regular grown-up visitor to Number 16.

Ian and Myra, home from the office one fine October evening, found little Pat at their garden gate playing with Puppet. As Pat had presumably no Negro, Jewish, Indian or Maori blood, she was put up for—and unblackballed from—an Aryan Club of Two. Apart from her negative qualification, she had no obvious social assets, being chummy but on the stolid side. Big for her age—at this moment eleven and four months—she had a round, impassive, pretty face, with a snub nose and brown eyes under a dark fringe. She was invited in to be presented to Lassie and to Gran. In that order.

'Ello, Lassie—is it a lady doggie? . . . Aye, I like 'Attersley but I do miss the traffic . . . Aye, I like telly bar t' gunfire, our Mam says it's voilence an' oughta be banned. Well, must be off . . . Ye mean termorrer after school? . . . *Black an' White Minstrels,* oh ta, our telly's on the blink, *Third Man* series smashin', ta Mrs. er er . . . Okay, I'll remember, it's Myra 'n' Ian. Ta for the orange squash, ta ra for now.

Pat's stepfather, Mr. Masterson, asked Elsie if Ian and Myra were married, and Elsie said she thought they might be—otherwise he wouldn't have let Pat visit them. Then the week after Angela Dawn was born, Myra arrived home with one of a litter from the Smiths' dog, Peggy ("They got no use for a puppy now") and christened him Duke after Gran's Duke in Bannock Street that had been run over. Pat, he's a present to ye frae Ian an' me.

Which of the two initiated the triangle? He had been, for him, solicitous; the orange squash, for example, and—yes, fatherly. And she had taken her cue from him, instinctively, easily. With so much on Pat's mother's shoulders, nice to ask the kiddie in, bring a bit o' color into her life.

It did. Pat, what d'ye say to askin' your mam if you can drive wi' me and Ian Saturday, up to the moors? We're fetchin' some peat—you know *peat!* It's sort of grass an' stuff that's got all messed up together for donkey's years, an' marvelous for the garden, Ian says.

And Pat's mam was delighted to have *one* out of the house, all that fresh air too. Oh Mam, it was super, we drove first to Long-sight an' Myra'n me waited in the car while Ian went in to see 'is mam, Myra told me she never goes in, as Ian's mam will keep 'er talkin'. Then Ian come back an' we drove back an' up to the moors, an' Ian said, to keep me warm 'e'd let me sit on 'is knees. Then we got to a place they said belongs to *them,* an' we got out an' Ian dug some peat an' Myra 'n me 'eld the sack. Then we got back in the car an' they turned on t' music, Ray Conniff, Hello Young Lovers, Smoke Gets in Your Eyes, Thanks for the Memory —Ian says 'e likes the oldies. Then we sat for ages an' they give me some stuff to drink, wine or summat, not a bit nice . . . Oh, I only 'ad 'a drop but Ian drank a dollop, then we started for 'ome, Ian was *funny!* . . . Aye, he sat me on his knees like before, an' kept laffin' an' singin', Night and Day There's a Yearnin' and a Burnin' or summat, an' jiggin' up and down like a proper clown, talk about laff! . . . What? . . . O' course Myra was there, don't be daft, our Mam, she was right next to us, drivin'!

Christmas is a-coming, and the goose is getting fat.

Wha' am I doin' on me knees? Why, Hess love, jus' fixin' a lock on your bedroom door, so that when I'm developin' me snaps, people can't come bargin' in. Hessie, d'ye ken what I'll gie ye this Christmas, ye'll nivver guess! I'd like to see ye wi' black hair for a change . . . Aye, I ken well I wanted ye blond, but now I'd like to see ye darrk . . . No, no' dyed, a lot o' gerrls go in for wigs now, an' I want ye to get yourself a stylish black one for special nights out—right?

An' now, Hess—is Gran's door shut?—a wee playback on the tape. Listen, *bitte*—what d'*you* think this sounds like? . . . A bit o' love, how right ye are! All that pantin', kinda sexy, huh, *jawohl!* . . . Listen now for the actress to scream oot, "No no, you're hurting me!"—there she goes! An' then *he* growls an' groans, mmmm—what's *your* guess it is? . . . No, daftie, it's no' from a blue talkie, it's the sound track of the BBC thriller last week! The Buchenwald I stayed in for, remember?

Let's put it on again—oh, talkin' o' Christmas, what would I like? Well, a down payment on a tape recorder, ta very much . . . Aye, I ken well we got this one already, but what's wrong wi' *two*? Ye can record from one to the other, great larks . . . thanks, Hess, a lot.

All over the Overspill, preparations were aswing for Hattersley's first Yuletide; perhaps that is why they were more noticeable than in the old Gorton streets. Peeping in between the curtains, on every mantelpiece you saw the Christmas cards, glistening with plastic frost, aglow with loving white beards and mince pies and haloed Virgin Mothers and plum puddings and Babes in mangers, Peace on Earth and Mercy Mild. Scraps of holly and mistletoe everywhere you looked.

But every community has its rebels. Last night outside Number 12, there hadn't been much Mercy Mild when a roistering neighbor had—as Mrs. Masterson put it—"gone bersick" and beaten up her twenty-year-old son. It is unlikely that Jim, less tough than Dave, retaliated with a teapot; he and his little fiancée, Anita, fled for succor to Number 16, where Ian and Myra, evidently imbued with seasonable charity, "looked after Jim's face." Myra even drove to Hyde Police Station to report the incident. Ten months later, her visit was to be recalled with a scratching of constabulary heads.

But tonight, the eve of Christmas Eve, all is calm. The carol singers knock at Number 16, Gran produces threepence (Bless 'em), Ian adds sixpence. Then he goes back to his writing, and Gran rejoins Myra and Pat and Pat's mam, who has dropped in to see snaps Ian took of Pat with Puppet and Lassie. They are watching telly, nice thriller, *Ring Out an Alibi*. Somebody shoots somebody, Puppet and Lassie start to bark, and two doors away in Number 12, blowed if Duke doesn't bark back, saucy. Gran says it can't be very nice for the Braithwaites in between, bugger the Braithwaites. Myra steals an occasional glance at Ian, to see if he is all right.

Funny, with him having hated Christmas more every year, this time it doesn't seem to have got on his nerves at all. Look at the way he was nice to the carol singers, an' 'twas him who got the bits of holly and that bunting with the paper bell, an' when I drove him into town last Saturday, to get a Christmas disk from the record library, I couldn't believe it—Ian, when we goin' to hear it?

He turns off the telly and puts it on, a long-player by Ray Conniff (natch) and his Singers, a medley called "We Wish You a Merry Christmas." Gran loves the sleeve: a colored photo of a swinging teen-age girl in red, flecked with snow, besieged by five grinning young men all dressed as Father Christmas and carrying sacks laden with presents. The prettiest exhibit ever to feature in a murder trial.

The sweet strains echo through the cozy room. First "Jolly Old St. Nicholas," fresh young voices in harmony: *Whisper what you'll bring to me, When the clock is striking twelve* . . . Gran stops her knitting to beat sentimental time with her needle. She is about to say something when Ian puts finger to lip: the tape recorder is on. He's making his own tape of it, which of course is always the idea behind borrowing the record—if people are real sharp they can get the whole of flippin' Wagner that way, and we'll be able to hear this next Christmas as well, and all for nowt!

Then into "The Little Drummer Boy," and beyond the thin wall several dark heads are raised in smiling appreciation: Number 16 ain't meebe such forthcomin' neighbors, but they got music in there. The high, fluting voices sing of the poor lad who only has his drum to give to Baby Jesus: *I have no gifts to bring, Rumpa-pom-pom Rumpa-pom-pom, To give a King, Rumpa-pom-pom.* In Number 16, the rhythms rock them all into dreams.

The only male in the room (apart from Puppet) stops writing and opens the Gorton *Reporter*. Carefully, to avoid a crackling noise. At the ads. The music dies away, he clocks off. Gran sighs: Myra, that was loovly, your grandad an' your mam would ha' fancied that.

He turns to Pat's mother: Elsie, Myra 'n me thought for a Christmas present we'd take Pat out tomorrow night, Christmas

Eve. Let's look in the paper . . . "Ashton Palais, Gala Ball," pity she's not a wee bit aulder—"Ashton Market Wish You a Happy Xmas" . . . "Your Greatest Gift Is Life, Be a Blood Donor" . . . I've got it—Belle Vue circus! What d'ye say, Pat?

He puts down the paper and picks up his pen again. What's he writin', a letter? No, it's an exercise book.

As on the telly the nice announcer is warning to drive carefully over the holidays, to ensure that the festive season stays festive, she watches him take up his ruler and draw.

Columns.

The next morning at the office, Christmas Eve, an early finish because of the holiday. Then the traditional "bit of a do" over at Haxby's. Everybody working as usual, but it's the joky atmosphere of the last day of term. The two of them sit next to each other at the long desk. Nobody taking any notice.

Okay, Myra. Dear Serrs, Kindly send an extra container of Sodium-Hypochloride, bla bla bla, break for elevenses. Myra, I'll slip over to auld Nellie wi' her bottle o' port.

And then she'll have five minutes to try and break through to him. Mechanically she takes out colored paper, scissors and Scotch tape (ha ha) for wrapping up her presents. He's back, tea and a cig, it's now or never. Somehow easier to talk if you're fiddlin', an' folk movin' about, than in the car, which we never have done. And in case anybody hears a couple o' words, we can do it in double-talk like. An' that makes it easier too, more like a game, such as B.V. for Belle Vue, and S.P. for secret place.

Ooh Ian, I got something to dictate to *you!* Dear Sir said she timid like! Wi' reference to taking P. to B.V. tomorrow night, is it proposed to forward the Consignment by road to the S.P.?

Somebody laughs, a phone rings, a rustle of silver paper, somebody calls out, Pass me some colored string, Tony loov! And at her center she feels a warmth, and knows that he is feeling it too. The warmth of complicity. Aye, he answers. Just aye.

But Dear Sir, surely when Consignment is missed by owners, this office will be held responsible as being last seen in charge of

Consignment? Dear Sir—you mean, start off for B.V. with Consignment, and then change direction and up to S.P.? But *after* Op S.P.?

Click of typewriters. Oh, ta very much, how did you guess this was my scent? Merry Christmas.

Ian, I mean it, after Op S.P.—what? Down to B.V.? *Without* Consignment? How d'you mean, pretend to start lookin'? For Consignment? All over B.V., you mean? . . . But what will this department report re Consignment?

In his monosyllables, he explains. And up to a point it sounds feasible, even ingenious: Officer, we're worried, we brought a little girl here a couple of hours past, and a quarter of an hour ago we put the wee thing on the merry-go-round. Well, she went 'round and waved to us, then it stopped with her on the other side, we walked 'round to where she'd climbed off and she'd gone, vanished into thin air . . . No, my young lady here looked in the ladies', first place we thought of. We're that worried, Officer . . .

But doodling on her pad, staring intently at the whorls of a shell she is shading in, for five minutes she turns onto the situation the searchlight of her own common sense. For the first time. It can throw an effective beam, and up till now she has deliberately swiveled its face to the wall and floated in the outer twilight. Swivel back. Take a good look. Work it out, inside yourself.

It'd leak out that he an' me's been takin' 'er to our Secret Place an' the wine an' that, our photos'd be in the papers as the last people with her. Suppose somebody remembered seeing us at some traffic lights, also they might say what was the three of you *doing* in Belle Vue all the two hours, show where you took her and have the staff identify you, an' Christ, there might be mud an' stuff on the car. Oh no, it's too risky, I must tell 'im, now or never, brace up. An' if 'e won't see sense, I'm goin' after that Naafi job in Germany, I will I will, I'll clear out . . . 'Ere goes.

Ian, about the Consignment, it's dynamite, blow right up in our faces, get the firm a bad reputation. No, I wash me 'ands of it, that's final. Hello, Olive, just goin' to wash me 'ands, must be time for the do.

She has not dared look at him; she crams her presents into a shopping bag and follows him out. But he is in his coat and down the stairs before she has time to say "Hey." She is joined by two other girls and they walk over to Haxby's, where Tom Craig stands to greet his flock with his holiday face on, nicest moment of the year. Where's Neddie?

Over in t' corner talking to Gloria Brister. Laughing and clowning, he's got a whisky, her giggling and blushing like a Jim Idiot, she must be knocked all of a heap, he hasn't stood like that alone with one girl since he came, never never, always been me and him and nobody else— Thank you Tom sherry, Merry Christmas. Now he's pointing to the mistletoe, and my God, just for a giggle he's kissing her, all polite but it *is* on the lips, and now they're whisperin'. Well, if they leave together I'll die I'll die— Merry Christmas, sherry please. He's got another whisky, oh God, make him look this way, if it's only that sarcastic old Scotch bow-from-the-waist. No, he's turned his back— Merry Christmas, sherry please.

Out in the parking lot. It's like that terrible early time, I expect to see him get on that motorbike and off.

Worse than the early time. They're gone. Together. No no no.

She drives home, unseeing, stunned, dead. Rain . . . where's the bluddy wiper, what's the matter wi' me, I moost be real gone. After everything I've been through in this car, it's *now* I feel terrible, I just don't want to do anything but die, an' if I see another shop with a bit o' mistletoe I'll scream blue murder.

Still raining. Gran having an afternoon nap in her chair, but the house might as well be empty. Never been in it without 'im an' there's the buntin' 'e put up— No Gran, 'e's shoppin'. An' now she's goin' to tell me about Uncle Bert bringin' the Gorton *Reporter*—Myra, 'e *never* misses 'is Fridays—I couldn't care less. I'm all right, Gran, just lookin' out to see if it's stopped rainin'— 'Ow can I tell 'er I'm watchin' Mottram Road for the buses in case he's on one? *Him* on a bus, hasn't been on public transport for close on a year an' this'll teach him—oh my God, here he comes, stridin' down the path. It's all right, Gran, I'm curlin' up for a nap.

Gone straight upstairs, but not the bathroom. The bedroom.

Two minutes. Four. Five. She can bear it no longer. Up the flowered stair carpet. The door is open. He has his back to her, and holds in his hand a photo album. The one with a tartan cover. *Their* album, their very own. He stands in front of a suitcase, which he is packing.

He turns, they look at each other. Both faces empty. His eyes have the diamond glitter she dreaded to see. But now that he is home, any look is better than none.

She walks forward, takes the album from him and drops it back into the drawer of the wardrobe. Then she takes a suit out of the suitcase and hangs it back. Ye're wearin' a wet coat, she says. I'll dry it an' I'll brew some tea. Okay, he says and goes downstairs. She unpacks the suitcase, lifting from the bottom the two guns, and the binoculars. Then she follows him, locking the door.

High tea. The long festive weekend is on.

CHAPTER 20

SUFFER LITTLE CHILDREN

"Remember, Christ our Saviour
Was born on Christmas Day
To save poor souls from Satan's power
Which had lost their way."

Anon.

SEVEN O'CLOCK, Christmas Eve. The New Inn had filled to overflowing (Same all around, loov, an' keep the change for Santa), while in the little houses the television carols boomed matily from one hearth to the next, and on every floor of the seven skyscrapers, impromptu parties were starting up. Walking up Sundial Close and Pudding Lane in the crisp winter air—will it be a white Christmas?—the high hard-hitting amber light of the street lamps was softened by the carnival feel in the sky.

But Pat's mother, Elsie, was in the dumps, hubby trouble. And it had dampened her Christmas. "So I *was* pleased when there was a knock—Myra to say Ian was at his mother's in town for a Christmas visit an' back soon, an' 'ow she liked my little tree in our window wi' the colored lights, our Jim had fixed it. I said why didn't she get one nex' Christmas, for 'er sister's little Angela Dawn?

"Then she told me that after all Ian wouldn't be able to pierce Elsa's ears for 'er earrings on 'er tenth birthday, an' then Myra give me ten bob in stamps to pay for Elsa's piercin'. An' then she says, 'Oh oh, 'ere's soom figures for your sideboard.' I 'ad the idea it'd be like a tableau o' Baby Jesus an' Mary an' Joseph i' the stable, but when I opened it there was every sort o' cut-out animal stood oop wi' cello-tape! I said, ' 'Ow nice,' but I *was* disappointed. I thought to meself, we got enough animals about the place without paper ones, wi' so many dogs you expect the budgie to start barkin' next . . .

"Then Edwina come downstairs, wi' her gettin' on for fourteen she was off to a teen-age party. She looked *loovly,* all mod. Well, she 'ad some money an' felt sorry for me because I got no Christmas cheer, so bein' under age she asked Myra to go across with 'er to the New Inn to buy me soom mild beer, an' Myra did. An' while they was there, Pat took Puppet for 'is evenin' patter 'round the 'ouses, with 'is little blanket on against the cold.

"Well, after my beer, Myra asked our Edwina in to 'er place and Edwina come back 'ome wi' five presents, each in a loovly wrapping and with a card wi' the child's name an' 'Love from Myra and Ian.' They was perfectly done an' I could ha' cried at the loovly gesture to my kiddies, the time an' care that must ha' gone into the wrappin's. Then Edwina off to 'er party, then Pat off to Myra's with a box o' chocs for Ian, an' for Myra a jelly mold she'd made i' the shape of a rabbit. Then I give little Ruby an' Pete their bath, then Elsa to bed to wait for Father Christmas, then at nine-fifteen Pat run in to say Myra an' Ian was expectin' me.

"Myra's gran 'ad gone to bed, so it was just Myra an' Ian an' Pat an' me watchin' the telly, Frankie 'Owerd an' then the carols, nice fire an' drinks all laid out on the coffee table. Ian made me 'ave a gin an' Pat soom wine, the attitude of him was sittin' in his chair smokin' a cigar an' lookin' very cool an' manly. Then 'e told Myra to pour him a whisky, which she did. She looked funny at him, never seemed to take her eyes off. Then Myra said, joost chattin' like, 'Well, Elsie, 'ow's your Jim's face?' I said, 'It's better, thank God.' Then I asked Ian—because he *is* bright, is Ian— 'Ian,' I says, *'what makes a man go bersick?'*

"Well, 'e took a long pull at his cigar, still very cool an' thoughtful like, an' Myra watchin' him. Then I said, 'Ian, to do that, is there soomthin' wrong with a man's *brain?*'

"Well, 'e started off all right, I managed to get my answer. '*When a man goes berrserrk,*' he says, more an' more 'Arry Lauder, '*when a man goes berrserrk, it is nuthin' to do wi' his brain, it is a question of how much provocation he can stand.*'

"An' then he took off. An' that wasn't Scotch he was chantin', they *could* ha' been big words I never heard of that's far beyond my vocaburry, if it had a' rhymed or summat I could have put it down as Unknown Poetry. Then Gran started shoutin' down from her room, was her cuppa tea ready, and Myra shouted back, 'In a minute,' an' pulled a face at the ceilin'. Then she stared back at Ian carryin' on, I couldn't understand one word an' gettin' fed up, Pat lookin' puzzled too. Well, about ten-thirty he shuts up an' asks for another whisky.

"Then I went into the kitchen with Myra, she put the pork in the oven and a shillin' in the meter. The 'atch was open an' I could see Ian an' Pat drinkin' an' Pat watchin' the TV. 'Any other news, Elsie?' says Myra. 'Oh,' I says, 'I meant to tell you both, I'm pregnant again!'

"Well, Myra jumped past me an' shut the 'atch with a slam, then she ran to the kitchen door. 'What was that in aid of?' I said. 'Well,' she said, 'I just didn't want Ian to 'ear the word "pregnant," he doesn't like anything like that at Christmas with all this unto-us-a-child-is-born stuff.' Well, I just couldn't sort that one out. Then she said, 'Are you goin' to shift it?' I said, 'No fear,' then we went back in. An' Myra sat on the rug in front o' the fire with a glass o' wine, an' Puppet on 'er knee, an' still lookin' at Ian all the time. An' once when Ian stubs out 'is cigar, she picks the bit up an' lights the sloppy wet thing an' smokes it. Quite comic, reely.

"Then Ian says, 'Pat, what d'ye say to a run?' Then Myra says, quite worried like, 'Oh Ian, isn't it a bit late to go down there?' Then 'e says, 'Down where, we're goin' *up*, love, up up to the moors to see Christmas Day in. Come on, Pat, get your coat, an' Myra, don't forget the wee transistor!" Well, I thought, a funny way to see Christmas in, but they'd been up there so often I made nothin' of it, an' bein' Christmas I thought I'd overlook the late hour like, so I wished 'em a happy Yuletide, but nowt about a newborn babe, as you can imagine.

"Well, I took Pat 'ome an' got 'er into the warm coat an' waved 'em all off, an' as I saw the red light go out o' sight toward the moors I thought again, funny way to see Christmas in. An' then I turned out our lights, all except the 'all an' the tree in the window wi' the red bulbs, it looked eerie, then I got ready with me cotton-wool beard for the kids at midnight, an' lo an' behold, it was Christmas Day!"

At the lights in Stalybridge, with Pat prattling away on Ian's knee, he turns his head idly—and then the driver turns hers—to the poster outside the Palace: Tomorrow Sun Dec 27 THE PREMATURE BURIAL. Sun Jan 3 KILL HER GENTLY. Well I never.

"Midnight Christmas Communion." The same hallowed harmonies and the same bells that ring out the Holy Birth to every family party in Longsight and Gorton and Ancoats and Ashton-under-Lyne and Hyde and Hattersley—the same bells fill the little car parked out in the icy wind at the Secret Place. Not one other car, everybody at home. A warm li'l island of a car.

With the heat and the wine and the lateness of the hour—the latest the child has ever been up—she is falling pleasantly asleep against the sleeve of the girl at the wheel, who eleven years ago was the same age as she is now. But the one at the wheel is not falling asleep. The bells wake the child. Meek and mild.

'Appy Christmas, Myra, where's Ian?

Ian's to fetch some peat, loov, like he did before, says it's lucky to dig peat first thing Christmas Day.

But Myra, you can't dig peat without a spade!

It was in the back o' the car, loov, wi' the sack, that's what give him the idea.

Myra, can't we open a winder, it's that warm.

Pat, give over botherin' me, I like 'em shut.

But Myra, you're all of a shake!

The transistor has faded out. The dreaded silence. The child drops off again. Silence, silence. Around the car, the giant figures. Motionless, watching. No, that's not the wind, you can't fool me, it's *them*. She is glad to be terrified. If she weren't, she'd go out of her mind. He is suddenly back, and at the rear of the car.

He heaves in the sack of peat, then throws something after it. The spade falls with a clang which startles her out of her skin and wakes the child. Then he is swiftly around the other side, and into the car, on a great wolfish howl of wind. He crashes the door shut and sits back, frozen and still. But breathing hard.

She waits. The child is nodding off again. He speaks at last. The child stirs.

Myra . . .

Yes?

I reckon we go back an' drop the little lady an' pick up a coupla more rugs, an' the two of us spend the night up here, wha' d'ye say?

Her heart leaps, he's seen sense. God thank God an' he wants to come back up. With me.

The child is fast asleep. Myra, listen, you stop the car outside Number 10 an' I'll lift her out with the rug over her an' carry her along the path. Elsie'll be at her door.

And when they get home, sure enough Elsie is: Pat, I thought you was *never* comin', it's past one. You get upstairs this minute, you're droppin'. And Pat fell into her Christmas-morning bed, to sink into the dreamless sleep of the luckiest little lady in all the land.

And her mam wishes happy-Christmas-Myra happy-Christmas-Ian, you're *not* goin' straight back up there! I must say you *are* devils for picnics, talk about sleepin' rough. Well, nice work if you can get it, thanks again for the gifts, ta ra.

The taillight disappears again up to the hills. Everything all right.

They did sleep rough, and it was nice work. They were back in Number 16 by dawn, then beauty sleep for a couple of holiday hours.

But everything not all right.

For once she sleeps while he is awake, awake to the rhythm of distant revelers' cars swishing home along Mottram Road. The swishing begins to have an echo, the echoing swish of water in the sewers of Münchester. The dripping message. Disastrous Loss of Face, Immediate Coup Essential, code word S.C. for stock clerk, end of message.

Friday, Christmas Day. After midday dinner, telly, *Pinky an' Perky*, daft, it's for kids but you 'ave to watch, then the Queen's Speech, gude for a giggle, then *Disney Time*. In the evening, as they exercise Puppet and Lassie just before *Xmas Night with the Stars*, she notices him pacing by her side, along the front path, with deliberate concentration. Shut up, I'm countin', eighty-eight, eighty-nine, ninety, bugger. Ninety paces from the front door of Number 16 to the pavement outside Number 10, forget it.

Well, he couldn't. For this was the drawback to Number 16 which he had not fully realized at first, why should he have? It was all right for him and Myra to scramble up and down "the slope" in and out of the car, but once they had an unathletic companion such as Gran, or—more important—heavy luggage, they were forced to park next to the sidewalk beyond Number 10 and walk with the luggage past the three houses. Ninety paces. If Gran had been allotted 10 instead of 16, the future might have been different.

December 26, Boxing Day. Late rising, lazy hangovers from food and drink.

Unluckily for Myra it was a Saturday, and she was due to take Gran for her fortnightly visit to her son Jim Burns in Dukinfield. So at ten o'clock she trundled Gran along the footpath and into the car with Lassie, "doomped" them both at Uncle Jim's, four miles off, and left immediately, with the usual arrangement to come back for her at nine-thirty that evening.

It's a chore, she thinks as she drives home, but it does mean that for the whole day Neddie an' me'll have the house to ourselves.

Boxing afternoon, people flop about. Snooze. Watch telly. Make lazy love. Free country. If it occurs to you to make notes, you make notes. Between ruled lines. Jottings.

And if you feel like pottering about in a bedroom with gadgets, you do just that.

"I says to our Edwina after Boxin' Day dinner, 'If you're to make that dress for Myra by New Year, you pop along now and measure 'er.' Well, back she comes wi' Myra, who says rather red, 'I don't like takin' my clothes off in front o' Gran an' Ian, she can measure me here.' An' Edwina did: bust thirty-eight, waist twenty-six, hips forty-two."

And then Myra drove Ian down into Manchester and waited as usual in Dallas Street while he went into his mother's with belated Christmas presents. He seemed fine. Not only one from Myra, one from Myra's mam. And not only one from Myra's mam, one from Myra's gran. As Ian's mother was still not known to her, Myra seemed to be forcing the Christmas pace.

Sky overcast, light snow.

For Inspector Chaddock of the West Riding Constabulary, this Boxing Day was not entirely a respite—he was on his beat. And he looked the part, a fresh-faced country policeman, the country being a large slice of the moors. At the first mention of snow on the radio he was out in his little car, patrolling the mountain roads looking for trouble in the way of ice and drifts, spending the whole day "knocking about in the area."

Snow on the tops of the hills, but traffic flowed normally all day. Then at three in the afternoon the meteorological office issued a snow warning. At five o'clock it started to come down, not a heavy fall, but as a precaution, "salting" was started: the process of strewing the road with a mixture of rock salt and grit. The snow never became a problem, but the ground was definitely frozen "oop there." Boxing Night on the moors was clearly for Eskimos. Or for people who have traveled way out of the reach of cold or of heat, of laughter or of tears.

Dark by teatime, the estate is already glittering with lights; while last night was family parties, tonight is the night out: Opera House, *Dora Bryan Show;* Palace Theatre, *Sleeping Beauty* (pantomime), the dog races. *And* the Christmas fairs. Here's one advertised in Ancoats. Finish your tea an' wrap up weel, it's tryin' to snow again. I've put a new battery in the wee transistor . . . Did ye put in the cardboard box, have ye my binoculars, will the car start?

Oh memo . . . pop in to remind Elsie we're frantically busy tonight doncherknow, tapin' a concert. Hello Edwina, hello Pete, hello Elsa, hello Pat, hello Elsie, how's tricks?

Oh fine, Ian, only our Edwina 'ad a nightmare, like kids do after Christmas dinner, all that plum pudding, woke up gassin' about goblins an' that—What? . . . Pat? Oh, Pat slept like a top, ta ra for now.

The car starts all right. The enemy streets are bursting with revelers. And we know what they're celebrating. Last night's fiasco. At every traffic light, exultation written on every smug face, and ridicule.

Turn down this alley, stop. And while the male secret agent holds the hand mirror, the other opens the box and fits on the black wig. Fine. To the left, here.

In the distance, music. Exciting. Nearer. Nearer. The fair. Lights, crowds, enemy laughter melting into the martial heady merry-go-round music in the light snow. Binoculars. Slow down.

He lowers the window. Happy Christmas to ye, love, are you waitin' for somebody? . . . Weel, a wee gerrl like you can't hang aboot gettin' wet. Nip in an' we'll drop ye hame—what? . . . But your mam meant gangsters, not people like us! Nip in, loov . . . Charnley Walk? Well, you just show us—is this Iron Street? Okay, like to blow your nose? I got a hanky—there, we're off.

As the toy music of the merry-go-round dies away, the shawffer sniffs the faint sweet smell of the ethyl chloride. Nice girl, Ethyl. Kiddie's sleepin' like a top, won't wake up till we're safe an' sound by our own fireside. To the left here, into the alley—stop. Wig put away, brunette secret agent replaced by blond. Headquarters will be astonished. And the car goes steadily home. Nine miles. At traffic lights, women give warm Yuletide smiles as they glimpse the curly dark little head nestling against her young father's shoulder (Goin' home from the Panto most like, an' the little thing worn out wi' Christmas) .

The little thing is breathing peacefully. And if on the journey a childish nightmare were to invade her sleep—the hot breath of the wolf in the nightdress, the snarl of the giant, the dragon's fiery nostrils—she would wake, crying, to the instant comfort of strong warm arms.

Hyde, Mottram Road, and before we're home an' dry, big hazard. The ninety paces. Dark all right, moon won't be up till later, perfect timing, but the four houses are just about floodlit from that fuckin' tall lamppost i' the road. The Fryers in Number 10's lights are out—gude, now pass the rug an' wrap it around like las' night, now anybody that knows us will just think it's Pat lookin' smaller. You get out your side and open my door an' shield it while I lift her out—wait, there's a door openin'. Elsie Masterson—Christ, fiddle wi' the handle. Wait, she's pickin' up the evenin' paper, gone in again, closed the door, right. You walk in front, I'll stick close behind, an' whatever ye do, don't hurry, an' kindly note we're only leavin' two lots o' footprints in the snow.

Ninety long, long paces. In through the toy garden gate, boots scraped dry on the doormat. As she puts the key into the lock, she turns to give a swift look at the New Inn in case anybody is hanging about: in the light of the lamp, it is the face of a sleepwalker. And as the front door shuts softly, on the three inside the secret little dream house far from the slums, the child stirs and begins to wake.

To the nightmare.

Was there, motionless on the hill beyond the New Inn, a ghostly figure she had missed? A friend of Neddie's who had been watching out for them, on horseback, perruque under tricorn hat?

They say ghosts know everything. If the Marquis did linger, to watch the lighted window at the heart of the Overspill Estate, he cannot have stayed long. For it must soon have come to him that his pupil had made such strides that from now on, the pupil was the Master. And the ghost, smiling a thoughtful smile, rode away.

CHAPTER 21

NIGHTS OF WINE AND ROSES

"One o' these days these Boots
Are gonna walk all over you . . .
Are ye ready Boots?
Start walkin' . . ."

Pop song

MONDAY still a holiday; Tuesday, Millwards. 'Ello Myra,
'ello Ian, you were off in the car, were you? . . . Oh, joost family,
the usual overeatin' an' drinkin'. . . . I observe several empty
places this mornin', soom people got no sense o' responsibility . . .
Aye, that's right, I allus say Christmas is for the kids . . . Oh,
very quiet, y'know—joost family.

She is suddenly startled to hear him say to Tom Craig, "Tom,
how did Lesley Ann enjoy her Christmas?" She had a wonderful
time, says Tom; o' course, Tom has a daughter named Lesley
Ann (Ooh, it did give me a turn. Neddie is awful). Then Tom
said, "Did you see in the *News* about the poor little lass o' the
same name?" an' then they all started to natter. (Like bein' on a
tightrope sort o' thing, quite scary.)

Tuesday evening, Ian's duty supper at his mam's. Pat Brady:
"He didn't seem upset about anything. I didn't ask 'im how 'e'd

spent 'is Christmas as 'e was old enough to please hisself."

A present from Ian to Myra, a large calendar for 1965 with a splendid head of an Alsatian dog, and she hangs it straightaway on the hatch. Is it unlucky to put up calendars before the New Year? Anyway, there comes one cheerily unobtrusive pointer to 1965 and what it will bring: Millwards . . . Ian, the phone—a Mr. Smith.

Hiya Ian, long time no see . . . Oh fine, Angela Dawn in crackin' form an' sayin' dada, only don't tell Myra, tell her she's sayin' bowwow. Well, we got a coupla buddies in for New Year, Madeline an' a lad named Keith an' maybe two or three more, so knowin' auld MacDoonigle's feelin's 'bout Hogmanay, we thought you 'n' Myra should be along on December thirty-one for a booze-up in the auld 'omestead frae dark till dawn . . . Ah, that's great, only don't bring Lulu, I mean Gran, you know 'ow she will sit oop. Cheerio.

Ritz Hyde Dec 30 *Murder Most Foul.*

December 31. Ian and Myra arrived early at Number 13, in time to catch Myra's mam leaving with little Angela Dawn, whom (not for the first time) she was taking off the Smiths' hands. Myra gave the bundle a quick casual look; but Ian, whom nobody had ever seen kiss anybody, not even Myra, bent down and gave the infant a peck on the forehead, "just ferr luck, the Scottish New Year." (" 'E showed the kindness of a father— didn't 'e, Mo?—as much as I could meself.")

Dave's dad was home, but had been out celebrating during the day and was upstairs having an early night. It was a good party; with only a handful of people the front room was bursting with young folk, few holds barred, tons o' booze, pop music on radio and record player and enough paper decorations to mask dirt, cracks and scars. Guests remembered afterwards Myra's extraordinary vitality—vivacity almost: she had had her hair specially done in a great honey-colored bubble and wore a tight, short black sequin dress with a diamond-type brooch and her slim diamond-meshed legs looked especially striking.

She jived a bit. Somebody remarked lightly that it was as if any minute her engagement, so long kept secret, was about to be announced. Ian, considering he was a professional Scot on the most important Scottish night of the year, did not seem to drink too much, if anything less than Myra did. Once, when she got overexcited and too talkative, "he says to her, under his breath like, the two words that was always enough to do the trick. '*Shut* . . . *up*,' he says, joost like that, '*shut* . . . *up*.'" He was more relaxed and amiable with strangers than the Smiths had ever seen him.

Midnight, Big Ben, cross hands, "Lest auld"—no no no, "*Shude* auld acquaintance"—three years ago to the night. I woonder if he's thinkin' the same as me, I'll catch his eye—ooh yes he is. He's like one o' them racin' cars, terrific on the track, scare the daylights—an' yet can brake any minute, switch engine off, dead calm an' not to worry.

He is thinking, Silly lot o' bletherin' sods, they think they're the cat's whiskers. Jus' get a load o' that coupla schoolboy thugs i' the corner boastin' aboot this an' the ither. Let's give 'em the shock o' their lives an' watch their mouths drop open—no, the password is Incognito, mum's the word.

Myra and Ian were the last to leave. It was after six in the morning, and while Maureen and even Dave felt pretty whacked, the two from Hattersley were fresh as larks.

As Myra backed the smart little white car down Wiles Street past the Reades in Number 9, they must both have thought, in the ghostly early-morning light, Let's have a quick run around, "*Shude* auld acquaintance be ferrgot"—around the tight little circle of former haunts. Eaton Street, razed Bannock Street, the Bessemer, the Shakespeare, the Steelworker's Tavern. Then east out of Gorton, to the new home.

Only one call. At seven o'clock they stopped as a sleepy news-dealer unlocked his door, and Myra picked up the Gorton *Reporter*, hot from the printer. (Won't look till we're home).

Hattersley dead to the world in the brand-new New Year light, overspill oversleep. Park car in avenue under Number 16, and scramble up wall. Even Puppet asleep, just wags a delighted tail.

Coffee in the kitchen. Their heads still buzzing with the

night's music and drink, side by side at the table, with the paper unfolded across it.

They had expected a great deal, but it startled them. Right across the front page: HAVE YOU SEEN 10-YEAR-OLD LESLEY? Then the big photograph of her, smiling at you as gaily as little Johnnie did. The two of them, though, cannot have thought the picture was very like her. They had never seen her smile.

Later in the morning a little gathering, the record of which was to be very conveniently preserved. A knock at the front door, Pat wanting to show off a dress Edwina had made for her. Ian made quite a fuss of the kid, more than usual. Then they had some wine, quite a party, the three of them plus Gran and Puppet and Lassie and Joey the budgie. Just sittin' around, Myra peeling potatoes for lunch.

I see that pop singer Gerry from the Pacemakers 'as announced 'is engagement . . . I keep thinkin' it's Saturday . . . Oh Myra, *Watch with Mother*'s on the telly at 'alf past . . . Then, Pat, why don't you get your mam in 'ere, then we can all watch it . . . 'Ere, Pat, d'ye want to read the *Reporter?*

Pat took the paper and glanced at the front page: Oh look, a boy with a dog called Nigger. Myra, y'see this girl from Ancoats, she lives near my friend Glenys . . . Oh, did your friend know her? . . . I dunno.

Just sittin' around, the morning conversation of a thousand homes. Well, I think my mam'll be waiting for me . . . No Pat, sit a minute, 'ush that dog, quiet all, *listen* . . .

Watch with Mother *'ere Pat d'ye want to read the* Reporter *oh look a boy with a dog called Nigger. Myra y'see this girl*— But Myra, that's *us* natterin'!

Aye, loov—look, it's a machine, ye see, an' Ian turned it on an' it can be played back whenever convenient.

Saturday, January 2, daylight reconnaissance. Just to check everything's okay. In Stalybridge, next to a flower stall, they look at the flowers, then at each other. Same thought (Well, perhaps we *ought* to, at that), same sly smile, same naughty feeling.

Cold but dry, conditions satisfactory for recky. Standing in the wind, wonder if Neddie feels the same, sort of quiet and sad as if you'd lost two kiddies a long time ago, and got over it, and sort of thinking about it in a way nobody else knows about and nobody ever will. Home for high tea.

Then indoor snaps, flash flash—Gran and Pat and the dogs and Myra; Ian's doing some developing in the bedroom and wants to finish off the reel.

At work, the Gorton *Reporter* had made a tremendous effect: Isn't it terrible isn't it mad, there was that boy too, wasn't there, up Ashton way, isn't it mad isn't it terrible, I mean it's like one o' them werewolf film things, ooh. (Hard to keep a straight face sometimes. And just wait for *next* Friday! That Lord-Lieutenant will be at it again to his troops through a bluddy megaphone: SUNDAY'S SEARCH WILL BE THE BIGGEST THE WORLD HAS KNOWN, every Man, Woman and Child will scour Ancoats and all Suburbs from end to end. The Bereaved Family have received—an Unprecedented Move—a Message from the Queen, who will Next Week announce a State of National Emergency.)

Friday morning. They buy the paper on the way to work, and again purposely don't unfold it. They stop in a side street to have a good read over the front wheel. She turns the paper to the front page.

CONSTABLE CHASES SHOP THIEF. Five-year-old girl in Newton Heath spoken to by man, she screamed and kicked him, he ran away.

Nothing. As he crumples the paper slowly and throws it out of the window, she dare not look at him. They drive to the office in silence. Not unusual, but this silence is loaded.

Even upon one who has turned his back on reality to the extent of creating his own, unwelcome facts will keep obtruding. A second fact will loom later; the first one, as he sits at his office desk staring out of the smudged winter window, fingertips together, is upon him now.

It is the elementary truth that not only must the spy start off invisible, if successful he *stays* invisible: success and anonymity are inseparable. The blown-up bridge, the brilliantly impudent theft of the plans, they are nine-day wonders which blaze up only to wane inexorably to ashes, first red-hot, then cold. If only *something* would come through from Headquarters. Just a sign. One word.

Nothing.

And there is an added frustration. The blown-up bridge is at least there for all to see; the papers carry stupefied reports of how brilliantly the plans were stolen . . . But what of the hostage who has been so successfully liquidated that there is not one hint of the unique audacity of it? This spy is like an author who, having completed the greatest book ever penned, realizes with a pang that it can never be admired by the waiting world because it is written in invisible ink which only he can read; he and one woman, who is already stupidly taking his genius for granted.

Looking somberly around at the office workers circling like shadows outside his mind, the dreamer contemplates the dream that can't come true.

The dream that this morning the Story Broke. The Full Account. *Smack,* it hit the front page of every paper on the globe. Every hour the radio is being interrupted to convey more details, to a terrified and admiring world. As he entered Millwards, didn't every soul rise and stand with bowed head while he walked to his desk? And when later he strolls along Deansgate, he will be stared at by an awed and hatless crowd. The Beatles not in it. Unique.

Ian, this letter wants more detail on the kind o' soap we mean. Let me have it by eleven, will you?

The bubble has burst.

And up bounces his typist, what's-her-name Hindley: Ian, Tom says there's a mistake in this. Oh Neddie, ye give me a turn every time you ask how little Lesley Ann is. Don't do it again, for Pete's sake. (But she knows, damn her, she *knows, and even she has no respect!*)

In the Gorton *Reporter* of the following week, a headline on an inside page suddenly caught the eye, and the eye lit up: LANDMARK ON MOORS IS A MILESTONE IN HISTORY. It turned out to be a feature called "Country Ramble," describing a tower built in 1832, miles away.

Not a word. Might never have happened.

What are we goin' to *du?*

As week trails after winter week, the second truth begins to sink into his consciousness like a great stone that will not budge. A fact which he realizes must have entered the Lieutenant's mind too, though the Lieutenant knows better than to acknowledge its existence even to herself.

It is a fact—scaring to the nervous citizen, but any policeman will confirm—that while you will be in danger if you try to poison your next of kin, it is quite easy for a respectable man to pick up a stranger, murder him or her, dispose of the body, and never be found out. And when he is abetted by an equally respectable young woman, it's like falling off a log. Meaning that any moron could get away with it? When you feel low, it is a humiliating obstruction across the mind.

And then, slowly, the mind starts up again. Far, far away, drum drum.

Pat, don't you or your mam come knockin' this evenin', Ian's workin' on his tape-recordin's . . . Aye, he's makin' copies . . . No, loov, ye can't hear it, it's grown-up stuff, very scientific. Oh, by the way, ask your mam if you can come up to the moors tomorrow night, full moon an' it'll be just right for a little stroll. We might pick up some peat, it's done the back garden all the good in the werrld, Ian's delighted with it, ta ra.

No, Mam, I'm just sleepy, that's all. Oh, it was funny, we sat in the car wi' the music an' the wine an' Ian nattered . . . No, I only 'ad a drop, 'onest, but Ian 'ad 'is dollop an' then the moon was out, fab. Then Myra said, Ooh Pat, listen, that's the record I brought back from the office, Gene Pitney singin' Twenty-four Hours to Tulsa, an' Myra started hummin', As-We-Were-Dancin'-An'-I-Caressed-Her-Only-One-Day-Away-From-Your-Arms-Dearest-Darlin'.

Then, you see, Mam, Ian said, Now for our stroll, so the three of uzz walked along for the view, wi' yours truly i' th' middle.

Then Ian said, We'll stand just 'ere an' not move nor say nothing—as a tribute to Nature or summat. So we stood for two minutes like Remembrance Day, them on eether side 'oldin' me 'and—ooh, it was cold, I'd 'a been scared without them there. Then Ian said, We should ha' had some music, and 'e 'ummed a bit o' song, foreign I think, then I was thirsty from that wine. And Ian said, Oh look, a wee stream wi' fresh water, you bend down an' scoop it up, an' I did.

Then back to the car, we sat a bit more wi' the music on, an' soom wine—Pet Clark Downtown, then the Beatles Hard Day's Night, super, then some more wine an' we come 'ome. Ooh, I'm dead sleepy now.

Week after leaden week. He is so bored that he spends evenings pasting snaps into the family album. With the tartan cover.

Ritz Hyde Feb 15 *Black Sabbath.*

February 15, Manchester *Evening News,* front page: £100 REWARD FOR NEWS OF LESLEY "offered by Mrs. Ann Downey today for information about her missing daughter. The money has been raised by neighbors. Mrs. Downey called today at the police station, but there was no news for her."

Myra, we'll skip the moo-errs Saturday, we'll lay in a stock o' wine at Grey Street an' pay 'em a surprise visit at Number 13.

A great get-together in Wiles Street. Weel, weel, little Snow White herself, Dad caught in the act! And Myra and Ian are as struck with Dave's act as her Uncle Jim had been: the father, just seventeen, with his four-month-old daughter upside down on his knees, changing her diapers prior to giving her the bottle.

Gin with a d-dash o' milk, what d'you think. When Angela Dawn is right side up, Myra concedes that "she doesn't look bad, for a baby." Hush, our Myra—now, Dave, don't get mad, it's just her silly way of talkin', you wait till *you* start a baby Myra 'Indley—what about it, Ian?

But Myra was much more concerned that the Smiths had had to have their dog, Peggy, "put away." She was only pacified when they said they were getting a replacement, Bobbie.

Well, you p-posh 'Attersley lot, take your last look at the ole 'omestead, we're condemned as the man i' the dock said, out nex' month on the b-bloomin' ear, leastways they *say* it's condemned, maybe they just want us out. We'll go to me dad's in Ardwick for the time bein', not to worry . . . Oh, on an' off; had a coupla weeks at M-Moseley's, they make rubber an' that, then I got a touch o' t-tonsillitis an' 'ad to lay off but we got the dole, s-something'll turn up, not to worry—what's that, Ian? *'Attersley?* What, uzz in Mayfair, don't be daft, but 'ow d'you get there . . . just put yer name down, you mean? . . . Ye will? Well, ta very much—Mo, wouldn't that be just the ticket.

Ian more animated than for weeks. More like that first night last summer, the wedding night—what a relief! Two bottles. Three, four. Myra had more than usual and said she didn't want to drive. Ian suggested she tuck up with her baby sister in the marital bed, and he and Dave could sleep on the two chairs in the front room. Leaving the men to muzzy small talk, the girls went up.

A fifth bottle. Dave, ye gotta learn *Deutsch,* the only civilized language . . . My books? I got millions, d'ye want a giggle? Myra'n me walk into the big public library opposite the Midland Hotel, Myra's got her big bag. We take a cultured look around the shelves. Amazin' what that bag takes in the way o' culture, an' the bill goes straight to the ratepayers, how's that for a giggle? Your health, friend.

(Friend . . . An' me, Dave Smith, ten years younger'n 'im, an' Ian wouldn't say it 'less 'e meant it, Ian wouldn't. Ian, the choosiest chap goin', nobody gets 'is confidence, nobody, an' here we are. Terrific honor, really.) An' 'ere's *your* 'ealth, friend.

Meanwhile, upstairs, an episode which Maureen was to forget, for eight months.

With Angela Dawn asleep in her cot, there came the old routine, Mo recognized it. She, as usual, stripped completely, pulled on her nightie, threw her sister a spare, and slipped into bed. Myra took off her sweater, then turned off the light to undress (Ooh Myra, you are funny). Then Myra clicked on the light again. She was in her nightie, and got into bed.

But Myra, you 'aven't turned the light out . . . Frightened o' the dark, big deal, what's all this? But you don't leave the flippin' light on all night in Number 16, what would your bill be like? . . . You mean you're okay so long as *Ian's* there? Well, that's love, I must say. Pass me that *Evenin' News,* I'll have to put it over me 'ead if I'm to sleep—Oh, did you see, that poor Mrs. Something-or-other is offering a 'undred-pound reward to anyone who finds 'er little girl, must ha' thought the world of 'er. Goo' night. . . . Our Myra, what are you shakin' for, are you cold? . . . But you're laffin' —you're drunk, our Myra, that's what you are. Goo' night . . .

Our Myra's mirth subsides, and under the reassuring dusty bulb she drifts into hazy sleep. Nice change going on a visit.

Under her, the snores of menfolk. And over her there crawls, like a beetle across a grey wall, a trail of unease.

From then on, the weeks seem to fly. Spring. The front garden a treat, giant nasturtiums on their side, which Gran hates. Jealous. And the back lawn shows the benefit of the peat, beautiful green grass, best on the estate.

The drums. That bit nearer. And the Giant Rat on its way. Drum, drum, drum.

On April 5 the white mini-van was replaced by an even smarter little mini-Countryman, "color surf-blue, can drink less fuel than a camel and carry a family with *all* their luggage in style, 4 seats convertible to 2 plus 35½ ft. max. baggage capacity."

Ritz Hyde Apr 12 *Act of Murder.*

Sunday, April 25, noon, a timid knock. On the doorstep two orphans, Maureen and Dave. Her eyeblack smudged, his eyes sore too. Last night in Ancoats Hospital, six-month-old Angela Dawn, whom Ian had kissed at the New Year, for luck, had died of bronchitis.

The wine helped, as well as looking around the little house and admiring everything, then cans were opened and they had a snack, Ian's favorite macaroni cheese. It was such a fine day that Ian suggested a run, a christening for the new car. The Smiths' first excursion since the Lake District, just what they needed.

Off in the sun, picnic outing to Whaley Bridge in Derbyshire, smashin' beauty spot. Ian introduced his guests to what he called his secret valley. Nothing special, just a scoop with a bit of a cave, shut in and free from trippers.

Sandwiches, wine, then it got dark. Home by nine, snack, and then Ian had a lot more wine, very chipper, an' says, I 'aven't seen Braithwaite for days. An' then he says, in 'is Neddie voice, Funny we got a spade i' the scullery an' five Spades nex' door, ha ha, an' now we're awa' again, to another special spot of our own—an' then off in the dark, different direction. Myra fine at the wheel, but her sister did notice that once, when she accidently jumped the lights and spotted a policeman walking toward them, she jerked down on the brake and said, "Oh my God, I'm for it, oh my God." But the bobby went by.

Up to the moors, somewhere. Neddie had been drinking steadily, and when he got out he was lurching, unusual for him. Maureen turned down the idea of a stroll because of her shoes, and anyway, it was chilly. As Ian and Dave walked off in the moonlight, Myra shut all the windows, locked the doors and turned on the headlights. Maureen asked her what on earth for; she said she just felt safer that way.

Ian, on the stroll, got on to all the old political stuff. Dave couldn't follow a lot of it, a load o' b-balls about Churchill, Ian callin' 'im a cigar-smokin' twit, an' wi' the old boy only gone a coupla months it seemed a bit m-much, an' anyway, what about Ian's cigars, but let it ride. "Then Ian stopped an' said, You stand just 'ere, this is *the* view. But you really couldn't see much, water miles below an' everything still an' ghostly like."

Then the two walked back to the car, Myra drove the Smiths to Gorton, dropped them, and drove Ian home. The little outing had achieved its object, and taken the Smiths' mind off tomorrow's pathetic little ordeal. The burial of their baby daughter.

Then Myra read in an article in the Woman's Mag about smoking giving you cancer and gave it up. Just like that. And nearly every night the Four Musketeers met, either at Wiles Street or on to Hattersley. The month of May brought proof that where fiction fears to tread, real life flourishes the coincidences—

Gran suddenly read out from her *Reporter:* "The mother of Lesley Ann Downey has applied for fresh accommodation a reasonable distance away from Ancoats. Sympathetic Manchester Corporation has allotted her a house in Hattersley, near Hyde."

About this time, Myra and Ian paid a rare visit to a pub. Not the New Inn opposite, but the Chapman Arms on the other side of the estate. Not far from 4 Bowden Close, Mrs. Downey's new address. She and Alan West used to drop in of an evening, and the occasional habitué would offer sympathy. Whether a young couple ever accosted her who answered to such and such a description (Mrs. Downey, the change will do ye good and the fresh air blows in fresh from the moo-errs) she could not later recall.

The days fly faster, somehow. July 1, the Ross Ensign camera sold in exchange for a Fujica, super Japanese color job. And Maureen noticed that Myra too was living beyond her means, and joining more and more "clubs," a North Country variation of installment buying. "She 'ad a dress for every day of the week, didn't she, Dave?" Elsie Masterson: "Oh, that July Ian an' Myra was kind, our Elsa got knocked down by a car and in Ashton 'Ospital and of a Saturday, on their way to Gorton to the Smiths', to arrange the move, they give me a lift, Myra was quite concerned about Elsa."

And on the twenty-third the Smiths made the same giant step as the others ten months before. After eight weeks with long-suffering Nellie Hindley in Eaton Street, they moved. Not only to Hattersley, but to a home that suited Dave to a T and made him feel "p-proper with it"; not one o' them sissy little houses, but a flat in one of the seven skyscrapers, the one that towered just behind Wardle Brook Avenue with the super-posh name of Underwood Court. Flat 18, third floor. The host had got some wine in—they had acquired the taste, too—and that evening Ian and Myra walked up for a housewarmin' booze. If you cut through Sundial Close and across Pudding Lane you were there in three minutes, as near as in Gorton. In the serenely fading summer light, the late gardeners were pottering about: the Overspill at its best.

To the Smiths, Underwood Court was a Garden of Allah lifted out of Hollywood. Outside the glass doors, a row of buttons, you pushed the number you wanted then you spoke into a little grill, and there was a printed sign: WHEN THE BUZZER GOES PLEASE PUSH FRONT DOOR. Beyond the spacious hall, a great Notice Board for Tenants, a door saying LAUNDRY and TENANTS' STOREROOM, and a sign saying NO DOGS ARE PERMITTED. Sez you—coom on, Bobbie, straight into the lift, loov, an' don't bark. The only indication that the estate was not always what it might be, was another prominent sign outside the front portals: WILL PERSONS PLEASE KEEP THIS DOOR CLOSED FOR THEIR OWN INTERESTS.

And from the roomy flat a marvelous view: frontways, from the bedrooms, the doll's estate, with the back garden of Number 16 lost in the scramble like a crumpled handkerchief—and sideways, outside the big sitting-room window and its glass door, a real Hollywood balcony, overlooking the rolling countryside of roofs and fields shelving up to the skyline of the moors. Whoopee! Mr. and Mrs. Elvis Presley joost planed in from the coast and are at the Waldorf Towers, kindly open up the wine, the fillum stars are 'ome . . . What's that, Mo? *Fillum?* Did I say it like that, I reckon it's a thing I must ha' picked up from Ian.

Not the only thing. Mrs. Masterson: "I asked Phoenix Braithwaite if 'e'd conversed wi' young Dave an' 'e said no, an' then 'e said one day 'e was passin' Dave an' Ian, an' 'eard Dave say soomthink not very nice."

The drums. Nearer. And the Giant Rat has left the message. And is paddling back. Urgent. Two words: Enlist . . . aid. Drum, drum, drum. ENLIST AID.

Ritz Hyde Jul 26 *Never Mention Murder.*

A couple of evenings later, the film stars descended from the Towers and dropped in on what Dave called the Small Fry at Number 16. The usual, Gran went to bed, fish an' chips an' wine; then at twelve Maureen got sort o' fed up and walked home to the Towers; then Myra went into the kitchen to rustle up some sandwiches. While she was gone, more wine and Ian started talking about "the crime situation."

Soon as Ian got on to one of his p-pet things, talk about gift o' the gab, he'd fix you with them eyes an' you gave 'eed. 'E'd 'a made a swell politician, an' if there'd ha' been a N-Nazi Party I swear he'd 'a got votes, very novel his views were.

Bank jobs were touched upon. Guns, we got two. Dave pricked up his ears, he was still enough of a telly-fed teen-ager to find guns glamorous. Hobby that could lead anywhere, you interest me.

Then they got on to general topics, rock-'n'-roll, birth control, Jews, Negroes, violence. Murder. Now listen, Dave—when ye consider that dyin' is the one thing tha' happens to everybody, what's wrong with it happening errly rather than late, an' as Nature makes murder the easiest thing in the world if ye have the gumption, then wha's so wrong aboot it? Listen, kid, didn't Nature murrder your own wee gerrl at the age o' six months— Oh, the d-daftest line o' backchat, 'e got a gift o' the gab, all right.

Then he got on to sex.

I'd knocked about a g-good bit in my time, but as a rule it's been s-straightforward stuff, if you know what I mean. But Ian said, You 'aven't lived till you've been on a s-sex kick, an'—same as the bank-job bit—he said it so quiet an' strong like, you just 'ad to 'ark to 'im. Well, I said, spill the b-beans, Dave's broadminded. Then he said, I wouldn't do this for many guys, but I'll open your eyes. Give give, says I, an' he goes to a drawer an' takes out these three or four books. One o' these, he says, ye'll read carefully, and I've marked passages for you to get by heart, it's on the top. Thanks, Prof, I says, f-fabulous.

Justine, or *The Misfortunes of Virtue.*

Myra back with sandwiches, another bottle. Two A.M., whispered good-nights, and young Dave emerges from the garden gate of Number 16. His slim silhouette in the watery moonlight, bundle of books under arm, is of a callow student wending his way home from his tutor. Set texts. A bookish boy, and if Elsie Masterson were at her window instead of asleep since ages, she would murmur that there's 'ope for teen-agers yet. After the student has jumped the white rail, and down the wall by Myra's car, as he proceeds around into Sundial Close there is a slight weave in his walk, but that is corrected by Pudding Lane.

Maureen is asleep, and the student settles eagerly if heavily at the sitting-room table. As he sits with his books before him, next to a glass of wine, he would look, from the balcony, as if he were studying for a scholarship. Burning the A.M. oil. He looks at titles, *Tropic of Cancer, The Perfumed Garden, Mein Kampf,* that's a funny one, then takes the one recommended by his tutor and opens it at random.

A couple of long words, like fishbones. He frowns, and tries to mouth them. Perhaps he won't pass after all. He turns to the beginning.

The first line, without galvanizing him, nearly makes him call into the bedroom, "Our Mo, soom old foreign boogar's wrote a book about you!" For *Justine* kicks off with "There were two sisters, very unlike each other." But before Dave can have a good look at Juliette, "carefree and gay," she is off on her primrose path, in search of "money and love's delights." And hell he is landed with Justine. After a ten-page crawl the truth dawns: the old boogar's a flippin' cheat.

To start with, where the 'ell are the four-letter jobs? And on top of that, there suddenly appear words of dropsical size which would baffle a professor: "The third bandit forced on her his outlandish fancies; he was a scatalogomaniac." The irritated student murmurs "Shit" and presses on, nearer the mark than he knows.

Turning more pages of "an important cultural event," he arrives at the Count's Hymn to the Comforts of Sodomy. The Count is addressing Justine, who badly needs comforts, but these seem unlikely. " 'My dear, the sweet illusion of being no longer a man, but a woman! What delirium to be, during the same twenty-four hours, the mistress of a porter, a Marquis, a valet and a Duke!' " "L-little Man," Dave mutters thoughtfully, "you 'ave had a busy day."

He picks up the book and mooches into the bedroom. Maureen stirs: "Dave?"

"That Ian's dead kinky, listen to this for kicks!"

She sits up, acquiescent as always, and reaches for cold cream and tissues. "What is it, summat smutty?"

Laboriously he reads the words out one by one: " 'The whip was a s-stimulant to their l-loobricities—' "

Maureen's hand, rubbing her face, is arrested. "To their loo what?"

"Search me, all I know is the old Marquis does top it up a bit. ''E p-punished the girls by l-lashin' them—'"

"Ooh, what a nasty man—"

"'Thirty lashes for anyone not up at the prescribed hour in the mornin'.' Well, our Mo, that's you b-black an' blue for a start!"

She is nodding off, the student undresses and slips into bed. And there, as like as not, the vicarious sweetmeats hoped for from *Justine* are replaced by a spot of matrimonial conjugation. Before shut-eye, the teen-age hubby has another quick look at the old French freak. "'Ark at this, 'Why should a woman enjoy while a man is enjoyin'?'"

But Maureen is asleep. And in two minutes so is Dave, with the Marquis flat on the floor. The author of one-of-the-greatest-forbidden-books-of-all-time has missed the bus.

Give the ole boogar a second chance. Next evening, dead sober, Dave settles to his homework. One of Ian's shorthand pads, ballpoint. First, as advised, he writes—in admirably neat backward-sloping capitals: NOTES TAKEN FROM BOOKS I HAVE ENJOYED, COPYED FOR FURTHER ENJOYMENT, JUSTINE. Hard to find the hot bits, but here goes: "HE SAID THAT WHAT SHE REFUSED HIM HE WAS GOING TO TAKE BY FORCE . . . LET JUSTINE STRIP HER-SELF NAKED—"

The buzzer. Ian's voice: It's me . . . Come on oop. Suite 18. Maureen in the kitchen.

'Ello Ian, I'm s-surmisin' ole D-Dee Sad.

Ye mean "summarizin'."

That's right, s-surmisin' . . .

Weel, Dave, wha' does it do for ye?

Wow, says Dave, lifts his head and meets a sly, steady smile. No question of physical seduction, but it is the same dry-mouthed, equivocal look which the homosexual gives to the young friend whom he knows well, but is in the one direction unsure of, and whom he has just tried out with some extreme drawings—weel, wha' does it do for ye? And the embarrassed friend, to save feelings, pulls a face and in silence turns the page. The silence, by mistake, implies complicity. And when Dave pulls a face, it is a young face but not an innocent one; if he puts on his sexy puss, as he does now, projecting the lower lip and narrowing the eyes, he looks a proper lecher, which the fastidious tutor could never ·do.

And the tutor is taken in. *It's going to work.*

Saturday afternoon, the four up to the moors. Afterwards Dave wasn't able to locate the place, but it was somewhere near a spot which Myra and Ian seemed to know well. Myra parked the car and they all hiked across a mile of rough ground to a wild part, with hills around, which Ian said was his second Secret Valley.

Then, out of her big leather shoulder bag, Myra produced the two loaded revolvers. Puppet was scampering excitedly around her feet; she hardly ever brought him up to the moors, but for some reason he was there. The girls hung back while Ian and Dave walked off to practice shooting at old oil drums.

As Dave's shots reverberate and birds squawk up from no- where, he feels the power creep pleasantly through him. Then he watches his friend. In his narrow sports trousers, black shirt and dark glasses, Ian looks a proper James Bond. Crack crack, he's a shot as well, can hit a stone at thirty yards, must get meself a pair o' dark glasses. Dave, have I impressed you? Ian, you 'ave.

"Then, without Ian nor me noticin', over the hill there come a ruddy crowd o' sheep wi' one o' them funny countrified blokes, I suppose you'd call 'im a shepherd, an' in two ticks Puppet's havin' a mad go at the lot of 'em.

"Well, it seems that fellows like that 'ave a license to carry firearms and shoot dogs that worry their sheep, though it doesn't 'ardly seem right—anyways, this shepherd lifts his rifle an' aims at Puppet just as Ian rests his pistol on one o' them broken-down stone walls an' takes a steady aim at the shepherd. Honest, I thought the chap 'ad 'ad it. Then Myra rushes forward at the shepherd, screamin', 'Don't shoot the dog, for God's sake *don't shoot!*' Then everything calmed down, but it was a near go."

In the evening, back to the Towers, lashings of wine; then the girls went to bed and the men sat up, like that time in Bannock

Street. This was to become routine, but always at the Smiths', never at Number 16. There the idea somehow never came up because—though the room upstairs was after all "Myra's bedroom"—there was never any question, if Maureen wasn't there, of her leaving the men, going up to the single bed and sleeping in it alone. Never.

And that night Ian talked. Since the baby died Maureen had been back at her job, part-time machinist with her mam in Gorton, but Dave had been off work from Moseley's (tonsillitis again?) and any minute they were going to be behind with a li'l thing called rent. Ian certainly knew the ropes. He showed Dave his exercise books with the bank lists: Watch Premises, Count Staff, Work Out Slackest Period, ecksettra.

Well, try anything once, but just a minute, Ian, these guns—I sound a bit chicken, but they'd have blanks, huh?

Ye leave that to me, mate, I'm nickin' 'em, an' for why? 'Cause they're more painful that way, believe you me, but we only use 'em in a real tight corner. Now, I want you to go next Saturday mornin' and watch the back door o' this bank I've wrote down, in Stockport Road, and make a list of the employees who come out, and of any heavy cases being carried, ecksettra ecksettra. (Well, li'l Dave could do wi' some cash.)

And on Saturday morning, there he was, stationed at the prescribed spot, making laborious notes. Nine to twelve-thirty, a good timekeeper for once. He'd have liked to wear his new dark glasses, but realized they would draw attention. He made believe he was James Bond, but after an hour's jotting he felt more like those nippers running after train numbers. Not so long ago he was at it himself, in Central Station.

He was not having half such a good time as the Master, sitting in Number 16 with the glass of wine and picturing him obeying the secret orders. When that evening the four meet again, the new Lieutenant's report is passed as satisfactory.

On August 27 a link was broken: Pat and Peggy moved from Westmoreland Street to Heywood, ten miles away. A much better district, yet Ian made no move to visit them there, with or without Myra. It seemed part of the closing in on himself.

September. More and more evenings with the Smiths, shuttling between Number 16 and the Towers. Heck, what's it all in aid of?

Saturday the eighteenth, the two were to start their week's holiday (Gosh, is it on us already). And Ian abruptly announced they would spend it in Glasgow. With the Sloans. It was startling, for not only had he never expressed any wish to return there with Myra, he had so much avoided discussing his beginnings that she did not know he was illegitimate.

On first thought, the plan would seem a contradiction of his withdrawal into his own shadows. But was it? Could he be feeling a premonition? Having just lost Westmoreland Street, was he suddenly impelled, before a half-glimpsed door would slam and lock, to burrow backwards into childhood?

Or with the increasing momentum of his inner life, was he being driven back to his home city in order to leave on it his own special mark, invisible but devastating? Was the restless ablebodied young hunter thirsting for the thrill of the chase?

Myra did know that the Sloans had been much more his family than his own mother, whom he had kept so consistently from her, and she was touched and elated. "I felt," she was to be quoted in a rare gabble of revelation, "I felt he was accepting me, proper. Oh, after all that time it was a *loovly* feeling!" With a racing win, he bought her a little methylated stove so they could camp out on the way, and even up there.

Elsie, this is Ian, can I come in? What d'ye say to Myra'n me whizzin' Pat up for a campin'-oot holiday, Loch Lomond? . . . But Pat just started school again, Lakes Road Secondary, Dukinfield. Bad luck, Pat.

'Bye Mo, 'bye Dave . . . Och Dave, mind ye keep Saturday for the auld session!

But Neddie, we don't 'ave to be back before Sunday night . . .

Ah, but we canna miss our Cotter's Saturday Nicht, can we, Dave?

Off to Glesga. A beautiful day, exactly like the honeymoon trip, and as they follow the same route through the Lake District she is reminded of a missing presence. She knows, as surely as if

he spoke, that he is reminded too, and that he would sooner have
David Smith at his side.

(What's this dirty-books bit? What's he after, a foursome?
Well, it's been done wi' four, so I'm told, all strangers—but me,
Neddie, Dave an' Mo, *crikey*. Well then, a threesome, Dave an'
him an' me? Dave wouldn't fancy it any more than me, not with
an in-law, but all I know is, I can't go through last Christmas Eve
again an' watch him go off with a girl, I dunno.)

And so she flounders. (I don't fancy a row in the car, he'd just
walk out with it on the move an' sprain 'is ankle again. In Pollok
I'll bide me time an' *then* tackle 'im. I must keep it up about the
robberies, but I will mention that it's tricky 'avin' David Smith
around so much, because he *might* latch on an' that would never
do.) D'ye want some wine, loov? It's in the basket.

Pollok. 'Lo Ma, 'lo May, 'lo Jean. John Sloan had died several
years before and May was married, Mrs. Smellie.

Smellie, ha ha, this is Myra, everybody.

Pleased to meet ye. . . . Behind the monosyllables, the nervous
tension of the age-old confrontation: the foreign bride-to-be
(understood) being presented to the family. And the family noticed how childishly anxious Ian was to prove to her—as if it
needed proving—how Scottish he was.

To Ma Sloan, tinier and more deaf than ten years ago, it must
have been a strange reunion. The foster sisters high-spirited and
friendly—trousers an' that—could make little of tongue-tied
Myra miles from home, but she desperately wanted to be liked
and did her best.

But "the lass seemed absent-minded—not *with* ye. Werrse than
Ian used to be." In a trance, self-sufficient, smiling the fixed smile
and answering with the useful phrases. She only came to life when
showing snaps of Puppet. Ian had the Japanese camera and a lot
of color film and took endless photos. Outwardly a successful
reunion plus girl friend.

Marked by one incident which the Sloans were to recall. Ian
and what's-her-name had been to the pictures. They had a good
choice that week: Central Glasgow *Peyton Place* plus *Secret
Agent FX18* in cinemascope. Waverley Shawlands *The Killers*.
ABC Govan *The Killers*.

When the two got back to Templeland Road it was clear—the way a close couple will betray sudden disharmony—that they'd quarreled: he paler and more silent than ever, she flushed and shaking. It could be that she had "tackled him" and that he had snapped back, reminding her between clenched teeth that he needed neither David Smith nor her nor anybody in the whole fuckin' werrld. He was off for the night "to look up some pals."

For the Sloans that evening, it was distressing to watch this alien girl in their midst, utterly at a loss. Having appeared "tough as nails"—not the first or last time for the phrase—she was suddenly a bewildered child. They brought out family snaps, Ian at five outside Camden Street in the Gorbals, the two growing girls behind him, Jean's protective hands on his shoulders. Look, May, what I'm showin' Myra—isn' he sweet, an' them wee socks, an' look, I mind weel, your auld sneakers!

(Oh, it's a loovly snap, there he is, lookin' up past me at a grownup in the street, with a funny little 'alf smile as if he's too shy to smile proper. Where have I seen that before—o' course, little John on the poster, it's the *same!* . . . It's like family. Makes you want to sniffle. Nobody but me could understand how I feel.)

When he returned, it was certainly well into the night. Where he had been and what he had done, nobody knows. And it is fairly likely that nobody ever will, though that is not for lack of later zeal on the part of the Glasgow police.

If that night he *was* up to "mischief," the agony of mind which tortured Myra Hindley—in a strange bed in a strange city, alone and with the light on—was the oddest form of jealousy ever to rack a human being. But even if he wasn't up to mischief, lying there she must have thought he was; dreading that for the first time she was excluded, forcing herself to the agony of picturing him. And she had a choice of pictures. On the rack because she was imagining him, at that moment, being unfaithful to her, by . . . All right, say it. Unfaithful to her by disposing of a Commodity behind her back, in a secret place she will never know.

But nothing. Next day back to normal, second visit to Loch Lomond, more snaps. Several in the Pollok house: Myra having tea with May and Jean, one of little Ma asleep on a sofa with her shoes off, and of course endless views of the Loch. One afternoon, in a specially cynical mood, he took Myra sightseeing in the Gorbals, producing for the tartan album some particularly sordid snaps of Camden Street.

Gudebye Ma, gudebye Jean, gudebye May, wavings from the car window. Ma had been touched by the visit, but knew him less than she ever had: he kissed her goodbye, which he had not done before. Was there again a premonition?

Back to the routine: Saturday night, the rotten old session, and Monday, Millwards. She certainly feels better for the change, one should get away more often. Dear Serrs, in answer to yours of the twenty-therrd, the wine, the outings. Dave seems pleased they're back. With his time lying heavy, he fancies his mornings exercising Bobbie in the "valley," a countrified dip behind the houses. I'm doin' the landed-gent bit. Look, I've cut meself a stick, I throw it an' the ole 'ound runs for it doncherknow Jeeves, but you can't spend your life on walks. Good to have Ian back.

More outings, more sessions, more color pics. The owner of the camera, oddly, features in none of these, not even the scenic ones. Except once, by accident. In the foreground of an idyllic sunlit shot of Puppet and Lassie bounding up with sticks in their jaws, there lies a black shadow thrown from behind the camera. The murderer.

Then on several fine mornings, six o'clock or thereabouts, there was Ian up at the Towers, on the buzzer to wake Dave up and tumble him out of bed to come down and trample smartly up and down the "valley": Ian dressed for the office, not a speck of dust anywhere, up and down, down and up, my philosophy this, my philosophy that. One morning he'd keep this up right till office time; another time he'd be gone after barely five minutes.

Then comes the evening the exercise book is out, ruler, abbreviations, Maureen in the bathroom, Myra in the bedroom. Dave peers over: What's cookin', Ian, bank job? Weel, it'll be in a coupla Sundays, depends how I feel, but no' a bank, Crossley Brothers in Pottery Lane, or maybe the Electric an' Gas Board Showrooms in Hyde Road, they only have two on staff Saturdays as opposed to eight, easy as pie. Dave is impressed.

Myra returns and looks across the room at them. (Funny how

different the two are, Dave lolling about like an overgrown kid, and Neddie . . . He's bubbling up to some sort of boil, every day faster.) She cannot help catching it. Faster. Nothing she can do. Like watching your own car, the brake kaput, reversing down the slope leading to the precipice. Slow at first, then less slow . . .

Saturday, September 25. A heavy night at the Towers. Dave in his sharp new Beatle jacket, dark grey, no lapels, high at back of neck with red lining. There was one comic incident that had to make Dave laugh every time he thought of it.

Ian was sitting there by the open door to the balcony, excited and drinking and humming Walk in the Black Forest when all of a sudden something sort o' flurried across the light, and Ian jumped two feet into the air. "Myra," he shrieked like a kid, "get it out of 'ere! That ruddy big daddy-longlegs—get the paper an' shoo it onto the balcony—kill it, *kill it!*" She killed it, all right. Dave was highly amused, but Ian had been dead scared.

Then the excitement subsided, and Dave did notice Myra with her eyes fixed on Ian.

(Neddie's chantin' that German an' then lookin' absent-minded, watch out.)

The drums. They're here. At last. At the city gates. Enlist aid. IMMEDIATE.

The girls to bed as usual, leaving the boys in the sitting room. The real drinking started. Dave, how's the notebook? Well, Dave had kept it up fitfully, but his copying-out was inclining more and more to long furtive extracts, in the same good neat capitals, from two favorite novels. The furtiveness hardly seems necessary, considering they had both been American best sellers, once found in Park Avenue drawing rooms and now on the shelves of British public libraries. *The Carpetbaggers:* "RINA WAS STANDING CLAD ONLY IN A BRASSIERE AND A PAIR OF PANTIES . . . HIS HAND REACHED UP AND TOUCHED HER BREAST . . ." *Eternal Fire:* "ONE BY ONE THE BUTTONS SLIPPED AWAY, EXPOSING POPPIE'S MILKY BACK, THE PINK BAND OF HER BRA PRESSED IN HER FLESH . . ." There was enough philosophy, though, to please the Master. From the Marquis: "RAPE IS NOT A CRIME, IT IS A STATE OF MIND, GOD IS A DISEASE WHICH EATS AWAY A MAN'S INSTINCTS, MURDER IS A HOBBY AND A SUPREME PLEASURE."

Three bottles. Four. Five. Ian looking at him as if sizing him up. Six. Almost looked as if he was going to put a proposition sexwise; half as a joke Dave said so. His friend took offense, rose to his full height and said, "What d'ye take me for, a bluddy perrverrt?"

Then they got yakking about the bank job, and Dave reiterated about if the guns had real bullets, no deal. A long pause, then Ian swayed to his feet and looked out into the blackness. Dave realized afterwards that it was the window facing east. The moors. When Ian turned around he looked strange, excited, like somebody about to jump off something. It was like a sex thing too.

Then he took up Dee Sad and read aloud from him: " 'Nature is sufficient, and needs no creator . . . Did not Romulus permit infanticide?' " It was all the disciple needed; in a couple of minutes he was snoring.

Saturday evening, October 2. Same deal, the Towers, wine wine wine. Pencil, paper, ruled lines. The girls to bed. Wine wine wine. Dave asked if the payroll snatch was on.

Long pause, then Ian swayed to his feet and looked at him. Same look again, as if he were going to jump. Then he said thickly, "Would ye consider yourself capable of murrder?" Dave shrugged at the age-old question popular at parties, muttered something about extreme circumstances and t-temper and provocation, but pretty well said no.

Pause. Then Ian said, "Dave, ever 'ated anybody?" Then Dave said, "Well, there's people I like, there's people I don't like— quite a few—an' there's two or three I 'ate."

"Gie me the name o' the one ye hate the best, an' I'll let ye watch me polish him off."

"Come again—'ow d'you mean, polish 'im off?"

Then Ian said, deliberately and clearly, never taking his eyes off him, "I have killed several people, and *you* have stood on the grave of one of 'em."

"Oh yeh?" A leg-pull, but was he supposed to play along, you never knew with Ian. Not knowing what else to do, he returned the steady look without flickering. The stoned mates holding their liquor. And to the older of the mates, the younger one's look again conveyed connivance. "Aye," Ian went on, the words that had been so long pent up spurting gleefully out, "there are two ways to murder, either to see somebody in a quiet street an' get out an' do it, or bring them home an' do it in the house. Ye find that it's tricky pickin' 'em too young, they attract too much notice. Teen-agers is a better bet, they get forgotten an' labeled as missin' perrsons." Pause. "I do one every six months."

Pause. "Oh aye?" Pause. "I'm no' due for anither one till Christmas." Pause. "Oh aye?" Pause. "Aye, this one will be out o' sequence." Pause. He was swaying, but the look had not flickered.

Dave yawned and drained his glass. "Don' know 'bout you, mate, but I'm 'ittin' the sack." He turned out his light and curled up in his chair. As he closed his eyes he felt the other still looking at him, then heard him say, clearly, "It will be done." And then Ian flopped onto his chair.

Wha' was all that in aid of? 'E *is* a rum card. Woonder which Saturday he's plannin' bank job for. And Dave was asleep.

Weel, weel. He doesna believe me, the little pip-squeak just doesna believe me. Harrd for him to take, in so many werrds. Flatterin', reely. But that settles it. *It will be done.* He too is asleep.

They are all asleep. The Four British Musketeers, family type.

Tuesday, October 5. Just after five, Ian and Myra driving home from work, a wonderfully balmy evening. After a long silence, in Knutsford Road he clears his throat. And she thinks, Here it comes.

By the wa', tonight we put awa' the stuff.

The stuff, Neddie?

Aye, anything offbeat, guns an' that, get it awa' frae the hoose i' case. I'm givin' Dave orrders too, to bring his stuff.

She thinks, That'll be dirty books, he's never put stuff away before. It's to show off to David Smith.

As they turn into the warm twilight of Hyde Road, and east for home, she says offhand, What's David Smith to do with us? A pause, then his level voice continues, He's in on it, he doesna ken yet, but he is. Her heart sinks into her stomach. Then, carefully, and getting Scottish as she always does when trying to pacify him: But Neddie, we've always managed, why a therrd party noo? He answers in the level voice, Because cerrcumstances change; as things get more complex, help is essential. An' if we're caught, which will *not* happen, ye must imagine yersell in an airport wi' your luggage searched, it's full o' contraband. Well, ye're just to say ye dinna ken a thing aboot it, it must ha' been planted on ye. Contraband's the key word an' don't ye give away a thing, an' tonight in case o' trouble—*which will not happen*—I'll teach ye a code, what a superrb evenin'.

And that was that.

After high tea the Master, close on seven o'clock, walked up to Underwood Court and spoke to Dave on the buzzer. Dave went down, and "Ian said for me to bring the books, in case my dog Bobbie got at 'em an' corrupted 'imself." At about eight Maureen noticed Dave leave with a brown-paper parcel. The student returning his textbooks, exam over. *Mein Kampf, Tropic of Cancer, The Perfumed Garden, Orgies of Torture and Brutality, Kiss of the Whip, Justine.* And his notebook.

Dave found Gran and Myra in the sitting room. Myra took the parcel, put it on the table, went to the door and called up the stairs, "Ian, Dave's brought the books." Ian came down from the bedroom and took the parcel. By this time Gran was out in the kitchen, and Dave asked Ian and Myra, as she was getting into her coat, what was the big idea? Ian replied that whenever planning a B.J., it was his precaution to get incriminating stuff off the premises.

Then he took the books upstairs into the bedroom, and three minutes later came down with two packed suitcases. Dave took one, they went out, Myra vaulted over the railing down the slope while the others heaved the cases down to her, and Ian—in high spirits—called out, "For God's sake, don't drop one, it'll blow us all up!" Then Myra and Ian drove off, Manchester way, cases in the back. Dave went home, apparently under the vague impression that the B.J. would be the following Saturday and that he would be briefed between now and then.

On the short walk between the little houses, he may have wondered two things. First, what a bunch of sex literature—which you can buy in Manchester's posh bookshop—could have to do with a bank job. Secondly, why the hurry to clear the "incriminating" stuff out on a Tuesday, when the job isn't being plotted till Saturday at the earliest? He was never to mention that either of these thoughts had perplexed him, though it would have been in his favor if he had. He may have been so much under the older man's thumb that he shrugged his shoulders and thought, Well, Big Boss must know what he's doin'. Home to the Towers, telly, end of *Z Cars*, supper, bed.

By now the other two are home. Next to the sleeping Master, the First Lieutenant, faced with new and alarming marching orders, lies realistically awake. Neddie's mad, it's dangerous, mad mad mad.

But there is more than just realism to her disquiet. She is more filled with hate than if he were at this moment in a hotel bed with another woman. For she is threatened with having something, more precious than life, wrested from her and shared with a stranger. The Secret.

As she dozes off, she sees the nightmare car retreating, inch by inch, down the slope. Faster. That lump David Smith.

Wednesday, October 6, 1965.

CHAPTER 22

THE NIGHT OF THE DEAD WEIGHT

"Who would have thought the young man
to have so much blood in him?"
Macbeth, approx.

THE MOST BEAUTIFUL Indian summer day anybody in Greater Manchester could remember.

At Millwards, for months brains were to be racked for anything that happened during it. Nothing did. Dictation, cards in the lunch hour, Ian and Myra sitting in the car "eatin' sandwiches an' jokin'." And as frustrated reporters were to discover, nothing seemed to be known about them; Olive had left some months before, and anyway, Myra had confided in her only in the very first stages. Their colleagues had even accepted that Ian was still living at his mother's until the day, soon after the Bradys had moved to Heywood, when he had been given a form to fill in with his domicile and had caused office hilarity by looking it up in his diary.

Three minutes to five. Dear Serrs, Regarding your advice note No. A 21 A/64 two containers have now been found to be damaged and although the storeman signed top copy accepting delivery the damage was not noticed then as there was no leakage will you kindly arrange for the faulty drums bla bla bla Yours faith-fully I. Brady. The last letter. "She was my typist, I dictated to her and I suppose it overlapped into everyday life." It is signifi-cant that to him, by now, everyday Millwards was the fantasy, the other the real thing.

And at five they were off: two office workers who for years had been no more noticed by their colleagues than their colleagues had been noticed by them. Off into the glorious evening sun. Did she give last unknowing glances? At the playing fields of Ryder Brow School, at little Sunny Brow Park, evenin', thou waterfall, evenin', thou Sacred Heart?

Home by six. Maureen: "Gran always 'ad a smashin' high tea waitin' for 'em, didn't she, Dave?"

The account of the next twelve hours is based, where there is a choice, on the evidence of David Smith.

It had not been the best of days for the Smiths, happy-go-lucky though they were. Out-of-work Dave had returned from his land-owner's walk in the "valley," swinging his dog stick with Bobbie at his heels, to find a letter which hardly went with Elvis Presley at the Waldorf Towers. "Mr. Page, the janitor, is doing his job in reporting you, and I want the £14 rent money by Sat, or I shall take legal proceedings. And if that dog is still there I shall have you evicted." Ah well. A sit-around looking through the papers. When Maureen got home from work, she read the letter and gave a resigned sigh. It was no help that they were pretty sure—and happy in one way—that she was pregnant.

Mo, we won't tell Myra yet; if it makes 'er feel any better we'll call 'im Puppet. By the way, is Angela Dawn's pram still at me grandad's in Aked Street? It'll look fab on that balcony . . . Mo, don't worry, the future'll look after itself, I joost looked up my stars in *News o' the World* an' it says Capricorn's in for a surprise an' a windfall, *soomthink*'ll turn up. I'll nip down an' ask Ian's advice.

And he did. 6:15. The clocks having last Sunday been turned back an hour, the special night was already turning lingeringly, seductively dark. He found Ian and Myra at their tea, and informed them (according to Brady, a sly bit of reminiscence) that Maureen was "home readin' *Fanny Hill.*"

Dave gave him the letter, but Ian the oracle was no help at all. "He give it me back without sayin' anythink." Then Dave, for the first time out of three that night, walked back to the Towers, 6:30 P.M. An hour later Maureen discovered they were out of tea, so hubby loped back to Number 16 to "borrow" a quarter-pound from Gran's bedroom store. One of the few occasions when it was remembered that she was Maureen's gran as well as Myra's. He found her already preparing to bumble up to bed with the nice strong sleeping pills Myra said were so good and which Elsie Masterson had got her on prescription. He ran upstairs for the tea.

SMITH: "Ian was fixin' 'is cuff links an' jacket, so I knew they was goin' out, Myra doin' her 'air, then she went up an' come down in a sort of leopard-skin dress." As Dave left for home the others left too, without saying good night to Gran. That can hardly have upset her, as Myra hadn't spoken to her for months except when absolutely necessary, and Ian not since she didn't know when. As they stalked out, she might have been more concerned to have them look her way if she had known she was never to see them again.

As Myra followed Ian, Dave noticed three things. First, she was looking particularly smart in the leopard-skin thing, white high heels, hair and make-up fixed to a T. Second, she was carrying not a neat little handbag to go with all that, but the ruddy big shoulder bag she kept the two loaded revolvers in. Third, she was holding something you don't expect to see on somebody leaving home for a night out. Ian's binoculars.

Dave watched them nip down into the car and drive off into the still beautiful evening, toward Manchester.

8 P.M. Dave home through the dark with his packet of tea. "Nothin' on telly, so we went to bed with a book." Maureen was presumably still deep in *Fanny Hill.* By eleven-twenty, light out.

HINDLEY: "Ian an' me left at eight, we drove to Gorton to the off-license we know in Grey Street, I got some wine. Then in Old

Ashton Road we nearly run over a dog, then we cruised around the middle o' Manchester, then we stopped in a side street an' chatted, then just after ten Ian said he'd pick up some beer at the buffet in Central Station. I waited outside in the car, I didn't go in with 'im because it wasn't werrth messin' aboot wi' parkin' the car for three shillin's, and Ian was only away ten minutes."

10:45, Hattersley. Pat's mother, in Number 12, just off to bed, heard Phoenix Braithwaite coming home along the path, "sliding his feet as per usual." She heard nothing after that. Even Duke didn't bark.

BRADY: "Just as I got to the buffet, I found it had just closed. I was just comin' away when I saw a young chap standin' there, at the milk-vendin' machine." Edward Evans, aged seventeen years and nine months, apprentice fitter, frail, dark, tight jeans, suede jacket, new suede shoes, who had left home in Ardwick at half past six to join his mate at Aunty's Bar, missed him, and left to go to a football match. "He was just terrnin' to go when I minded his face, from having exchanged a werrd wi' him in the Barrowford Bar, name of Eddie . . . The Barrowford's in town, a hangout for homosexuals . . . Aye, I have been once or twice, it amuses me to watch their antics." It sounds an amusing hobby, antic-watching. "He said he'd just got off the Liverpool train." The boy's invention makes sense, it explained his visit to the buffet. "I asked him if he'd care to come back for a drink, my sister was doon in the car. At the car I just said, 'Myra, this is my friend Eddie.' We drove back." Eddie must have been puzzled by the setup of the snazzy blond bird who waits at the wheel while her brother cases the railway stations, but stranger things have happened.

Anyway, he's glad of her. (Wi' the shockin' tales you hear, a bloke with a sister's bound to be okay. Not mooch of a talker either of 'em, but things often start slow.) Loovly night.

It is indeed, and a gude moon, it'll be full by Sunday. D'ye fancy wine, Eddie? . . . Beer, too bad we're oot o' beer. That's a nice wee jacket ye have on, Eddie, I dig that button arrangement, must copy it, how many buttons on it?

And Eddie's new friend takes a wallet, writes something in

pencil and lays it on the shelf in front of his sister at the wheel. (Rum card. But a nice run out, and the bloke's promised a lift 'ome. Wonder why he's not drivin' now.)

BRADY: "We got to Wardle Brook Avenue about eleven-therrty." That meant that when the three climbed up the wall from the car the terrain was fairly quiet, the New Inn having some time ago waved off the last regular. But even if Brady lied about the time in order to conceal the fact that the three arrived at Number 16 much earlier—a possibility which will crop up in time—any acquaintance who might have glanced up at them from the New Inn would assume that the second young fellow was Dave, and forget about it.

BRADY: "The dogs rushed at us." *Dogs*, Eddie must have thought, doubly reassured as he stepped shyly into the little house as a guest, dogs make it nice too.

BRADY: "Myra seemed annoyed an' switched on the telly an' then took the dogs for a wee run as she did every night. I had some wine; no beer, so Evans didn't drink anything." The telly was showing "Soccer Highlights, a film of tonight's Old Trafford match," followed by the Reverend R. T. Brooks giving the Post-script, which one can assume was switched off, ach awa'. Ian—it is Ian?—what's that, a tape recorder? Wizard.

BRADY: "Then Myra returned and opened some dog food, jurin' which Evans went up to the bathroom. I said not to make a noise, as there was an auld lady." Whether the three of them had just arrived at Number 16, at 11:30, or had been in the house for some time, the host's "sister" now left the house, leaving the lads together. Eddie and Neddie.

SMITH: "At eleven-forty our buzzer went, we was still readin'. I allus sleep n-naked, so Maureen got up to look out o' the window to spy Myra's car, at that hour it couldn't be anybody else. No car, so she went to the buzzer an' said 'Yes?' Myra said back, 'It's me,' an' she come up an' into the lounge. I was puttin' on me jeans an' a cardigan thing an' went in . . . No, not dressed to go out, just bein' p-polite to a visitor like.

"First thing I n-noticed, and it really hit me, an' my wife like-wise, was that Myra wasn't lookin' anything like what she had when she'd left home at eight, all dolled up. This time her make-up was all smudged like, and half off, her hair tousled up an' she was in a scruffy old sweater an' skirt wi' the hem 'angin' down, and on her feet she had sort o' tartan pumps. It was the sort o' get-up she only got inside of on weekends when she was cleanin'.

"Well, we talked, an' then Myra said, 'Oh Mo, I want you to give a message to our Mam at work, tell 'er I'll call in at Eaton Street tomorrow night for her to bleach me hair.' An' M-Maureen said, 'Is that all you've come to tell us this time o' night, an' anyway, our Mam wants you to bring back them white shoes of 'ers you've still got.'

"Then M-Myra said, 'Dave, see me home through the 'ouses, it's dark and I'm scared.' Then Maureen said, 'Myra, you are daft—why didn't you come in the car, then you wouldn't need Dave's company back!' An' Myra just says, 'The car's locked, that's all,' so I got into me suede m-mocassins an' me jacket and took me dog stick as usual. Myra says, 'Don't bring Bobbie, you know how he fights wi' ours,' an' Maureen says, 'Leave me some cigs,' an' I says, 'I'll be back in a coupla minutes.'"

He didn't take Bobbie, but he did take his dog stick. He was later to wish he hadn't, for it was to turn up uncomfortably often as an exhibit. Not a formidable object, fairly slender and flexible, with a length of stout cord which he had wound around the top to form a loop around his wrist. Not a required article, obviously, in the "teen-age trend," but we must allow that in any other circumstances it would seem no more than an eccentricity.

11:50, across Pudding Lane, down Sundial Close, into Wardle Brook Av. The conversation en route is not preserved and was most likely nil. "Myra'n me together was never great talkers . . . Then she says, 'Would you like to see some miniature bottles?' I says, 'Okay, I'm game, I might even empty a couple.'

"Then as we was turnin' into the av, an' I was just goin' to skin oop the slope by 'er car, she says, 'No no, you wait across road by the New Inn wall, i' case Ian's doin' something. If he isn't I'll flick the landin' light coupla times.' 'Okay,' I says." This sounds more suggestive than it need: Myra could be implying that Ian was taping a record, it had happened before.

Dave stood idly by the New Inn wall for half a minute, long enough to make out, on the wall in chalk, "Harry Loves Linda."

Then the light flicked on twice, he crossed the road, skinned up the slope, creak of gate, tap on front door.

Opened by Ian. Jacket off but waistcoated and cuff-linked, alert, very much at home. "Hello, want to see those miniature bottles?" His voice was unnaturally loud, as if he intended to reassure somebody in the sitting room, the door of which was closed. The kitchen door to the hall was open, so Dave went in while Ian nipped upstairs, came down with three miniature bottles, set them on the kitchen table and went back into the sitting room, leaving the door ajar.

After a few seconds, during which Dave stood alone in the kitchen—Apricot Brandy, mmm—there came from the sitting room a sudden sharp scream followed by Myra: "Dave, help him! Help him! . . ."

Thinking Ian was being attacked by the visitor, whoever he was, Dave seized his stick and ran across the tiny hall and into the sitting room, a couple of long paces. Only the red-shaded lamp over the television was on, the room was in a livid half-light.

What he saw in those shadows he was never to forget. On the floor next to the couch, a screaming figure writhed on its stomach while another stood carefully bent astride it, holding the back of the neck in one hand and in the other, something with which he was flailing the back of the head: something moving so fast that for the first couple of seconds it was impossible to see what it was. An axe. Brady was smashing it down—not the edge of the blade but the side, so as to save blood—time and time again and with all his strength. A butcher felling a calf.

David Smith had been in rough houses, but this was something so new that his split-second impression was that his friend was playing a grim practical joke, with some sort of life-size marionette which he was pulling spasmodically about to make the limbs twitch with uncanny life. To Smith, it was just not possible that the savagery could be anything but feigned: Brady's muttered imprecations (quoted now from Smith's spoken evidence, in court) sounded so deliberate that they might have been directed at a nuisance which has caused endless trouble and is finally being dealt with, like a fire or a mad dog: You dirty bastard *crunch* you fuckin' cunt *crunch*. Then it came to Smith, like an electric shock, that the marionette was in stockinged feet, spouting blood all over the room, screaming for mercy, wearing jeans, and was a lad of his own age.

Asked in court what he did when he saw this, he replied, "I moved." The creature on the floor was on its stomach, and as it crawled spasmodically for life, the rest of the fourteen blows followed in rhythmic succession, *crunch* cunt *crunch* bastard *crunch crunch crunch*. Brady: "When I hit him I thought he'd shut up, but the axe kept bouncing off." The screams crumbled into groans and gurgles, which in their turn were swamped by a sound (Smith) "like when you brush your teeth an' gargle wi' water." The death rattle.

Then Smith: "He's a gonner." Brady: "We'll have to get rid of him." Brady then took a cushion cover from where it lay ready, bent down, lifted the boy's head by the long wet hair and cautiously pulled the cushion cover over it. He then took a length of electric cord, also at hand, drew it around the neck and pulled it tight. The rattle died away. The marionette, with the blood already seeping into the mass of the cushion cover, lay still.

The whole phantasmagoria had taken a few seconds, no longer than a direct hit, including the whine of bomb, explosion, rocking and collapse of brick and mortar. And in the midst of the explosion, like something glimpsed by lightning and never to be erased, Myra Hindley upright and watching, motionless and dull of eye like a woman drugged. Silence.

Then came the sudden shrill barking of the two dogs, who Smith realized were in the room and who must have yelped wildly through those seconds of scuffle and scream. With their familiar voices the room returned to life, and the slaughter had to turn into some sort of domestic crisis. As it did so, the dead boy at their feet became, forever, an object.

Myra patted and soothed Puppet and Lassie, who slunk muttering into corners. This must be one of the few indoor murders witnessed by two dogs, and surely the only one ever attended by a budgerigar. There is no record of any reaction from this last. An excerpt from Joey's limited vocabulary would have been, in that silence, impressive.

David Smith was standing near the half-open door. The question which had to be asked in court was: "Why didn't you run for it?" A house he knew well; front door directly behind the door behind him; Brady had already discarded the axe, and he would have been down the garden and over the wall before the other could have reached the doorstep.

But by his own account he must have been, at this moment, in a state of profound shock—the heart-in-the-mouth dream when the attacker is winging toward you and your feet are glued in terror to the ground. He explained afterwards that he felt himself—even *saw* himself, from outside—crash through the front door, down the garden, over the railing and up Sundial Close. Then Brady straightened up.

His look turned like a searchlight onto David Smith, and stayed there. It seemed, to the other, that his thought had been read. Brady stooped and picked up the axe. It was dripping blood. He was breathing evenly. He lifted the axe.

Then "Feel, Dave," he said, "feel the weight o' that." Dave felt, and handed it back. The other's look was still on him and it said, I've been waitin' for this for weeks and *now* d'ye believe me? Mate, ye're in this now up to the waist, and ye'll stay here in this house an' carry oot my orders until the moment I give the werrd for ye to go. Then the eyes left him and the hand laid down the axe. He could not go.

Two points to his story. First, he could easily have told the police that Brady stood between him and the front door, and held the axe longer than he did. Secondly, to anybody who at the trial was to see Ian Brady in the witness-box, great bony hands clutching the rail before him, lashing white-lipped and white-knuckled against the police, he was a wild animal at bay.

Even in the suave, cushioned afternoon light of a British law court, he struck terror. You could just sniff what you would feel if you had just seen him wield the exhibit which lay a couple of yards from him.

The axe.

Brady laid it bloodstained on the body, took Myra's Woman's Mag from the rack under the telly, wiped his hands on it and said to Myra, "That was the messiest yet."

She turned on the top light, and the living room was nakedly revealed.

Even the side of an axe, wielded fourteen times in a clumsy frenzy, can create havoc. Blood everywhere. Splashed on the rose-pink walls, on the blue door, on the floor around the fireplace, on Neddie's trousers, on Dave's jacket, on Hessie's skirt, on Dave's stick on the floor, on Joey's cage. And steadily it seeped from the mangled head of the object. The object had suddenly become obscene, a real-life obscenity which Smith, the student of vice, had never glimpsed in either book or gangster film or television serial. He felt a violent desire to be sick.

Then a sound.

A call. Smith looked at Brady: for one freezing moment it sounded as if it came from the back garden. It was repeated, querulous, sleepy. "My-ra-a!" Myra wiped her hands with a grimace, like a nurse summoned by a tiresome patient, went out to the stairs, then called out very loud, "Okay, Gran, it's the dogs, I dropped a tape recorder on me foot, okay." Then she came back, and looked around to assess the state of her home.

She had called very loud for the benefit of the Braithwaites next door. Puzzlement has been caused by the fact that a noisy murder was committed in a tiny house, with paper-thin walls, surrounded by many similar houses, with nobody lifting a finger. But nobody ever does, unless somebody rushes out of a door and yells, "Help help, somebody's being killed!" and even then, as a notorious New York case proved in the early sixties, it is hard to get outsiders to involve themselves. The noise was loudest to the Braithwaites but they were the last people to interfere; anyway, they heard Gran's voice and something about dogs. And then thought they'd kissed an' made up. Families quarrel violently late at night, never more than in an Overspill Estate; and nobody looks more of a fool than the man who knocks to ask what's the matter, only to be insulted. (They've quieted down, leave things be, get back to sleep.)

"Get cleanin' stuff," Ian said to Myra, "an' rags." Not even out of breath; he might have been a welfare officer who had arrived into a slum home to investigate a very ugly incident. Myra went out into the kitchen, then the domestic noise of running water.

Ian looked at the other, saw he was about to faint, crossed to the coffee table, steadily poured out two glasses of wine and handed one to Dave, who gulped it. Then "Go and help," said the Master. The boy went into the kitchen. She was in an apron and had everything ready, buckets, bowls, basins of water, rags: Lady Macbeth had merged into Mrs. Mop. On the drainboard, the cleaning stuffs were at hand, Gleamo, Spick, Sheeny. Everything but the perfumes of Arabia.

They returned to the sitting room, keeping their eyes high from the floor. "The walls," said the Master, who had lit a cigarette, and the three set to work. Luckily the rose-pink gloss paint took to water. The task was a thorough one, during which no one spoke: a spring-cleaning against time. Ian and Myra rubbed and scoured, scoured and rubbed, while Dave saw to the cage. Under the curious stare of the budgie, he wiped the blood from the bars.

The walls by now in excellent condition, Ian produced from behind the couch a shopping bag stamped ADSEGA, the big Manchester discount house where Myra's mam had shopped for years. They now turned their absorbed attention to the linoleum and the rugs. The bag was needed because cleaning up the floor was not only a matter of blood. Myra was picking up bits of matted hair when she recoiled. Dave, who was scrubbing, looked up: on the rug in front of her, a small red-grey sliver of something no bigger than a bean, which he guessed to be a mash of bone, brain tissue and blood.

"Pick it up," said the Master. She raised her eyes to him slowly, like a trained animal. "I can't," she whispered, "I can't," and retched. He gave her a look of contempt, scraped up the mash as if it were spilt turnips, tossed it into the shopping bag and went on with his scrubbing. Showing off.

"Now white sheet, blanket, polythene." One of the most appalling details of this night was that, to the pair, the removal of the body from the room had been a less urgent matter than the spring-cleaning; the fact that it lay in their midst right through caused them no discomfort. By now Myra was showing off too.

She went out to the scullery and returned promptly with exactly what had been ordered. The murderer spread the blanket, on top of it the semitransparent polythene, on top of that the sheet. Then the difficult part.

He took one square of the polythene, whisked the soaked cushion cover off the corpse's head (the face still on the floor), swiftly undid the electric cord, which was by now almost embedded in the neck, wrapped the polythene around the head, then, to keep the polythene in place, tied the cord around it, at the neck, then pulled the cushion cover back over the head. He then turned the body over (face up, but mercifully masked), raised it by the armpits while Dave took the stockinged feet, then they dumped it on the white sheet; as they did so, Dave observed that the waistband of the jeans was unbuttoned and the fly unzipped to its farthest extent.

During all this, Myra went into the kitchen to wash the blood-soaked clothes, and then to bring more water to clean up where the head had lain. Ian felt in the jacket pocket, brought out a shabby wallet and opened it. A green insurance card with the name Edward Evans, a pay envelope and an old letter from a girl named Wendy in Penrhyndeudraeth, North Wales, where the boy had been for his summer holiday. All this was tossed into the shopping bag with the rubbish, then the suede shoes, the axe. "Your stick's wet," said Ian with a smile and washed blood from it. He was more perfunctory with the stick, though, than he had been with the walls, for it was subsequently found to have hair and blood adhering to it.

Wanted, stout string. Myra went into the kitchen to look, none. It is odd that with all the other objects at hand, such an essential ingredient had been overlooked; odd too that Ian found the perfect substitute at his elbow: the cord around the top of Myra's brother-in-law's dog stick. "Just the ticket," said Ian. "Can you undo it?" And Dave said, "I bite my nails, *you* 'ave a go." Ian undid the cord and cut it into strips.

Then, while Myra cleaned up a bit more, the parcel. As neat and swift a job as in the mailing department of any big store. The object was first turned on its side; then, while one of them bent the knees and brought them right up till they touched the bowed and shrouded head squelching with blood, the other tied pieces of cord tight around calves and back. As tight as when the packer says to the helper, in the middle of a knot, "Press a thumb there, will you." Polythene, sheet, blanket.

Then Ian stood thinking, and said, "Damn." Myra said, "What's up?" and Ian said, "We can't heave it over the railin' and into the car, it might burst; neither can we hump it those ninety paces past three bloody houses at this time o' night. Upstairs." He rose briskly, then one of his legs sort of doubled up and he said, "Damn, the little bugger kicked me on me weak ankle—remember, Myra, when it went the other time?" But he was able, with Dave, to lift up the parcel.

As he did so, he grimaced, said, "Eddie's a dead weight," looked at Myra, and they giggled. He and Dave lugged the parcel through the door, Myra stepped over it onto the stairs with the shopping bag, went up on tiptoe and held the handle of Gran's door while they maneuvered the parcel up the stairs and into "Myra's" bedroom. She followed them in, then they all tiptoed downstairs. The room was back to normal. Myra said, "I'll brew some tea, did you notice how when you hit him, his eyes registered astonishment?" and went into the kitchen. Showing off. Ian lit another cigarette and poured some wine. Relaxation after a job well done. They could hear the rattle of teacups. The witch's brew. With milk and sugar.

Then Myra made up the fire, which during the last hour had been neglected, and they sat around drinking tea.

For David Smith, the dreamlike quality of this night was underlined by finding himself in a room he knew well, and in the company of two young people whom he looked upon as family. He stared with dull eyes at the square blank face of the television set, and thought of the number of times they had all sat around watching its noisy fake terrors—bang, groan, wallop, thud— terrors followed each time by lush dream girls crooning sexily at bits of chocolate or bars of soap. Well, tonight there'd be none o' that.

And on top of it all, it was not only the murderer who was behaving as if there had been an accident, one which had called for his skill and his fortitude, *the girl was too.* Two against one—was he himself mad? Was the thing upstairs a haul of pinched cigarettes?

Then follows a pictorial detail as authentic as it is bizarre, one of unparalleled callousness. The girl—who was wearing a skirt with black nylons, not trousers—sat in her grandmother's chair, holding cup and saucer and with her tartan-slippered feet on the mantelpiece. Which was only just low enough for them to reach. There was blood on the tartan slippers. Stirring her tea in this pose, she said, "Ian, d'ye remember the time we went on the moors with a body in the back, and you were off burying it, and a police car stopped, and a copper came up to the car and leaned over an' said, 'What's the trouble?' an' I said, 'I'm waitin' to dry my spark plugs,' an' I was prayin' Ian wouldn't appear, then the feller drove off. D'ye want another cup . . . Now, what about tomorrow?"

It was decided that Ian should take the day off from the office to nurse his ankle, and that in the evening the parcel would be "moved to the moors an' ditched there." The word "ditched" has an authentic ring. The problem was how to get it inconspicuously out of the house and along that path. It was agreed that in the afternoon Dave should proceed to his grandfather's, 39 Aked Street, Ardwick (a few streets from Edward Evans' home), pick something up from the backyard, bring it to Millwards by five o'clock and load it into the back of Myra's mini-Countryman: little Angela Dawn's old pram. In the North of England, "baby trolleys" are often seen being pushed along, stacked with heavy luggage in the way of coal or bedding. A date.

After three A.M. And at last the visitor rose to go. The murderer saw him to the front door: "Weel, so long, I'll be seein' ye," and Dave said, "Okay, ta ra for now." The front door closed softly.

He had prayed it would be already light, but of course it could not be. He had the feeling they were both at the front-room curtains, so took his time pacing the couple of yards to the garden gate. It gave the same comfortable little creak it always had. He took his time, too, vaulting the railing and even in walking to the corner, just restraining a look back at the curtained bedroom window.

It was the very middle of the dark desert of the night, halfway between the last revelers and the first workers; he was alone in a sleeping world. And he ran.

Ran, away from a terrible dream. And in that sleeping world, the clatter of his feet echoed so loud that he was convinced there must be another runner behind him. He streaked up Sundial Close and across Pudding Lane, with on either side dozens of sleeping figures capable of waking and gliding swiftly down through any front door to meet him with an axe high in the air.

But his real fright was that the two of them had got out and down the slope, and that the car was racing around by the road and would be in the shadowy forecourt waiting for him. To him, after what he had just been through, they were superhuman beings, all-knowing, all-powerful, whose move to him out of that stationary car would be as sure as the approach of a shark's fin through deep water. He ran.

Underwood Road, a frantic look to the right, nothing, across, a dive into the forecourt, his key out, and in: "WILL PERSONS PLEASE KEEP THIS DOOR CLOSED FOR THEIR OWN INTEREST." He was home. A great box rattling with strangers, but home. Up in the elevator, into the flat and into the bedroom, where Maureen lay dozing, "between awake an' asleep, 'alf an' 'alf like."

Still panting, he ran through into the bathroom, threw some cold water over his face, and was violently sick. As he turned he saw his dog, Bobbie, in the doorway. Was it imagination or was it shrinking from him? He got into bed, turned out the light, then ten seconds later turned it on again. Maureen rolled over, saw his face and was instantly awake.

English law forbids witnesses to give an account of a conversation they have held in the absence of the accused, but what these two said in the small hours of that night is not hard to reconstruct. Dave loov, you've gone too far wi' the vino . . . Then what is it—an accident? . . . Soombody bashed soombody? . . . God, them Irish laborers—*what*?

Everything must have been stammered out, between gulps and retches and clutches at cigarettes and swipes at perspiration. Maureen made tea, but with the taste of his last cup still with him, this was not one that cheered. In between, she listened open-mouthed to what sounded like raving. It is possible that she had had an uneasy idea of the payroll jobs and had certainly thought Myra and Ian were a nutty pair, but *this* . . .

It was many minutes before she finally accepted the fact of

murder. And so found herself, a simple, slow girl of nineteen in the middle of a suburban night, faced with an urgent dilemma of classic proportions, as hideous as any of Antigone's or Clytemnestra's. The claim that there were other bodies, she dismissed immediately as bragging—but the truth remained that at this moment, her own sister was inextricably involved with a killer.

She stared at the husband who had turned into a quaking schoolboy. What were they to do?

If Dave went through with this and turned up with their pram—a detail which must have turned her stomach—there was every reason to believe that with luck, the parcel would be disposed of forever. And the alternative—going to the police—bristled with hazards. Dave's record of violence, his intimacy with the pair, how to prove that he had no idea he was to be present at a murder, when his stick at this moment lay next to the parcel—when even his wife had just said, But Dave, how *could* you stay all that time, *and* help to tie it up—*how could you?* Well, he had, hadn't it just made him sick as a dog? *What were they to do?*

Then his wife said, suddenly, "We're goin' to the police." And somehow that settled it. As she dressed he looked down from their window: still dark. Below him, the black mass of the little houses, faintly lit by the glow from their own skyscraper's stairway. Somewhere down in that mass, Number 16. And such was his superstitious fright, caught by now by her, that nothing could have drawn them out of the safety of their fortress before the blessed light of day. Like two scared children they stood at the eastern window, watching a stray car snaking its lights along in the distance. Then, gradually, the sky turned grey. It was over, the longest night of their young lives.

A quick look out over the balcony, even now, to make sure that there was no car parked; and Dave's fear of maniacal attack was still so obsessional that he insisted on taking with him, hidden under his coat, a bread knife and a large screwdriver. Not a soul in elevator or hall. They crept out into Underwood Road. First light, getting lighter. They looked across toward the shortcut leading to Number 16, at the moment when suddenly out of the shadows a figure appeared; Dave shrank back into the doorway, tense and trembling. A little colored workman, adjusting a hearing aid.

More light every minute, and in several of the little houses lamps were switched on, people getting off to work. Off Underwood Road—the side away from Number 16—they cut through paths called Underwood Walk and Paynton Walk, emerging onto the main road, Hattersley Road West. In the distance, dim hillsides with factory chimneys and pylons. A red bus loomed up and passed, "PICCADILLY," a couple of tired charwomen off to city offices. For the estate, the day was beginning. And another beautiful day too, radiant, fresh.

On the corner of Hare Hill Road, a red phone booth. A quick look around, and Dave entered it while Maureen pressed herself against the outside, the side away from the estate.

Hyde 3538. He was not a great one for the phone, the first thing he saw written up was "Phone Your Greetings Telegram From Here." Then he found what he wanted: "Emergency Call, Do Not Insert Any Money Dial 999 Ask Operator For Fire Police Or Ambulance."

A last look around, and up the road. Three feet from him, a yellow garden gate, with beyond it a little house shrouded in sleep. He drew a breath, and dialed. 6:07 A.M.

The murderer, having in the black stillness of the middle of the night shut the front door noiselessly on Second Lieutenant Smith, re-enters the sitting room and gives a quick, refreshed look around. Checking up. First Lieutenant has drawn the cloth over the budgie and she is now pulling the pillow out of its cover, the oother cover's ruined, have to tell Gran we spilled coffee on it and will she run another up on her machine, will that David Smith turn up at five?

He will. An' in a coupla days it'll be the auld routine, out wi' the tracker dogs an' the police posters an' the Biggest Search Ever. He'll turn up at five.

And in the Master's mind, the picture of young Dave lingers pleasantly: the chalk-faced choirboy, Gorton toughness melted away and leaving the fascinated eyes, which all those hours never left the Master's face while we went impeccably about our tasks: it was the same look we had seen in her, then got used to, only this more intense. So intense ye'd ha' thought it was fright.

Fright? No no, it had been adoration. Lick my feet, David Smith, for they are the feet of thy Lord, Dave'll be there at five. Their clothes in a heap on the rug. Top light out. He to bed.

She undresses by the television lamp. The secret is one no longer. I hate you, David Smith. Ah well, lamp out. Bed.

In the fireplace, cozy glow of embers. Quite a little houseful, doggies asleep, budgie quiet, Gran in the Land o' Nod. Which leaves three young people. All solid working class, two born and bred in these parts, and the third as near as dammit.

Central Station. Eddie, this is Myra; Myra—Eddie . . . Back for a drink, Ed? Why should the evening not have ended up with the two men locked in embrace, and the violated female trussed like a chicken ready for disposal in an old pram? No, this is the way it was ordained, on the three days they were born. January 2, 1938; July 23, 1942; January 3, 1948.

Upstairs, crushed and corded, the consignment of adolescent flesh and marrow and bone slowly loses its heat. And imparts it, down through cheap lath and plaster, to the two young bodies warming up together. For the last time.

Far away a train, bearing dull people from one dull place to another. In the trees by the New Inn, the first questioning twitter of birds. In the room, the squeak of the budgie's perch as he sways in sleep. To the east, beyond the dark of the moors, the inexorable stirring of the dawn.

" 'Ello . . . yes? This is Hyde Police Station, what is it?"

PART FOUR

DOWN TO EARTH

CHAPTER 23

THE GHASTLIER
MORROW

"O dream, where art thou now?"
Emily Brontë

JUST the one sparrow, come over to perch on the garden gate, is enough to wake her as usual at half past seven. Neddie fast asleep. Sun already strong through the curtains. Tired, it was a big night, and a job this evening. Consignment of Contraband. Then an early night, wash me 'air.

Cloth off Joey's cage, kitchen, kettle on, bathroom. Depressed about David Smith.

When she takes Neddie his breakfast he's still asleep. 'Course, he's stayin' home. They don't speak much—"converrse," as she now calls it—but they never do at this time of day. His ankle aching quite a bit. No mention of D.S.

She's just off when he says, Oh, I better write a note for you to take to Tom, pass the pad. She knows he'll take his time, she does hate to be late but can imply to Tom that she had to wait outside 18 Westmoreland Street. Bradys don't live there any more but might as well keep it oop. Gran calls down for her milk, trust *her:* Myra, is your foot better? On the way upstairs, she hears a knock at the back door.

Milkman must want his money, cheeky monkey—

Man in white coat, surgeon or summat, 'Oosband, I 'aven't got a oosband.

I am a police officer. I'd like to see upstairs.

She has never thought of it happening, and now that it's here it's going so quickly it's as unreal as it would have been in her imaginings. Give me the key. It's not coonvenient. Give me the key. He bends down and feels the parcel and looks back at her. Contraband.

When they were out on the landing just now and she had to stand close to him, she knew she was forcing him to be conscious of her sexuality. His look now is different.

Talbot closed the bedroom door carefully, locked it and followed her down the floral stair carpet, liking his white breadman's coat better than when he had climbed the stairs behind her two minutes ago. An open-and-shut case. But the guns . . . *Had* the young chap got them in the sitting room? But she went in first.

As she did so, he nipped into the kitchen and to the back door, gave the signal to Wills to close in with their men, and with a couple of long steps was through the little hall and into the sitting room, thinking swiftly, May get that holiday after all. He went in.

It was as still as Every Picture Tells a Story. Chubby Sergeant Carr stood with his solid back to the fireplace, the lady next to the budgie, the dog next to her, and the man of the house still sitting in bed in his undershirt, green ballpoint gliding over the envelope as he finished an address. All through their two minutes upstairs he had been writing, and Carr had been looking at him. And for another second, not a word was spoken now. The young chap looked up at the young lady.

(Would ye believe it, Mr. fuckin' Smith's squealed on us, the whole thing wrapped up as usual and *alles* been *in Ordnung* for years and he crawls on his yellow belly into the enemy lines, the shit, the fuckin' shit, I'll split his head open wi' brains all over the ceilin', steady Neddie, carry on Scottie.)

Under the drinks table with the plastic chrysanthemums, something twitched; Talbot realized that what he had taken for a crumpled mat was a second dog. Cowering. And they aren't supposed to react to death. An' *he's* been finishing a blinkin' letter. In that second Talbot thought, Hello hello . . . A faint first prickle of unease. Open-and-shut?

He broke the silence. "Get a couple in," he said to Carr, who hurried out and into the kitchen and returned immediately with two constables. The room was suddenly crowded.

Talbot signaled crisply to Carr, who followed him out and upstairs. He pointed to the parcel under the window. "It's in there," he said, "you go and do the necessary." "Right," said Carr, and went. Talbot locked the door, took the key and followed him. As they entered, the two constables edged tactfully out. The young chap was still sitting, everybody waiting. "I'm afraid," said Carr to him, "there's a body." A pause. "Aye, I know." Two Scotsmen. "In that case," continued Carr, "Mr. . . . Thank you— Mr. Brady, I shall have to—"

A sudden scuffle, and Puppet, who had stood immobile next to his mistress, was into the kitchen and out of the back door. "Oh no," she called, "he'll be into Mottram Road an' the traffic's wicked, get 'im quick!" Her first sign of agitation. A constable got the dog back in, and she held him by the collar. Talbot noticed that this animal was cowering too.

"I'm afraid," continued Carr, "I shall have to ask you to come along to Hyde Station and answer a few questions. I must formally caution you that anything you say . . ." 9:02 A.M.

The two detectives moved their eyes from him to her. Carr had the same look on his face as Talbot upstairs. A look neither Ian Brady nor Myra Hindley had ever seen before. A mixture of wariness and aversion. But their own faces betrayed nothing.

Never have, and won't now. (So it's happened, we're in the open at last an' the work in the dark over, war declared an' us in enemy hands. Sort of a relief really, 'cause now we can sit back, quite amusin' really, think o' the cause, Hess, customs, contraband, not a word even under torture, chin up.)

Brady turned back the bedclothes. He was naked except for the undershirt, but made no haste bending to pick up his shorts

(259)

from the floor. He did not even pull the shirt down and tuck it between his legs. "Eddie and I," he said, "had a row, an' the situation got oot o' hand."

"I see," said Talbot. Glib—it had been a signal to the woman to say just that and no more.

She bent down and picked up shirt and trousers. As she arranged the shirt over a chair, he could tell she had washed and ironed it; she turned the socks back and lay them on the shoes. When he was ready—a neat dresser—she held out his jacket, like a wife seeing hubby off to business. "I'll get a tie," she said, "from upstairs."

"Never mind a tie," said Talbot, "right?"

"I'm comin too." She wasn't asking, stating.

"All right, no law against it."

Talbot peeled off the white coat and was moving out with official dignity, when he caught Carr's look of please-sir-adjust-your-dress-before-leaving and realized he had left his policeman's cap in Craig's Pantry Van, blast. A constable was dispatched with the white coat and the loaves. Talbot asked the woman her name, and about the old lady upstairs, though she was plainly more concerned about the dog, and she told him old Mrs. Hill over in the Walk was an old friend of her gran's. Talbot sent another constable for Policewoman Slater. Hindley sat fiddling with a corner of fingernail, Brady sat looking from fireplace to window. Certainly knew the value of silence, no need to have cautioned *him*.

Talbot stood with his eyes thoughtfully on the rug. The kind of hiatus which years ago had ceased to embarrass him. The woman opened her handbag. On the floor he espied a tiny fragment of what looked like jelly, but decided to leave it to the forensic department. Just as well. She was fluffing out her hair in her hand mirror, while the budgie filled up the silence with a twitter.

Carr returned from the kitchen, followed by Policewoman Slater, and handed Talbot his cap. Talbot instructed Miss Slater to come back from Hyde by noon, get the old lady moved to her friend's, and tell her that Myra'd had a car accident and that the injured man had been brought into Number 16.

Then, leaving Wills in charge—Oh, send for the local doctor—they were off. Talbot, then Brady, Carr, Hindley, the policewoman. Brady limping. Without a tie, shirt collar up and top button undone, he looked as if he were off on a holiday to the seaside. Talbot wondered if it crossed his mind that he was leaving the house for the last time. He didn't think of Myra. Early yet.

The five took the footpath past the other front windows. Would have been more convenient, Talbot thought, if they'd lived in the house at the other end. Luckily, the Estate did not find the sight of a couple of stray policemen so very startling, and few heads were turned. One door opened, Number 12, lady with little girl, " 'Lo Myra, 'lo Ian!" " 'Lo Elsie," said the two together, " 'lo Pat!" In the road near Number 10, the window with the plaster dog and cat, two police cars. Brady and Carr got into the back of the first, and Myra was just getting in up front on the other side when Talbot stepped forward. "Sorry dear, the other vehicle, with the lady."

She stood in the sun, as if she had been struck. Looked from him to the pleasant woman in uniform, then at Brady. He stared back at her thoughtfully, his hand rubbing his chin.

Talbot got in next to the driver, and as the car moved she looked after it like a dog that has been left behind. Then she entered the second car.

As they followed, Policewoman Slater realized they had an extra passenger, one dog that had not been left behind: Puppet, on his mistress' knee, her hand absently patting his head. During the two-mile run, nobody in either car spoke a word.

Hyde. They serpented through the narrow old streets. Police station. Talbot, Carr and Brady climbed alertly out and in, then the second driver emerged and opened the door for his passenger. She stepped down with a half smile of acknowledgment, her dog bounding after her and wagging his tail. The policeman might have been an important doorman, and she returning from the shops. So gentle are the first rhythms of the British legal engine that there was nothing to tell the vanmen, the delivery boys, the hurrying shoppers that in the October sun of Hyde something very sinister was stirring.

Into the dimness of the station. Like entering a quiet, shabby little old-fashioned school.

The first thing to check, everybody knew, was that the Smiths were out of the way. But the Smiths had seen to that; they were in a room on the other side, and were to remain there till the evening—guests of course, but you never knew what might develop during the day.

As Hindley entered, her eyes met Brady's. And Talbot noted that both faces remained absolutely blank. The blankness of complete complicity. "Miss Slater, will you take the young lady to the canteen?" and the young lady followed the policewoman, the dog trotting beside her.

"Now, Ian," said Jock Carr, "Ian is it?—if ye'll step in here" —they filed into the C.I.D. office—"ye are free to make any statement, which I will take down in front of Constable Fairley."

"Cerr-tainly."

9:33. Carr sat at the desk and Brady opposite. "I formally caution you . . ." The sergeant brought out note pad and pen. Brady started to speak, in an impersonal voice, slowly enough for Carr to take it down on the statement form in longhand. "Last night I met Eddie in Manchester. We were drinking, then we went home to Hattersley. We had an argument and we came to blows . . ." It was so clearly and concisely put that he might have been reading it. Carr was used to every sort of statement-maker: the eager, the inarticulate, the defiant, the evasive. This was something new. He almost felt he himself was the man in trouble writing down the statement he was to stick to, at the dictation of his lawyer. "There was a hatchet which I hit Eddie with . . . The gurrglin' stopped . . ." Unusual. "Sign here, please."

Carr took the statement in to Talbot. "Mmm. Ten for neatness."

In his little book, Talbot started his careful notes. Then more phone calls, the sort to continue all day: Detective Constable Leighton in Cheadle Hulme, to go now to Number 16 and photograph everything; Bancroft and Dr. Noel Jones, forensic scientists from the Preston Labs; Dr. St. Hill, Home Office pathologist; coroner to arrange hearse for removal of body; clothes to be examined for blood; fingerprints; full-face mug-shot photos, plus close shot of Brady's leg to show the minuscule puncture where kicked on the ankle; contact Mrs. Campion, their leading woman officer, out on a case; ring Manchester City headquarters to send police car to break news to dead boy's mother and bring her to identify him, nasty assignment.

Then, from David Smith, telegram to his dad, J. J. ditto, in London (funny how these families stick together); routine call to Public Prosecutor in London; car-rental people (Miss Hindley will no longer be paying installments, as financial responsibility taken over by Police). As Talbot made out the slip he thought, Taxpayers' money, here we go . . . And in between there were the chores such as traffic control, seeing kids safely across and all that.

After a quick shave Talbot felt he had the case sufficiently in hand to phone *his* superior, at the County Constabulary Office in the ancient walled city of Chester.

Arthur Benfield, fifty-two, was an old workingmate and a good foil. Where Bob was spare and serious he was rubicund, a baldish, beaming bachelor with a tolerant chuckle agreeably masking the dogged realist which every good detective has to be. A Cheshire man, son of a policeman, he had had much the same local career as Talbot: twenty-six years of slow-but-sure promotion, Ellesmere Port, Runcorn, Stalybridge, Sale. And just as five weeks ago Talbot had been made head of the Stalybridge Division, so on October 1, six days before the Smith telephone call, Benfield became Detective Chief Superintendent for the whole of Cheshire.

After their years of uneventful industry—everything from car accidents to pickpockets—they had joked about their futures. "Well, Bob, now that we're a couple o' big noises, what's the bettin' you strike the Million-Pound Drug Ring in Stalybridge?" "No, Arthur me lad, too tame. I bet on you, Train Robbery in Chester Station." 11:02 A.M. "Yes? . . . 'Ello Bob, I thought you were on your 'olidays!" "Not this time, Arthur. Looks as if we've got our first murder."

Benfield arrived from Chester on the dot of noon, and after being told everything, he went around, the benevolent new pipe-smoking headmaster: across the building to shake hands with the

Smiths, then back to Myra, then down to Brady, no handshake
but the amiable approach: "Well, Jock, an' how are the Glasgow
Rangers?" In the office, waiting for the doctor, quick sandwich, a
look at the typed-up notes. When Benfield saw the murdered
boy's address, 55 Addison Street, it was a shock of recognition: he
had himself, as a boy, lived a couple of doors away. "With my
gran, like Myra, but I trust that there the resemblance ends."

Millwards, same morning. Ian and Myra's lateness was com-
mented on at once, it's very unlike *them*. Then just after one
o'clock Tom Craig was sitting in his usual corner having his
lunch when Irene ran in with a startled face: "It says on the news
there's been a young chap murdered in Myra's house, doesn't
give the name!" Ian's dead, Tom thought immediately and was
deeply shocked, the lad got himself into a fight wi' some thug, an'
wi' that temper of his, good God . . .

As the truth gradually came out, the effect on Millwards was
one of prolonged shock. They were never to recover from it.

Hyde Station, 1:05 P.M., Dr. St. Hill with Gladstone bag. 1:15,
Number 16—Benfield, Talbot, St. Hill. A knot of people staring
up from the road, word had got around there'd been an accident.
Washing being hung, man gardening, pigeons being fed. Sergeant Carr opened the front door an inch. "Doctor," said Talbot,
and Carr gave a little bow and opened the door a little wider,
looking as if he had been doing exactly this for years, he might
have been in an apron. A flash from the kitchen, Leighton taking
his last routine photo.

Talbot hurried upstairs and unlocked the door; he was followed by Benfield, St. Hill, Carr, the local doctor, Ellis, and
Leighton. St. Hill was as old a hand as the policemen—age of
violence, Manchester a tough spot, folk lying stabbed in the
street—but the parcel on the floor next to NEW-LAID EGGS stopped
him short. My word, they were right, it *is* a small bundle. Leighton checked his camera, the others stood by, as if to watch an
operation in a hospital theater. Flash. Go ahead.

St. Hill lifted the three paperbacks from the parcel—*Among
Women Only* by Cesare Pavese, *The Red Brain, Tales of Horror*

and *The Road Ahead: A Children's Poetry Book*—and laid them on the lace runner next to a half-empty bottle of Yates' Amoroso Sherry. Flash. He undid the blanket. Flash.

The contents looked like an egg: a large, luminous oval catching the sun, the narrow end darkly steeped in brown. Polythene, whether tight or flapping loose, has an obscene look, all semi-transparent stickiness like a pig's bladder. It was skin-tight. And knotted at the top. He undid the knot and rustled the polythene away. Flash.

The inside of the egg was wrapped in a white bed sheet except for the narrow end, which was bulky with a cushion cover, stained brown and stiff. Removed, it revealed a polythene hood secured around the neck with electric cord. The hygienic neatness of the job was only marred by the fact that the hood, in a material scientifically devised, for housewives, to hold moisture, was nursing a human head bursting with blood. Flash.

He unwrapped the sheet. Lying sideways and trussed brutally tight, like a butcher's shipment packed off by an expert with a late truck waiting, there was the curve of an adolescent hip, in jeans, crushed hard against a stockinged foot: rough concertinaed working-class sock, the heel visible through a worn hole. Flash. As Benfield put it later, somebody's been determined the poor lad should leave the world as he entered it, in the foetal position. Flash.

The doctor cut the cords. They sprang back. The arms had been crossed hard and jammed between chest and knees, so close that the body now slowly uncoiled as if alive. Flash. The soaked cushion cover was prized from the head like flesh from a wound. Flash. Then the body was swiveled onto its back, and the dead face exposed to the suburban sun.

At any post-mortem, there may be sights to turn the stomach: heads wrenched off, features erased by bombardment. But this was peculiarly a face to disconcert a hardened doctor. For a moment, St. Hill had to wonder if he'd got his facts right, having understood he was to examine a boy of seventeen.

What lay before him was the frozen mask of a depraved, blown-up tramp of fifty, bleary eyes half closed, nose swollen, mouth split open, teeth bared in a grotesque snarl. Over the eyes, gobbets of hair doubly blackened with blood, stiff with it. The boy who last evening had swaggered gracefully down the warm dark of Oxford Road, best jeans and not-best socks, on his way to cheerio-mud-in-your-eye, looked like a clumsy make-up in a horror film.

It seemed as if the evil of the deed had seeped into the victim's face instead of the killer's.

The door opened, two constables were maneuvering an adjustable stretcher up around the staircase, like furniture movers. The doctors consulted: "Any use trying to straighten it up here?" . . . "Worth a go, it'll be some time before the hearse." Benfield and Talbot felt a bit queasy and went downstairs.

Rosy-faced Dixie Dean had been nosing about: Detective Sergeant Roy Dean, the nickname deriving (every male institution has its schoolboy jokes) from a famous North Country football player. Under the sitting-room couch he had found the letter Brady had been finishing that morning. An immature hand, but dead steady. You couldn't have told that in the middle of penning it the writer had had his life torn in half.

Talbot into the bedroom for a quiet look-see, while Benfield kept clear of the sitting room, where Bancroft, the forensic expert, was working his way around, and poked about in kitchen and scullery. He noted the gardening touch, peat, spade. Very nice.

Meanwhile, Hyde Station, 1:30, Policewoman Campion. She was quickly briefed. On her way to the canteen, trays being taken back to the café next door: the remains of three meals. Brady's in the C.I.D. room and the Smiths in purdah.

"Miss Hindley? Lovely day. 'Nother pot of tea?" My goodness, I agree, she does look older than twenty-three . . .

"Aye, that's r-right." Scottish accent. "Thanks, d'ye think ma dog cude 'ave soom Kit-E-Kat, he's starved."

"Certainly—oh, Sergeant," and Puppet was catered for. "I have a dog too," said Mrs. Campion.

"Oh—what's 'e called?"

"Mango."

"Mango—what a foonny name. Pooppet, sit!" Proper Manchester she sounded then. Not easy, yet somehow at her ease. The policewoman felt what they were all gradually to sense about them both: that they were like two people from another world who had suddenly been parachuted down into this one, word-perfect in the local dialect but somehow not *with* you.

"Smoke?" Thank God for cigarettes.

"No thanks, me boy friend smokes but I gave oop six months ago." The smile was social, empty.

Mrs. Campion noted, pretty strong will, not to give way to a puff *this* morning . . . In another way, it was like being with a person who's just had something dreadful happen, like an arm torn away, and sitting there as if she's under a local anaesthetic and not feeling a thing, and you think, What if it wears off, the screaming agony she'll be in—but somehow she doesn't look as if it *will* wear off . . .

The guest nibbled a biscuit. "The bobby told me ye've been away?"

"Yes, in Bramhall, on—a case." She somehow didn't specify.

"That's right," said the girl, "they told me, the murder there, fancy sendin' a woman on things like that."

"Well," Mrs. Campion found herself saying, "all in the day's work . . . Sugar and milk?"

They drank, she asked about Puppet, Myra asked about Mango. Then the inevitable pause. "Now," said Mrs. Campion, "I understand the body of a—"

"Here it cooms," said the other, "the Kit-E-Kat—Pooppet!"

As she fed the dog, Mrs. Campion felt entitled to a question. "Have you anything to say, after I have formally cautioned you . . . ?"

The girl looked at her, and Mrs. Campion realized this was the toughest she'd ever struck. "Nothing at all. Ian an' me came home from werrk and it was joost a normal evenin' till all this happened. Ian didden do it, I didden do it . . . What are you goin' to do with Ian because what he's done I've done."

Loud and clear. Said Mrs. Campion, still over tea, "David Smith says you helped clean up the mess." They had both forgotten their dogs, a moment of truth. "An' I suppose," said the girl cuttingly, "David Smith also told you he sat benevolently lookin' on. Ian didden do it, I didden do it, ask Ian." Apart from her nervous habit of holding her handkerchief to her mouth with both hands, and pressing its corners several times, she was unshakable. "The only thing I did find out," Mrs. Campion said afterwards, "was that she's mad on that dog."

Hyde Station, 2:30, Benfield and Talbot back.

"Mrs. 'Indley, sir." Nellie with her brother Uncle Bert fetched from work, both worried to death. "Mrs. Campion, tell her they're here, will you?"

Down the corridor, she saw the open canteen door; the girl had gone to the wash place and Puppet sat on her chair, waiting for her. Mrs. Campion saw her return, Puppet jumped down, she sat again and folded her hands. Just as the dog had waited for her, so, until she was taken away, she would be waiting. Like a dog. And the policewoman, like all who were to come into contact with her from now on, felt no pity.

" 'Lo Mam, 'lo Uncle Bert, this is a nice 'ow-d'ye-do, isn' it?" Then Nellie burst into sudden tears and clasped her daughter, then Uncle Bert wiped an eye, and Myra seemed to sort of sniffle too. Then noses were blown and Myra brought it back to normal. "Mam, ye herrd it on the radio, did ye, that lad David Smith's got us into a proper pickle, ringin' the police like that, didn't I always tell ye . . ." Nellie had to feel relieved, it must be a dreadful mistake after all—oh, when she'd realized the man at the door was a *bobby* . . . They all three sat like strangers in a railway station.

Benfield was having a long look at the letter Brady had been writing in the morning. "ATTENTION MR. T. CRAIG." Then neatly dated 10/7/65. "Tom, Sorry I could not phone yesterday, my family are in Glasgow this week. I was crossing road in town last night when someone on a bike came around the corner and knocked me down, except for a few bruises I was alright until I got up this morning, my ankle would not take my weight. I must have weak ankles or something, if it's no better tomorrow, I shall have to see doctor. Ian."

But he was *with* Craig yesterday, we've checked that, he must mean "last night" . . . And the family "in Glasgow this week"?

His mam's in Heywood, Lancashire, and his foster mother's never been *out* of Glasgow . . . Even in trivia, this was a peculiarly devious mind: at the time when he lived at his mother's and was once or twice on the sick list, she had gone out to a phone booth to tell the office: so now, in order to keep up the pretense that he is still living there, he has to explain her not phoning by pretending she has gone to Scotland. Otherwise a normal excuse letter.

3:55. Bert and Nellie took their leave, with the arrangement to come back in the evening with a complete set of Nellie's own clothes for Myra to wear, because Myra's had to be examined. Mam, it's a *formality*, don't go on so. And they were off.

Then a second mother. The dead boy's. Five minutes earlier, the two would have met on the pavement. "Mrs. Evans, sir" and they all rose as a pale woman in black entered timidly. Used as they were to the arrival of grief, they bowed their heads before the visitor's dumb bewilderment.

"Sit down, dear, and rest yourself a minute." As she did so, she saw something on the table, and stared. The suede shoes. She looked at the others. "Yes," she said, "they're his, new, his best."

She went on looking at the shoes. "He was all right," she went on in a whisper, as if to herself, "when he left 'ome for the football, what 'appened, where . . ." She did not finish. "Right next door," said Benfield as if to comfort her, "over the way." He had avoided the most chilling word in the language. Mortuary. Yet would the Anglo-Saxon sound any better, death house?

"Just sit quietly for a minute, eh?" Across the courtyard, the doctors had already started incisions, and the policemen were awaiting a sign that the body was re-covered, all but the face for Mrs. Evans to identify. They visualized what she would see, then thought of the man downstairs, having a nap after the café's special fruit pie, the strong hand digging into the crust, d'you wonder policemen are cynics?

"We'll get you some tea first, then Sergeant Carr'll look after you." Benfield rose. "An' I'll pop into the canteen and get my little spiel over." Mrs. Campion went with him. They found the girl friend still sitting, Puppet at her feet. "Hello Myra, 'nother cup . . . Mind me pipe?" She hadn't been offered a meal, being technically an intruder. They chatted a bit, the dog was again useful, then the formal caution and "From information I have received, you were present when . . ."

"I deny everything. Smith is a liar. I didden do it, Ian didden do it . . . Ask Ian, let me see Ian."

"I'm afraid you can't."

"Then I've got nothin' to say."

4:30, the station sleepily quiet. The open window overlooked the courtyard. There came to them, suddenly, a woman's voice. A desolate moan: "No, no . . ." It died away. He turned to her, his face set grimly. "That's his mother. She's identifyin' him. Now." From across the way, a gulping sob, then the silence of anguish.

Benfield looked at Mrs. Campion. A woman inured by her profession to tragedy, she was pale and near tears. They looked at the girl. She looked at them, then at her dog, who wagged his tail. Then she slowly stirred her tea, picked up the cup and took a deliberate and steady sip.

It was then the detective smelled that they were involved in quite a case.

CHAPTER 24

IN KING IAN'S OWN
FAIR HAND

"The Moving Finger writes; and, having writ,
Moves on . . ."

FitzGerald

HYDE STATION, first Police Constable: "'Bout Brady callin'
young Evans a bastard . . . Last thing poor lad was to 'ear,
funny . . ."

Second P.C.: "Why funny?"

First P.C.: "'Cause 'e wasn't, an' Brady was."

Pity for the mother pervaded the bleak station and softened it.
And those who had seen the corpse in the bedroom were later
relieved by the last photo Detective Constable Leighton had
taken of the face in the mortuary, not long before the mother
entered it. For although the moment when she stood under
the merciless top light and the sheet was drawn back was the
worst she had endured in a bumpy life, what she saw was not
what they had seen. Heartbroken, she cannot have been appalled.

The photographs had been taken with the same camera, and
with every minuscule mark showing. But the face bore no relation to the gargoyle of the morning. Things had happened the
wrong way around: the death's-head, had come to light next to a

housewife's window curtains, while now, on the mortuary slab, there lay something quite different.

True, the doctors had had the back of the head shaved in order to expose the multiple gashes biting deep, right down to the ravaged back of the neck. But the face had been washed, the eyes had been closed, the fashionably long hair flowed ascetically back from the brow and ears, so that the dead boy, except for a deep cut next to the right eye, resembled a figurehead of a drowned poet, on a ship forging ahead to a world he was at peace with. A chin not strong enough for beauty, and the teeth, under childishly curved lips, a millimeter too prominent. A life-loving mouth, more articulate in death than ever in Greater Manchester. And weak as a flower. But he looked now inviolable.

Another photograph showed the hands, in close-up, their backs plainly marked with "defense wounds." But these again were the gently tapering fingers of a statue. A third photograph showed the marble-smooth trunk. It could have been a torso dredged from the Aegean Sea, perfect except for the nibblings of erosion. The gargoyle had integrated into the child untouched by time: Dorian Gray in reverse.

Hyde Station–Number 16–Hyde Station, to and fro, fro and to. Mellow dusk, mellow dark. 6.30 P.M. Benfield emerged from Number 16, and at the garden gate glanced back at the house. All lights on, curtains closed, it looked as snug as next door, you'd never know. The car. Well, give it the routine once-over. He walked along the path—no vaulter he—around into the Avenue and down to the mini-Countryman, CNC 153 C.

Neat little job, transparent plastic covers on the seats. To keep them nice and clean. Nothing. Then his eye caught something. On the shelf in front of the wheel. A man's shabby wallet, in it three sheets of ruled paper off a shorthand pad. They were covered with what looked like an abbreviated shopping list. He walked up and in again, settled at the kitchen table, took out the three sheets and studied them.

Black ballpoint, except for the phrase "10 BUT" added in pencil. Capitals where indicated, the rest in Brady's neat schoolboy writing. The first two sheets in five ruled columns.

IN KING IAN'S OWN FAIR HAND

First sheet:

N° all List/u/   1+2   Destroy
all lists

Note how many pages EACH

OB	DET	CARR	STN	END
HAT	Clean before wipe pts place in paper container which has been cleaned After use, replace in container	×		Burn shaft bury head
CAR	Remove all moveable objects, clean cover floor and seat fresh Poly. at night Count all moveables, Keys etc.		×	Destroy Poly. inspect car for spots
GN	Polish, Bulls Polish	×		Dave
TICK	Place P/B		×	
REC	Check periodically unmoved			W/H
PROP P	STIMULATE			
CARR	For Hatch, paper bag			Destroy

Second sheet:

OB	DET	CARR	STN	END
ALI WE THEY HEYWOOD	Period of termination? Dave Carr 7–8.30 Use bus, pick-up and CARR Belle Vue, bus back HOTEL		×	14 days vague no memory after 14
METH	Drop me off, pass agreed Point ever five mins		×	
Dump	have container Hatch for Dave Carr Discuss		×	
CLOTH Keys	Check & Polish all buttons & clasps. Brush hairs, clean shoes, wear glov Packamac? Delete key ngt. 1 Pen	× 10 BUT		

Third sheet, no columns:

2 GN   5 Bulls EA   (Money)

    MATCHES   IF I AP Store Gn &

    CIGS   WALLET   Bulls where? New

    WATCH   10/–Note   Story

    GLVES

    2 PR Shoes   Dist   Why

Benfield, no longer the headmaster but the pupil, opened his notebook and wrote his answers. They were mostly easy. OB, object. HAT, hatchet. DET, detail. GN, gun. "Bulls," bullets. REC, reconnaissance. ALI, alibi. This was helped by remembering that Heywood was where Brady's mother now lived. METH, method. AP, apprehended. Packamac, isn't that one o' these newfangled raincoats that fold up into nothing?

But STN, CARR, TICK, *P/B*, *W/H*, PROP, BUT, "pass agreed Point ever five mins" . . . ? TICK, as in bed ticking? STN, station? Or stationery, writing paper? Or stationary, not moving?

Then he sat back and took in the whole picture. A plan. A plan to murder a man and dispose of the corpse.

He looked thoughtfully at the teakettle, and next to it the package of Sifta Salt, "Jolly Good Salt," with a picture of an old sailor, quite comic that. No, the details were so fussy they sounded phony. And the wallet left in the car—had Brady planted it there? As a leg-pull?

Talbot came in from upstairs with a suitcase, opened it and took out a pile of loose photos and a tartan-covered album. Twenty-two pages of tiny snaps as folksy as the cover, well over a hundred, pasted in more skillfully than most of them had been taken: holiday groups, arms around one another, babies dogs, dogs babies.

"If he'd 'a stuck to photography," said Benfield, "he'd 'a been all right."

He spoke too soon.

"Oh, and the cardboard boxes contain two guns."

Benfield stared, he hadn't somehow believed that part. "Six chambers each, loaded." "No!"

This was the real thing.

Talbot then took out two round cans enclosing yards of something around a spool. "They're tapes," said Talbot, "off a tape recorder, my son has one at home. There's two though there, in the sitting room."

"Two, *and* a car, marvelous what installment buying has done for the votin' classes. What d'you make o' this, Bob?"

He handed him the list, with side by side his own guesses. The first of many informal conferences, think-alouds really. Talbot studied both . . . Proper Agatha Christie stuff, eh?

Aye, Bob, that's why I—I dunno . . . P.B., that's the tough one.

Talbot remembered that Pro Plus was a mild stimulant, and after Reconnaissance, doesn't W.H. sound like a place? West Ham?

They drove back to Hyde. In the car: "P.B. . . . Pillar box?"

"Could be, that's where he'd mail letters . . . Park bench?"

"Not bad. Peat bog?" Well . . . Smith *had* mentioned the moors. "No, peat bog's not an expression, is it?" Then they broached a decision they had to face: assuming Smith was telling the truth, how much importance to give to Brady's talk of "other bodies." Empty boast? Leg-pull, like this list? Yes, but the list *has* got a murder attached to it. And guns. Anyway, if there *had* been other bodies, how the devil could he have disposed of them, he hasn't got a car! Settles it.

And yet as they drove, Benfield thought, The lad could ha' borrowed Myra's. And mentally he filed a question.

Hyde Station, 8 P.M., the long day beginning to go stale. C.I.D. room. "The Chief Superintendent is ready to see you. This way, please." Headmaster Benfield behind a desk, a bit of uncle thrown in: "Well, Jock, how d'you like it among the foreigners?"

"I dinna ken yet, only got here ten years back." Mmm, saucy. "Cigarette?" "Thanks." Smokes like a chimney, cool as a cucumber. "Now, Ian"—taking a paper, as if to give a pupil in trouble a chance to clear himself—"this is the statement you signed—"

"It is. And I stand by that, that's it."

"I see." Cheeky bugger. Well, caution him an' then police on trial as usual, but we'll have a bash, an' I bet I'm the first policeman whose first question to a murderer is, Have you got a driving license?

No, Jock hadn't, used to run a bike but can't drive, don't know one car from another, Myra drives. To a dull question, it was an answer which was to become more and more interesting.

Stand on your statement, do you? Then Benfield eased in with a routine question about the letter to Craig. "I had to tell him something to cover up."

Here we go, Jock. The Head, his manner slightly changed, took the wallet from his pocket, and still looking at the other's face, unfolded the first of the three sheets.

The eyes flicked down, up again. But no reaction. Not even the ripple of the Adam's apple as the dry throat is dealt with. It might have been a card in a big poker game.

The Head put a smooth question: "Could you tell me what these abbreviations—"

"Aye, the disposal plan." The pupil didn't seem to care if he got disgraced or not. "Smith and I planned it after it had happened, we sat up doin' it."

After? Let it pass.

"Now, Ian, couple o' things puzzle me. 'Destroy all lists'—now, that explains itself," and as he said it he realized, If these pieces of paper are to become evidence, how ludicrous the three words will sound in court, "these abbreviations . . ."

Brady agreed readily to the detective's renderings. "CARR?" "Things to be muved"—an obscure explanation unless it is realized that the word "carriage," with this meaning, is in daily use in an office like Millwards, such as "Carriage Paid." They got to "TICK." "Means 'tick off items.'"

"P.B.?"

A jolt of a pause. "Penistone Burrn." And Benfield knew that the glibness after the pause meant an improvisation. And he had an answer. He rose patiently and stood next to the wall map. "Look, Ian," he said patiently, pointing to a small town in Yorkshire, "this is Penistone and this is what they call the Penistone Road across the moors, but 'burn' isn't a word we use in these parts, we say 'river' or 'brook.'" "That's right," said Brady, "Brook," and it was left.

"You wrote all this *after* the murder?"

"Aye."

"*After* you had tied up the body and got it upstairs?"

"That's right."

"You mean that with the hatchet—now, don't answer unless

you want to—you mean that with the hatchet lying in front of you covered with blood ready to be cleaned up, you solemnly jotted down a reminder to clean it up?"

"I've allus been methodical."

Benfield looked at him, long and steady, and knew this list was no leg-pull. A schoolboy showoff, yes, but genuine and could be trusted to prove premeditation. The headmaster rose, and the pupil after him. 8:21 P.M. "I have to inform you I am arresting you on a serious charge"—taking up a paper—"this is the charge form."

In the pale, proud, hostile face, no change. "I stand on this morning's statement."

"You will of course be granted legal aid, the Clerk of the Court will help you there, that is, Mr. Pickup." Not the happiest name at the moment. Then an aside to Constable Fairley: "Take him down, will you." Brady put out his cigarette, leisurely lit another and followed down some stairs into the basement. A narrow passage with doors. The policeman opened the first. A cell.

The traditional kind, dark and cold and brutally empty. High up, the tiny barred window filtering in a dirty light, a rickety kitchen chair, a grey mattress sloping up from the stone floor, and a toilet bowl cemented to the floor, the wooden seat missing. The latter detail was somehow the major slap in the face. After all the jolliness upstairs, and the cups of tea, and the almost deferential questions, it was a cell. And often the new arrivals would recoil in sudden shock: "You mean *this* is where you expect me to . . ."

The policeman stood back. Brady stopped short, gave a quick look around, wrinkled his nose with distaste, said, "Well, thanks a lot," dragged on his cigarette and walked in. The distinguished foreigner. Alone. The door closed on him.

Report back to HQ—code word stock clerk—that in spite of traitor Smith doing his nut, the morale never been higher. We got the old buggers in the cop shop running around in cerrcles, they found disposal plan but not to worry, we have the werrld puzzled, Lieutenant Hess loyal and will remain loyal. We now relax to watch fun as everything now revolves around us, we are invincible, Sieg Heil.

. . .

His first visitor was Dr. Ellis in quest of specimens of saliva and blood swabs and samples of hair, including pubic, and particles of dirt from fingernails; same in a minute from Hindley and Smith. The seamy side of the whodunit.

Benfield, Talbot: Now that we've nicked Ian, do we knock off Dave? Myra? Neither? We're talkin' as if we'd known 'em for weeks.

One thing—if we let *him* go, we let her go too, she didn't even help wi' the tyin' up, and if we accept him bein' too scared to move, a husky young chap, we accept her too, the helpless girl friend. Yes, but she *is* the girl friend . . . Thought o' that; no, if she's out and about, she can't destroy any fresh evidence because in a case like this, any fresh evidence we need is in her house, which we're searching now and she can't get at.

I tell you one thing, just as well the case *is* as clear as it is. Because he is never going to break. And neither is she. Never.

8:45 P.M. First make sure Myra's still in the canteen, then let the Smiths out of their hideaway (We'll be in touch, ta ra), and off in a police car to Underwood Court. After the last twenty-four hours, they were done in. Wire from Dad to say he was coming up night train, fair play good ole Jack. Was a collapse into bed preceded by a couple of bottles of sparkling Moselle? Why not?

9 P.M. Benfield into the canteen. Immobile family group: Myra with her mam and Uncle Bert, and looking like a displaced person in a coat and skirt of her mother's. "Well, folks, that's all for today, sorry to ha' kept you hangin' about. Where d'you want to go, Myra?"

She stared. "Home o' course, with Ian."

"I'm afraid that's not possible."

"Why isn' it?"

Tough. "Because the house is under police supervision."

"Then I want to see Ian."

"You can't, you'll have to leave without him I'm afraid."

She stared again. (*Without him?* But I've never been without him—God, not without him . . .)

Once again she looked the foreigner: absolutely no relation to the two next to her, her uncle and her mother.

"Then I'll stay with Ian."

"I'm afraid you can't, he's under arrest." Five minutes later

she was outside getting into Uncle Bert's little car, to be driven
to Gorton.

Benfield to his bachelor quarters in Chester, Talbot to the new
house in Stalybridge and a philosophical wife who had packed
away the holiday stuff until further notice. Daughter Brenda, in
her twenties, was back from school; she taught at St. Paul's Primary, on the hill leading to Mossley and the moors. Dennis,
twenty and musical, was fiddling with his tape recorder. Talbot
had a whisky, he needed one. "It was on the one o'clock news
about a murder in Hattersley, anything to do with you, Dad?"
Family joke. "Aye, that's why your mum and me aren't sitting in
the London Palladium at this very moment. How was school,
Brenda?"

He looked out into the gentle evening, at his cherished garden
with its view of mucky old Stalybridge. In the morning, early,
there'd be just time for half-an-hour's pottering. Funny, Brady's
a gardener too. Been a long day. Longer ones to come.

"Myra, like to sit in front next to Uncle Bert?"

"No thanks" ('Ow *could* I sit in front, I'd keep on thinkin' I
was in *his* seat and that I oughta be the driver like always,
Neddie Neddie).

"Loov, should we go in by Hyde Road or through Ashton?"

"Ashton? I don't mind."

Not a word between the three, all the five miles to Eaton
Street. Uncle Bert has to think once again, God, what a dump,
and it's the house she was born in, and to see her standin' on the
doorstep in that smart hairdo, between an outdoor lav and a
condemned house. You have to feel sorry for her but she doesn't
seem to be taking anything in. He drove home to Clayton.

Knocker still on the blink? It is. Front door still peelin'? It is.
And as she looks at it she thinks, This is the first night him an'
me hasn't spent in the same bed since the beginning of time.

'Lo Dad, I got a terrible 'eadache, them police put you
through it something awful. Mam, 'ave ye got any o' that German wine Ian left here? It's the only thing for it, like Wincarnis
(Neddie Neddie . . .).

No, Mam, not the telly, I'll just 'ave a squint at the papers.

Woman's Mag, How to Make Diapers Last Twice as Long . . . Where's the corrkscrew? . . . Manchester *Evening News*, RHODESIA CRISIS—USA WARNS SMITH NOT TO DO IT. (Oh heck, I wish they'd warned 'im earlier, David Smith you're a fuckin' fifth columnist).

'Ello, what's this, BODY FOUND IN HOUSE IS IT MURDER, *a man is helping our inquiries at Hyde, Mrs. Maybury lives there with her granddaughter Myra Hindley, aged twenty-three*—gosh, I'm famous (No use lookin' to see if Neddie's horse won, Neddie Neddie), fill me glass again, Mam, I'm pooped.

('Alf past ten. Less than twenty-four hours ago I was at the wheel of our joy boat, an' wi' that lad in the back Neddie 'e pressed his leg next to my knee, it was warm through the cloth. I wash an' iron 'is underthings like he was a little boy.) Mam, I'll take the bottle up to bed for a nightcap, it's verra mild . . . No, no, not the radio (The Very Thought of You), goo' night Dad Mam, call me early for the 'Yde bus, Ian needs me there by nine, goo' night.

Christ it's dark, top light on quick. What a bedroom, I'd ferrgot, hello Baby Mo-Bee's bed, where's the bottle. Puppet darling, onto the bed an' not a werrd to Mr. Benfield about last night. Oh Neddie, ye'd 'a been proud of Hess today, I never said a thing an' even under torture I never never never never will, we'll win through an' beat the world. Oh, Neddie Neddie, gute Nacht mein Liebe Hairy Schottische . . .

And she sleeps. Better than Benfield or Talbot.

Ian? Ian didn't need his German wine to drop off, always slept like a log, did Ian. You bet he missed it, though.

Friday, October 8, Hyde Police Court. 9:30, Myra waiting. Manchester *Evening News* same day: "At a 3-minute hearing at 10:00 A.M., a man was charged with the murder of Edward Evans. As he left the dock he nodded at a blond woman friend."

10:30 A.M., Hyde Station, next door. Brady back in his cell. Myra wants her driving license back, is told she can't have it, goes. With the Smiths off the premises, and Myra, atmosphere more settled.

Talbot and Benfield. Review of position.

First, through Mrs. Evans, Eddie's friend Jeff Grimsdale had been contacted and shown a photo of Brady. Not a friend of Eddie's. Positive.

Mmm. Got to face it, the first idea—jealous quarrel over girl friend—doesn't fit. It looks as if that business you're always reading about is cropping up here too. Homosexuality. Brady had picked up a boy of seventeen and brought him home.

How?

How d'ye mean, how—oh, you mean not drivin' a car—well there, there's buses stop right opposite Number 16, change at Hyde!

True.

To a couple of policemen with a working knowledge of the half-world, Brady didn't seem to fit into any of the recognizable homosexual categories. But they knew enough, too, to know that you can never be sure of anything.

Myra.

Well, we know that sort of girl, if she *is* that sort. Well, there are *two* sorts. First, the manly Lesbian who runs around with the womanish man-lover. And that sort, this lass isn't. She's a big girl wi' no nonsense, but she's potty about Ian and that's that. The other sort is the girl that falls for a homosexual an' begs to live with him an' cook his meals an' doesn't mind the boy friends. And when he gets into trouble, she'll shield him by swearing she was with him all the time and so he *couldn't* have picked up a boy . . . Also, if he's homosexual it accounts for him taking up Smith, a kid of sixteen, day after his wedding, can be a challenge to that sort to nip a lad right out o' the orange blossom . . . No, I mean it, I've knocked about, old friend, and so have you.

But when he brought the lad back to Number 16, she was home . . .

Aye, but he may not have known that, she might have been supposed to be visitin' her mam in Gorton and something had mucked up the visit an' there she was, spoilin' the picnic. Then Brady gets her out o' the house to go an' give a message to her sister, then he—shut the door, in case o' Mrs. Campion—then he makes 'is overtures, which explains the lad's shoes being off, fly undone and the medical evidence of the dog hairs found on the back of his legs where he'd sat on the bed presumably with his jeans an' his shorts around his feet—

Mrs. Campion's head around the door, hope she missed that bit. "Myra's back."

"Oh heck, *an'* Puppet?"

"An' Puppet."

"Well, give her the old cuppa."

"And the Kit-E-Kat?"

"Goes without sayin'." She goes.

"What does our Myra want?"

"I give you three guesses, an' it isn't from me an' it isn't from you."

"Well, she won't get it, not here she won't."

A think. No, doesn't fit into the picture . . .

How d'you mean?

I mean, Brady bein' that sort of a homo who'd pick up that sort of kid for that sort of thing. Too strong. He's as strong as the blade o' that hatchet. No, he was playin' the lad up.

But why?

Search me, can't ha' been money, kid obviously hadn't much. No, he picks up a lad—

You mean, *they* pick up a lad.

That's right, they. And there's another thing. Brady says the three of 'em got back to Number 16 "at eleven-therrty" and that Myra left pretty well immediately to go up to the Smiths'. But Dave swears she'd changed all her clothes—in that short minute, why?

You mean, they'd brought the boy home much earlier?

Could have. Another thing—accordin' to her they'd been "cruisin' around Manchester" for a good two hours—well, Dave swears Ian wouldn't stand for that, he just went places an' did things an' came back, no hanging about.

But suppose they *had* come home earlier, why should that explain her changin' her clothes?

Because she might ha' changed 'em unintentionally, like . . .

How d'you mean?

I mean that in the bedroom she may have stripped off the leopard-skin dress and all that went with it—wasn't it found over the armchair next mornin', here it is in the photo—an' when, in good time, she dressed again to fetch David Smith, she happened to get into old clothes.

You mean—it was a case of three's company?

Well, it's as believable as her driving Evans home with Ian so that the two lads could get chummy . . . An' then, with her an' her brother-in-law lookin' on, the old boy friend kills the new boy friend . . . *And* accordin' to plan. It's a blinkin' puzzle.

Mrs. Campion again. "Says she can't stay at her mother's any longer, wants to go to her Uncle Bert in Clayton."

"All right, get a driver."

"An' a rug."

"An' a box o' chocs. An' a transistor. What d'you say we go all U.S.A.?"

"How d'you mean?"

"Slap her into his cell for the night, just him and her and the 'idden microphone makes three."

"Don't be daft, have you had a look at the new Judges' Rules, out just in time for this little caper? . . . *I* know what she's come to do."

"What?"

"To tell us *Ian* didden do it, *she* didden do it, ask David Smith."

And so it went on. Until 7 P.M., when Dixie Dean breezed in.

He had been back to Number 16, to " 'ave a look around."

In sitting room, tiny brown spots on wallpaper above fireplace, also in a corner of wall and brick hearth. If you lift up linoleum and scrape with point of a penknife, it's all crusty wi' dry brown powder. Blood. Puts you off your grub.

Umpteen empty bottles, lot o' junk from the wardrobe, scribblings, accountancy exercises, letter from him to her, nothing to it, more photos.

From among it all, Talbot picked a shabby school exercise book. More accountancy sums, drawings, then in black ballpoint a page of names lazily doodled in the same schoolboy hand, down and across, fairly higgledy-piggledy, a bored twenty minutes at Millwards. In the middle, a sketch of two heads—quick but fluent, firmly adult as opposed to the handwriting—two melo-dramatically bad men, high cheekbones, slit eyes, broken nose, long thin cruel lips. Throwback to Mexican thriller of the forties in a Gorbals flea pit. Psychiatrist might make something of it.

The sprawled names didn't seem worth a look, but Talbot gave the look.

Christine Foster, J Mcready, Jean Simpson, Robert Uquart, James Richardson, Joan Crawford, Gilbert John, Ian Brady, Jim Robertson, Ian Broderick, Jim Leonard, Ian Brady 18 Westmore-land St. Bradford Yorks, John Sloan, Jim Idiot, John Birch, Frank Wilson, Alec Guineas, Jack Polish, J. Thomson, John Gil-bert, Mieklerig Cres, Ian Cresent.

At the end of a tiring day, this was a bind. Had farce set in? Had all these been done in with an axe? Jean Simpson—garbled film star or dead Glasgow teen-ager? Wouldn't ha' thought Brady'd heard of an oldster like John Gilbert, and why take that street of his in Longsight and dump it into Yorkshire? As a contemptuous nickname, Jim Idiot was serviceable, John Sloan's his foster father, isn't John Birch some funny political chap in the States, and Ian Cresent showed that the doodler's invention had expired.

Talbot was about to close the exercise book and put it away to be marked "Irrelevant to Case," when between Frank Wilson and Alec Guineas his eye caught a name. He'd seen it before.

Film star? Politician? But he *knew* it . . .

Then he remembered. A schoolboy. John Kilbride.

CHAPTER 25

A LITTLE CHILD SHALL
LEAD THEM

"I know a bank . . ."
A Midsummer Night's Dream

IN THE LONDON TELEPHONE DIRECTORY, which can produce
a dozen duplicates of an unusual name, there are only four Kilbrides. If David Smith had been surnamed Kilbride, and vice
versa . . . Following Frank Wilson, John Smith would have
passed unnoticed.

Talbot sat with a growing light in his eye. A think about
spelling. Judging by this little lot, our Ian isn't too hot at it. One
of the mistakes was obviously a wry joke, typical and not bad,
nice gossip headline about the film star who signs a contract for a
million: "Alec Guineas." But "Urquhart" shouldn't have defeated a Scot, and Kelly's Directory for Glasgow was to show that
he should have been able to spell Meiklerig, as it was the Cres-
cent, parallel to Templeland Road in Pollok, in which his childhood sweetheart Evelyn Grant had lived—and what about
"Cresent"? Now, if your spelling wasn't dead-on and you knew
the name Kilbride only by hearsay, wouldn't your instinct be to
write "Killbride"? But this chap had got it right. Could he have
been helped by the Ashton *Reporter?*

Evans had been seventeen. Twelve, was John Kilbride. But big for his age. Certainly uncanny. You never know.

Then, instantaneously, he thought, Uncanny, yes . . . *but you do know*. Moors. Other bodies. Kids are dangerous they get missed, switch to teen-agers they get labeled as missing persons. Get this photostated. *This is it.*

Well, we've said it. We don't believe it, not yet . . . But just the same, put a call through to Ashton-under-Lyne headquarters. Detective Chief Inspector Mounsey.

Mounsey, the man who called regularly to see Mrs. Kilbride and was determined to find the boy ("he's Mounsey's Lad, is John"). Or was, maybe by now Joe's lost interest.

Talbot's approach was tentative. "Joe, this may be nothing, but we've got a spot o' bother here in Hyde you'll have heard about. Well, on a bit of paper I've got in front o' me now, somebody wrote the name John Kilbride."

At the other end, the big combative-looking man sat right up at his desk. Dead silence. Talbot was not to know that staring at Mounsey in Ashton Station, two years after the event, was the smiling poster of the missing boy. Then Joe said, "I knew it'd come . . . First thing in the morning? I'll be there."

Well . . . Of course, they told themselves, one reason why he's accepted the clue unconditionally is that he visualizes the suspect as a psychopathic sex maniac, probably a crazed older man. How will he feel faced with a presentable young couple from next door?

But his reaction had been a shot in the arm. Suddenly the activity in the old station—the clacking of the typewriters, the phone calls to Glasgow, the search of Number 16 and of the Smith flat, arrangements for Evans' funeral, the delving into the past history of all concerned—it was all worthwhile. They arranged, tomorrow morning, for a police car to fetch David Smith.

Then another arrival, Detective Chief Inspector Tyrrell from Manchester C.I.D. A gentler type, more scholastic, but just as determined. There was a child missing from Ancoats, and Ancoats was in his area. Lesley Ann Downey.

P.B., P.B. . . . Potboiler? Don't be daft . . . Prime beef?

Check on all Myra's cars; during less than two years she's had three.

So as not to get too identified with one car?

How are they off for luggage? How are what off? The cars. Oh . . . sort o' mini-vans, you open the doors at the back and slide the rubbish in. I see, handy.

Jokes of course. Kilbride Kilbride Kilbride.

Saturday, October 9, Talbot's office in Stalybridge. Mounsey was five minutes early, the bulldog with something between his teeth which he would never let go. They told him the story, with every emphasis on Brady and Hindley being unlikely candidates: typist daughter of Catholic father, Scottish clerk in reputable firm, practically betrothed.

The bulldog face did not change, Mounsey seemed almost not interested. Just asked for the exercise book.

He stared at the names. For quite a minute. He had the exact mind of a watchmaker or a miniaturist, the sort of man that can stare a jigsaw puzzle into creeping together. And as the minute crept on, it seemed to the others as if the name they were all looking at, upside down on the paper, grew in authority till it filled the room. Frank Wilson John Kilbride Alec Guineas John Kilbride JOHN KILBRIDE. I, John Kilbride, call to you. Find me. Find me.

Ian, this is Detective Chief Inspector Mounsey. Brady had never heard of him and Ashton-under-Lyne was not mentioned. But the reaction of both was instantaneous. They were fighters suddenly in the ring, opponents who have known of each other all their lives and face to face at last. This is it. Right. The detective wasn't even saying to himself, I have a feeling we've got the right man—not even, I know in my *bones* we've got the right man. You could see him thinking, So *this* is what he's like . . .

Back to cell, then David Smith. As he entered, more composed and confident than that first day, Talbot and Benfield realized his sudden importance. Realized too, that as he told his story yet again, stammering but coherent, Mounsey believed him. N-no, didn't know the name Kilbride—oh, wait a m-minute, wuzzen it a lad that went missin' . . . Moors? Picnics an' such, an'—well . . . t-target practice . . . You mean the night he tuke me to see the view? I cude f-find that all right, the road's got them p-posts all along an' a lake on the right—ah, I've remembered the name. Woodhead.

The others looked at one another. Reconnaissance, W.H. Not bad. When do we s-start? Tomorrow, right.

When he had gone, Mounsey did not even discuss minor queries re his statement, just got out all the photographs and spread them. First the tartan album, the twenty-two pages of family fun.

Wee Ian laughing with foster sisters by the banks of Loch Lomond, smiling on doorstep of 21 Templeland Road, Ian in black shirt and white tie, Ian sunbathing on his back stripped to the waist next to transistor, Ian and Myra snapping each other crouched in the snow, just a couple o' kids playing at spacemen, top boots, crash helmets, goggles, rifle aimed up at the sky, pom pom pom, Myra on back of bike looking forty—who said crime keeps you young?—Ian stripped to the waist again, grinning and pouring an empty bottle onto his head, Myra and Ian on sofa looking up at budgie, Maureen, dogs, Myra with puppy, Myra on boulders, Ian on boulders: he with feet apart, sweater, hands easy in trouser pockets and smiling easily through dark glasses, personable young Unspoiled Film Star, on the intellectual side, savoring the British way of life. "Why the hell," growled Mounsey, "is he wearin' specs when there's no sun?"

No background to these last, so no possible way of placing them. Never mind, get 'em enlarged, you never know. More dogs. Myra as a film star too, in those dark glasses that give you the devilish eyebrows; Myra in Number 16, fur collar, glass in hand, sitting next to the telly. Ian in a Pollok back garden, holding a two-year-old baby. Myra at the wheel holding Puppet, photographed from back area of car. More babies. Too bad.

Then a long look at the collection they had settled to call the "Moorland Views." Wi' most of 'em, it's the Sherlock Holmes joke, you know—unusual thing is the people in the foreground—

Oh, but there *aren't* any people in the foreground—

I know, that's what's unusual . . . I mean, look at this one of the white mini-van, against them ugly rocks, flat light, no scenery —and all these, just a lot o' land, stony valleys winding away from camera, ribbons of mountain roads. I mean, look at this one, just a flat patch of soil and stones, like a devastated area. It's like those shots the film units take when they've picked their locations and take a photo for reference, such as places on the way to the site where they'll shoot the scenes when the fine weather comes—

Site?

Yes, the site of the big love scene. The site of a fight with the villain over a cliff. The site of a grave.

The grave is on the moors. Puzzle, how can a man who can't drive convey a victim into wild country and then get home? No puzzle, the girl drove him both ways ("Wherever he has gone I have gone, he has never been anywhere without me"), just as she drove him to Central Station to pick up Evans. The girl who had stirred her tea when she heard the cry of a mother was the same girl who had stirred her tea resting her crossed feet on a low mantelpiece and said, "Remember the night we were burying a body?" The terrifying improbability of it—that they swept aside. The grave is on the moors.

Yet another look at the Disposal Plan. Long look. "Check periodically unmoved," what does that convey to you? . . . Yes, but who would ever have found a dead body and then moved it without reporting it? Or, come to think of it, moved it, even without reporting it?

Ever heard the word "viable"? It's what peat is. Wi' time peat breaks up. Shifts about. *Moves.* Winter is a-comin' in, the peat is gettin' soft. On the moors, lot o' peat. No, "Check periodically unmoved" means: check that through the action of the peat the body isn't getting near the surface.

And let's look at "Drop me off, pass agreed Point ever five mins." Put baldly that means, "I tell Myra to stop car, I get out with spade and leave the road for a spot o' diggin', but she's not to park like she did before, and have the police stop to ask is anything up—no fear, she's to drive a few miles, slowly, to an' fro past the spot, till she finds me standin' thumbin' a lift an' waitin' to take the goods out o' the car." What's wrong wi' that?

Nowt. Except we don't know the spot . . . By the way, occurs to me—didn't Brady mention that when they hadn't a car they occasionally rented one?

Aye, and then couldn't for the life of 'im remember where from . . .

Well, no harm in combing through the car-rental firms. Call Nimmo, Manchester City.

Before parting, the four looked down at the other item, the open exercise book. The page had acquired the importance of a Bible manuscript. "Well, we start right in on Monday, eh? Lookin' for Mounsey's Lad."

"True," said Tyrrell quietly, "but Manchester City's got a stake too." He lifted the exercise book, smiling, and held the page to the light as if looking for a name in the watermark. Then he took a pencil, and on the blotter wrote the word LAD. Then he put in a couple of dots. L.A.D.

He didn't have to explain to the others. It had been in their minds too.

Now, if instead of Christine Foster or Jean Simpson or Joan Crawford, he had doodled Lesley . . . Ann . . . Downey. It would have taken him only a second. We would like to have been given a lead, 'cause we're very tidy up North, we are.

But you never know. Start in.

Meantime, in adjoining office, routine jobs. Some truculent chap brought in, had lunched too well, in trouble.

First Police Constable: "That's one thing our Ian won't be found guilty of."

Second P.C.: "What?"

First P.C.: "Drunken driving."

Sunday, October 10, 1:30 P.M. A police car called at Underwood Court, Mounsey at the wheel, Talbot in the back. Maureen sat next to Mounsey, and Dave in the back so as to be where he'd sat in Myra's car and see the road that way. It was a fine afternoon and he was as excited as a schoolboy; the others felt a quickening of the pulse too.

The lake he'd mentioned made it easy: it would be the Woodhead reservoir. Out on A57, the winding road known as the Snake, to the moorland town of Glossop—Myra had said they'd been there—and on to A628 toward Penistone, where the reservoir would be on the right before coming to the beauty spot called Woodhead. W. H. They were in great spirits. Approaching Glossop, Mounsey handed Dave a sheaf of "Moorland Views": Any of these ring a bell with you Dave?

Ian's, are they? He was allus queer for cameras. I never seen *these*, a bit dreary they look to me . . . No, don't remind me of anything, sorry.

Through Glossop. The reservoir, said Talbot, will be showing on our right, any minute now. So it will, said Dave, peering to one side, then to the other, staring at the posts. The car bowled along, primed to slow down at a signal from the back.

But the signal did not come. Just as passengers always know instinctively when a driver has lost his way and is trusting to luck, so now Talbot felt that the lad was losing confidence. Finally Talbot turned to him. Dave was sheepish. "It's them posts," he muttered, "they was whiter some'ow, an' lower. An' the water doesn't look right neether. Too near an' too 'igh up . . . No, the wife won't remember any better, she never notices a thing."

Never mind, nice day for a joy ride, no bones broken. Let's face it, Davey lad, half the time on those jaunts, wasn't the old elbow working overtime? Never mind. This time the informer had misinformed.

But never say die, hadn't the four picnicked in more than one place—here we are, Woodhead. And just beyond, sure enough, Dave thought he recognized a steep rocky valley. And they *were* on the Penistone Road. Somewhere 'ere, I think . . . Dunno.

In the car going back, less chat. You have to think . . . It's rare for a murderer who kills in a rage to have killed surreptitiously already . . . And if he's going to make false boasts of such murders, what more natural than to pretend he's disposed of the bodies on the same moors which are proved, by the "Moorland Views" and indeed by the present outing, to have been his favorite haunts? You have to think . . .

Same afternoon. Myra and Uncle Bert and Auntie Kath went to Hattersley and called at Mrs. Hill's, where Gran was staying, 2

Wardle Brook Walk. It was so near the back of Number 16 that they hadn't thought for a minute that Myra would go, but she did. And what was odd was that as they walked across from the bus, with Number 16 staring down at them and a couple of pass-ersby staring at Myra—after all, that teen-age lad *had* been clobbered in her house by her boy friend—she looked utterly unconcerned. Just gave the house one quick look and walked on with Puppet, who of course made a dash for "oop the slope" and had to be caught and carried past.

At Mrs. Hill's, Gran was resting, so Myra didn't have to go up and cope with her, Uncle and Auntie did that, Elsie Masterson there but wi' poor Mrs. Hill bein' blind and the girls not knowin' what to say or not to say, not an easy visit. Aye, Mrs. Hill, the pedestrian's died but it wasn't my fault, he ran straight into me on the wrong side. Ian an' me was lucky not to get killed, Ian's fine. It was arranged that later in the week poor Gran should go to daughter Annie in Railway View and later to daughter Nellie, 20 Eaton Street. Myra back to Clayton with Uncle and Auntie, just like any other house but at least *not* the one she'd been born in.

Myra loov, look at Puppet lookin' up at you as if 'e longs to speak. I think dogs know all don't you? Myra, I wish they wouldn't keep askin' your Uncle Bert about it at work, very bad for him, you see, bein' a foreman. "Oh Mr. Maybury," they say, "you mean *your niece* knows the chap that done this?" I mean, it isn't nice. Myra, don't you think it might take your mind off of the waitin', to come to Mass? . . . Oh Myra, what d'you mean shurrup, what a thing to come out with, what would Father Theodore say? Did you know he'd written to the Catholic priest in 'Attersley? Sorry I brought it up I'm sure.

(Neddie, your Hess loves you, and loyal mein Liebling forever and ever, amen. See you tomorrow.)

Monday, October 11, Stalybridge Police Court, 11:30 A.M.: "A man was charged with the murder of Edward Evans, and re-manded." Myra, can we give you a lift to Hyde? Sitting next to Mrs. Campion, dog talk. Hyde Station, 2:05 P.M. Carr: "Miss Hindley, I'm afraid we have to charge you with being an acces-sary to the murder of Edward Evans."

Caution. "It's not true, Ian didden do it, I didden do it. Ask David Smith."

"This is the charge sheet, sign here please."

"I want the same solicitor as Ian." Mr. Fitzpatrick of Hyde, a kind and sensitive man, was to be compassionately known right and left as "poor old Fitz."

(An' yet it means I'm *with Neddie*, no more o' that hangin' aboot, thank God we're in it together an' we'll get out of it together, Sieg Heil.)

Mounsey to his ace photographers in Ashton, Detective Constables Gelder and Masheder: immediate enlargements of all outdoor photos, however unpromising.

Then, after cautioning, a series of chats. Brady and Hindley v. Mounsey and Tyrrell. Talk talk talk, tea, talk talk talk, cigs. The police behavior perfectly correct, but gone was the how's-tricks-Jock approach. Both detectives, each in his way, straight as an arrow. Jock was right up against it, and so was she.

MOUNSEY: I have reason to believe that, with David Smith, you discussed the subject of killing people and burying them on the moors.

BRADY: There are no others.

MOUNSEY: Have you discussed killing people and burying them on the moors?

BRADY: It was all part of the fiction to impress him—

. MOUNSEY: Have you discussed burying people on the moors?

BRADY: Yes.

MOUNSEY: David Smith has told us that when Evans was killed you said it was the messiest one yet.

BRADY: It was to do with the situation we were in. (An evasion which has served at many a top-brass crisis conference.)

MOUNSEY: The remark can only indicate that you have committed other crimes.

A steady drive, courteous, unflinching, admirable. But the two never showed one crack, not a hair's-breadth of one. Before the question the unblinking stare: Your inquisitiveness is an impertinence but I'll try tae co-operate; then, after the question the shrug: I really don't know how to help ye on such a trivial detail.

TYRRELL: You went on the moors at night to dispose of the victims you killed?

BRADY: What I told Smith was only to build up an image.

TYRRELL: Smith says you said that he had almost been on a grave where you and Myra had buried a body. Is it off the Penistone Road?

BRADY: In that general area. It was the situation we were in. I spoke in general terms. It was to build up an image.

And that was that. He had talked, but the shoddy generalizations had somehow kept him in his depth. And from her, the monosyllabic answers followed one another with the same heavy trying-to-rise inflection, as mechanical as the flat call of a bird: No, no, no, no, no . . . To go from one stone face to the other, the two in impregnable conspiracy, was grueling. Unprofitable. The loaded name of Lesley Ann Downey produced the same two stares.

All right, here we go. And Mounsey played his card. Flipped out the photostat of the "Kilbride doodle."

Brady was clearly puzzled by the list, as anyone would be by an absent-minded jumble of names scribbled in an old exercise book nearly two years before.

Mounsey spoke in the end. "John Kilbride?"

No reaction. Aye, it was his writing, just a muddle of names, fillum stars an' that, must ha' been testin' a pen—

"John Kilbride?"

A fellow he'd known at Hull Borstal. No, knew nothing of any perrson missin' from Ashton, ye mean I've buried Kilbride on the moo-errs as well as John Gilbert an' Joan Crawford an' Jim Idiot? Quite a cemetery there must be up there, it's an amusin' idea.

Mounsey thought of Mrs. Kilbride, then stifled the thought. No point in losing your temper.

And so round the mulberry bush. Round and round and round. At the end of the day the two prisoners were put in cars—Brady handcuffed to his escort—and taken to Risley Remand Centre, on the other side of Manchester, where they would henceforth be "detained." What a relief to have him out of the place. As Tyrrell remarked, he and Mounsey looked so whacked it could have been a day of Brady and Hindley grilling the police.

Conference. Mounsey couldn't hide the fact that he had hoped for results and hadn't got them. He had hoped Brady would make a vital slip, or even suddenly turn cynical and tell all, just to see their faces. Neither. Brady had acknowledged boasting to Smith about other bodies, but hadn't that merely confirmed one of their first ideas, that he had made it all up to impress Smith?

Quite right, they were exhausted. Oh, let's make that long-distance call to Hull, get that over. Suppose, by a million-to-one chance, they say, Oh yes, John Kilbride's an old boy now doing well in New Zealand . . . Hello?

No, never been a Kilbride here, a Kilmarnock once, not at all a pleasure—oh, wait a sec, somebody's 'ere sayin' they do recall the name, hold on . . .

(God no no no . . .)

Are you there? Yes, they do know the name, it's on a list here. Isn't John Kilbride a boy down your way a couple of years ago who went missing? . . . Not at all, 'bye 'bye . . .

That's all right but we're nowhere. Joe, what do we do tomorrow?

Mounsey's bulldog jaw stuck out. He had talked to Prescott, Benfield's opposite number in Lancashire, and Prescott agreed. "Tomorrow," said Joe, "we do what *he* bluddy well did. Dig."

Meanwhile, Hyde Station.

Benfield, to David Smith: "Dave, *you* know our Ian better'n anybody—what would you say would be the best way to persuade him to talk?"

David Smith: "Lock 'im up in a room with a couple o' daddy-longlegs, an' in two minutes he'll be up the ruddy wall."

As the politicians say, any avenues unexplored? Oh, one thing might help, give it a try, one o' them questionnaires, around Hattersley door to door: Kindly fill in anything untoward, et cetera. And the questions were duly composed, duplicated, delivered and at the end of the day the results collected.

None had anything constructive to tell. Some were inane: "They were eatin' chips, we thought nothing of it at the time." Some abusive: "Yes I did notice their car was outside their house and next minute noticed *my* car was *not* outside *my* house and you damn well find it for me."

One reply passed unnoticed: "Can give no information. (Mrs.) Ann Downey."

Personal calls of course were made on immediate neighbors. The Jamaican Braithwaites were polite. They answered, in their musical voices, like good children. "Yessir, the hole lady shouted 'Myra, Myra,' then something about dogs. . . . They seemed a quiet couple, flyin' high over the railin's an' down into the car. . . . No sir, we keep ourselves to ourselves so didn' chat so much . . . Thanks for callin', sir."

"Good morning, Mrs. Masterson."

"Oh yes, our Pat knowed them well, she used to sit wi' them an' Myra's gran, an' 'elp collect peat for Ian's garden, didn't you, Pat? Like a little niece she was, an' she can't believe there was that lad murdered in the 'ouse, and as for me, the idea of Ian bein' an 'omosequel an' not mindin' what sex the other person is, oh dear . . . It's been a proper shock to the system, I never set ears on the word 'pornography' 'fore this week an' now it's on everybody's lips, when I meet strangers now I go all reserved.

"Foonny, old Mrs. Hill, bein' blind, used to send Myra's gran over to the New Inn with a bob to put on a 'orse for 'er, an' always won—well, since this bother she's sent somebody else an' never won a sausage since. Oh it's terrible, isn't it? Is it true Ian 'n' Myra's goin' to be made into wax an' on show in Madame Tussaud's in Blackpool? . . . Oh yes, like a little niece to them our Pat was."

Back at Hyde, these sentiments produced a couple of deep sighs. So that's what we're up against, Uncle Ian an' Auntie Myra. God, I vote we give up.

No, dig.

Hyde Station, same afternoon. Mounsey, Chief Inspector Lowe. Notes for project, shall we call it a Disposal Plan? Tracker dogs as before. Contact Mr. Broadhead in Wakefield, surveyor for West Riding County Council, for most detailed ordnance maps available. Recruit fifty Manchester City police and C.I.D., particularly any knowing the terrain. Shepherds. Beg or borrow spades from civil defense, farms, gardens. In case of bad visibility, fluorescent coats. Endless copies of "Moorland Views" for reference during reconnoiters, and to be distributed to expert farmers and hikers all over, with the faces blotted out. Long canes, like they used at El Alamein looking for mines.

Next morning, Tuesday, October 12, 9 A.M., Operation W.H. Woodhead.

The Penistone Road. Cold, damp, territory savage. Vans, portable canteen, it was like a film unit on location for a drab documentary. But the fluorescent coats gave a touch of gaiety, like poppies, and for an hour spirits were jaunty. Then the long grim day. "Proper needle-in-a-'aystack job an' no mistake!" The river Etheroe, very damp. Snake Pass, brr.

As Mounsey stood and surveyed the miles of rough grass and stone, an area nowhere smooth enough for even recent disturbance to show, his heart sank. But his face gave no hint. He might have been a farmer directing a fleet of laborers engaged to turn every square yard, from here to the horizon, into priceless property: "This corner looks a bit ragged, try it—no, leave that, it's all stone underneath, waste of time . . ." The men with the long canes kept sinking them deep into soft ground, and then putting them to their faces and standing immobile, so that at certain moments, against the sky, a gang would resemble a frieze of wintry flutists playing music beyond the human ear. The truth was less romantic. They were carefully smelling the ends of the canes.

The press had somehow, with uncanny skill out of the empty air, deciphered the bush telegraph of the Woodhead activities. Manchester *Evening News*, same day, across the front page: POLICE IN MYSTERY DIG ON MOORS. "A piece of paper bearing the name of a person who vanished two years ago has come into their possession." The name Brady had not been mentioned in the papers, not even in connection with the Evans case.

From that moment, the air started to crackle. Wednesday the

thirteenth (Benfield in London, conferring with John Wood of the Director of Public Prosecutions Office), out of the void, crowds materialized at Woodhead, among them reporters and photographers craning necks over operations which the diggers knew were leading nowhere. The moors stretched for mile after misty mile. Manchester *Evening News*, same day, was perforce mysterious, the laws of libel being what they are: FORENSIC MEN COMB TERRACED HOUSE OF SECRETS "for clues which might connect any former occupant with the disappearance of certain persons."

Dig dig dig. Nothing. Had that other idea been right, that he'd buried nobody and said Penistone as a name out of the blue just to impress Smith? Or *had* he buried somebody and said Penistone to put them off the scent of the real place, miles and miles off? Look for any disturbed ground. Dig dig. The bulldog face was set, but it was hard going. Coldharbour Moor, rightly named, brr.

Hyde Station. The going was not helped by reports filtering in from the experts. "Myra in front of the waterfall" turned out to be Shiny Brook Clough, six whole miles from the Penistone Road; the one with a stream and the promising wood was taken at Whaley Bridge, fourteen miles; another background was identified as Leek in Staffordshire; another desolate valley was Ladybower in Derbyshire. And nobody could place the Unspoiled Film Star on the rocks, or Myra ditto. Brady said it was Whaley Bridge, how to tell?

Then a stroke of luck: phone call from Nimmo in Manchester. After intensive inquiries at every sort of car-rental firm, he had in front of him a slip of paper witnessing to the rental, from Glazier's Autos in Liverpool Road, of a Ford Anglia 9275 ND for the period of twenty-four hours, 10 A.M. to 10 A.M., £4/10/0, signed "Myra Hindley." Date? November 23, 1963. John Kilbride's last day on earth.

God, takes your breath away. Lifts your spirits, though.

Thursday the fourteenth, Woodhead. Spirits needed lifting, bitch of a day, scudding mist and fog, rain, even the tracker dogs rebeled and one tubby little explorer with a dog as big as himself had to drag him up the crags. Waders, oilskins, the lot. That sneering face lying on the Dunlopillo mattress in the warmth of Risley bluddy Remand Centre blowing smoke rings . . . makes you feel proper upset. Heavy excavators? Out of the question, might reduce valuable evidence to pulp.

The wind howled. In a coffee break, a fanciful policeman remarked to his mate that if you listened you could almost think that the sudden shrill gusts were a kid's voice. Calling. Find me find me find me. Nothing.

Risley Remand Centre, 12 noon. Chief Inspector Tyrrell, to Myra Hindley: "David Smith says you said a policeman stopped and spoke to you while a body was being buried."

"Rubbish."

"Did Ian say, 'It's the messiest yet'?"

"Rubbish."

Hyde Station. The quick sandwich in the office, the talk turns to gardening. Bob Talbot warms to his subject: . . . An' the best for the soil mind you, bar rich manure, is peat.

Never knew that, says one of the constables, not bein' a gardener. Where d'you buy it from?

Don't be daft, you don't buy it, you do what a lot do, go up on the moors an' dig it up.

You don't say . . .

Why, what's the matter, remembered something?

Yes, I 'ave—that Mrs. Summat in Number 12 told me her little girl used to 'elp 'em get peat.

Talbot's sandwich stopped in midair.

"Aye, I'm Pat, twelve last July . . . Aye, they got chummy wi' me over Puppet—ooh, I do miss Puppet . . . Oh yes, up on the moors. Mam, there's nothing wronk in tellin', is there? Yes, a lot at night . . . Well, sometimes a sip of his drink when I sat on 'is knees in the car, sometimes two or three glasses and once whisky an' gin.

"Always the same spot, they says if I wanted a change I could stop 'ome . . . No, they never give it no name, just the moors . . . I dunno, I can't remember proper, just grass an' stones an' muck an' that, like all the moors is, for miles an' miles . . . One side o' the road goes up an' t' other down . . . No, I don't know any think about no water, an' I been up there in the day as well—just one tiny stream wide as your 'and . . . Well, I don't mind, I can *try* an' find it, but when I got 'ome nights an' our mam asked me where it was, I could never remember."

The two officers walked over to the New Inn. "Poor little soul," said one, a father, "trouble was, it was long past the kiddie's bedtime an' all that fresh air."

"Trouble was," said the other, not a father, "the kiddie 'ad mixed 'er drinks."

Hyde Station.

P.B., P.B. . . . Puss-in-Boots? Could be at that, Myra in them German jodphurs. Beats me.

Listen, Dave, in the car you flipped through the "Moorland Views" right fast; now you sit here and give every single one a good long stare . . .

No, I n-never seed any o' these in Number 16, where'd they keep 'em? They told him. What d'you say, in one o' the *suitcases*?

Aye, the two in the bedroom.

Anything he felt, he looked. And he looked startled. Guilty. What is it, Dave?

He had just remembered something. Something he should have remembered before, and now blurted out: There's t-two other cases. Evenin' before the Evans n-night, Ian and Myra drove off wi' them, "Don't drop one, it'll blow us all up." He made a clean breast of the books he'd brought. Oh, j-just ordinary suitcases—you know, one blue and one brown or could be grey. Ian said he was plannin' a p-payroll snatch an' wanted everythink out o' the way. The detectives showed him the two cases from the bedroom. Sorry, I j-just can't remember if they was like these—no, n-not too like I don't think . . . Oh, they just drove off toward Manchester. Ta ra for now.

Talbot, Benfield: Them sort o' books in private houses aren't going to get you into trouble unless you're selling 'em. Was Brady playing Smith up again, or *was* there something incriminating in those cases? Couldn't be ammunition, when he'd left two loaded guns in the bedroom, doesn't make sense . . . But even if there *was* incriminating stuff, Brady may have destroyed the lot, he never told Dave he wasn't going to. And even if he did put the stuff away, where d'you start looking? Left Luggage, somebody said facetiously. No, if those two cases still exist they're in Uncle Bert's attic or more likely wi' some shady chum in town . . . He could 'a even *buried* 'em—no, I'm serious.

Well, no harm in asking Uncle Bert and other relatives. Left Luggage *is* pretty hopeless but might as well start a look around —ever see the mountains of stuff waitin' in Victoria Station? Then the nagging thought again—they'd left Myra free as air from Thursday night to Monday morning, free to get at anything she liked to lay hands on. Blast the lad, why didn't he remember about this that first morning?

Damn damn damn. It's getting so that we need help. Put Carr on to it, wild-goose chase. And there's Pat, not-sure-if-I'll-remember-anything-but-I'll-try. Never say die. But please, help.

She did try. Friday the fifteenth. After early midday dinner Detective Constable Clegg, Mounsey's aide-de-camp, called with a car at Lakes Road Secondary School, Dukinfield, with Policewoman Slater and a box of chocolates, and took her off for a little outing. Pat in the back with the police lady, where she had sat when she wasn't in the front on Uncle Ian's nice warm knees. The day was greyer than for Dave's outing, and so were the prospects.

"No," Pat said suddenly, as they were about to go forward on A57 for Woodhead, "to the left 'ere. Can I 'ave anoother choc?" Well, give it a try. Through Stalybridge, this is new. They stopped to buy the Manchester *Evening News*, early edition. Right across the front page: POLICE HUNT MOORS FOR GRAVES. Kilbride Downey Downey Kilbride, shouldn't be surprised if Manchester bookies aren't starting bets, which'll they find? Fat chance.

Past the Palace Cinema and up the hill, due north. The choc had made the guide quite chatty. "Oh yes, I like the Braithwaite kids, but Ian an' Myra told me not to speak to 'em on account they're black. Our mam says there's been a lot o' folk gone missin', she says it's the atom bomb . . . Take this road," she said suddenly, and this road they took: A635 to the east, the main route over the moors into Yorkshire, and six miles north of A628, where the men were at this moment digging, and parallel.

Clegg looked at his colleague. They bowled on. Pat turned to him. "I've thought o' summat." They stiffened. "Yes?" "We're in a car, an' the other bobby's name is Carr." She shook with silent laughter. Come to think of it, it was quite funny.

Up, and on. Then Clegg turned to her. "You said there was no water, what about down there?"

She looked down, to the right, and frowned. "Oh, I thought you meant right next to the road, like a river wi' bridges an' that. That's the rezzervoy down there, it's scenery, you didn't ask the question right . . . Slow down."

Clegg slowed down, stopped. He looked at her. "Well?"

"Well what?" said Pat. "We're there." It was 1:30 P.M.

They got out. Signpost: HOLMFIRTH 7, OLDHAM 7¼. "Pat, how can you tell?"

"By them two road signs, 'Steep Hill' an' 'Bend.' " Down in the valleys there had been no breeze, up here a strong wind. "Oh," said Pat, "this is flippin' nothin', soom nights you get blowed off yer bloomin' feet."

Bleak, but a grand view, in summer perfect for a picnic. Knolls of scrubby autumn grass and boulders and rocks undulating up to a low skyline with driving clouds. In the Yorkshire distance the slender mast of the Holme Moss television station. Far below, the strip of water.

"What did you all do up 'ere?"

"Sit in car," said Pat, "pull up windows an' natter."

"Did you see him diggin' for peat?"

"Oh yes, Saturdays 'e digged in the day, an' Myra or me 'eld the sack or our old bath, and 'e put the peat in. One time it was dark, an' he took the spade an' went off."

"Where?"

"Oh . . . up 'ere somewhere. Over the top, I think."

Miles and miles of inscrutable moor. As if to tease them, the mountain wind gave an extra tug at their coats. Clegg looked at his ordnance map. Hollin Brown Knoll. He marked it faintly with a cross. Then he noticed a name just along from it. Wessenden Head Moor.

W.H.

He marked the cross again, blacker, and they all got back in. "And where we're parked is where they parked?"

"Oh yes," said Pat, "I told you, it's the same. Only, Myra and Ian 'ad a nicer car."

"That's right," said Clegg, avoiding Miss Slater's eye, "more room i' the back," And radioed Mounsey.

Hyde Station. Jack Tyrrell, for the twentieth time, staring at "Frank Wilson John Kilbride Alec Guiness." Why shouldn't there be *more* doodles in the house?

Sorry Jack, Dixie Dean's been all over, four times, nosin' around the cockloft behind the cistern, under the lining paper in the kitchen drawers, wires down the lav, not a hope.

Mind if I have a last go? And Tyrrell took a car to Hattersley.

The inevitable was happening, to Number 16. It had to sooner or later, even in phlegmatic Britain. From hour to hour, there had been glances at the house (I *think* that's the one, not sure), but today, where Myra had parked the car, twenty people stared up the wall at the house. Then thirty. Then forty. The police were digging up the garden.

First the front, where the giant nasturtiums were the first to go, then the pretty back lawn, then the paving from the front path to the door and around the gable. It looked like a pocket battlefield. "If Ian knew," one of the wreckers said, "what's bein' done to 'is garden, 'e'd go out of 'is mind." And Talbot the manic gardener had to mutter, "If we find nowt, we'll *have* to apologize to him." They found nowt.

But as the day matured, across the plot of baby ash trees in the main Mottram Road, the line at the bus stop remained steadily turned toward the house, and kept being reinforced by the curious idle who had traveled to have a look. The secret li'l dream house wide open at last, to the world. Any day now, Wardle Brook Avenue will be News. As if with prescience, the Hyde

Guide had on map and index misprinted the avenue twice: Wardle Brock Avenue, Nardle Brook Avenue.

There was also industry inside the house, of a quieter kind. Jack Tyrrell was working his way through an autumn spring-cleaning.

To tell the truth, to go through a murder house with a fine-tooth comb once the body's out is every bit as dull as spring-cleaning somebody else's property. Not made any more interesting by the fact he knew Dixie'd been over everything he was touching. Dixie, though, *might* not have spooned around in the soft sugar *and* the syrup, or turned the two horse ornaments on the mantelpiece upside down and shoved a pencil up the hollow part. But near everything else.

Tyrrell was a great reader and somehow gravitated toward the books. Not that there were that many. He took each in turn—*Peyton Place, Sexus, Goldfinger, Forever Amber*—turned it upside down and riffled the pages smartly in case something floated out. Hardback and paperback.

Paperback? P.B. . . . That was funny. He even looked for notes in margins. Nothing. One book, a hardback, looked somehow special and he took it out again to have another glance; much smaller than the others, bound in ivory and gilt. He opened it.

Redeemer of the World . . . I believe that Thou art truly the Christ, who hast come into the world to save sinners of whom I am the chief . . .

On the cover the initials I.H.S. and a gold cross, and on the flyleaf: "To Myra from Auntie Kath and Uncle Bert, 16 Nov 1958, souvenir of your first Holy Communion."

A prayer book. P.B.

He looked through it again. And again. And was about to replace it when he noticed the back. He bent the covers.

An action which displayed a gap of hollow spine. In the gap there nestled a flimsy paper, tightly folded.

He wheedled it out, unfolded it. A ticket. TICK. Tick for ticket. Number 74843, Central Station, Manchester, Left Luggage Office, One Shilling Each, Two Suitcases.

CHAPTER 26

THE DAY OF THE VOLCANO

"A policeman doesn't know what the day
may bring forth, so he makes sure of a
bluddy good breakfast."
                    Det. Chief Supt. Benfield

BY THREE O'CLOCK Pat was safely back in Number 12 after her
jaunt to the moors, the earliest she'd ever managed to get home,
even from the day outings. And it must have been the first time
she'd ever got home from the country without a drop having
passed her twelve-year-old lips. As she settled down to a comic
and another choc—normally she'd still be in school, loovly—she
had no idea what she had started.

At Woodhead, with the morale at an ebb, plod plod plod
squelch prod prod prod squelch, the press lads playing gin rummy
in cars . . . suddenly, a stir. And the press, like gambling blood-
hounds, pricked up ears: What y' say? Whole thing moving
where? Look, that's Eckersley's car—isn't it—Clancy—an' that's
Mattin surely tearing off, there goes a bus—and another. It's a
flippin' policeman's outing. Pack in the chips, get crackin'!

And they left valiant Inspector Lowe to his battle with Woodhead. It was like a film chase, only this was the police being
chased, by the press. Back through Glossop, then Stalybridge

(What is this, a mystery tour?), then to the right. And up. Up.

Hollin Brown Knoll. Mounsey had not long arrived there himself. As he stepped out of his car and looked around, he stopped in his tracks. Then he leaned quickly back into the car, fished out his photographs and found the one he wanted: Myra's white mini-van, VDB 893, against grim rocks silhouetted blackly against sky. He looked from the photo to the rocks before him. Identical.

The swarm settled. A careful reconnaissance, and the digging was on. Not easy terrain either and what a wind, but thank God not anything like so hellish as the other. The press pencils out, Hollin, Brown—how d'you spell Knoll? And on the ordnance map, the other age-old Saxon names, Ox Rake Brow, Wildcat Moor, Raven Stone Brow.

Spirits are up, but now it's the light that's sinking, into Manchester. Pack up, chaps, nine tomorrow. Wonder what Mounsey knows.

Mounsey knows nothing ("Yes sir, I can tell it was 'ere because o' them two road signs") . . . "If necessary," he told a *Daily Mirror* man, "we'll dig until 1968."

Hyde Station, 8:05 P.M., Talbot. Detective Constable Barrow speakin', sir, from Railway Police, Central Station. I've got out the two suitcases you mentioned.

Splendid, Carr'll be straight over.

Talbot phoned Benfield. As he hung on he thought, Central Station . . . After Brady'd picked up that poor lad at the buffet, as they walked away had he thrown a glance at the Left Luggage Office?

He told Benfield the news. Pause. Then Arthur, hardly a dramatizer: "Y' know Bob, I keep gettin' the feelin' we're like they say in books, sittin' on our behinds on the edge of a volcano, an' it's a funny sensation."

Saturday, October 16, 9:30 A.M. While spades clanked like armor out of the vans up on Hollin Brown Knoll, and the diggers stamped their feet for warmth, Bob Talbot settled at his desk in Stalybridge.

First, a brisk checkup with the staff as they reported on interviews with members of the two families, the Bradys and the Hindleys. Nothing worth going into further, mostly comments stupefied and unhelpful. "We never noticed anything out o' the ordinary, they was just Myra an' Ian . . ." A chat with Myra's Uncle Jim had elicited a picture of her family image if nothing else.

"She may ha' been my half sister Nellie's lass but I never saw eye to eye wi' Myra an' less than ever the last couple o' years. All her bad points seemed to go from bad to worse. More an' more pigheaded. Stand-offish. Not a bit thoughtful. I remember once we 'ad a proper dustup. It come about this way.

"She'd dropped her gran in the car at our place, 21 Combermere Street, Dukinfield—that is, four miles off Hattersley. It was of a Saturday mornin' which she did every other week so her gran could spend the day with us, then as per usual Myra went back home wi' the understandin' she'd drive back to us for her gran at nine-thirty P.M.

"Well, Myra never turned up. Her gran went on noddin' in front o' the telly but by eleven she wasn't noddin', she was fast asleep. An' for the third time I says to my missus, Nellie—she's Nellie as well—I says, 'Whatever 'as 'appened to the girl?' Then I went to the front door to see how the weather was shapin'. Well, it wasn't snowin', just corners o' drift like, in the road, so it couldn't be the weather against 'er.

"Well, eleven-thirty, sharp knock. An' Myra walks straight into our front room like she'd only got a minute to spare, all flushed up like as if she's been runnin'. Well, nothin' much was said, but believe you me, it was to the point. 'Sorry Gran,' says Myra, 'I can't take you 'ome, you'll 'ave to stay the night.' Well, I stared at her. 'What's up?' 'Weather,' says Myra, 'that's what's up, roads is too bad.' 'Too bad?' says I. 'Then 'ow did you get here?' 'We nearly didn't,' says Myra, 'an' it's gettin' worse.'

" 'Well,' I says, 'looked all right to me just now. Anyways, you know your gran can't stay the night, there's no bed for 'er an' that's that.' 'Well,' says Myra, sharp as a knife, 'what about the back bedroom?' 'Myra,' I says, 'you know quite well nobody's slept in that room for six months, not since our Peter died, the bed's not made up. Where's that Ian?' I says.

"Then she says, 'Ian's waitin' in the car on the corner, we can't risk an accident wi' Gran in the car an' ye'll have to make a bed for her in 'ere. I'll fetch her in the mornin',' she says, 'an' that's that.' An' she was off.

"It was a cold night sure enough, but the roads was okay, we knew folk that drove 'ome from a local concert an' no problems. We 'ad to make a bed on the sittin'-room floor for my mother, Mrs. Maybury, an' I remember sayin' to my Nellie that that lass o' Nellie's 'ad got a tough side to 'er. My guess was that she an' that Ian 'ad got a rock-'n'-roll session up at Number 16 an' Myra was ashamed for 'er guests to realize she was livin' on her gran's property. I remember thinkin', There's only one word for Myra. Inconsiderate . . .

"Oh, it wasn't lately, it was nearly a year back. I remember it well on account of it was my birthday, my mother brought me a present. December the twenty-sixth."

Then Carr came in, the rest of the staff left, Carr cleared the desk and heaved onto it the two suitcases.

Dirty books and ammunition won't get us far, but all in the day's work. Carr prized open the locks, then stood with pen ready for the routine list.

As Talbot raised the first lid he thought, Suppose they're the wrong ones? Then his eyes lighted on an insurance policy in the name of, and a tax form addressed to, Ian Brady. Had he *set out* to be identified?

The dirty books, all right. Cartridges, .45, .303. And the old snaps, here they come—albums, haven't we got enough "Moorland Views" already?

A blackjack. Ah well. Two blackjacks. What's this, a busby? A guardsman's black busby?

A wig. A woman's wig. Amateur theatricals? In a case where anything was possible it had to cross the police mind, which everything travels sooner or later: Did Ian Brady fancy dressing up as a woman? It was a quick cross and right out the other side. No, it was Myra's. Well, imagine that.

Three or four cans. Tapes. He placed his son's recorder on a low table, then onto it the first tape. It turned out to be the usual amateur hotchpotch: snatches of martial music, comedy dialogue from some television series, more music. At the end of it, he put the other tapes aside, to be given a routine check later.

A rusty old can with a smudged label, "Halibut Oil," what next. About to throw it away, he noted that what he had thought was paper lining the can was the back of a small snap. One of several snaps. More "Moorland Views"? He turned them over.

As he sat looking at the top photograph he thought, How long have I been doing this, without moving? Then he thought, Now I know what it means, that expression—what is it—your eyes starting out of your head. He looked up at Carr, who was staring down at the photograph.

Looking straight into the camera, a little girl. Her mouth was gagged with a man's scarf tied behind her head, tight enough for the childish cheeks to bulge over it. Except for shoes and ankle socks, she was naked.

Talbot, the father of a daughter who not too long ago had been the same age as the child in the photograph, found himself filled with a horror he had never before experienced. And yet the next moment, almost before he had absorbed the shock, his mind was transfixed by a tremor of a different order. One to make a detective's heart leap.

For despite the bandage, the little head with its halo of tight dark curls and the wide eyes looking straight at him were un-mistakable. The poster last New Year, smiling from wall after wall: HAVE YOU SEEN THIS LITTLE GIRL?

Lesley Ann Downey.

Missing since Boxing Day. Boxing Day. Saturday, December 26. Uncle Jim's birthday. The evening Myra had said she couldn't drive her gran home.

It was a lot to take in, and for a moment Talbot sat limp. Then he braced himself, and carefully, between finger and thumb, took the pictures one by one and laid them on the table. Nine pornographic pictures, each a different pose. They were to stimulate such exaggerated guesswork, orally retailed with every sort of ghoulish embellishment, that it is important here to ap-praise them in their proper perspective.

First, aseptic facts, as noted by Talbot. All taken indoors, flash lamp, worked from a wall socket and not very strong, about 150 watts. Camera stays put, same lens, six feet away from subject. Single bed sideways to camera, with on it one white sheet; low bed head, no pillow; behind, plain wall. It was to be technically possible to work out from the photographs the order in which they were taken.

When he was later to examine them microscopically, for vital clues, he realized that he had anticipated worse than he saw. For in each the child is alone, either sitting, standing or kneeling, with hands and feet either together or separately extended; from the expression in her eyes and from her physical bearing, it is plain that she is a puzzled and scared little girl whose one idea is to get home to her mother ("I got to get back by eight o'clock") and who has been told by this strange couple that she can't do that until she has obeyed these crisp and mysterious instructions: "Now sit down, now raise one foot . . ."

She has settled that this is some sort of weird grown-up game, involving exercises and your clothes off like in them school medical things, only there's summat fishy here. And she has schooled herself to do exactly what she is told, with serious eyes wide open on wherever she is told to look. (All right, I'll put my foot up in the air. Ooh, it's cold, can I go home now?) In one photograph her arms are stretched horizontally and sideways, which was to give rise to the fanciful whisper of "in the crucified position," but judged as poses, eight of the nine might be of basic ballet exercises attempted by a raw pupil.

I purposely emphasize that compared with the rumored atrocities, the real thing is comparatively mild. I do this not to minimize the vileness of the act, but to stress it. If in these photographs the utmost bestialities had been committed, involving one or both of the adults—and this camera allowed for the latter—their uncontrollable psychopathic madness would have moved the crime straight into the clinical field. And in these times, the two could have pleaded insanity.

But these pictures were taken, by a cool and cynical man, for his own fun and for his partner's. And the fun consisted of seeking to degrade a child by sniggeringly exposing her to the camera and having it—as it were—despoil her.

"Ooh, it's cold, can I go home now?" On top of the cumulative infamy of this night, it is somehow—comparatively unimportant though it may seem—the last straw that the little girl, who had not even been given the inevitable Lancashire cup of tea, was taken into an unheated room—its electric outlet was already in full use—and on an icy northern December night, was made to undress. The thought of it is not to be dwelt on without rage.

Then, too, the photographs all have one characteristic: the one which first had to catch Talbot's eye. It is a detail which in its fiendish simplicity dominates each innocuous posture, and sickens the beholder. The scarf across the mouth.

And when it is realized that Lesley Ann Downey had been calmed down enough to obey nine detailed orders, and so was unlikely suddenly to utter a hysterical cry, it becomes clear that there was no practical need to use a scarf at all. A childish symbol of cruelty, vented on a child.

All that need be added is that in the ninth photograph she is kneeling on the floor, facing the camera. The hands are held up just below the gagged mouth, clasped in an attitude of prayer, while the eyes look anxiously past the camera. The last pose. The photographs are a dreadful collection.

Yet when one looks at the victim's face . . . Like the picture of the dead youth in the mortuary, they are not unbearable. If Brady were to learn that they fail in the ultimate revulsion, it would enrage and baffle him—how, he would ask, how *could* they fail? Because he had counted without the child.

"Can I go home now?" The nine photographs are completely innocent. Obscenity is in the eye of the beholder. No, Brady and Hindley, you killed her and you buried her, but the dirty pictures were a failure.

His thoughts collected, Talbot made notes. Where taken? Nothing identifiable in the room, nothing, clever that. Could it be the same camera as for the "Moorland Views"? But even if it is, can we prove it, wasn't it sold? Brady's bound to say he was slipped the snaps from under the counter in one of those magazine shops, under the impression they'd be of an older chick, and aren't we told *Lolita*'s a masterpiece? The wave of elation was ebbing.

Operation Hollin Brown Knoll. Helped by the return of the autumn sun—though up here, still that wind—from nine to eleven they toiled doggedly, as if Digging for Victory. Cars parking and folk staring, they'd read the things in the papers. Mid-morning break, diggers crowding at a van, tea. A woman leaned out of her car and said, "What film is it? I don't see any stars."

Back at it—stab stab—but the morale was sagging again, it had to: What's wrong wi' two young people picnicking in a favorite spot with a grand view, when the bloomin' weather takes pity on 'em, and the wind isn't nippin' up your trouser leg like a mongrel dog? Tommy, here's a more likely bit, bit of a dip an' then a bump—stab—hello, something hard, what's this . . . A broken milk bottle. God, these trippers—stab—gettin' nowhere very fast.

Lunch break, few miles down the road to the Clarence, nice country pub with good beer, others to the canteen van, sandwiches and more lashings of tea. Pressmen everywhere you looked, jokes about "How you diggin' this diggin', man?" You laugh but it doesn't come that spontaneous when you've got an afternoon comin' on of this hit-or-miss stuff. Well, cheers, once more unto the breach. Paper headline "EXCAVATIONS BEING CARRIED OUT" sounds like ancient flippin' Egypt.

From two o'clock they worked, and as beer and tea wore off they got colder and more dispirited. Saturday afternoon. City's day off. Football, et cetera. Didn't help. It was only when Mounsey approached, walking from group to group, that the men took their pride out of their pockets and strained with a will. Mounsey had on his face what one of the older men called the "Dunkirk look": the square, unshirking eyes, we're on the losin' side, fellows, and our backs to the sea, but don't give it away. Dig.

They dug. And nothing happened. Corners of pots left from age-old picnics, a shepherd's old stick, a blackened penny (not even a bluddy sovereign), peat, stones, soggy muck. Another half-hour, lads, an' then we call it a day. Sunday tomorrow, and something made the lads feel it might be a call-off, for good.

Then the wind suddenly dropped, and as if to let them off for their last half-hour, it was still and warm and they were reminded of the mild autumn in the valleys below. The clouds parted to show the moon waning in the afternoon light, and there was a gentle mist in the air.

Right, lads, three o'clock, we said an hour and we've given it an hour. A great burst of home-going activity, canteen packing up, spades stacked into the backs of vans, buses backing up and men piling in. One bus set off.

The second started its engine. "Excuse me, sir." Police Constable George Spiers rose in the bus, rather red in the cherubic face; a Scots boy straight out of Police Training College, he had only been in uniform three days and this was his first sortie. "Excuse me, sir, but before we start could ye excuse me a minute, it's all that flippin' canteen tea." A roar of mirth, he jumped down redder than before, up the hill and over the ridge, away from where the digging had been.

Distant laughter, the bustle of departure. He stopped, then with a policeman's propriety stole a quick look behind to make sure there was no lone hiker around, it would hardly do for a copper, first week out, to be charged with a minor offense. Coast clear.

He was turning to hurry back when something half behind him caught his eye. A yard away, in a rain-logged depression in the peat.

Something white. The bus driver was hooting. He looked again. It was sticking out. A bone. The mutilated forearm of a child. The driver hooted again.

Lurching over the ridge, Spiers was met by a cheer, but by now he was more white than red. His superior, Sergeant Eckersley, was standing on the steps of the bus, which was bursting with chat; Spiers halted, called breathlessly "Kilbride" and they both went running back over the slope. In the bus, the chatter died away. The policemen said afterwards that the arm looked, eerily, as if it was trying to beckon. Find me find me.

2:57 P.M., Saturday, October 16. The volcano had erupted.

From that moment, a supersensitive ear would have heard, in

the still mountain air, the steady grind of the official machine as it accelerated. Spiers fetches Eckersley, Eckersley fetches Mattin, then Clancy, Leach, then Mounsey, Tyrrell, Nimmo, Mr. Eric Cunningham, Assistant Chief Constable; buzz of field telephone, ambulance out of nowhere, men with canvas screens on spikes to plant around the spot; Dr. Gee from the forensic department of Leeds University, Dr. Bartley from Harrogate, Police Constable Rylatt, photographer, more and more and more. Stand back please, nobody except officials (they've found him, John Kilbride), stand back please, stand back (John Kilbride—that boy —they've found him), stand back. By now it is dark. A dreadful dark.

Inside the screens, watched by the important few, the doctor heaped back the soil, flash. Mounsey craned forward, heart beating, eyes pricking.

At the foot of the huddled body, a tangle of mud-soaked clothing. But not so stained that when Gee lifted up the first item you could not see, by the flash, that it was a little tartan skirt. Lesley Ann Downey, died December 26, 1964, aged ten years and four months.

CHAPTER 27

REGINA VERSUS

"The heart is dead since infancy,
Unwept-for let the body go."
Emily Brontë

HALF AN HOUR LATER, by a fluke Ernie Lewis, an enterprising
journalist on the *Sunday Mirror*, got through to Hollin Brown
Knoll, on a private line, to Eric Cunningham himself. The conversation was short.

"Found anything?"

"Yes, can't say more."

"Just one thing, Chief—man or woman?"

"Woman."

BBC Television carried the story that evening, and the *Mirror*
the next morning.

7:30 P.M., work in progress. Inspector Chaddock, summoned to
the home ground which he had for years cherished acre by acre
like Talbot with his garden, came to find it desecrated forever.
He "witnessed the remains," and at 9 o'clock they were covered
with a plastic sheet and carried on a stretcher to be taken
to the mortuary at Uppermill, a town along the moors. The
scraps of clothing, more valuable than they looked, were bundled
into a plastic bag and taken along too. When later they
were extracted, there fell out the blackened white beads which
the child's elder brother had won at the fair and given her
for Christmas.

. . .

The next day, Sunday, October 17. In Uppermill, from dawn, under the supervision of Professor Cyril Polson of Leeds University's forensic department, the examination proceeded slowly and unflinchingly. Photographer Rylatt stood by for each stage, flash, flash.

Stalybridge. Talbot up early, working at his flower beds. Waggish neighbor, over hedge: "Hello Bob, don't you ever do *anythink* besides dig?"

At eleven, as he settled at his office desk for a Sabbath of catching up on routine on the case, he did think that though the momentum of the whole thing was increasing at a dizzy pace, today might at least afford an emotional respite. For him the worst was to come.

He carefully reviewed the contents of the suitcases, then went into the detail of the Downey pictures under a magnifying glass. Funny how you get used to everything—hello, there's a very faint pattern in the bed head. Isn't there a low bed head in Myra's bedroom? Get a picture of it blown up tomorrow.

Then he noticed the unplayed tapes he had set aside the day before, decided he might as well check them now, and put on the first. Another hotchpotch: first a snatch of the Goons, then for no reason a familiar BBC voice, the much respected Freddie Grisewood. (Except there *was* a reason, he was describing the rise and fall of Hitler.)

Talbot resigned himself with a sigh and started to check through statements, listening to the commentary with one ear as he did so. The door was open and Mrs. Campion was working in her room. Not a sound from the deserted Sunday street. A dull extra morning in the office. Distant church bells. He put on the second tape.

At about the same time Mrs. Downey, pathetically young and fair, came out of Bowden Close, Hattersley, through a knot of sympathizers and got into a police car. Uppermill, to identify.

The child's face, in profile, was intact enough for that: the little snub nose was unmistakable. To make things less hideous, the clothes had been washed and dried and then coaxed onto the body: ankle socks, shoes, slip, red tartan frock, pink cardigan,

royal-blue coat. Over the whole, a shroud. The shroud was drawn
back, and the mother looked down at the sight which, for close
on three hundred days and nights, had never been quite ban-
ished from her mind. She nodded slowly and her dead child was
reshrouded. Nothing was said. There was nothing to say.

From Bostock-Yates-and-Chronnell-Solicitors-Hyde-and-also-at-
Old-Street-Ashton-u-Lyne: *Dear Mrs. Masterson, Mr. Fitzpatrick
from this office will represent Miss Myra Hindley in certain proceedings against her and she is concerned as to the future of her
dog. She asks for you to be good enough to look after the dog for
her, and if and when she is able to do so, she will do her best to
recompense you for your trouble and would be extremely grate-
ful. Yours faithfully,* Bostock Yates and Chronnell.

Listening as he sorted papers, Talbot found the second tape
even duller than the others, sounded as if it had been left on by
accident sometime. On the tape, noises of doors slamming,
thumps, footsteps, low unintelligible mutterings. He waited for a
musical item—nothing. He continued to write. Mumble, bang,
meaningless pause, bang, mumble. Then he looked sharply at the
machine. What was that?

A scream? Couldn't be . . . Muffled voices and—yes—another
scream, and the words *Don't . . . Please God, help me . . .* A little
girl, screaming. He shot up in his seat and dropped his pen.

The telephone rang. "Bob, I want to check up on a couple
of—"

"Sorry, something terrible . . ." The tape was still going on. At
the other end they were convinced that a minute before, Talbot
had had some sort of seizure. "I just don't know what we've got
into here, I don't know . . ." He rang off.

Church bells. And the tape went on. He rose, shut the door,
and sat again. His hands clasped hard on the arms of his chair,
for fifteen more minutes he sat watching the revolving ribbon,
around and around, unhurried, ruthless. Staring at a snake. For
a man who sixteen hours before had seen a dead child lifted from
the shadows, it was an experience.

This tape was to become the most scaring object ever to lie on
the exhibits table below a judge at a murder trial. Before then, it

was to be listened to, for session after grueling session, by the police, by expert R. J. Weeks of BBC Sound, working to eliminate extraneous noise, and by shorthand transcriber L. O. Milner. Talbot was even, for identification, to have to play the beginning of it to Mrs. Downey: the first mother to sit in a room ten months after the death of her child and hear that child's voice call to her by name.

The judge at the trial, April 26, 1966: *"There is a question whether this piece of evidence should be heard in camera or not. There has been so much talk that in my opinion we have no right to exclude the public. Anyone who wishes not to listen should leave now. During it I request complete silence. The Attorney-General will beforehand read out the transcript, at dictation speed."* And he did, clearly and dispassionately, confessing afterwards that it was the grimmest ordeal he had ever faced in court. Then Weeks stepped forward, an efficient witness doing his job, though pale and set, and in front of a frozen assembly turned on his machine. They were first startled by a commanding voice which rang through the courtroom: *This is Track Four.* Brady's, added afterwards. Then the tape began. And played for seventeen intolerable minutes.

To listen to it was made doubly so by the very nature of the invention which made the experience possible. In the course of murder trials, for centuries dreadful things have had to come to light, not only visually but mumbled by unwilling witnesses. Never before, however, has the modern phenomenon of preserved sound been put to such a grisly use as was "the Moors tape." All of us, following the radio performance of an imaginative play of suspense, have experienced the creepy effect of long pauses punctuated by sudden sounds: footsteps, the shutting of a door, a sharp exclamation. Such things can work on lone listeners so successfully as to frighten them, badly.

The effect of the real thing went so far beyond this that it was to linger inescapably in the minds of those who heard it, for many many months. At the end of the tape there occurs "music, during which various nonvocal noises can be heard, ending with 'The Little Drummer Boy,' growing fainter. Footsteps. Sounds on tape cease."

Four points of detail.

One phrase of Myra Hindley's sounds improbably Victorian ("Don't dally") until the listener realizes that it is a Lancashire idiom. So much so that Myra Hindley, in court, said she could not believe she had said it (the tape had been played) because "It is not an expression that I normally use."

Some way through, Myra Hindley thinks she hears somebody at the front door, runs down, turns on a light and runs back up. It would seem so much more logical, if one wished to discourage callers, to turn *off* a light rather than turn one on; one can only assume that she turned on the television light in the sitting room, which she may have known would discourage a neighbor from interrupting.

The music heard at the end of the tape, Weeks opined, was added by Brady, *at the time,* from a second tape recorder playing a tape which he had previously prepared from a commercial record: a disc which (by a coincidence, for though it is popular, it is not a "must") was in young Dennis Talbot's collection. He identified the music immediately as the first two items in the Ray Conniff LP "We Wish You a Merry Christmas." One of the suitcases contained not only the original tape but two copies of it, which means that the copier had listened to the tape right through at least twice.

Lastly, a problem which, at the trial, was not to be made an issue of, by either side. But it is a major one. Puzzle: in that bedroom in Number 16 on December 26, 1964, which happened first, the photos or the tape?

The prosecution's opening address told the jury that a tape recording had been "followed by photographs of a child." And naturally this was the claim of the defense: if the two accused could maintain that the photographs came second, then clearly the child was alive after the end of the tape, and there could be at least a shred of credibility to their claim that she was taken away from the house alive and well, by "the two men who had brought her."

Their second solid assertion was that while the tape was running, they were forcing between the child's teeth the gag which they maintained is in her mouth in the photographs, behind the scarf. The words heard are just ambiguous enough to fail to

disprove this claim entirely; it would even appear to be sup-
ported by one sentence: *I want to take some photographs, that's
all.* But the fact that the word "more" is not included does not
prove that photographs (the nine) have not already been taken.
The meaning could be: "You were frightened just before I took
those pictures; well, it wasn't too bad, was it? Well, nothing
worse is going to happen now." Another detail which points to
photos-then-tape is that the child's appeal, *Don't undress me will
you?,* sounds as if she were afraid they would, which surely could
only occur to her *if they had done so already*—for the photos—
and then allowed her to dress again.

No, as has been proved a thousand times in cases of burglary,
it is not difficult to gag even grownups, to stop them calling for
help; two strong people can do it in fifteen seconds. So it is hard
to believe that it took nearly seventeen minutes to gag a child of
ten.

There is a more powerful argument. In typewritten description, words like "distress" and even "screams" look disturbing
enough; but when you have heard the frantic sounds echo like
jagged knives of pain through an appalled courtroom, again and
again, it is not conceivable that after those cries the victim was
able to pose obediently for nine arranged photographs.

And if this is so, then the silence on the tape after those cries, a
silence which merges into the tender Christmas music of "Jolly
Old St. Nicholas"—*When the clock is striking twelve, And I am
sound asleep*—and worse, the plaintive drums of "The Little
Drummer Boy"—*I have no gifts, To bring a King*—then that
silence is a nameless one.

The Attorney-General (at the trial, to Ian Brady): *Why did
you preserve this tape?*

Ian Brady: *Because it was unusual.*

Ian Brady, one morning in his cell in the Remand Centre,
talking at random: "D'ye ken what this country deserrves this
minute, an' what I'd like to see it get? The atom bomb."

12 noon, the playing of another tape. The voices of Brady,
Hindley, and a child. But the child is Pat Hodges, anti-

climax: an endless, aimless New Year's Day conversation: *Let's listen to* Watch with Mother . . . *omelette* . . . *Shakespeare's ruddy 'Amlet you mean?* . . . Well, not entirely boring, made you sit up to hear Myra discussing with Pat the news about the missing child on the *Reporter* front page . . .

12:30. Good God . . . What's up? . . . That morning you went into Number 16 and found Evans—wasn't there a tape recorder open in the sitting room?

They scrambled for it and turned it on. Second anticlimax. Nowt.

2:30. At Ashton headquarters, emergency top-level conference of heads of C.I.D. for the five police forces involved in the case: Cheshire, Manchester City, Yorkshire, Lancashire and Derbyshire. With Eric Cunningham in the chair, immediate Regional Crime Squad activities were swiftly mapped out and allotted in detail. Presiding over the conference, on the wall from which he had looked for nearly two years, John Kilbride—HAVE YOU SEEN THIS BOY?

It was decided that Hyde headquarters, in spite of modest and antiquated premises, should become the fulcrum for an immense operation which automatically placed Chief Superintendent Benfield at its head. He gulped. A far cry from car crashes and burglaries.

But on Monday the eighteenth, even he was taken aback by the force of the eruption. Hyde Police Station had turned into a tiny railway junction the day war is declared. It was immediately thronged with workmen trying to bring it up to date overnight: canteen became the press room, sergeants' office "Murder Inquiries," and C.I.D. quarters were set aside solely for the case and christened the "Murder Room." Instant Maigret.

Instantly too, it was swamped with five-fold police and newspapermen from everywhere. And yet, so circumscribed is English law that the names of the two prisoners had still not been printed in connection with the diggings, the papers still going no further than the melodramatic HOUSE OF SECRETS SEARCHED. The Paris press was less reserved and one reporter flourished a splash headline: LES DEUX DIABOLIQUES DE MANCHESTER.

Benfield, whose experience of the press was pretty well confined to cub reporters, presided that day at a press conference of fifty journalists from all over the world, the first in British criminal history to be televised. All over the little station, country policemen stared at teen-age girls in stretch pants running around adjusting lights.

And Benfield didn't do so badly. When asked anything which he wanted to dodge, he would say, "Evidential factors are being considered."

Somebody shot at him, "Is there witchcraft and black magic in this?"

"Definitely not witchcraft."

"But what about black magic?" Rumors were rife, and it was a loaded question. Benfield blinked through his glasses at the assembly and announced, "Never eat 'em myself, they put my weight up." Quoted in *Time,* he earned a footnote; "Black Magic: brand of British candy."

Later in the morning Tom Craig was telephoned at Millwards —those two chairs at that desk—and with the typewriters chattering around him in the cubicles as they had for years and years, and trusted faces floating past his door, he was informed by a reporter that his two long-standing employees were the stars of "the murder case of the century." The typewriters chattered less after that: "Folk stood talkin' for an hour on end, you just had to go an' break it up."

Two press conferences a day, boasting by Wednesday an attendance of eighty-five "global correspondents." And Dixie Dean was created Exhibits Officer. The heat was on.

And the volcano was spilling over. By Thursday, although the Downey photographs and tape, as well as the doctors' findings, were top secret—as if by telepathy every other person in Manchester knew that out Hyde way there was being unpeeled, like a monster onion, a very special story.

The doctors had reported that like the forearm, the center of the body had been gnawed by animals, this being the part most likely to be sought by a starving rodent. The case was already horrific enough, but the public is like a child in a candy store, not satisfied until it is sickened; within three days, wherever the case swamped the conversation—which was everywhere—to the rumor of crucifixion (based on accounts of the photo with arms extended) there was now added the hint of disemboweling before death.

Jokes too. Bitter jibes at those two, for Lancashire was hating them, a loathing exacerbated by the new rumor (true) that the pair had applied for permission, before entering the dock, to get married. The last cynicism. One exchange, over beer: *"Church weddin'*, would you say?" "Aye. A case of 'Until Life do us part.' "

As people flocked into Manchester, one broken woman left it with averted head. When Peggy Brady had learned of the Evans matter she had been appalled, but as revelations seeped through to envelop her like a miasma, she broke down. Reporters knocked at her door and offered a fiver for a photo of Ian in his pram in the Gorbals ("I couldna do it, Pat—how could I, what would the neighbors think?")

Pat took her off to Glasgow to share her bewilderment with gentle Ma Sloan ("I never had reason to believe he was anything but a stable, normal boy"). Then she echoed, over and over again, what Nellie Hindley was saying, what three other women had said before them, only for these two it was even worse, and for Nellie—parent not only of the murderess, but of the wife of the prosecution witness—worst of all. A Greek chorus of tragic mothers: "O God, what have I done to deserve this, what have I done . . ."

So it is a relief that one parent braved the limelight with gusto. Mrs. Masterson. Overnight her Patty was a celebrity, a combination of Pollyanna and pocket Sherlock Holmes, and Elsie answered the many knocks at her door with alacrity. "I took our Pat this afternoon to the valley be'ind the 'ouses, for some ferns for our rockery. We took the old bath I used to lend Myra an' Ian for the peat. Well, when I give Pat the ferns to 'old, she shudders an' says, 'Mam, I can't touch it, it's soil' . . . Well, the welfare people come an' suggested 'er goin' away for a change before the bad weather, like pot-'olin' on the moors, if you please. I don't think that would do *at all*."

. . .

Hyde Station. In the daily swelling crowd, there was one policeman who could not share one hundred percent in the rejoicing. The man in search of Mounsey's Lad. Joe, in a quiet fever, was going to go on searching.

Come off it, Joe, one needle out o' the haystack, right? But where's the chance of another one? Not an earthly—oops, sorry Joe.

And his photographers had caught the fever from him. Last Saturday at five-fifteen, as the light was going and the crowd around the Downey grave waited for the doctors, Gelder walked a few steps over the hill to look at the view to the south: the road, then the reservoir miles below and the mountain sweeping up from it into the sky to a tooth point. He looked at the mountain. For quite a time. Then at the boulders at his feet. Then from a sheaf under his arm he selected two enlargements, studied them, paced a bit and then—very odd—just turned his back on the grave and took a snap of the scenery.

And on Monday morning, the eighteenth, while the press conference raged in Hyde, the enlargement of that snap lay in front of Mounsey: boulders in foreground, water and mountain at the back. Next to it, the enlargements of two snaps in the tartan album. One: Unspoiled Film Star, Brady in the dark glasses, hands in pockets, smiling into camera. The other: Myra, sideways to the camera, low heels, skirt and hair blowing in the breeze, hands in pockets of leather coat, smiling into camera.

And Mounsey had been right. While the snaps had shown no background at all, the professional developing had worked marvels: the background in both was hazy but perfectly recognizable. *And it was the same as in Gelder's empty enlargement.* Same water, same mountain, same tooth point. Ian Brady and Myra Hindley had photographed each other, smiling at each other, standing not many feet away from Lesley Ann Downey's grave, with, on a rock near the feet of each, the smart little transistor. Had it been playing ghostly pop music?

And then he had stuck the two pictures in the family album, placing his snap between one baby in a pram and another baby in a highchair.

. . .

An hour later Mounsey's fleet drove up to Hollin Brown Knoll. Canvas screens stand by. Spades out. To work.

Talbot and Benfield. Photos and tape . . . Would you say this Downey case is the first ever where a murderer doesn't just leave evidence by accident—like the Kilbride exercise book—but goes to incredible lengths not only to manufacture but to *preserve* that evidence?

Too bad it wasn't Kilbride we found instead . . .

How's that?

Well, we need him more than we did her. Even without her body, wi' the photos and the tape we already had the makings of a case—but the other, just a name in a book, makes you mad.

I've got an idea, what's wrong wi' sending for Spiers the water diviner?

In the meantime though, the darkroom diviners were at it again. Back in Hyde, photographer Gelder handed photographer Masheder the negatives of three snaps from the tartan album, to be enlarged. Then Detective Constable Leighton and Dr. Jones produced an enlargement of one of the Downey pictures which showed a very slight pattern in the bed head behind, and beside it an identical photograph had just been taken of the bed head in the side bedroom of Number 16. Moreover, the camera had been traced and forensically proved to be the same. And Sergeant Jarvis of the fingerprint department had identified, on three of the Downey photographs, Myra Hindley's fingerprints. It all helps.

During the next wearying bulldog days, Joe Mounsey drove himself and everybody else. Nobody was helped by the hordes of reporters and avid sightseers, on tiptoe for another miracle. Nowt. And yet with all those folk gaping, and hearing that all over Manchester people were taking transistors to work in case of a news flash—well, you just had to look as if you'd got something. Jack Tyrrell a tower of strength: Tyrrell the ticket collector. Dig.

Tuesday the nineteenth. A reporter called on Mrs. Kilbride. "Yes, a neighbor told me. Oh, I am sorry for Mrs. Downey, they say she believed all along Lesley was alive." He tried to persuade her to come up to the moors and be photographed. "Thank you, I'd rather not." She was told that on the following Tuesday the little girl was to be reburied, in Ancoats. "I still 'ave the feelin' some 'ow that our John was burnt. I would like 'im to ha' 'ad a decent funeral."

Myra Hindley, a letter to Elsie Masterson: "HER MAJESTY'S REMAND CENTRE, IN REPLYING PLEASE WRITE ON THE ENVELOPE W/605, *Dear Elsie, This is just a few lines to ask you if you've still got Puppet. I gave my mother £5 to give you so you could spend 10/- per week on his food. Ian said to the solicitor that the £100 he will receive for the pension contributions he's been paying over the years is to be given to whoever has Puppet as we don't want him to have to be put to sleep as he's only a baby. No more at the moment as I want to catch the early post.*"

2:30. Detective Constable Gelder snapping scenery again. Joe wandering about just looking absent-minded, leaning against the back of a car, or feet in a bog. He was always looking up, away from the ground where surely, if treasure there was, the treasure lay. Wasn't that why the RAF reconnaissance bombers were circling ceaselessly overhead, taking pictures, to pinpoint disturbed areas? Also, he was walking about with a book under his arm, and if he'd been a poet instead of a policeman, you'd have thought he had his eyes on the horizon.

He had. And the book was "Moorland Views," by now supplemented with enlargements of snaps from the tartan album. One loose. He kept on looking at it. Myra with Puppy.

From the tartan album. An insipid picture. The girl seated not ungracefully on the calf of one leg, the other knee almost on the ground: bareheaded, tight light trousers, rough lumber jacket, double-breasted and thigh-length with four big plonky black buttons, big shiny almost knee-high black boots with pointed toes, and holding under the jacket, for warmth, a very young dog, little black-and-white nose just peeping out. She looking down, head half averted from camera, but not so much that you could not glimpse the affectionate half smile hovering on her lips. In the back, any little boulders which might have been distinctive were disguised by wings of snow. The far skyline a row of indeterminate rocks, of the same kind as the ones in the photo above Myra's car, which he had identified on first arriving there last Friday.

But working to the right and then to the left of the Downey grave, he could not for the life of him fit this distant silhouette into the horizon of Hollin Brown Knoll. And the view down over the road, the reservoir and the mountain—this time it offered nothing. His mouth tightening, he looked again at the snap. Could have been taken anywhere between here and the Brontë country.

Elsie, now known throughout the estate as "Pat's mam," was walking Duke past Underwood Court with Pat when they espied something in the gutter which was glittering, a lot of wire. They went to look. "It was Joey's cage, and 'ow it got there God knows. A lot o' blue feathers nearby—well, when they cleared the furniture out I suppose they didn't know what to do with Joey, so dumped the cage an' Joey flew away." One hopes. "Oh, but the cage did look nice"—after all, hadn't David Smith given it a good wipe-over not too long ago?—"we took it 'ome an' bought a budgie for Elsa an' set the whole thing up in the front room an' Elsa called him Ringo."

Wednesday, a boost. Detective Constable Gelder's snap of yesterday corresponded exactly (skyline, the lot) to Brady's "Devastated Area" picture. Only one thing different: Gelder's showed, background extreme right, the mound of earth excavated from the Downey grave. Right, try this patch. The beauty spot was acquiring the look of one vast bomb site. Dig. Circling up in the sky, a *Daily Express* plane, taking photographs. Well, we'll do our best for you, we really will; try a couple of square yards up yonder.

Report from Nimmo, Manchester City: 13 Wiles Street, now empty, had been searched from rotten floorboard to peeling ceiling, and even Tyrrell hadn't found a sausage. "And why," said

Talbot, "did the Corporation have to pull down 7 Bannock Street just to spite the police?"

Late afternoon. Mounsey was still patrolling Hollin Brown Knoll, photo in hand, when a thought struck him. He had been confining his search to the north side of the road, where the bank sloped steeply up and over the rise to the grave; suppose "Myra with puppy" had been posed for on the *south* side, where the bank sloped down to the valleys and the reservoir?

He crossed the road and skirted it westward for a dozen yards, then stopped and looked back over his shoulder. Up against the sky, rocks. Good God, of course . . . The row of rocks in the far background of "Myra with puppy" was not just "the same kind" as the row in the near background of Myra's car. *They were the same rocks,* photographed from much farther away. From the south side.

He went on walking, looking back regularly at the skyline. Every twenty yards, it changed. A stone shape would creep up out of the foreground and form an entirely new graph, then a curve of grass would swell gently up and obscure that.

Then he stopped, looked again. Well . . . it was not unlike. They were the same sort of jagged rocks up there, though the shapes were different, somehow. But it *was* the first formation he had spotted which was at all possible. One chance left; to leave the roadside and walk at right angles to it, downhill.

Though it was a gentle incline, the ground was rough and boggy, with little rivulets turning the clay to mud, and strewn with small boulders. Slow going. When he had stumbled a good eighty yards, he braced himself. He did not need to open the album under his arm, he knew the silhouette by heart. He turned around.

Beyond and above the road, the shadowy lines of digging men, the occasional fluorescent jacket standing brightly out in the fading afternoon. He fixed his eyes on the distant skyline above them.

The silhouette. There it was . . . Well, as near as dammit.

Was he deluding himself? He opened the album with urgent fingers.

It *was* like. Very like.

But he wanted it to be exact. God, it had to be. The light was going, and that alters things, doesn't it? And with its going, the silhouette on the horizon seems maliciously to waver, to change. It seemed to say, Any bunch of rocks against the sky looks much the same all over the Yorkshire moors, what's all the fuss?

Call it a day. Home. There was talk of moving after tomorrow, fifteen miles across country, Whaley Bridge way.

He did not sleep well, hiking in his sleep, tramp tramp tramp, valley after valley, skyline after skyline, all wavy and all exactly the same. Hundreds of them.

Thursday, October 21.

Hyde Police Court, 9:40 A.M.: Ian Brady and Myra Hindley were charged with the murder of Edward Evans and of Lesley Ann Downey. "She wore a red coat, he an open-necked shirt."

During which time Joe Mounsey was driving up to Hollin Brown Knoll with his second photographer, Detective Constable Masheder. A fine morning. More people than ever, cars, vans, motorbikes, push-bikes. And press press press: *Life, Time, Paris-Match, Der Stern, Quick,* eighty-flippin'-five of them. And digging going on all along the upper side of the road, around where the grave was, sticks rhythmically stuck in the ground and held to the nostrils.

Good morning to Inspector Chaddock and to Talbot, who'd popped up for half an hour. The sun came out, and they remembered once again that they were at a beauty spot. "Y' know, Joe," said Talbot, "for a time to come, those two, on top o' what they're charged with, have spoilt a lot o' good things for a lot of folk—picnics on the moors, glass o' wine, music on wireless, holiday snaps, dogs, giving sweets and outings to kids—oh, they've done their work, all right. Couple o' miscreants."

Mounsey knew roughly where to lead Masheder. He did not dare to look behind him, up at the morning skyline. Would it have changed even more?

But the photographer did turn, and looked. He put fingers and thumbs to his eyes, then looked briskly at the photo. Then he did some what he called "aligning": one pace here, check, one pace there, check, one back, check, half left, then back with fingers and thumbs. He trained them along the horizon like a telescope.

The telescope rested. Then he started spearing the three legs of his camera into the soil, then looking swiftly from photo to viewfinder, then readjusting the legs. Several times, down to the last millimeter. A knot of sightseers. Finally he was satisfied and beckoned to Mounsey, who gave a last glance at the photograph in his hand, then looked through.

The two settings were so alike that the shock was that the girl with the puppy was not in the middle of the frame, the illusion being that she had just vanished from it, gone with the strips of snow. Identical.

Calm down. Just a holiday snap. Myra with puppy.

He took out his magnifying glass and studied the photo once more. This time he concentrated on the blond head bent over the puppy.

Was it his imagination, or was she looking, with that funny sort of veiled smile, not at the puppy, but past it? Down at the ground?

11:30 A.M. Chaddock arrived, holding one of the long sticks. With Chaddock looking over his shoulder, Mounsey took more searching looks at the photo and at the ground before him, darting his eyes from one to the other, to and fro, to and fro. Then he pointed, as near as he could—he felt like a phony magician, but he did it—to the exact spot on the ground at which the girl seemed to have been looking. He nodded to Chaddock, who stepped forward, bent down and drove the stick, without too much difficulty, a couple of feet into the ground. He pulled it out again. He looked at it, and was about to drive it in again a foot away when he stopped, seemed puzzled and frowned. Mounsey and Masheder looked steadily at him. As they did so, they smelled something; then they saw Chaddock put the stick to his nostrils and recoil sharply. 11:45 A.M.

Steady on. It could be a sheep; yesterday, on the other side of the road, hadn't a dead dog been unearthed, making a lot of people wish they'd waited before making fools of themselves?

Chaddock knelt and scraped away the clotted soil. Minutes passed. In the half distance a couple of onlookers drifted away. Then his hand seemed to feel something. He looked up at Mounsey. Carefully he pulled it up through the muck. A shoe. A boy's shoe.

Chaddock laid it carefully by, delved again and groped underground. "Feels like a sock," he said, "an' it's got a foot in it." John Kilbride, died November 23, 1963, aged twelve years and six months.

Like Talbot five days before, Mounsey felt two opposite emotions: distress and triumph. So opposite, indeed, that they canceled out and left him completely calm and practical.

A lot of work to be done. And in the right order. First a cordon, and only just in time did twenty policemen drop their spades and sticks to form one. For word spread magically and the whole world seemed to converge on the spot now to be known as Sail Bark Moss. Second move, the canvas screens to be rushed down; then a call to Leeds University, to pathologists Polson and Gee. Then, for what seemed hours, the essential people stood around the disturbed soil. Each was to remark on what seemed, lying on its side in the sludge, the most important object in the universe. The muddy shoe.

The lunch hour was the strangest period of adjustment, or rather of nonadjustment. Both police and press had to feel, to a less poignant degree, Mounsey's conflict of emotions—but the shock was quickly stifled by the rising tide of excitement. God, what a story! The drinks flowed at the Clarence; you felt guilty in a way, but no doubt about it, a great victory had to be celebrated. Like a war being over.

After the meal everybody trooped back to the field of operations in high spirits flavored with hysteria, helped by the arrival, from the Queen's Hotel in Hyde, of Benfield, Talbot, Cunningham, Prescott, Nimmo, Mattin and a cohort of police and press. Just as they had all been sitting down to a lunch to celebrate the Brady-Hindley charge that morning, Benfield was handed a note giving the news, and had had the self-control to keep it to himself till after the coffee. God, what a story! 2:30. Rylatt photographing the shoe.

Then, like a reproof, the good weather left the sky and the mountains. While the air stayed unnaturally warm and still, it darkened perceptibly.

3:30. The two doctors arrived, black overcoats and black bags, and the crowd watched them pick their solemn way from the road, across the smashed slope of the hillside. In the already baleful light, the two disappeared behind the screens. And the crowd had nothing to do but stand around and wait.

For the guards inside the screens, it was to be a long and gruesome vigil. In spite of the fact that the body lay only eighteen inches below the surface, the uncovering took nearly three hours. It had been buried at right angles to A635, head to the south, away from the road.

The corpse of the first child had of course deteriorated, distressingly so. But the second had not only been in the ground thirteen months longer, it had been lying—except for shoes—fully clothed. It was in such an advanced state of decomposition that the doctors did not dare use implements which might pull away flesh or snap bone, so were forced to use what they called "excavation by hand," a procedure requiring endless skill and patience. For it meant first kneading away clay all around the body without touching it; then gradually, with the tips of fingers, frittering away as much soil as possible without damaging what was capable of being damaged, which was a great deal.

They then "undercut" the body, delving under it deep enough to be able, ultimately, to extricate it lying on a bed of soil strong enough to give support. A long job. Gradually, from the clay and sludge—flash—there emerged a shape. It was so thickly covered in black soggy clay that it looked like a large misshapen poodle. But it was short enough for a child.

A glorious sunset, down behind Manchester. And nobody who was there, in the swelling crowd, will ever forget it. As great swathes of blood-colored mist suffused the distant upper air, people felt that on this particular evening, a whole city lay mantled in anger and shame. Then, as the acetylene flares snapped on and rasped brutally over the second sequestered place, their garishness painfully recalled Ashton-under-Lyne, the jolly market. The moorland scene under the naked lights—

shadowy figures looming past the coke braziers and faces peering around the screens, in the foreground the black outline of the two scientists, crouching absorbed and dedicated—was like a macabre Biblical painting.

6:20. The scientists were lifting the child from the grave. Tenderly, by order of both head and heart. Night having taken over all around, the wind slyly changed.

And there crawled along the thickening dark, like a fearsome reptile which clung to the knees and rose to lick at the nostrils, a smell. Savage whiffs of something so beyond the normal effluvia of refuse and city drains that it had a sweetness. It filled the sky. The sweetness of abomination.

6:30. Inspector Chaddock arrived, and supervised the remains being measured (4 ft. 9 in.) and then being rolled with infinite care onto a galvanized sheet, which was then lifted onto the stretcher—flash flash—and shrouded by two policemen holding cloths to their faces, to ward off what another policeman described in his notebook, in a shaky hand, as "the puterfication." They took the stretcher, stumbled up the treacherous ground to the road, and slid it into the van behind the inspector. For Uppermill Mortuary. The same slab.

And as the lights of the van disappeared down the road, so the flares clicked off and the night took over. And at that second there was a scramble. As if for protection, every headlight was turned on, and then began a feverish exodus of every sort of vehicle.

Helped by the all-pervading smell (when the men who had handled the remains and the clothing reached home, their first imperative need would be an immediate bath and complete change of wear), the presence of evil that night on Hollin Brown Knoll was so strong as to cause a physical shrinking. In fifteen minutes the place was deserted: policemen thanked God they were not one of the two constables left up there to keep watch all night, and only breathed easily again when they got to the lights of Stalybridge. Seeing a child skip across the road, drivers found themselves staring at it, bemused. Pedestrians at Ashton-under-Lyne traffic lights, seeing the police cars thread through, said afterwards that the looks on the faces were extraordinary: the faces of dazed survivors from some great communal disaster.

At the mortuary, the doctors worked again heroically, cleaning the remains for examination. In the photograph of the head ("features obscured by post-mortem change") only the teeth are discernible; they were later identified by Professor Saunders (Dentistry). Strands of brown hair were also put aside. In a court of law, that would hardly have been enough without the clothing, to be identified by the mother, including the father's undershirt she had "taken in" for the boy. One fine bonus for the prosecution: the buttons on the jacket had the pattern of a football, and she had kept an extra one, which was to be produced in court.

As in the Downey case, Professor Polson could find no proof of violent death, but strangulation could not be ruled out. There was one peculiarity.

This detail, the vilest in the story, was also the last in the vital sequence of discoveries which sealed the case. It is as if the Goddess of Justice, having arranged for the detail to come to light, then averted her blindfolded head and said, No more no more, the victory is to the law.

It was to be attested by the professor, and proved by a photograph passed to the jury, that the victim's trousers had been rolled down to the knees, and the undershorts down to below the thighs. The undershorts had then been pulled from behind to the full extent of the elastic band and then knotted hard behind the legs in order to pin them together. Finally the body, in a last infantile attempt to degrade a departed spirit, had been buried face down. No more, the case is complete.

The next morning Joe Mounsey called at Mrs. Kilbride's with the boy's shoe, which she identified. He then arranged with her to ask Father Kelly to conduct a Mass for her son on Sunday, in St. Christopher's, his old church, where his younger brother Pat was an altar boy. Then they made plans for Monday's funeral; the choir of St. Damian's, John's old school, to sing from the gallery and the interment to follow in Hurst Cemetery.

Then to Hyde to consult with Benfield and Talbot, etc. Routine business on the case was piling up, the Murder Room would be busy for weeks, day and night.

They were all so engrossed in detail—addresses of prospective witnesses, copies of tape, copies of photos, more fingerprints—that when a couple of them had to drive over to Risley and a door was opened to them, they were taken aback.

It was then they realized that in the rush of work they had forgotten who the whole caboodle was about.

Ian Brady and Myra Hindley.

The two sat facing the door, staring straight at the visitors as if to say, next time please knock ferrst, 'cause we're with our lawyer, Mr. Fitzpatrick. Fuck off, an' the same to the trick cyclists—mental experts, my eye, the two of us is saner than the lot o' ye put together.

They are side by side in two wooden chairs with arms, exactly as they sat in Millwards. She even holds her ballpoint and her ruled notebook, a duplicate of the one she kept her diary in, a thousand years ago.

And they sit exactly as they will soon sit, for seventy hours, behind the bullet-proof glass wall of the dock. They are even dressed as they will be, every day of the trial (fresh linen every other morning, washed and ironed by unwilling Remand Centre staff): he in a conservative grey-blue suit, waistcoat, folded handkerchief in breast pocket, white shirt, plain blue tie, a shadow behind it under the Adam's apple because he is getting thinner; she in the pepper-and-salt suit with the demure little blue collar and her mam's white high-heeled shoes. Her hair is blond but already wearing an ominous frown at the roots. Not to worry: by the trial it will have blossomed into a film-star halo of gold mashed up with platinum. Nicely made up, black eyes lined with black just like any smart cookie on telly.

The business the officers were here on, was one they had shirked: a piece of news to be broken to Myra. Once again farce, always just around the corner, popped out its head, and this time at its most outrageous.

That morning Mrs. Campion had phoned Benfield. It was

most important to prove that the photo of Myra on the Kilbride grave had been taken after the boy's disappearance and not before, by establishing that Puppet had been born around about that date, or after. Myra, suddenly vague about her darling, was inclined to think it had been well before, and Mrs. Campion had arranged for the dog (photographed first, Leighton again) to be taken to Gorsey Lane Kennels to have its age ascertained by means of a dental X-ray examination by an Edinburgh surgeon.

When Mrs. Campion phoned, Talbot was with Benfield and could just distinguish her voice. "Oh, Mr. Benfield, I don't know how to tell you . . ."

Benfield sat up. "Yes, what is it?"

Talbot couldn't make out her answer but saw Benfield's face fall. "Good God . . ." Talbot thought, Her husband, accident, hospital . . .

Benfield turned to him. "Puppet's passed away, under the anaesthetic. Now we *are* in trouble."

And now, in Risley, two police officers faced the dog's mistress, like shamefaced schoolboys, and blurted out the news. She stared at them, incredulous and white with rage, then spoke a phrase which is, deservedly, her last recorded saying in this book: "You police are nothing but murderers." Her dog had died in Oldham Road, Ashton-under-Lyne, three quarters of a mile from John Kilbride's home.

When she has somewhat recovered and the normal careful interview is under way, the two are behaving exactly as they will during those seventy hours. Building up an image.

She looks straight at the lawyer, moodily; then, when he makes a point, she takes up her ballpoint and bends short-sightedly over her ruled pad, again as she did at Millwards and as she will in court. Where time after time she will rise, lean over the dock wall and give an imperious tap on the shoulder of one of the defense lawyers; seven months before, if either of the latter had paid an official visit to Millwards, she would have been standing respectfully with the other girls. Now, having made her note, she looks back at the lawyer, unblinking under level brows. A faintly scornful stare which she has learned from film posters and close-ups on television. An empty look. Imitation. Synthetic Messalina. (Talbot: "Lookin' at her, you have to keep on thinkin', This is a girl that's lost her soul.")

Brady sits as he often sat in Number 16. And will sit, at the trial, when he is not drawing rapidly on his pad—endless aboriginal profiles, villainous men with thick beards and brows in their eyes. One hand on the bony knee, the other holding the chin. A thoughtful intellectual onlooker who has lost interest. Born thirty years too late, in the wrong country. Would have ended up at the top, Heil Brady.

She moody, he resigned. And in court the look will never change: continuously they resemble a couple sitting in a register office who have come to be married, are being subjected to endless delay, cannot conceive what the red tape can be (All these folk natterin') and are keeping their tempers with dignity.

To go further, they are carrying through to the end the fantasy of the Spy. For in their bearing, every detail is compatible with their being the Exiles who have Slaved for the Homeland, been Betrayed by a Comrade, and are determined not to let down that Homeland with either doubt or fear. "We report that in court today, our Hero and Heroine conducted themselves with exemplary dignity." No medals, though; the Devil does not reward.

Only once will Hess let her Neddie down. One afternoon descending to her cell after a day of horrors, she glances up at a journalist looking at her over the partition, gives him the stare, and then, for good measure, adds the utmost vulgarity to the utmost injury: she puts her tongue out at him.

But her only lapse. Otherwise the look stays immutable, whether directed at witness, jury, prosecution, defense, judge, or exhibit: at the axe being handed around a yard in front of them; at the little tartan dress held up even closer; at the mothers giving evidence (Mrs. Downey: "She looked at me as if *I* was the murderer"); or at Exhibit 1540, an album of stage-by-stage photographs (the little girl being unearthed), the pages of which they turn, head next to head, as if scanning items at an indifferent concert, she once blowing her nose.

It will be the same look when the tape will be played; when, at the heart of an appalled court, they sit making notes and passing candy. And most extraordinary of all—for while they know the tape by heart, this will *have* to be new to them—the look will not change when a reluctant policeman will withdraw John Kilbride's jacket from its polythene cover and hand it to the judge, and there will spread through the court the obscene smell. Unshakable.

And will be to the end: even when they will stand up to be sentenced to imprisonment for life, even when they are hustled into a special car with the execrations of the crowd ringing through their heads, and sit between the prison guards and face the fact, at last, that they are never to see each other again. Gone their little little world, gone the back streets, gone Gorton, gone Hattersley and the little dream house, gone the fillums and the music. For the dreams are over, and the powers. Only the desires are left. The same look.

Should they be hanged? It was a question to exercise many minds, and a petition to "bring back the noose" was signed locally by thirty thousand people. At the trial, as the sounds on the tape faded into silence, there was not a father in court— a lawyer declared afterwards—who would not have volunteered to pull the levers.

Even a century and a half ago, the two might have been marched, the one from Ashton Market and the other from Ancoats Fair, between miles of jeering and spitting and urinating; and if science had progressed more swiftly, the tape would have been broadcast, deafeningly, from loudspeakers every fifty yards. Then, in the heart of mountains covered with greedy spectators as thick as heather, the two would have dangled. Three hundred and seventy-three yards apart, one gallows planted deep in one grave, the other in the other.

No, that would have been the apotheosis not even of King Ian and his Consort, but of Saint Ian and his Lady. And now that the law is, by its own new law (capital punishment in murder cases had been abolished in Great Britain in November 1965),

forced to spare them, that is right. Not that we should feel sorry
for them. We should surely keep our pity for the poor maddened
rat gnawing at whatever it can find, for the poor maddened
lunatic impelled to rape and to destroy. Not for these two. If
they were to be hanged, they would march to the scaffold—a
goose step almost—invincibly united, the martyred Macbeths of
the Welfare State. But neither of these would be troubled by
remorse, or by fear of the hereafter; they would be martyrs to
their own inscrutable cause, and once again theirs would be the
only composed faces in an assembly of human beings either
nauseated or gloating, both conditions deplorable. And as Mrs.
Kilbride thoughtfully said, "What good would it do? It wouldn't
bring our John back."

If only the God of the Old Testament had come back into His
own! That flat afternoon in court, when the screams of the child
merged into music and the music into a silence that left hardened policemen pale to the lips and the judge himself with head
averted—if only the Almighty had then raised His thunderbolt
high, cleft Chester Castle in twain, and struck! Two screams, a
puff of clean smoke, and it would have been over.

God might even have done it less obviously, which He has
been doing for a long time now. One evening during the hearing,
when the fog was thought too dangerous for the two to be driven
back to Risley, they spent the night in cells in Hyde. If the
authorities had taken the risk, and if the car had somersaulted
down an embankment, throwing the driver free and killing the
two passengers outright . . . But He moves in a mysterious way,
and that was a wonder He chose not to perform. He elected
rather, a few weeks after the trial, at a moment when the murderer's mother needed all the moral help she could get, that her
husband Pat should drop dead in the street. Mysterious.

Their continued existence is indeed hard to tolerate. Public
feeling being what it is—and about these two the public will have
a long memory—it is unlikely that they will ever be released, and
it is natural for taxpayers to be incensed at the thought of their
being maintained, for life, by the state. But one word in that com-
plaint does not apply. These two are no longer alive.

They died at 9:02 A.M. on the morning of October 7, 1965,

without causing the degradation of either prison chaplain or hangman waiting to get home to wife and family. They died when, in Number 16, they heard the words "I shall have to ask you to come along . . ." and two policemen faced them with a look they had never seen before. The look people give in the zoo, at some unfamiliar and repulsive beast. The look which will confront them henceforth and forever.

Their sentence might not have been this mortal blow if they were to serve it together. But he went to Durham Jail and she to Holloway—her first visit to London—and with the cutting of the cord, they were unable to survive. Never a great reader was our Myra, or a girl to think. All she was good at was being the Slave of the Master.

And even the Master, without his Slave, is nothing. King Ian is dead, long live the Law. In a cell which is after all no smaller than the back bedroom of 18 Westmoreland Street, where most of his realm was founded, he may occasionally sink deep into old dreams and in spurts rebuild his razed Golden City as good as Warsaw. But he is sealed off as he never was before ("Prisoner Brady has requested to be kept in complete isolation from the other inmates"). He knows they might lynch him. And once a day, with the door of every other cell locked on the occupant, the one sacred monster takes his solitary walk. Pacing slowly around and around under the unearthly neon lights, cast away by castaways, he is the loneliest man in the world. Both dead.

True, they breathe and move. On the one hand, the stomachs of tough citizens have been turned by the innocent stench of two ravaged children, whose souls are at rest. On the other hand, the bodies of the murderers are in prime condition, young and clean; if at any time the authorities were broad-minded enough to lock them up together for an hour, the result might be incandescent. Their separated bodies are A-1.

But their souls are together, buried in one grave on moors of their own making. And when on Judgment Day those souls are dug up, they will stink to heaven.

APPENDIX

The Trial

The two accused were tried at Chester Assizes (April 19, 1966, to May 6). They pleaded not guilty to all three murders. Ian Brady was found guilty of all three, Myra Hindley guilty of the murder of Edward Evans and of Lesley Ann Downey, not guilty of the murder of John Kilbride but guilty of being an accessory after the fact. Both were sentenced to life imprisonment.

The Evans Case: Brady maintained that just before the Evans murder (Smith being in need of ready money, emphasized by the defense), he had discussed with Smith a plan to "roll a queer" (Smith vehemently denied this), Brady's plan being to go into town, pick up a well-heeled homosexual, bring him back to Number 16 and send for Smith. They would then "intimidate" the pickup into handing over money and valuables. It is believable that Brady might have deceived Smith into thinking he meant to do this in order to get Smith to the house to witness a murder; but not believable that Brady meant to carry the idea through, as Edward Evans was obviously a penniless adolescent.

The Downey Case: The two accused maintained that the child was brought to Number 16 in a car "by two men," with the idea of having her photographed by Brady for the pornographic market. Myra Hindley maintained that during the picture taking she was looking out of the window (she "was so embarrassed"), and turned on the radio "to ease the tension an' alleviate the child's feelin's." The window, on a snowy December night, was apparently open, the door open, the front door open, with one of the two men at the garden gate holding a conversation with the other man sitting below in the car, in the open, for at least fifteen minutes. The accused maintained that after the photographs were taken, the child left, alive and well, with the two men.

The Kilbride Case: As there is no proof that Myra Hindley knew of the Kilbride name in the exercise book, or that she knew it was the boy's grave she was being photographed on, it is apparent that she was found guilty of being an accessory on the supposition that she, and only she, had not only driven Brady and the boy to the moors, but had then driven Brady home, without the boy.

Four Questions

In the Foreword I mentioned having had to "surmise," which has to include offering answers to puzzling situations.

1. How was a timid child like *Lesley Ann Downey* taken nine miles, and then into a strange house, without protest or anybody noticing? Given Brady's preoccupation with gimmicks, to me the idea of her being "put to sleep" immediately she got into the car is a credible one. Some explanation is made imperative, surely, by one detail. If an adult gives a lift, even an innocent one, to a strange child, the obvious instinct, in order to ease the atmosphere, is to make conversation with the child, and the first question has to be: "What is your name?" Yet, on a twenty-seven-minute journey the question was not asked, for on the tape Brady is heard asking it.

2. *Pat Hodges.* The fact that this child was taken up to the moors less than forty-eight hours before another child was mur-

dered must (to me) mean that Brady had a plan which he realized at the last moment was too risky, and which he abandoned.

3. *The "Disposal Plan."* Brady's explanation of the "10 BUT (ten buttons) being added afterwards in pencil was that in the small hours after the Evans murder he accompanied Myra Hindley when she went down to lock her car, took the wallet out of the car, wrote it in and put the wallet back. As he was then limping badly enough for it to interfere with plans, it seems unlikely he would have limped round and down with a driver who was perfectly capable of locking her car by herself. The explanation I proffer is on page 239.

4. *The music on the tape.* The Ray Conniff record "We Wish You a Merry Christmas" was never found by the police at Number 16 or anywhere else. It is my suggestion (page 195) that Brady borrowed the record from a record library, and after taping it, returned it.

The only theory I have advanced which is not in answer to a puzzling question is the psychological connection between the Kennedy assassination on November 22, 1963, and the Kilbride murder the next day.

Two Mysteries

1. In addition to the fatal photograph of Myra Hindley bent over the Kilbride grave, there exists another one of her, taken a few hundred yards away. In this she is not bending but standing, among rocks and against hills and winter sky. It is special because the details are identical with the other photograph— clothes, hairdo, and of course the puppy inside the lumber jacket, being protected against the cold—and so prove that both snaps were taken on the same afternoon.

As with the first picture, the police photographers established after meticulous aligning the exact location of this second one. They then took their own photograph of it, exactly corresponding to Brady's except—again—for the absence of the girl's figure.

Instead of that figure, the police photograph reveals something which, in the Brady snap, Myra Hindley is completely obscuring: a metal sign a couple of feet high, embedded in the soil and reading, in bold print: "GAS M 83—2-6 DEEP—SIZE 14." The sign is to establish that two and a half feet beneath the surface, there lies the Methane Gas Pipe which travels crosscountry between Sheffield and Manchester.

Myra Hindley was slim and the metal sign is fairly wide. As one looks at the two pictures, it is obvious that Brady had placed himself with his camera in such a position that in his photograph his model could completely hide a landmark which, to a prying eye, would identify the location at once. He wanted to avoid that. Some yards away, beyond the camera's range, is the site of the Downey grave.

Was that why he took the picture?

The first thought which throws doubt on this is that since Brady had just photographed (or was about to photograph) Myra Hindley crouched with both feet on the Kilbride grave, would not his impishly symmetrical mind have insisted that his second photograph should show the same booted feet squarely on the Downey grave and not yards away from it?

A second thought does more than throw doubt. It proves that it is impossible for Brady to have been thinking of the Downey grave at all. The photograph was taken months before Lesley Ann Downey disappeared.

In this second photograph, therefore, has the exact spot on which Myra Hindley is standing its own significance?

If there is a possibility of that, why—it may be asked—have the police not probed, with their long sticks, down into the soil between the rocks on which Myra Hindley posed?

They have. And they struck the Methane Pipe.

During the summer of 1963, up at Hollin Brown Knoll there had been continuous daily activity: workmen were engaged in laying the pipe. This involved excavation to quite a depth, followed by exposure of the excavated parts for some days while the pipe was being prepared. Then, once it had been lowered into place, the workmen carefully shoveled loads of earth back on top of and around the pipe. Many loads. And long before the bad weather threatened, the lonely hillside was back to normal.

In that same summer *Pauline Reade*, sixteen, lived with her Catholic parents and her young brother, Paul, at 9 Wiles Street, Gorton, two doors from David Smith and his father. Paul was fifteen, having been born twelve days after Edward Evans and six days after David Smith. Pauline had attended Peacock Street Primary (Myra Hindley's first school), then St. Francis' School (Myra's father's), then St. James' Secondary Modern at the same time as David Smith and Maureen Hindley, being a year younger than she and a year older than he.

On Friday, July 12, 1963, at 7:30 P.M., Pauline left to join her girl friend Pat Cummings at a jive session at the British Railways Social Club in Cornwall Street, a walk of less than half a mile. Her way there, along Gorton Lane, skirted Eaton Street (Myra's mam's) and Bannock Street (Gran's). She did not arrive at her destination, and has never been seen or heard of again. Some months later her father said, "I think Pauline cannot still be alive. If she was, I'm sure she would have sent at least a card, she was a very nice writer." His daughter had disappeared eleven days before the twenty-first birthday of Myra Hindley. Pauline Reade, born February 18, 1947, aged sixteen years and five months.

No charge has ever been brought against any person or persons. The case is unsolved.

2. On Tuesday, June 16, 1964, at 7:45 P.M., seven months after the disappearance of John Kilbride, *Keith Bennett*, schoolboy, set out with his mother from his home at 29 Eston Street (not to be confused with the Hindley home, 20 Eaton Street, a mile and a half away). He was going to stay the night in Morton Street with his maternal grandmother, to whom he was as attached as John Kilbride had been to his. Although it was a fine summer evening and only a half-mile walk, his mother felt it wise to accompany him to the corner of busy Stockport Road, where he had only a few hundred yards to go, the length of a couple of short streets. She waved to him and called, Loov to Gran. One of

the short streets was Westmoreland Street. Brady's Street.

The boy did not arrive at his destination. His mother's first worry the next morning was that he was short-sighted and hadn't his glasses on him, having cracked one lens at the swimming pool. She was to keep the broken glasses in his drawer in the back bedroom for a long time. "If I had known, I would never have let him out of my sight." He has never been seen or heard of again. Keith Bennett, born June 12, 1952, aged twelve years and four days.

No charge has ever been brought against any person or persons. The case is unsolved.

During the first exploration of the moors these two names were mentioned freely in the press ("The dossiers of other missing persons are being scrutinized by the police"), but naturally, once the prisoners were charged with the three murders, the outstanding mysteries went into limbo. It is odd that at the trial, where those mysteries had to be constantly in people's minds, the only person who mentioned the two names, loud and clear, was Ian Brady: "Aye, the police questioned me not only aboot Kilbride and Downey, but aboot Pauline Reade an' Keith Bennett."

"Queerer Than Queer"

1967, an afternoon nine months after the trial. In the sitting room of 18 Underwood Court, Hattersley (on the third floor of "The Towers"), I sat with David and Maureen Smith. It was not long after his nineteenth birthday. On the balcony, eight-month-old Paul Anthony lay asleep in the sun.

"When all this c-come out," said Dave, brushing ashes off his jeans, "d'you know what come as a shock to me? That Ian was illegitimate. We 'ad no idea. 'Ad we, Mo?"

"No," said his wife, shaking the baby's bottle, "quite a shock." She went on, in her rapid, low voice, "Oh Dave, I meant to tell you, they told me in the greengrocer's that them new tenants in

Number 16 is a young couple, an' they got posh front curtains. Posher than Myra's."

A cat sidled around the chair. "We had to have Bobbie, the dog, destroyed," said Dave. "Terrible business. Wasn't it, Mo? Then we got a cat, an' now we got five, ye can't go against nature, can you?" He chuckled, then said jokingly to the cat, "Get along, you filthy swine you!" and gave it a pat forward with the *Radio Times*. "Mo, d'you see the new *Avengers* just started on telly?"

He saw me looking at the wallpaper around the fireplace, a pattern suggesting grained wood. I said it reminded me of the front room in Number 16.

"Aye," said Dave, "we got it same shop, only Ian's cost more. Always 'ad big ideas, did Ian . . . The other thing I couldn't go along with, like," he continued, dragging on his cigarette, "was the idea that Ian was 'omosexual. 'E wasn't. I mean, he was my friend, and if he'd been a pansy—well, he'd ha' been bound to make a pass at me. Wouldn't he, Mo?"

"Aye," said Maureen, stepping out onto the balcony to unstrap the baby, "stands to reason."

"Well, he never did," said Dave, "no, Ian wasn't queer." Then, after a pause: "I reckon 'e was queerer than just queer."

He was looking thoughtfully out of the window. At the sunlight beyond the balcony. It was then I knew that his mind was deeply shadowed, possibly for the rest of his life.

I said, "Has Maureen written to her again?"

"No," he said, "not since that last time. An' that was the fourth. Ye can't do more than write, can you? Even just to answer back 'Drop dead' would be something."

A pause. He turned and stared at the door of the room. "Mind you, I did squeal on them. If that door was barred an' bolted an' he was on the other side, he'd break it down into splinters to get at me."

Out on the balcony, Maureen was picking up the bundled baby. I said, "That's a nice pram."

"Aye," said Dave, "it's worn well, it was Angela Dawn's." I looked from him to Maureen coming into the room, then back at him. "That's right," he said, "it's the one I was supposed to fetch from my grandad's the day after Evans, to take Evans off in, to be buried. Isn't it, Mo?"

"That's right," said Maureen, setting Paul carefully back in the other armchair as he gurgled up at her. She took up his bottle, shook it again and laid it on the table, near a German pocket dictionary which looked as if it had never been opened. On the other end of the table, a red-jacketed book splashed with the words *The Monsters of the Moors*. "That's right," and she went on, "I'll just put the kettle on before I give Paul 'is feed, then I'll brew up some tea."

She disappeared into the kitchen. Dave took his son's hand, made a burping noise at him, did his chuckle and looked even younger than his age.

"He'd better make the most of the attention," he said, "because we've got another one on the way. Ye can't go against nature. Can ye, Paul, eh?"

INDEX

INDEX

INDEX

ABOUT THE AUTHOR

EMLYN WILLIAMS began writing novels at school in Wales, but stopped abruptly at the age of seventeen on reaching Oxford, where he became beguiled by the theater. He stayed beguiled for many years, writing plays and acting continuously on both sides of the Atlantic. His credits as a playwright include *Night Must Fall* and *The Corn Is Green;* as an actor he has created prominent roles in *Montserrat, A Man For All Seasons, The Deputy, Emlyn Williams as Charles Dickens* and *Emlyn Williams as Dylan Thomas Growing Up,* among others.

In 1962 Mr. Williams' first book, *George: An Early Autobiography,* was published here and became a Book-of-the-Month Club choice. *Beyond Belief,* a very different kind of work, is his second book.